QUEER CINEMA,
THE FILM READER

Queer Cinema, the Film Reader brings together key writings that use queer theory to explore cinematic sexualities, especially those historically designated as gay, lesbian, bisexual, and/or transgendered. The collection examines the relationship between cinematic representations of sexuality and their social, historical, and industrial contexts.

Sections include:

- *Auteurs* – examines the ways in which sexuality figures in the work of queer filmmakers such as George Cukor, Dorothy Arzner, Barbara Hammer, and the directors of New Queer Cinema
- *Forms* – explores how the horror film, the musical, film noir, and animated film construct queer cinematic spaces
- *Camp* – looks at how this reception strategy and mode of textual production, initially practiced by pre-Stonewall queers, retains its critical charge even in contemporary mainstream popular culture
- *Reception* – considers three historical case studies of queer fans interacting with media texts (Judy Garland, Underground Film, and *Star Trek*).

Contributors: Jack Babuscio, Harry Benshoff, Alexander Doty, Richard Dyer, Caroline Evans and Lorraine Gamman, Brett Farmer, Sean Griffin, Henry Jenkins III, Moe Meyer, B. Ruby Rich, Janet Staiger, Thomas Waugh, Andrea Weiss.

Harry Benshoff is Assistant Professor in Radio, Television and Film at the University of North Texas. He is author of *Monsters in the Closet: Homosexuality and the Horror Film* and co-author (with Sean Griffin) of *America on Film: Representing Race, Class, Gender and Sexuality at the Movies.*

Sean Griffin is Assistant Professor in the Division of Cinema-Television at Southern Methodist University. He is author of *Tinker Belles and Evil Queens: The Walt Disney Company from the Inside Out*, and co-author (with Harry Benshoff) of *America on Film: Representing Race, Class, Gender and Sexuality at the Movies.*

IN FOCUS

In Focus: Routledge Film Readers

Series Editors: Steven Cohan (Syracuse University) and Ina Rae Hark (University of South Carolina)

The In Focus series of readers is a comprehensive resource for students on film and cinema studies courses. The series explores the innovations of film studies while highlighting the vital connection of debates to other academic fields and to studies of other media. The readers bring together key articles on a major topic in film studies, from marketing to Hollywood comedy, identifying the central issues, exploring how and why scholars have approached it in specific ways, and tracing continuities of thought among scholars. Each reader opens with an introductory essay setting the debates in their academic context, explaining the topic's historical and theoretical importance, and surveying and critiquing its development in film studies.

QUEER CINEMA,
THE FILM READER

Edited by
Harry Benshoff and Sean Griffin

Routledge
Taylor & Francis Group

NEW YORK AND LONDON

First published 2004 in the USA and Canada
by Routledge
29 West 35th Street, New York, NY 10001

Simultaneously published
by Routledge
2 Park Square, Milton Park, Abingdon, Oxfordshire OX14 4RN

Routledge is an imprint of the Taylor & Francis Group

Designed and typeset in Novarese and Scala Sans
by Keystroke, Jacaranda Lodge, Wolverhampton
Printed and bound in Great Britain
by MPG Books Ltd, Bodmin

Library of Congress Cataloging in Publication Data
Queer cinema, the film reader / edited by Harry Benshoff and Sean
Griffin.
    p. cm. – (In focus–Routledge film readers)
1. Homosexuality and motion pictures.   2. Homosexuality in motion
pictures.   I. Benshoff, Harry M.   II.   Griffin, Sean.   III.   Series.

PN1995.9.H55 Q397 2004
791.43'653–dc22   2003024424

British Library Cataloguing in Publication Data
A catalogue record for this book is available from the British Library

ISBN 0–415–31986–2 (hbk)
ISBN 0–415–31987–0 (pbk)

Contents

Acknowledgments

1   Alexander Doty, "Whose Text Is It Anyway? Queer Cultures, Queer Auteurs, and Queer Authorship," from *Making Things Perfectly Queer: Interpreting Mass Culture* (Minneapolis: University of Minnesota Press, 1993), 19–23, 25–27, 29–33, 35–38. © 1993 by the Regents of the University of Minnesota. Reprinted by permission of the University of Minnesota Press.

2   Thomas Waugh, "Physique Cinema, 1945–1969: Hard to Imagine," from *Hard to Imagine: Gay Male Eroticism in Photography and Film from their Beginnings to Stonewall*, 254–269. © 1996 Columbia University Press. Reprinted by permission of Columbia University Press.

3   Andrea Weiss, "Transgressive Cinema: Lesbian Independent Film," Chapter 6 from *Vampires and Violets: Lesbians in Film*, 137–142, 149–150, 154–161. © 1992 by Andrea Weiss. Reprinted by permission of Viking Penguin, a division of Penguin Group (USA) Inc.

4   B. Ruby Rich, "The New Queer Cinema," was originally published as "A Queer Sensation: New Gay Film" in the *Village Voice*, March 24, 1992; reprinted and expanded as "The New Queer Cinema" in *Sight and Sound* (UK) Volume 2, Issue 5, September 1992. Reprinted by permission of the author.

5   Harry Benshoff, excerpt from "Introduction: The Monster and the Homosexual," Chapter 1 of *Monsters in the Closet: Homosexuality and the Horror Film* (Manchester and New York: Manchester University Press, 1997), 4–10, 11, 13–24. Reprinted by permission of Manchester University Press.

6   Brett Farmer, excerpts from "Fantasmatic Escapades: Gay Spectatorships and Queer Negotiations of the Hollywood Musical," Chapter 2 of *Spectacular Passions: Cinema, Fantasy, Gay Male Spectatorships* (Durham and London: Duke University Press, 2000), 74–90. All rights reserved. Reprinted by permission of Duke University Press.

7   Richard Dyer, "Queer Noir," in *The Culture of Queers* (London and New York: Routledge, 2002), 90–113. Reprinted by permission of Routledge.

8   Sean Griffin, "Pronoun Trouble: The 'Queerness' of Animation," *Spectator: The University of Southern California Journal of Film and Television Criticism* 15:1 (Fall 1994), 94–109. Reprinted by permission.

9   Jack Babuscio, "Camp and the Gay Sensibility," in Richard Dyer, ed., *Gays and Film* (London: BFI, 1997), 40–57. © Richard Dyer, reprinted by permission.

10 Moe Meyer, excerpt from "Reclaiming the Discourse of Camp," Moe Meyer, ed., *The Politics and Poetics of Camp* (New York: Routledge, 1994), 1–17. Reprinted by permission of Routledge.

11   Richard Dyer, excerpts from "Judy Garland and Gay Men," *Heavenly Bodies: Film Stars and Society* (New York: St. Martin's Press, 1986), 141–154, 193–194. © Richard Dyer, reprinted by permission of Palgrave Macmillan.

12   Janet Staiger, "Finding Community in the 1960s: Underground Cinema and Sexual Politics," in Hilary Radner and Moya Luckett, eds., *Swinging Single: Representing Sexuality in the 1960s* (Minneapolis: University of Minnesota Press, 1999), 41–45, 48–65. © 1999 by the Regents of the University of Minnesota. Reprinted by permission of the University of Minnesota Press.

13   Henry Jenkins, excerpts from "Out of the Closet and into the Universe: Queers and *Star Trek*," in John Tulloch and Henry Jenkins, eds., *Science Fiction Audiences: Watching Doctor Who and Star Trek* (London and New York: Routledge, 1995), 237–245, 258–265. Reprinted by permission of Routledge.

14   Caroline Evans and Lorraine Gamman, excerpts from "The Gaze Revisited, or Reviewing Queer Viewing," in Paul Burston and Colin Richardson, eds., *A Queer Romance: Lesbians, Gay Men and Popular Culture* (London and New York: Routledge, 1995), 24–27, 30–36, 38–41, 45–50. © 1995 Caroline Evans and Lorraine Gamman. Reprinted by permission of the authors.

Queer Cinema,

The Film Reader

General introduction

This volume is designed to bring together key writings that address issues related to the study of queer film. We have chosen to focus this anthology on queer film—rather than gay and lesbian film—because we feel it better describes our project. Our use of the term "queer film study" encompasses the exploration of cinema in relation to non-straight sexualities (including but not limited to gay and lesbian sexualities), and it also refers to a mode of cultural analysis derived from queer theory. While for many people "queer" is simply the latest trendy word used to describe homosexuals, for the purposes of this volume, "queer" should be understood as a theoretical approach to rethinking human sexuality. Queer theory posits that sexuality is a vast and complex terrain that encompasses not just personal orientation and/or behavior, but also the social, cultural, and historical factors that define and create the conditions for such orientations and behaviors. As such, queer theory rejects essentialist or biological notions of gender and sexuality, and sees them instead as fluid and socially constructed positionalities. The term queer, once a pejorative epithet used to humiliate gay men and women, is now used by academics to describe the broad, fluid, and ever-changing expanse of human sexualities. Queer can be used to describe any sexuality not defined as heterosexual procreative monogamy (usually the presumed goal of most classical Hollywood couplings); queers are people (including heterosexuals) who do not organize their sexuality according to that rubric.

At its most basic level, queer theory helps interrogate and complicate the term "gay and lesbian cinema." That label is confusing—does it refer only to films made by gay and lesbian people? Or does it mean films that have garnered large numbers of gay and lesbian fans? Perhaps it refers to films that depict gay and lesbian characters, even when they are made by avowed heterosexuals? And who decides when and if a character is gay or lesbian? Furthermore, the very meaning of the words gay and lesbian—how they are used and understood—has changed greatly over the decades. So have the conditions of gay and lesbian cinematic representation, since the characteristics that mass culture has used to signify homosexuality have also changed over the years. For example, while today's films can be relatively forthright about sexuality, films made before the 1960s could only hint at it in various ways. Thus, there are great cultural and historical differences between films made by gay and lesbian directors in 1930s Hollywood and today's independent gay and lesbian filmmakers.

Queer film study, then, understands cinematic sexualities as complex, multiple, overlapping, and historically nuanced, rather than immutably fixed. While often giving emphasis to traditionally ignored or censored non-straight sexualities, queer film study explores how and why the fluidity of all sexualities relates to the production and reception of cinema. As this volume will demonstrate, "queer" can be used to describe (among other things) an authorial voice, a character, a mode of textual production, and/or various types of reception practice. Filmmakers, forms, and audiences—not necessarily identified as gay or lesbian—can rather be understood as queer. Queer film study, especially queer film history, is often about locating the queer traces in texts, marks left there by their makers (who may or may not have been homosexual). Queer is descriptive of the textual (and extra-textual) spaces wherein normative heterosexuality is threatened, critiqued, camped up, or shown to be an unstable performative identity.

Despite its being a fairly new concept, "queer" is actually a more accurate and descriptive one when dealing with non-straight sexualities. It works to describe such sexual desires even before the coining of the terms homosexual and heterosexual. It can refer to the sensibilities of closeted or repressed homosexuals. It acknowledges the similarities (and hopefully underscores the differences) between gay male and lesbian perspectives, as well as bisexual or transgendered perspectives. It can be used to define a new generation of people (and the films they make) that resist being labeled into a heterosexual–homosexual binary. Queer also works to describe the non-procreative sexualities found in other nations and other cultures, places that often have vastly different ways of understanding human sexuality. (By design, due to Hollywood's global dominance and the need for brevity, this volume focuses primarily on twentieth-century concepts of sexuality and how they have been represented in English-language media artifacts distributed in Western nations. The history of queer sexualities and their representation in other parts of the world are complex and still being researched. For an introduction to non-Western queer cinemas, see Gever, Greyson, and Parmar [1993]; Jackson and Tapp [1997]; and Dyer [2003].)

Queer is thus a broadly used term, but as a theoretical approach, identifying something as queer is only the first step toward further analysis. Queer artifacts (like queer people) differ from one another in myriad ways, and it is the queer exegete's task to uncover and explore the various socio-cultural, historical, and institutional discourses that contribute to those differences. As such, this volume contains a variety of essays written both from within queer perspectives as well as several written before the concept became a theoretical tool. Several are written about films or figures that many people would not label as explicitly gay or lesbian. Almost all are grounded in specific historical contexts, and even the older essays (that may use the terms "gay" and "lesbian" in somewhat essentialist ways) have nonetheless been chosen precisely for the ways in which they illustrate concepts of queer media study.

From homosexual to queer: a brief history

As has been often noted by historians of sexuality, the terms "homosexual" and "heterosexual" were not coined until the late 1800s, and did not make their way into Western societies' public discourse until the middle of the twentieth century (Katz 1976, 1995; D'Emilio and Freedman 1988). This is not to say that sexual desires and acts did not exist prior to that time, but rather to acknowledge how those words themselves have shaped (and continue to shape) the twentieth-century understanding of sexuality. Furthermore, the terms homosexual and heterosexual were both coined in order to describe "abnormal" sexual behaviors—as well as the people who practiced them. A homosexual was someone who engaged in same-sex behaviors, while a heterosexual was someone who engaged in different-sex behaviors outside the bonds of procreative matrimony. Over the course of the twentieth century, heterosexuality came to mean the "normal" orientation of male–female attraction and desire, while homosexuality remained its "abnormal" shadow.

How homosexuality itself was theorized also changed a great deal over the course of the twentieth century. As the 1900s began, homosexuality was strongly associated with gender identity: it was believed that men who were sexually attracted to other men were actually female souls trapped in male bodies. Similarly, a female homosexual was thought to be really a man born into a female body. Contemporary theory and science use the terms transgendered or transsexual to describe this old-fashioned model of homosexuality, as it really was based on the concept of gender identity (i.e. do you feel like a man or a woman?). Today, sexuality is defined by object choice (i.e. do you find yourself attracted to men or to women, or both, or neither?). Early sexologists sometimes used the terms "invert" or "the third sex" to describe homosexuals, furthering this confusion between sexuality and gender. According to this definition, conventionally feminine women who had sex with other women were not often recognized as lesbian, and traditionally masculine men who took the aggressive insertive role in sex with other men were not considered truly homosexual (Chauncey 1994). To this day, certain societies and individuals (as well as media systems) still strongly focus on gender markings to distinguish who is homosexual and who is not.

For most of the twentieth century, homosexuality was considered a shameful, distasteful thing. Religions often condemned it as sin, medical and psychological institutions considered it an illness, and the law declared it illegal. People could be and were sentenced to prison for being homosexual, as was the playwright Oscar Wilde. Thus, while society had given a name to homosexuality, it simultaneously worked to erase it, to make it "the Love that dare not speak its name," as (Wilde's ex-lover) Lord Alfred Douglas most famously described it (1892, "The Two Loves"). For roughly the first two-thirds of the twentieth century, it sometimes seemed as if homosexuality did not officially exist (not to mention the variety of other sexualities that went ignored by the creation of the homo–hetero dichotomy). It was rarely written about in the popular media, it rarely appeared in motion picture stories, and it was considered inappropriate to talk about in polite conversation. Queer people generally had to live in secrecy—staying "in the closet" by keeping their sexuality hidden from friends, co-workers, and family members. As a consequence, many queer individuals remained isolated from each other. Many accepted the medical model of sexuality and understood themselves to be sick or diseased. In fact, some early homosexual rights advocates used the medical model to argue for an end to discrimination: homosexuals should not be punished, they argued, but rather helped via medicine and psychiatry to adjust to "normal" heterosexual society (D'Emilio and Freedman 1988).

Nevertheless, communities of queers did grow and evolve in the urban areas of many Western nations. These communities developed their own subcultural practices in response to the dominant heterosexist culture, and sometimes used the word "gay" to describe themselves. Interestingly, "gay" at this time meant something closer to the current usage of "queer": it described the myriad forms of sexuality (homosexuality, heterosexual relations outside marriage, prostitution, etc.) that defied the dictates of procreative monogamy. Living the "gay life" meant that one was sexually free, not necessarily homosexual (Weeks 1989). Ironically, the fledgling gay communities of twentieth-century America encountered a boost in population as a result of the U.S. military's anti-homosexual policies during World War II. Queer men and women who were dishonorably discharged from the Armed Services often settled in the port cities in which they had been disembarked, swelling the ranks of nascent queer communities. As those communities gained critical mass, many people in them began to speak of and fight for civil rights (Bérubé 1991; Faderman 1992). In Great Britain, the Wolfenden Report (issued in 1957) argued that homosexuality should be decriminalized, and it too brought new legal, moral, and sociological perspectives to the growing public debate over homosexuality.

The understanding of homosexuality as a civil rights issue increased in the 1960s when younger and more activist queers followed the example of women and people of color and began to demand fair and equal treatment under the law. The so-called Stonewall Riots that occurred in New York City in June of 1969 are sometimes said to be the start of the modern gay and lesbian civil rights movement, although various demonstrations, protests, and media events designed to bring publicity to the cause had occurred before then, both in other parts of North America and in Europe. As part of this new militant attitude, many queers rejected the term "homosexual" because it was associated with the medical and legal establishment. "Queer" was still an epithet like "faggot" or "dyke," so the terms "gay" and "lesbian" became the preferred labels most queers used to describe themselves. It became very important for queers of this generation to step forward and to self-identify as gay or lesbian. Such "coming out of the closet" was meant to show the straight world that lesbians and gays were indeed everywhere, and that they were no longer ashamed to be acknowledged as such.

Within months of the Stonewall Riots, many North American newspapers and news magazines were announcing the birth of a new liberation movement demanding fair and equal treatment for homosexuals. Gay pride festivals and parades began to be held in major urban areas every year in June, commemorating the anniversary of the Stonewall Riots. All sorts of lesbian and gay groups—both political and social—began forming. Activists challenged the legal and medical establishments that had discriminated against homosexuals in the past. A major victory occurred when, in response to pressure from gay activists, the American Psychiatric Association removed homosexuality from its official list of mental disorders in 1974 (Katz 1976; D'Emilio and Freedman 1988).

Many early gay liberation manifestos were surprisingly queer—calling for an acknowledgment of sexual fluidity that would deconstruct simple straight–gay binaries. Yet this initial flush of radical sexual activism waned during the 1970s into a more specifically lesbian and gay equal rights movement. Often activists used the essentialist argument that lesbians and gay men were "born that way" in order to justify equal rights. Doing so, though, often denied the fluidity of sexual desire and practice. Bisexuals and transgendered individuals, who more readily exemplify such fluidity, were often pushed to the sidelines in early gay rights organizing. By the mid-1970s, lesbians and gay men had gone into separate political and social spheres, as lesbian separatism severed ties from patriarchal society, and gay men set up all-male communities in urban centers. These lesbian and gay subcultures began to exert pressure on their members to conform to a certain lifestyle—policing what the truly committed lesbian would be wearing, saying, and eating; establishing the dominant "clone look" among gay men. Thus, while the rise of gay rights activism heralded a rebellion against heteronormativity, it ironically worked to fix more precisely rigid categories of identity rather than celebrate more queerly fluid ones.

In the 1980s, two related factors brought gay and lesbian communities together again: the AIDS crisis and the rise of Christian fundamentalist thought (which tended to figure AIDS as a holy curse against homosexuals). The policies of the radical Right—meant to uphold traditional heterocentrist values—prevented some governments from doing much of anything during the first few years of the AIDS crisis. In America, President Reagan mostly ignored it, funding for research was severely lacking, and educational campaigns went unfunded. As such, new coalitions of gay men, lesbians, bisexuals, transgendered people (plus their friends and families) came together to fight the crisis (as well as other heterosexist actions initiated by conservatives). Many activists in these coalitions began to use the term "queer" (as in the group name Queer Nation) to designate a "community of difference" inclusive of a broad variety of sexual *identities* and *behaviors* (Duggan 1992). Queer was not only meant to acknowledge that there are many different ways to be gay or lesbian, but also to encompass and define other sexually defined minorities for whom the labels homosexual and/or heterosexual were less than adequate: bisexuals, cross-dressers, transgendered people, interracial couples whether homosexual or heterosexual, disabled sexualities, sadomasochistic sexualities whether homosexual or heterosexual, etc. The term was meant to gather together multiple marginalized groups into a shared political struggle, as well as fling back at mainstream heterosexist culture an epithet that had been used to oppress people for decades.

While queer activists were demonstrating in the streets, academics across the United States and in Canada and Europe had begun to discuss what was soon labeled queer theory. As such, queer theory traverses many interrelated disciplines, including philosophy, history, literature, anthropology, sociology, and cultural/media studies. It emerged from the confluence of identity politics (e.g. the study of race, class, gender, and sexuality) and currents in poststructuralist and postmodern thinking—currents that questioned the stability of signification and the desirability of categorization. As such, queer theory is often closely associated with third wave or anti-essentialist feminism and newer approaches to understanding race and ethnicity as social constructions rather than biological facts.

Scientists such as Sigmund Freud and Alfred Kinsey had argued in previous decades that human sexuality was not an either/or proposition, but rather fluctuating in nature. Following that line of thought, queer thinkers in the humanities began to explore how sexualities were socially constructed—expressed and understood in time and place. The work of French historian Michel Foucault (1990/1977) argued that sexuality in Western cultures was not in fact controlled through repressive means, but instead regulated through the various discourses in which it was spoken. Thus, sociocultural institutions like religions, medicine, the law, and even Hollywood narrative forms each "speak about" sexuality in certain ways that inflect one's understanding of it. Queer philosopher Judith Butler (1990, 1993), drawing upon camp notions of role-playing, analyzed gender and sexuality as performative acts, not essential identities. For example, people have to consistently enact their sexual identity—by voicing their desires out loud, hanging up posters of idealized sexual partners, or (especially in the case of insecure heterosexuals) possibly by denigrating other sexualities. In her work, literary theorist and social historian Eve Kosofsky Sedgwick (1985, 1990, 1993) explored the dynamics of male homosocial bonding and the social ramifications of the queer closet, showing how homosexuality and heterosexuality are deeply connected to one another. Queer theory points out that heterosexuality is itself a multiple and varied thing, sharing similar acts, behaviors, and desires with other types of sexual orientations.

While "queer," as it has been reappropriated and redefined, speaks of and from a specific historical moment (roughly the 1990s through today), queer theory works to examine the entire history of sexuality. It allows us to examine both straight and non-straight sexualities, in order to deconstruct the ways and means that patriarchal hegemony constructs and maintains the idea that only one sexuality (married-straight-white-man-on-top-of-woman-sex-for-procreation-only) is normal and desirable. Importantly, queer theory allows us to study the various concepts, images, and discourses that have been (and are being) used to understand sexuality. Specifically, queer film study allows us to examine how those concepts, images, and discourses surrounding human sexuality have impacted upon the cinema, and vice versa.

Queers and early cinema

Motion picture technology was developed in the late nineteenth century, just as the concepts of homosexuality and heterosexuality were beginning to take hold in Western science. Thus, film can and does provide a record of how human sexuality has been understood and represented over its 100-plus-year history. Interestingly, one of the earliest films ever made provides an exemplary queer moment. A film by W. K. L. Dickson (made for Thomas Edison in 1895) showed two men dancing intimately together. Is the duo supposed to be homosexual? They might simply be two heterosexual workers in Edison's factory performing for the newly invented camera. Without a narrative context, the meaning of "two men dancing for the camera" is left open to interpretation. One thing is certain however—the dancing pair is queer: they are not the usual expected heterosexual couple.

As motion pictures evolved into mass-produced studio-based productions, they began to emphasize fictional narratives, and normative heterosexuality became fundamental to the story-telling formula. For example, almost every Hollywood film (historically and still today) contains at least one male–female romance. In contrast, evidence of other sexualities was (and is) exceedingly rare. When queer characters were depicted, they were usually relegated to minor parts and/or were the butt of jokes, by contrast reinforcing the central and socially appropriate nature of the heterosexual love story. Furthermore, the construction of those queer characters often reflected the early-twentieth-century model of homosexuality as gender inversion. From silent films onward, the most common way of cinematically representing a homosexual was to have the character act in defiance of traditional gender norms. Feminine men (commonly referred to as "sissies" or "pansies") or masculine women (sometimes referred to as "butches" or "bull dykes") quickly became the stereotypical clichés of queer representation. Early examples of sissified males can be found in *Algie the Miner* (1912), *The Soilers* (1923), and *Wanderer of the West* (1927). One notable example of this gender inversion trope for women can be found in *A Florida Enchantment* (1914), a film in which female characters eat magical sex-changing seeds that turn them into pants-wearing, women-chasing lotharios.

Films made outside Hollywood often had a more complex take on human sexuality. For example, arguably the first film ever to feature homosexual love as its theme was the Swedish film *Vingarne* (*Wings* 1916), directed by homosexual filmmaker Mauritz Stiller (Dyer 2003/1990, 8–22). Carl Theodor Dreyer's *Mikael* (1924), filmed in Germany a few years later, was drawn from the same source novel. Weimar Germany also produced the first film to make a plea for homosexual rights and freedoms: *Anders als die Anderen* (*Different from the Others*, 1919) was made in conjunction with early sexologist and gay rights pioneer Magnus Hirschfeld. A few years later G. W. Pabst's famous film *Pandora's Box* (1929) featured a lesbian subplot. Perhaps the most well-known German film of this era to deal with homosexuality was Leontine Sagan's *Mädchen in Uniform* (1931), a film about a schoolgirl's crush on her teacher. (It should be noted that if and when these films played in America, they were often censored in ways that elided their homosexual content.)

In Hollywood film, the gender-inversion stereotype lingered precisely because state and local censorship laws forbade depicting homosexuality in a forthright manner. In accordance with the Hollywood Production Code (written in 1930, and enforced in 1934), explicit representation (or even the mention) of "sex perversion" was banned from Hollywood movie screens for almost three decades. Thus, unable to show any overt marker of homosexual desire, but still desiring to characterize supporting characters as homosexual, filmmakers repeatedly employed the pansy or butch woman stereotypes. Actors such as Edward Everett Horton, Franklin Pangborn, or Grady Sutton (in films like *The Gay Divorcee* [1934], *Easy Living* [1937] or *Anchors Aweigh* [1945]) often made careers out of playing these caricatures. Similarly, character actresses such as Hope Emerson and Agnes Moorehead specialized in quasi-lesbian roles (prison matrons, spinster aunts, etc.). In other words, classical Hollywood films used connotation rather than denotation when dealing with onscreen homosexuality, and thus created moments and characters that were more queer than specifically homosexual. While often these moments and characters were played for laughs, queer gender-bending touches were also used to signify evil. They were used to enhance the villains in suspense thrillers (as in *Rebecca* [1940] and *Laura* [1944]), in horror films (as in *The Bride of Frankenstein* [1935] and *Dracula's Daughter* [1936]), or in World War II films (as in *Saboteur* [1942]).

Queer moviegoers also decoded classical Hollywood films in ways that often went beyond (and sometimes against) what their makers explicitly intended, a subcultural reception strategy known as camp that developed within the era's urban queer communities. Camp was a means of queering heterocentrist film culture, and it both celebrated and satirized Hollywood films and their "larger-than-life" characters and situations. Certain melodramatic movie stars, including Marlene Dietrich, Greta Garbo, Joan Crawford, Bette Davis, Lana Turner, Judy Garland, and Maria Montez became favorites among queer moviegoers, as did genres such as the musical and the melodrama. These stars and genres seemed to appeal to queer audiences at least in part because of their visual and stylistic excess. The overly mannered performances of "natural femininity" by these (and other) stars, and the overwrought flair of these (and other) genres in depicting heterosexual romance, allowed some audiences the opportunity to view gender and sexuality as performative, unnatural, and queer. Camp also functioned as a secret code among queers trying to identify one another in an often hostile world. For example, many gay men of the era identified themselves to each other as "friends of Dorothy," in reference to their camp devotion to *The Wizard of Oz* (1939).

Queer movie fans also speculated about the sexuality of certain Hollywood stars (such as Dietrich and Garbo) and, with the growth of auteur criticism in the 1950s, movie directors as well. Obviously, many queer actors and actresses worked (and continue to work) in Hollywood. Leading silent film stars Ramon Novarro and Billy Haines were homosexual, but as the Production Code was enforced and Hollywood grew more homophobic, their careers faded. Haines was fired from MGM because he refused to go along with studio publicity designed to hide his homosexuality. Such arranged publicity stunts included dates and even weddings —the so-called "marriage of convenience." For example, Rock Hudson was briefly married in the 1950s to persuade his fans that he was indeed heterosexual. Many queer people also worked behind the camera in Hollywood, many in costume design (Orry-Kelly, Adrian), set decoration (Jack Moore, Henry Grace), and choreography (Robert Alton, Jack Cole). There were also successful producers and directors who led queer lives, including David Lewis, Ross Hunter, Mitchell Leisen, Charles Walters, Edmund Goulding, Irving Rapper, Arthur Lubin, James Whale, George Cukor, and Dorothy Arzner (Mann 2001).

Due to the times in which they worked, how these artists defined their sexuality differed from person to person. Whether director Dorothy Arzner self-identified as a lesbian is still open to question (although she regularly wore mannish suits and smoked cigars on her sets). Director George Cukor allegedly preferred the term "homosexual" over "gay." Interviews and other historical evidence suggest how these artists negotiated their sexuality within the classical Hollywood studio system (Doty 1993; Mayne 1994; Tinkcom 2002; Hadleigh 1986, 1994, 1996). With the Production Code in place, none of these queer filmmakers could forthrightly depict homosexual desires on screen, and in order to continue in their chosen careers, they enacted, wrote, directed, or produced films that celebrated heterosexual romance. Nonetheless, it is often possible to find queer traces in their work. The work of director James Whale provides many examples of this: *Frankenstein* (1931), *The Old Dark House* (1932), *The Invisible Man* (1933), and *The Bride of Frankenstein* (1935) contain numerous moments that ridicule and/or critique heterosexist figures of authority, morality, and/or social convention. However, Whale may have paid a price for infusing his films with a fairly obvious queer sensibility—his career ebbed in the 1940s while those of more closeted directors continued to flourish.

Queers and film circa the sexual revolution

Throughout the 1950s and 1960s, Hollywood began to amend its Production Code and allow more "adult" topics to reach the screen. In 1961, the Code Administration agreed to allow the onscreen treatment of homosexuality, as long as it was done with "care, discretion, and restraint." In actual practice, that meant that homosexuality could now be discussed fairly forthrightly, but that it should also be condemned. For example, the British film *Victim* (1961), which centered on a gay blackmail case and argued that social prejudice against homosexuals was wrong, was denied the Code's Seal of Approval, while the first few American films to deal with homosexuality approved by the Code suggested that homosexuality could only lead to tragedy. In *Advise and Consent* (1962), a past gay relationship is shown to be cause for suicide, and in *The Children's Hour* (1962), a young woman hangs herself after admitting that she is a lesbian. Steeped within the era's medical discourse of "homosexuality-as-disease," such films routinely implied that queer lives were empty, lonely, pitiful, and all too often deadly.

That said, queer characters were still also objects of ridicule, and homosexual innuendo became a staple of 1960s sex comedies such as *That Touch of Mink* (1962), *A Very Special Favor* (1965), and *The Gay Deceivers* (1969). Queerness also continued to function as a signifier of ultimate villainy in action and adventure films like *Lawrence of Arabia* (1962), *From Russia with Love* (1963), and *Caprice* (1967). A few Hollywood films of the era attempted to deal with sexuality in more complex ways: *Reflections in a Golden Eye* (1967) and *The Sergeant* (1968) centered on (repressed) homosexuality in the military, even though their queer characters still met death and destruction. Two of the most famous (and least offensive) Hollywood films dealing with homosexuality during this era were *The Killing of Sister George* (1968, about lesbians in the British television industry) and *The Boys in the Band* (1970, about a group of gay friends in New York City). Both of these films were based on successful stage plays and explored issues of romance, the closet, the possibility of blackmail and job loss, internalized homophobia, and the burgeoning (but still mostly underground) gay and lesbian culture of many cities. While these films may seem overly melodramatic or stereotypical by today's standards, they did capture a certain slice of reality for many urban homosexuals of their era. Perhaps most importantly, no one died at the end of them.

The revision and eventual scrapping of the Hollywood Production Code (it was replaced with the MPAA Ratings System in 1968) was due at least in part to the growing popularity in America of more sexually explicit foreign and independent films throughout the 1950s and 1960s. A few European films that dealt with homosexuality—such as *Olivia* (1951, aka *Pit of Loneliness*), and *The Third Sex* (1957)—found release in North America on the exploitation circuit, as did American films like *Glen or Glenda* (1952), *Chained Girls* (1965), and *The Queen* (1968). The soft-core sexploitation cinema that evolved throughout these years, primarily aimed at heterosexual male spectators, also occasionally contained female same-sex or gender-bending moments. Physique films (shorts that showed men in homoerotic poses and situations) became available via mail order, and around 1970 they evolved into feature-length hard-core gay-male pornographic films. Prior to that, physique films were also screened in urban theaters that catered to gay men, alongside campy Hollywood classics and experimental works made by avant-garde filmmakers like Kenneth Anger, Jack Smith, Andy Warhol, and the Kuchar Brothers.

Each of these different cinemas might be considered broadly queer in some ways, as they often twist the monogamous heteronormativity of Hollywood film into something else altogether. Avant-garde or experimental filmmaking was especially able to explore polymorphous sexual desires because of its open-ended, fluid, and often symbolic form. Rather than telling explicit stories, avant-garde films are open to multiple interpretations and encourage queer border-crossing possibilities. At least one American avant-garde film had dealt with homosexuality before World War II (James Watson and Melville Webber's *Lot in Sodom* [1933]), but it was Kenneth Anger's *Fireworks* (1947), a surreal psychodrama about a young man's homosexual desires, that both scandalized and inspired a new generation of gay male filmmakers. Although Anger lived abroad for most of the 1950s, he returned to America to make his most famous film, *Scorpio Rising* (1963), a film that combined found footage, contemporary pop songs, and a host of other cultural artifacts to examine the social construction of homoerotic motorcycle cultists.

Many queer avant-garde filmmakers of the early 1960s were associated with the so-called Underground Film movement. Jack Smith's *Flaming Creatures* (1962) featured characters (slave girls, vampires, Roman guards, etc.) and overly dramatic music drawn from exotic Hollywood melodramas; it too was queer in content and style, campily framing gender and sexuality as nothing but performative parodies. Andy Warhol's films (including *Haircut* [1963], *Couch* [1964], and *Lonesome Cowboys* [1967]) also parodied Hollywood style and conventions, not to mention subject matter: his actors (many of whom were hustlers or drag queens who did little more than pose for the camera) referred to themselves as "Superstars" and behaved as if they were Hollywood royalty. Many of these Underground Films became enmeshed in various moral crusades and censorship scandals, but they also provided a source of cohesion and community for pre-Stonewall queers. They also inspired cult filmmaker John Waters, who in independent films like *Pink Flamingos* (1972), *Polyester* (1981), and *Hairspray* (1988) brought Underground Film style and transvestite actor Divine to broader audiences.

Independent and experimental lesbian filmmaking began to be popularized in the 1970s. Filmmakers, such as Jan Oxenberg (*Home Movie* [1973]) and Greta Schiller (*Greta's Girls* [1978]), made films that explored the growing lesbian feminist communities of their era. The most prolific lesbian filmmaker, Barbara Hammer, also began to make films at this time. Hammer's films —even her earliest—are excellent examples of queer cinematic practice. They cross borders (between documentary, fiction, and experimental filmmaking), and focus on the complexities of human sexuality—especially the ways in which those sexualities have been socially constructed across time and place. Her early work, including *Superdyke* (1975), *Women I Love* (1976), and *Sync*

Touch (1981), explores issues of love, sex, identity, humor, community, relationships, nature, and spirituality. Lesbian feminists also participated in what would be one of the first documentary features about North American queers, *Word is Out* (1977). The film, made by a collective of gay and lesbian filmmakers, remains a fascinating time-capsule of the nascent gay liberation movement.

Also during the 1970s, the study of gay and lesbian cinema became a growing concern for film scholars and queer activist groups. Gay and lesbian publications in North America and Europe started to pay more attention to media representations, and for the first time in history, queers began to lobby the entertainment industries for better, more well-rounded representations of themselves. Feminist and leftist film journals, such as *Women in Film* and *Jump Cut*, began to publish essays dealing with gay and lesbian representation. One of the first books published that addressed onscreen homosexuality was Parker Tyler's *Screening the Sexes: Homosexuality in the Movies* (1972). A few years later Vito Russo's seminal *The Celluloid Closet: Homosexuality in the Movies* was published (1981, revised and updated in 1987). In that book, Russo examined over 80 years of film history, exploring the ways and means in which gay and lesbian people had been portrayed at the movies.

However, while independent and experimental films were presenting new images of sexual desire, representations of queers in Hollywood films did not initially change very much. Lesbian vampires and other killer queers (such as the homosexual assassins in *Diamonds Are Forever* [1971]) were still popular at the box office. Occasional overtly queer Hollywood films, like *Myra Breckinridge* (1970) or *Something for Everyone* (1970), became the targets of homophobic critical backlash. Aside from *Cabaret* (1972), which presented heterosexual, homosexual, and bisexual leading characters, most mainstream Hollywood films shied away from the topic altogether. However, just as in the silent era, some European cinemas addressed sexuality in more complex ways. In Germany, Rainer Werner Fassbinder directed over 40 films about nationality, race, class, and (homo)sexuality, while Rosa Von Praunheim and Ulrike Ottinger made even more surreal excursions into the politics and pleasures of queer sex. In England, Derek Jarman began to make a series of highly stylized films (*Sebastiane* [1976], *Jubilee* [1977]) that critiqued sexual repression and the British Empire. In Spain, Pedro Almodovar began to develop his queer aesthetic in a series of short films. Interestingly, the one European film centering on homosexuals that became something of a hit in North America was the French film *La Cage Aux Folles* (1978). The film is far less theoretically queer than many of these other European films, and it arguably became an art house hit because it reinscribed decades-old stereotypes of gay men as silly drag queens.

As the 1980s began, Hollywood produced another cycle of gay-themed films. Some of these reworked the old queer psycho-killer stereotype: in *Dressed to Kill* (1980), *Cruising* (1980), and *The Fan* (1981), queer villains slashed their way across multiplex movie screens. Perhaps to atone for those images, Hollywood also released a handful of films that featured sympathetic queer characters. *The World According to Garp* (1982) featured a male-to-female transsexual played by John Lithgow, while *Personal Best* (1982) dramatized a lesbian relationship and issues of bisexuality. Twentieth Century-Fox released *Making Love* (1982), a melodrama about a married couple coming to terms with the husband's latent homosexuality. By far the most popular of these films was the old-fashioned musical sex farce *Victor/Victoria* (1982), a film that featured Julie Andrews as a cross-dressing nightclub performer and Robert Preston as her flamboyantly gay best friend. With those films in the theaters, and British gender-bending bands such as Culture Club and Eurythmics on MTV, it seemed as though Western culture was ready for a new approach to gender and sexuality. However, the growing AIDS crisis had the opposite effect on mainstream heterosexual culture, producing a hysteria around homosexuality and causing a backlash to the idea of gay and lesbian rights. Not wanting to court those controversies, Hollywood again withdrew from the arena.

Out of the closet and into the art house: new queer cinema and beyond

While Hollywood was ignoring the AIDS crisis (except within the metaphoric generic spaces of the horror and slasher film), independent filmmaking continued to grow and provide even more nuanced and complex images of queer lives and issues. The first batch of these films, including *Buddies* (1985, dir. Arthur J. Bressan, Jr.), *Parting Glances* (1986, dir. Bill Sherwood), and *Desert Hearts* (1985, dir. Donna Deitch), used realist storytelling conventions to explore coming out, romance, and AIDS. They were joined at the art house by critical hits like *My Beautiful Laundrette* (1985), *Kiss of the Spider Woman* (1985), *Maurice* (1987), and *Longtime Companion* (1990). Documentary films like *Common Threads: Stories from the Quilt* (1989), and *Silverlake Life* (1993), humanized AIDS and helped spur education and organization, as did video work by activist AIDS collectives. Other documentaries, such as *Before Stonewall* (1985) and *Silent Pioneers* (1985), revealed forgotten aspects of gay and lesbian history, while the Oscar-winning documentary *The Times of Harvey Milk* (1984) chronicled the rise to power of the United States' first openly gay City Supervisor (as well as his eventual assassination by an unhinged right-wing politician). Marlon Riggs's video documentary *Tongues Untied* (1989) remains the definitive statement on what it was like to be a black gay man in America in the 1980s; it too is very queer in form, combining personal history, fictional vignettes, and cinéma-vérité documentary footage with dance, poetry, and music.

The production of these and other films eventually led to the creation of a new crop of queer independent features—films that made waves at several international festivals in 1990 and 1991. These films (including *Poison* [1991], *Swoon* [1991], *Paris is Burning* [1991], *The Living End* [1991], *Edward II* [1991], and *My Own Private Idaho* [1991]) were made by more activist and/or theoretical filmmakers: Todd Haynes, Tom Kalin, Jennie Livingston, Gregg Araki, Derek Jarman, and Gus Van Sant. The films, many fueled by 1980s AIDS activism, engaged with concepts being formulated within queer theory, and collectively they became known as the New Queer Cinema. Christine Vachon, who has been dubbed the "Godmother of New Queer Cinema," produced several of these first films and has since then become a leading figure in the movement. Other important New Queer films of the early 1990s include John Greyson's *Zero Patience* (1993), Rose Troche's *Go Fish* (1994), and Cheryl Dunye's *Watermelon Woman* (1995).

New Queer Cinema makes use of postmodern ideas and aesthetic styles (as does queer theory itself). New Queer Cinema often questions essentialist models of sexual identity, and frequently shows how the terms "gay" and "lesbian" are inadequate when trying to define actual human experience. The films also regularly explore sexuality in relation to gender, race, class, age, etc.—in order to show how other discourses of social difference inflect our understanding of sexuality. In most of these films there is a focus on permeable formal boundaries—the crossing of styles and genres. New Queer Cinema simultaneously draws on minimalism and excess, appropriation and pastiche, the mixing of Hollywood and avant-garde styles, and even the mix of fictional and documentary style. For example, *The Living End* reappropriates the Hollywood buddy/road movie for HIV-positive queers, while *Zero Patience* is a ghost story musical about AIDS. *Watermelon Woman* is a mock documentary about an African American lesbian actress who played "Mammy" roles in 1930s Hollywood: the film is a witty interracial lesbian romance as well as a thoughtful meditation on queer visibility and historical erasure.

While the term "New Queer Cinema" has been mostly applied to a certain group of low-budget English-language independent films made by openly queer filmmakers in the early 1990s, queer filmmaking has continued to branch out into other national and industrial contexts. For example, coinciding with the initial splash of New Queer Cinema was the release of *The Crying Game* (1992), a higher-profile British film that interwove in complex ways the issues of national, racial/ethnic, gender, and sexual identity. It became a major box-office hit (perhaps because many people were fooled by Jaye Davidson's female impersonation), and it won multiple Oscar nominations. Queer films from around the globe such as *Farewell, My Concubine* (1993), *Wild Reeds* (1994), *The Adventures of Priscilla, Queen of the Desert* (1994), *Heavenly Creatures* (1994), *Carrington* (1995), *All About My Mother* (1999), *Our Lady of the Assassins* (2000), *Iron Ladies* (2000), and *Y Tu Mama Tambien* (2002) continue to explore the overlapping borders of various sexualities (as well as those of gender, race/ethnicity, class, and nationality).

Other independent American films—whether made by self-identified queers or not—such as *The Wedding Banquet* (1993), *Happiness* (1998), *Being John Malkovich* (1999), *Chuck and Buck* (2000), *Hedwig and the Angry Inch* (2001), and *Mulholland Drive* (2001) are queer in the ways that they explode formal boundaries and simple-minded classificatory schemata. Recently, due to critical regard, some of these newer queer independent films have even achieved more mainstream distribution. *Boys Don't Cry* (1999), based upon the real-life hate-crime murder of transgendered youth Brandon Teena, was nominated for several Oscars and won for Best Actress. Todd Haynes's *Far From Heaven* (2002), a queer pastiche of 1950s Hollywood melodramas, was also nominated for several Oscars, as was *The Hours* (2002), a film that explored the boundaries of female desire and sexual identity across three different historical periods. Each of these films "broke out" of the art-house circuit and into mainstream multiplex theaters (and were therefore seen by wider audiences).

The practice of New Queer Cinema is not without its detractors. The films often anger conservative filmgoers who feel such subjects should remain unspoken. Other viewers have accused the movement of recirculating negative stereotypes such as the queer psycho-killer. Although films like *Swoon*, *The Living End*, and *Heavenly Creatures* attempt to show how social forces and/or sexual repression can and do cause violence, some filmgoers still see them as reconfirming harmful stereotypes. New Queer Cinema has also been charged with elitism, since it is frequently engaged with issues of queer and postmodern theory. As such, New Queer Cinema can be rigorous and difficult both thematically and formally, and many queer spectators, like straight spectators, prefer "feel good" Hollywood-style movies with happy endings. Those types of movies are also now being made by gay and lesbian independent filmmakers. For example, *The Incredibly True Adventures of Two Girls in Love* (1995), *Beautiful Thing* (1996), *Edge of Seventeen* (1998), and *Billy's Hollywood Screen Kiss* (1998) draw upon the conventions of Hollywood narrative form and the genre of the romantic comedy, placing lesbian and gay lovers into previously heterosexual roles. Films such as *Love! Valour! Compassion!* (1998) and *The Broken Hearts Club* (2000) mix humor with drama, but represent predominantly middle-class white gay men. (It is still easier to find funding for films about white gay men than lesbians or queers of color.) Nevertheless, lesbian, gay, and otherwise queer independent films and videos continue to be made in unprecedented numbers.

Queer Hollywood today

The success of New Queer Cinema in the early 1990s led Hollywood to try briefly (and un-successfully) to market a few films that explored more open parameters of sexuality, such as *Three of Hearts* (1993) and *Threesome* (1994). Hollywood moviegoers were more comfortable with films that deployed the usual stereotypes. Drag queens were central characters in the Hollywood comedies *To Wong Foo, Thanks for Everything, Julie Newmar* (1995) and *The Birdcage* (1996), but the films used them more for comedic effect than a queer deconstruction of gender roles. The success of New Queer Cinema also led to the first major studio film to deal with AIDS, *Philadelphia* (1993), released more than a decade after the crisis began. While a major critical and box office hit, *Philadelphia* still relied on the "tragic-homosexual-who-dies-at-the-end-of-the-film" formula. The lesbian noir thriller *Bound* (1996) was also popular with some mainstream audiences, but it too reinscribed queers as devious criminals, much as did *Silence of the Lambs* (1991) and *Basic Instinct* (1992).

A few new trends dealing with queer issues in Hollywood briefly surfaced in the late 1990s. The first was the reworking of the Hollywood buddy film formula so that it now comprised a straight female lead and her gay male best friend, thus potentially attracting both women and gay men to the box office. *My Best Friend's Wedding* (1997), *The Object of My Affection* (1998), and *The Next Best Thing* (2000) explored the friendships that often exist between women and gay men. However, these films still tend to chafe at Hollywood films' need for happy heterosexual closure. (If the success of *Will and Grace* [NBC-TV, 1998 –] is any indication, the formula works better on TV.) Another recent trend in Hollywood's treatment of homosexuality are a handful of films that explore repressed homosexuality. It was played for laughs in the Hollywood comedy *In and Out* (1997), but a few other films (and recent psychological studies) suggest that it can have deadly effects. *American Beauty* (which won many Oscars in 1999 including Best Picture) dramatized how repressed homosexuality can lead to vicious homophobia, violence, and murder—a theme also found in *The Talented Mr. Ripley* (1999) and even the Comedy Central TV show *South Park* (1997 –). While these films seemingly present a wider range of queer subjectivities, many of them have been understood by moviegoers as simply new versions of the old killer-queer stereotype.

In an era of nostalgic Hollywood blockbusters based on fantasy novels and comic books (and aimed at teenage straight boys), mainstream Hollywood films that deal with actual gay and lesbian lives and issues are extremely rare. However, many of those fantastic Hollywood genre films do seem to be increasingly queer, if only for the ways in which they acknowledge the fluidity of identity and celebrate personal difference over mindless conformity. Films like *Addams Family Values* (1993) and several of Tim Burton's smaller Hollywood projects (such as *Edward Scissorhands* [1990] and *Ed Wood* [1994]) posit more or less overt queers as heroic and their straight counterparts as villainous or banal. In other examples, *X-Men* (2000) and *X-2* (2003) draw fairly explicit parallels between superhero shape-shifting mutants and queer sexual minorities: both are feared and hated by fanatical right-wing politicians because of their ability to undermine order and classification. Other recent films like *Moulin Rouge* (2001) and *Down With Love* (2003) revel in camp aesthetics. Hollywood is perhaps becoming more comfortable with queer sensibilities (no doubt because more and more queer filmmakers in Hollywood are able to be out of the closet), but Hollywood films are still reticent to feature actual queer characters.

This wariness about openly queer characters in Hollywood film helps to maintain the industry's closet mentality. While there are ever-increasing numbers of openly queer writers, directors, and producers in Hollywood today, many actors (and/or their agents and advisors) still fear that the public will not accept an openly gay or lesbian actor in a heterosexual role. The vast majority of queer Hollywood actors remains secretive, reinforcing the notion that there is something wrong or shameful about being gay or lesbian. However, in the late 1990s, a few Hollywood stars, including Ellen Degeneres, Nathan Lane, Rupert Everett, Rosie O'Donnell, and Sir Ian McKellan, have been leading the way in being openly queer media personalities. Many of these actors have worked predominantly in theater or television, two venues that arguably do a much better job depicting queer lives and issues than does Hollywood film. Theater is generally produced for more sophisticated urban audiences, while television's massive need for product has also allowed it to "narrow-cast" to queers.

In many Western nations, state-controlled television outlets (such as Britain's Channel Four, West Germany's ZDF, and PBS in the U.S.) have produced queer-themed shows and movies as part of their goal to give voice to minority filmmakers. Even network television in America is becoming more queer-friendly. After first dabbling in queer issues in the 1970s, gay and lesbian supporting characters were integrated into dramas and comedies like *Dynasty* (ABC-TV, 1981–89) and *Roseanne* (ABC-TV, 1988–99). The popular situation comedy *Ellen* (ABC-TV, 1994–98) broke down many barriers when its lead character came out of the closet as a lesbian, and the short-lived comedy-drama *The Education of Max Bickford* (CBS-TV, 2001–02) even featured a transgendered character. The current craze for reality television programming has also been insistent on including gay, lesbian, and bisexual characters in its line up. MTV's *The Real World* (1992–) has brought many queer people (including HIV-positive Pedro Zamora) into living rooms around the world, and, on *Survivor* (CBS-TV, 2000–), Richard Hatch proved that a gay man could outwit and outmaneuver an entire cast of heterosexuals. Even more recently, the cable network Bravo has aired the reality shows *Gay Weddings* (2002), *Boy Meets Boy* (2003), and *Queer Eye for the Straight Guy* (2003–).

At the start of the twenty-first century, some of the most interesting queer film is now being produced by (and/or distributed through) subscription television channels and global satellite networks. This development (along with the rise of video cassettes, DVDs, and the Internet) has made queer film work much more widely accessible. Some cable channels, such as IFC (the Independent Film Channel) and the Sundance Channel, now regularly program independent queer films and documentaries. Because they don't have to sell their projects to audiences one film at a time, pay TV channels like HBO and Showtime have also been able to produce a great deal of queer-themed work in recent years. Miniseries, original series, made-for-television movies, and theatrical adaptations (including *More Tales of the City* [1998], *Common Ground* [2000], *Queer as Folk* [2000–], *If These Walls Could Talk 2* [2000], *The Laramie Project* [2002], *Normal* [2003], *Soldier's Girl* [2003], and *Angels in America* [2003]) continue to entertain subscribers and win awards for HBO and Showtime. While not yet extant in 2003, the recent boom in queer television programming has even led some media moguls to announce plans for an entire "queer channel." Although heterocentrist imperatives still dominate the mainstream film and television industries, queer audiences don't have to search as intensely as they once did to find evidence of themselves. An ever-widening spectrum of overtly queer images are now available via art house and multiplex theaters, network and cable television, and the local video store.

About this volume

This book is broadly organized into four parts, but it can be read in any order. Part One: Auteurs problematizes traditional ideas of the cinematic auteur in relation to queer theory. It presents several case studies of queerly made work, including an essay discussing queer Hollywood filmmakers George Cukor and Dorothy Arzner, an essay on pre-Stonewall gay male physique films, and one on 1970s lesbian avant-garde cinema. It concludes with a reprint of B. Ruby Rich's "The New Queer Cinema," an essay that officially marked the ascendancy of that movement in the early 1990s. Part Two: Forms presents four essays that discuss how and why the horror film, the musical, film noir, and the animated film might be understood as queer. Part Three contains two essays on camp, one written in the 1970s and another from the 1990s. Finally, Part Four: Reception presents three specific historical case studies that demonstrate queer reception practices. The volume concludes with excerpts from an essay that attempt to rethink or otherwise queer classical gaze theory.

Aside from this broad four-part organization (Auteurs, Forms, Camp, and Reception), there are two larger overlapping systems that structure this collection. The first is a history of queer cinematic representation produced by and in response to Hollywood. All of the essays included in this volume attempt to shed light on this history in some way—a history that has often been overlooked and/or denied by mainstream film critics as well as many viewers. The second is a history of the theoretical models used by scholars to analyze these representations. Since its inception, a variety of philosophical and/or sociological models have been used to study film, up to and including queer theory. Thus the essays collected here often speak from and about different eras, and use different methodologies. It is hoped that the essays will speak to and inform one another. For example, while chiefly an examination of queer fan reception, Henry Jenkins's analysis of queers and *Star Trek* delves into issues raised in Part Two: Forms. Similarly, Andrea Weiss's overview of lesbian independent cinema in Part One: Auteurs discusses aspects of gaze theory that are the foci of Caroline Evans and Lorraine Gamman's essay in Part Four: Reception. Thus in apposite queerness, the articles contained herein refuse to stay neatly categorized. How queer theory will be used and applied in the future we cannot say, but this collection hopes to show where it has been, in order to suggest avenues still left to explore, and boundaries still waiting to be crossed.

PART ONE

AUTEURS

Introduction

Auteur criticism (assigning creative authorship of a film to a specific talent—usually the director) became popular in the middle of the twentieth century as a strategy for promoting cinema as a serious art form. If one could argue that artists were responsible for making films, then one could argue that films were art. Auteur critics found stylistic and thematic motifs across a director's oeuvre, and often linked these emphases to the life history of the auteur. For example, the emphasis on guilt and punishment in Alfred Hitchcock's films is supposedly tied to his Catholic upbringing. Yet, auteur criticism has also come under harsh reappraisal since its hey-day in the 1960s and 1970s. On a basic level, the auteur theory accords responsibility to one person, and ignores the literal army of creative talent that often comes together to create a motion picture. The auteur concept has also come under attack as poststructuralist theories have deconstructed the concepts of individuality and human agency. In exposing the matrices of complexity that inhabit each individual, poststructuralist thought seems to make the "creative genius" notion of the auteur overly simplistic. Thus, when one speaks of Hitchcock as a director, one is actually speaking of a set of stylistic and thematic traits derived from the study of his films, and not the actual man. The connections between "Hitchcock" the auteur signature and Hitchcock the man are necessarily complex.

In more recent years, the rise of cultural studies has reinvigorated auteur analyses. Critics and theorists are once again examining the social and historical background of filmmakers, especially in relation to race/ethnicity, class, gender, and sexuality. It is felt by many that such social discourses do have an important impact upon a filmmaker's creative imagination. For example, in the case of The Color Purple (1985), many people questioned how Steven Spielberg's white Jewish male subjectivity could adequately address the issues of black lesbian feminism. Similarly, is it appropriate to have a heterosexist (or even homophobic) filmmaker make a film about queer characters and issues, as has happened throughout Hollywood history? The rise of gay and lesbian independent filmmaking in the 1980s was a challenge to that situation: with those films (and later New Queer Cinema), filmgoers could be assured that queer stories and issues were being expressed from some kind of a queer subject position.

Queer auteur theory allows one to explore how a homosexual director in the 1930s might have expressed him- or herself in Hollywood films. Many critics have argued that some sort of gay sensibility or queer trace does indeed "shine through" the restrictions of studio filmmaking under the Hollywood Production Code, especially in work of directors such as James Whale, Dorothy Arzner, and George Cukor (Benshoff 1997; Mayne 1994; Doty 1993). Yet, queer traces in film can also arise from other sources, and other studies have explored how costume designers, actors, or choreographers might also be considered queer auteurs (Mann 2001; Tinkcom 2002).

This section begins with Alexander Doty's "Whose Text Is It Anyway? Queer Cultures, Queer Auteurs, and Queer Authorship," an essay that examines classical Hollywood filmmakers Dorothy Arzner and George Cukor. Doty's essay reviews some of the complexities of queer auteur theory, and stresses the need to understand how Arzner and Cukor themselves understood their sexuality. In "Physique Cinema, 1945–1969: Hard to Imagine," Tom Waugh examines the often anonymous auteurs responsible for making 1950s and 1960s physique films. Physique films were an offshoot of that era's physique magazines; both were forerunners of the modern gay male pornography industry, serving as soft-core erotica for queer men in the pre-Stonewall era. However, the films often presented themselves as "merely" non-sexual artists' studies in order to circumvent the obscenity laws of the times. The physique cinema, while little known today, was one of the first commercially viable film movements made by and for gay men.

Andrea Weiss's essay, "Transgressive Cinema: Lesbian Independent Film," examines the work of several lesbian avant-garde filmmakers of the 1970s and 1980s, including Jan Oxenberg, Barbara Hammer, and Su Freidrich. Weiss is careful to examine how historically specific forms of lesbian feminism impacted upon the films, and also explores how lesbian desire might be represented outside patriarchal forms. The last article in this section, B. Ruby Rich's "The New Queer Cinema," shows how, starting around 1991, a new generation of filmmakers began to use queer theory to structure their films. Rich's article also critiques the movement by examining how gender and racial/ethnic identity impacted upon the first wave of these films.

Whose Text Is It Anyway?

1

Queer Cultures, Queer Auteurs, and Queer Authorship

ALEXANDER DOTY

There is a moment in George Cukor's 1939 film *The Women* that I will use as a condensed illustration of the critical issues in this chapter. The scene is a luncheon at Mary Haines's suburban home. As Mary passes biscuits around, Sylvia Fowler refuses them because she is watching her weight. "Go ahead, dear. No starch, it's gluten!" Mary exclaims. Taking a biscuit, Sylvia sarcastically remarks to the other women: "Have you ever known such a housewife?" In a film abounding with in-jokes, this moment is perhaps the slyest and the most subversive of them all. For Sylvia is played by Rosalind Russell, who three years earlier had portrayed the neurotically "perfect" housewife Harriet Craig in *Craig's Wife*, directed by Dorothy Arzner.[1]

Linked by an actress who was to become a cult favorite for many lesbians and gays, Cukor's reference to Arzner pivots on an implicitly antidomestic wisecrack pertinent to the hidden agenda of both *Craig's Wife* and *The Women*, as well as to that of a number of Arzner and Cukor films. In terms of queer cultural history, Russell's retort also offers itself as a hidden homage by one queer director to another—that is, if you know Cukor was homosexual (Cukor disliked the term "gay") and Arzner was lesbian.[2] With this queer biographical information, the moment of closeted comradeship in *The Women* becomes both touching and provocative, placed as it is within the context of a conventional narrative film produced by a capitalist industry for a straight society.

The genesis of the following thoughts on Cukor, Arzner, auteurism, authorship, queerness, and queer cultures was an invitation to present a paper at a Cukor and Arzner symposium that was part of the 1990 Pittsburgh Lesbian and Gay Film Festival. The particular context for this lecture suggested that I consider traditional auteurist notions of Arzner and Cukor as queer directors expressing consistent, idiosyncratic stylistic and thematic concerns throughout the body of their films, as well as questions of how Cukor, Arzner, and their films might be meaningful in and for queer cultures, particularly lesbian and gay ones. Thinking about the critical approaches implied by this public context for the paper, the anecdotal cross-referencing of Cukor's *The Women* and Arzner's *Craig's Wife* seemed to point out how the demands of established critical approaches such as auteurism and other types of authorship studies might require reworking when set against the work of queer cultures and queer cultural analysis.[3]

[. . .]

Why should queers bother with Cukor and Arzner? If career survival and success within the Hollywood system were the issue, why not focus on a Howard Hawks or an Alfred Hitchcock, whose bodies of work have the added advantage of containing more obvious queerly erotic and crypto-queer elements than are readily apparent in all the films of Cukor and Arzner— excepting, perhaps, *Sylvia Scarlett*. Being erotically attracted to members of their own sex shouldn't automatically make these directors interesting to queer cultures. Indeed, a radical queer critique of Cukor and Arzner as auteurs would say that they were closeted homosexual collaborators who helped perpetuate a heterocentrist industry catering to the desires of a queer-oppressive society.

But while there may be something to this, there are ways in which the lives and works of Dorothy Arzner and George Cukor have been, and might continue to be, analyzed within the context of queer culture and queer cultural studies. Beyond this, a spectator's queer pleasure in Arzner and Cukor texts can be enriched by considering a critical approach that combines auteurism and queer cultural reception practices.

Relatively recent work to discover (and create) queer history in order to make it more visible (including the strategy of "outing") has encouraged discussions exploring the relationship of sexual orientation to cultural creation and production. It is important to recall, however, that these discussions have always been encouraged in queer cultures through the "guess who's lesbian, gay, or bisexual?" gossip grapevine. This informal and vital source of information has, for a number of decades, encouraged many gays, lesbians, bisexuals, and even some straights to develop their own specifically queer forms of auteurist analyses around certain cultural figures and their creative output.

Gay culture—and by this I mean, in this case, a gay culture fostered largely by white middle- and upper-class urban men—discovered individual Cukor and Arzner films before they recognized Arzner and Cukor as auteurs, or as queers/queer auteurs. Generally, gay cultural enthusiasm for these films was first generated and sustained through the women stars in them: Greta Garbo in *Camille* and *Two-Faced Woman*; Katharine Hepburn in *Little Women*, *Christopher Strong*, *Sylvia Scarlett*, and *Adam's Rib*, among other films; Jean Harlow in *Dinner at Eight*; Clara Bow in *The Wild Party*; Judy Garland in *A Star Is Born*; Joan Crawford in *The Women*, *A Woman's Face*, and *The Bride Wore Red*; Ruth Chatterton in *Sarah and Son*; and Rosalind Russell in *Craig's Wife* and *The Women*.[4] This being the case, gay cultural readings of these Cukor and Arzner films were (and still are) often worked out within star-as-auteur paradigms. That is, these readings are primarily concerned with analyzing, and actually helping to create, the meanings of a star's image across films by different directors. An important part of such star- as-text/text-as-"star vehicle" reading practices is using extratextual material: exploitation and marketing information (reviews, interviews, advertising, studio publicity), gossip, and even fantasies and fictions created around the stars.

Most of the stars and films I've just mentioned could also be cited as examples of how many lesbians first came to appreciate films directed by Arzner and Cukor. Through their own star-as-auteur cultural readings, lesbians developed cults for Garbo and Hepburn, for example.[5] An issue of the lesbian and gay quarterly OUT/LOOK contains a tribute to Garbo by the artist Margie Adams that begins: "Garbo is dead. And the grief that sits in the corner of my day is, first of all, simple. I have loved and admired her since the first time I saw her in 1964, in *Grand Hotel*. I was seventeen, an awkward, fierce, and angular young one, just come out three months earlier, and I knew, right down to my molecular structure, that the shimmering beauty with such a jawline up there on the screen was a dyke, just like me."[6]

Since erotic pleasure and identification are so central to these lesbian star cults, I would guess most lesbians who love such Cukor films as *Camille*, *Little Women*, *Sylvia Scarlett*, or *Adam's Rib* finally care very little that the same person directed all these films, even once they discover this person was a self-defined homosexual. Aside from perhaps taking some degree of incidental pleasure in the knowledge that a queer worked with Garbo and Hepburn on these films, I doubt most lesbian readings and uses of the films I've just cited are fundamentally concerned with director-as-auteur, or even director-as-queer-auteur considerations.

The situation might be different in Arzner's case, as knowing another lesbian was involved in the presentation of a figure of identification and erotic desire such as Hepburn is bound to encourage lesbian viewers to reexamine the films for signs of the director's narrative and stylistic articulation of lesbian desires and attitudes in relation to the star. And, of course, as knowledge of Arzner's queerness is becoming more widespread, her life and works are becoming important in lesbian (and more generally queer) cultural readings of film history, as well as in individual lesbian/queer readings of Arzner films. One can reverse these observations about Arzner and Cukor in relation to gays and gay cultural history. Whereas discovering Arzner was queer would not fundamentally alter most readings of those films gays had come to through star cults, or perhaps through genre cults (such as for maternal melodramas and musicals), knowing Cukor was gay could make a great difference to gay readings of his films, and to articulating gay cultural history in general. To mention just one instance, the critical commonplace about Cukor being a "woman's director" would take on different meanings when placed within the context of certain cross-gender identification practices in gay culture.[7]

Of course, an important consideration in all this formal and informal queer cultural work is the intersection of cultural history and the personal history of the reader. It is in this intersection that queers have mapped out the complex and diverse space of their interactions with mass culture. We enter cultural history at various times and under differing circumstances, which affect how we make sense of the personalities and products within a culture. For example, in earlier periods lesbians might initially become acquainted with the films of Garbo or Arzner through erotic attraction, lesbian star cult, or feminist scholarship, and they would develop readings and uses of Garbo and Arzner through these approaches. More recently, lesbians might first come to Garbo and Arzner upon hearing something about their lesbianism (or alleged lesbianism), information that might then develop into the central analytic focus for these viewers' appreciation of the star's and the director's films as "lesbian films." This reading process uses extratextual material as a way of "authorizing" the decoding and reading of certain narrative and style codes in films as specific to lesbian culture.[8]

Naturally, as audiences move through history as individuals and as members of groups, their initial readings and uses of culture are subject to additions and revisions. A recent piece on Arzner's films that examines earlier academic feminist work in the light of specifically lesbian critical perspectives is Judith Mayne's "Female Authorship Reconsidered" in *The Woman at the Keyhole*.[9] In this chapter, Mayne suggests that the central marks of Arzner's "female authorship" are to be found in the tensions between her narrative interest in female communities and friendships among women and her representations of herself through certain secondary characters coded as "mannish" lesbians. In relation to this, Mayne proposes that "textually, the most pervasive sign of Arzner's authorship is her use of irony." This irony takes the form of a general female/feminist "ironic perspective on patriarchal institutions," as well as more specific forms of "lesbian irony." Both of these ironic modes work to reinforce those tensions between the homosocial and the erotic Arzner develops in her films' narratives and characterizations.[10]

But aside from Mayne, and academic conference papers by Jane Gaines and Claudia Gorbman, most writers have ignored Arzner's sexual biography and its potential relevance to lesbian and queer cultures in terms of questions of authorship. Indeed, until feminist academics interviewed her in the mid-1970s, no one was much interested in Arzner's life at all. And because Arzner resisted discussing herself as a feminist or as a lesbian, even this one interview, conducted by Karyn Kay and Gerald Peary, carefully avoids the topic of Arzner's sexuality and how it may have influenced her work.[11] In spite of Arzner's hesitancy, though, the interviewers do constantly return to a straight feminist agenda, often asking Arzner to discuss what it was like to be a woman working within the studio system, or about the ways in which she may have paid more attention to coaching actresses and developing women characters.

However, there is a moment in this interview where Arzner, consciously or not, offers an opportunity for a discussion of cross-gender identification within erotic narrative situations as one means of establishing a lesbian mode of expression within traditional film forms. This moment comes when Arzner deflects another attempt to link her identification to the actresses and women characters in *Christopher Strong*: "But I was more interested in Christopher Strong, played by Colin Clive, than in any of the women characters. He was a man 'on the cross.' He loved his wife, and he fell in love with the aviatrix. He was on a rack. I was really more sympathetic with him, but no one seemed to pick up on that."[12] Understandably, the straight auteur-as-feminist program of Arzner's interviewers kept them from pursuing the potential auteur-as-lesbian coding in this statement.

Unlike Arzner, George Cukor was interviewed many times by journalists and scholars outside the Hollywood publicity machine, once at book length. The continued availability of this material has allowed the interested general public to indulge in some form of biographical (if not necessarily queer) auteurist readings of Cukor films. Cukor also has the advantage of an interview with Boze Hadleigh that touched upon issues of sexual identity and creative production within the Hollywood system. This interview, reprinted in Hadleigh's book *Conversations with My Elders*, became part of Cukor's personal and professional coming out.[13] This process was continued after Cukor's death with Patrick McGilligan's *George Cukor: A Double Life*, which considers the director's personal life and professional life within particular gay cultural contexts, with reference to Cukor's own attitudes about his "homosexuality."[14]

In "Cukor and Authorship: A Reappraisal," one of the first academic articles on the director after his coming out, Richard Lippe takes issue with earlier auteurist critics who devalued Cukor's authorship by pejoratively categorizing him as a "woman's director" or a "stylist." While Lippe makes clear his desire to "indicate why [he] think[s] Cukor deserves recognition as an auteur," he also suggests that his interest in reevaluating Cukor's films isn't only focused on "their status as auteurist works" by a gay man. From his position as a gay cultural critic, Lippe is also concerned with how Cukor's films and his career are "relevant to a discussion of the Hollywood cinema which remains to the present day a homophobic institution," as well as how Cukor's films examine "an extremely crude and barbaric social and economic system . . . which is constructed on sexual inequality."[15]

[. . .]

In constructing an auteurism to fit their gay and lesbian critical agendas, Lippe and Mayne reveal some of the range of approaches available to queers in developing forms of authorship that consider how ideas and information about directors (or other important creative collaborators), whether they are queer themselves or not, have been, are, and might be significant in queer cultural readings of individual texts and bodies of work. This would be a use of auteurism that considers that meanings are constructed within and across film texts through the interplay of creators, cultures, and audiences. As a result, queer auteurs could either be "born" or "made"; that is, a case could be developed for directors (or stars, or scriptwriters, etc.) as queer auteurs on the basis of their being queer (Cukor, Arzner, Mitchell Leisen, Isaac Julien, Sergei Eisenstein, Richard Fung, Edmund Goulding, Marlon Riggs, F. W. Murnau, James Whale, Michelle Parkerson, Luchino Visconti, Ulrike Ottinger, Barbara Hammer, Kenneth Anger, R. W. Fassbinder, and many others), or on the evidence that many of their films hold, or have held, particularly meaningful places within queer cultural history, with or without knowledge of the director's sexuality (Cukor again, Vincente Minnelli, Alfred Hitchcock, William Wyler, Josef von Sternberg, Leontine Sagan, Ernst Lubitsch, Max Ophuls, Douglas Sirk, Rouben Mamoulian, Billy Wilder, Susan Seidelman, Joseph L Mankiewicz, Busby Berkeley, and others). Perhaps another way queer auteurs are "made" happens when the films of non-queer-identified directors become interesting to queerly positioned spectators for their queer (sub)texts (Hitchcock, Seidelman, Jacques Rivette, Diane Kurys, Howard Hawks, Martin Scorcese, Carol Reed, Nicholas Ray, Blake Edwards, Joseph Losey, and others). Of course, there is always the possibility of queerly reading the oeuvre of any director (star, scriptwriter, etc.) by conducting a queer analysis of textual discourses articulating sexual desire and sexual identity, whether these concern queer or non-queer subjects.

As part of queer cultural authorship practices that employ some form of auteurism to establish queer auteurs, queers might borrow the notion from Andrew Sarris and other early auteurists that certain unconventional elements of a director's biography and ideology could be expressed within the conventional texts of a capitalist industry—even if sporadically and in heavily coded forms. To this we might add *Cahiers du Cinéma*'s structuralist reworking of auteurism in 1969, which separates films into seven categories, "a" to "g." Each category is defined according to how clearly and coherently a culture's ideological agenda is conveyed through the text. Of particular interest for queer auteurist readings of Arzner and Cukor films is Category "e," which is defined as containing films in which

> an internal criticism is taking place which cracks the film apart at the seams. If one reads the film obliquely, looking for symptoms; if one looks beyond the apparent formal coherence, one can see that it is riddled with cracks. . . . This is the case in many Hollywood films, for example, which while being completely integrated into the system and the ideology end up by partially dismantling the system from within.[16]

Viewed as Category "e" films, the works of many commercial directors, but even more those of queer directors such as Cukor and Arzner, might be "obliquely" examined by queer-positioned readers for textual signs that complicate or resist the coherent presentation of conventional straight ideology.

Finally, feminist work with auteurism in the 1970s and 1980s provides queer spectators and critics with analytic models linking auteurist analysis to the articulation of certain theories and polemics. Implicitly basing many of their readings of traditional narrative films on the *Cahiers* Category "e" paradigm, feminist critics would search the works of directors such as Raoul Walsh, Alfred Hitchcock, and Dorothy Arzner for textual gaps, contradictions, and excesses around which to construct radical readings of these directors' works from positions critiquing patriarchal ideology.

As part of this feminist auteurism, studio directors such as Arzner, Ida Lupino, Lois Weber, and Alice Guy-Blaché were rediscovered and their careers and works reread as part of a feminist project to construct their own film history, film theory, and film practice. To this end, feminist uses of auteurism initially concentrated upon identifying "female discourses" within and between the films of female (and a few male) directors. Although critically examining the production contexts in which these directors worked was important to feminist auteurist readings, as they exposed various institutional and aesthetic impediments to directly expressing female discourses in film, the personal biographies of directors appeared to hold little interest for the first wave of feminist commentators, aside from these directors' status as (implicitly straight) "women" or "men."

But since queerness is not usually visible in the ways gender is understood to be, biographical information about directors (and stars, writers, etc.) and spectators often becomes crucial to examining queer authorship. For queer people on all sides of the camera— before it, behind it, and in the audience—the problem of expressing ourselves from our positions as invisible and oppressed "minority" sexual cultures within a hypervisible and pervasive straight culture offers a compelling parallel to auteurist notions that certain studio directors expressed their unconventional views by developing oppositional practices within conventional production and narrative models. The signs of such oppositional practices, whether intentional or not, would be found in those elements of textual tension and contradiction created through formal emphases—whether narrative or stylistic.[17]

Following this line, we can say that directors—and certainly queer directors—who had particularly unspeakable ideological programs found it necessary to continue developing a repertoire of sly working-within-the-system expressive tactics even once they achieved stature within the industry. Arzner and Cukor were among those commercially successful studio directors who eventually attained a degree of creative choice and collaborative control in developing their projects. This could mean making casting suggestions, as well as influencing the choice of scenarist, cinematographer, and other crew members. Perhaps this explains such daring projects as Cukor's *Sylvia Scarlett* and Arzner's *Christopher Strong*, as well as startling moments such as Maureen O'Hara's class- and patriarchy-dismantling, working woman-bonding speech in Arzner's *Dance, Girl, Dance*; young Mary's comment as she jumps in bed with her mother in *The Women*: "You know, that's the one good thing about divorce—you get to sleep with your mother"; Clara Bow's "You see, I love her too," in *The Wild Party*; or the last line of *Our Betters*, delivered by a heavily made-up fop observing the reconciliation of two socialites: "Ah, what an exquisite spectacle! Two ladies of title kissing one another."[18]

Apart from *Sylvia Scarlett*, these films and scenes almost, but don't quite, openly express queer positions within conventional narrative texts. These particular Cukor and Arzner films do invite spectators to view "obliquely" the conventions of straight narrative construction and the straight ideology these narratives attempt to naturalize. As such, they become crucial in developing queerly authored auteurist readings of Arzner's and Cukor's films.

[. . .]

Arzner's *Dance, Girl, Dance* has been the subject of straight feminist analyses, but what's here for queers?[19] Some aspects of potential queer pleasure overlap with straight feminist pleasure: for example, having women at the center not only of the narrative but of the narrative action, becoming as much agents-subjects as they are spectacularized objects. The men in this film can't quite get a purchase on the narrative. Just when it seems as if one of them will begin to control the action, Arzner narratively neutralizes them, and Maureen O'Hara's Judy, Lucille Ball's Bubbles, Maria Ouspenskaya's Madame Basilova, or Katharine Alexander's Miss Olmstead ("Olmie") steps in to move the plot along. And the narrative often moves along in terms of these women's work and their relationships to each other through their work. Mayne suggests that "female authorship acquires its most significant contours in Arzner's work through relations between and among women," and that this includes establishing a "female gaze [that] is defined early on in [Dance, Girl, Dance] as central to the aspirations of the women as they are shaped within a community of women."[20]

At first glance, the burlesque performer Bubbles seems to be a conventional straight golddigger who is the romantic opposition to ballet-dancing Judy for rich alcoholic Jimmie Harris (Louis Hayward). But look again: Bubbles is jealous of Judy not primarily or ultimately because of jealousy about Jimmie. Bubbles enviously admires Judy's dancing talent, her "classiness," and her quiet strength of character. After she becomes a successful burlesque queen called "Tiger Lily White," Bubbles finds Judy and offers her a job as her lead-in act. Of course, Bubbles knows Judy's ballet dancing will be mocked by the crowd. And we know Bubbles herself will derive some satisfaction from Judy's humiliation, but not so much because Bubbles is mean-spirited as because she hopes it will place Judy on the same personal and professional level as her.

And this is just the queer point—not only is most of Bubbles's jealous energy directed toward Judy, it is ultimately about Judy, in the sense that it is about Bubbles's envious admiration of Judy. She wants Judy with her, and she wants Judy in a situation she controls. Indeed, a lesbian/queer reading of Dance, Girl, Dance would recognize the obvious: the most compelling emotional energies and tensions develop around Bubbles's and Judy's inter-twined professional and personal lives. Arzner (and Bubbles) uses Jimmie in the narrative in the same way women characters are traditionally used in "straight" male narratives—that is, as a public vehicle for transgressive erotic exchanges between same-sex characters.[21] Bubbles loves the money and fame her solo career brings her, but she can't forget high-class Judy, so she attempts to combine the personal with the professional by convincing her manager she needs a lead-in act, and then hiring Judy for the spot.

A reading along these lines would see Bubbles's sudden decision to trick a drunken Jimmie into marriage as her way of removing a romantic and sexual threat to her partnership with Judy. This interpretation seems reinforced by Bubbles's attempts to provoke Judy to display visible signs of jealousy about the marriage. At this point they, and we, know Bubbles doesn't really care for Jimmie, and that even Judy is more devoted to her dancing career than to him. So what would this jealousy be about if it were not an indication of lesbian (or perhaps bisexual) desire?

But Judy seems more concerned about herself and her career than she is about Bubbles, although Arzner makes Judy's spectacular show- and narrative-stopping, woman-bonding, straight man-bashing speech seem to be Judy's response to the news of Bubbles's marriage to Jimmie. Thus positioned, the speech makes one wonder a bit about the possibility of Judy's repressed queerness, especially as she implicitly defends Bubbles in her indictment of straight male sexuality as the illusory base for patriarchal empowerment: "We'd laugh too," Judy shouts out to the burlesque show audience, "only we're paid to let you sit there and roll your eyes and make your screamingly clever remarks. What's it all for? So you can go home and strut before your wives and sweethearts, and play at being the stronger sex for a minute? I'm sure they see through you, just like we do!"

However, Judy's deconstruction of the straight sex show in and out of the burlesque house (and, by extension, the movie house) also signals the end of her partnership with Bubbles. Realizing this, and incensed that Judy has ruined their act, yet perhaps also encouraged by Judy's man-bashing rhetoric, Bubbles rushes out and instigates an onstage wrestling match with Judy. Although this match can be appropriated for straight uses, as it is by the cheering men in the burlesque house, it seems less a conventional "catfight," given Arzner's narrative contextualization, than the wild, confused expression of Bubbles's thwarted and not fully conscious desire for Judy.[22]

Earlier in the film, Judy, substituting for Bubbles, auditions for a job by attempting a hula. Failing to impress the club manager with her restrained movements, it appears as if Judy and the entire troupe will continue to be jobless. Enter Bubbles, who looks at Judy, sizes up the situation, and launches into a sexually suggestive hula. Bubbles's dancing here seems designed as much to show herself off to Judy, and to impress her, as it is to impress the lecherous club manager. But a full reading of how this sequence helps to establish a space for articulating lesbian desire within or alongside positions that represent straight male desire needs to consider the part played by the character of Madame Basilova in this scene, and throughout the narrative.

Madame Basilova is a once-famous Russian ballerina who has been forced to make her living by training troupes of chorus girls for nightclub floor shows. Bubbles and Judy both work in her current troupe, but Judy is the only one with a talent for classical dance, so Madame Basilova focuses her attention on training Judy for an audition with a major ballet company. Wearing plain tailored outfits and ties, Madame Basilova offers, in appearance and narrative function, striking parallels to the many publicity pictures of Dorothy Arzner at work, usually showing her gazing intently at the more traditionally feminized actresses she is directing.[23] Basilova's name also suggests that of one of Arzner's more famous lovers—the Russian actress Nazimova, who also produced films, the most notorious of which was a 1922 version of Oscar Wilde's *Salome*.[24]

Both Basilova's work training dancers—whether classical or burlesque—and Arzner's directing Hollywood actresses in straight, patriarchal narratives are concerned with presenting women as erotic spectacles. So Basilova and Arzner find themselves in rather queer positions vis-à-vis the women they work with. The dance instructor and the film director are women whose jobs encourage them, indeed require them, to assume an erotic gaze while preparing women for public presentation. In an interview, Arzner recalled the time she visited the set of a never-completed "Tarzan-type picture" in order to discuss *Christopher Strong* with Katharine Hepburn. "She was up a tree with a leopard skin on!" the director recalled, adding, "She had a marvelous figure."[25]

In *Dance, Girl, Dance* Arzner appears to acknowledge the erotics of her own position as Hollywood film director through her treatment of Madame Basilova. Simultaneously, Arzner demonstrates how easily supposedly straight male erotic spectator positions might be claimed as sites of lesbian/queer pleasure. The scene I mentioned in which Bubbles dances the hula for Judy (and, one might add, for Madame Basilova) is one example of how a lesbian erotic gaze is negotiated in *Dance, Girl, Dance*. Even more striking is the sequence Arzner constructs around Madame Basilova's secretive and pleasurable gazing at Judy while she practices a dance.

Lured by music playing above her office, Basilova climbs the stairs. Before reaching the top, she stops and positions herself behind the balustrade, glancing off at Judy. As Basilova places herself to gaze at Judy, the camera makes a graceful tracking curve away from Basilova, positioning itself so that our first sight of Judy is clearly *not* Basilova's; it is a spectator position emphatically established as being *next* to Basilova's, which offers Judy as a (sexual, entertainment, identificatory) spectacle for those "not Basilova" viewers—straight men, by traditional feminist theoretical convention, but also, potentially, gays, bisexuals, and straight women. Subsequent shots of Judy, however, will represent Basilova's gaze in their angle and distance, until Basilova sneaks down the stairs and the shot of Judy returns to a non-point-of-view one, which now encourages a range of erotic responses from viewers, as the previous sequence has marked at least two different eroticized spectator positions in relation to the spectacle of Judy's dance.

In this sequence, by the simple expedient of making a culturally invisible spectator active and visible in her spectatorship, Arzner suggests something extraordinary: the space for queer expression has always existed within, or alongside, what traditionally have been considered straight cultural forms and conventions. These forms and conventions only seem inevitably bound to express straight positions because, historically, they have been used most often, and most visibly, to promote straight ideologies and desires. Make queer positions visible and differentiate them from straight positions, Arzner implies in *Dance, Girl, Dance*, and we can articulate queer discourses right in the heart of existing cultural forms—no secret (sub)cultural coding, recoding, and decoding necessary.

[. . .]

Cukor's *Sylvia Scarlett* is one of the queerest films ever made in Hollywood. This is the film in which Katharine Hepburn plays a teenaged boy for most of the running time. It opens with a printed prologue that hints at the queerness to come: "To the adventurer, to all who stray from the beaten track, life is an extravagance in which laughter and luck and love come in odd ways; but they are nonetheless sweet for that." Cukor had wanted the film to begin with Hepburn already dressed as a boy, but the studio forced him to modify this opening: "We had to add a silly, frivolous prologue, to explain *why* this girl was dressed like a boy, and being so good at it. We weren't allowed to give the impression that she liked it, or that she's done it before, or that it came naturally."[26]

Although a commercial failure in 1936, many critics were taken with Hepburn's abilities as androgyne. *Time* magazine's critic noted the film revealed "the interesting fact that Katharine Hepburn is better-looking as a boy than as a woman." The *New York Herald Tribune* effused, "The dynamic Miss Hepburn is the handsomest boy of the season."[27] Discussing *Sylvia Scarlett* in his first book on cult films, Danny Peary finds it "quite remarkable that during a period when such things as transvestism and bisexuality were taboo no one even mentioned the strange sights found in this picture."[28] Peary proceeds to enumerate some of these "strange sights" in language that veers between the heterocentric and the homophobic. "We actually see Katharine Hepburn kissed on the lips by another woman," Peary breathlessly notes. And he feels compelled to follow this observation with the straight-comforting explanation that this queer kiss occurs when Maudie thinks Sylvia is a boy and tries to seduce 'him.'"[29]

Peary then goes on about the scene in which the artist Michael Fane invites the person he knows as Sylvester to share a bed with him. Though Peary tries to suggest that "Fane's intentions may be innocent," he adds, "but how many men in their thirties are such good friends with teen-aged boys?"[30] "Then, of course," Peary concludes, "there is Fane's famous line to

'Sylvester': 'I don't know what it is that gives me a queer feeling when I look at you.'"[31] Actually Peary misquotes the line. What Fane says to Sylvester is "I know [not 'I don't know'] what it is that gives me a queer feeling when I look at you." Peary's rewriting bespeaks denial and repression of queerness; Cukor's film of the recognition and assertion of queerness. And it is a queerness that ultimately has bisexuality as the foundation of its erotic politics: Michael Fane, the painter (Brian Aherne); Jimmy Monkley, the con artist (Cary Grant); and Lily, the countess (Natalie Paley) are all shown to be attracted both to Sylvester and to Sylvia. Since we know Sylvester is Sylvia, even Maudie's (Dennie Moore) flirtations with Sylvester carry some bisexual charge in addition to their lesbian suggestiveness. The narrative concludes with the union of two bisexual couples: Jimmy and Lily (after she leaves Fane) and Fane and Sylvia-Sylvester.

The public and critical silence in 1936 about the "strange sights" in *Sylvia Scarlett* is not so remarkable considering that a commentator in 1981 can't even see what the film is really about—or, perhaps, can't comfortably accept what he sees because it gives him the same "queer feelings" Fane gets when he looks at Sylvester. After homophobically declaring that "modern thinking has added unfortunate connotations" to "trans-gender impersonation," Cukor critic Gary Carey admits that audiences who find cross-gender material "embarrassing and alienating" do so because "too often it cuts close to our own suspicions about the actors involved or to our fears about ourselves."[32]

Queerly seen, *Sylvia Scarlett* is an erotically daring film whose seriocomic uses of transvestism within the conventions of a mistaken identity plot playfully invite all spectators to experience "queer feelings" as they move through the range of homo-, bi-, and heterosexual desires articulated in the text. And the film gains added dimensions if you know that Cary Grant's real-life bisexuality could be playing a major role in its gender- and sexuality-blurring proceedings. While Cukor and Hepburn often joked about the film as a failure, Cukor said he was pleased about its "sexuality before its time" cult status, admitting that although *Sylvia Scarlett* was "a flop" it was "still [his] favorite picture."[33] No doubt much of Cukor's fondness for the film had to do with what he called the "impertinence" of the project, and his collaboration with Hepburn, Grant, and scenarist John Collier ("a daring kind of writer").[34] "But the picture did something to me," Cukor told one interviewer. "It slowed me up. I wasn't going to be so goddamned daring after that. I thought, 'Well, kiddo, don't you break all sorts of new paths, you just watch it.'"[35]

Three years before *Sylvia Scarlett*, Hepburn revealed her butch potential for the first time in film as record-breaking pilot Cynthia Darrington in Arzner's *Christopher Strong* and as Jo March in Cukor's *Little Women*, in which she cut off her hair to raise money for her mother. A queer-cultural-history-meets-auteurism question occurs here: Would Hepburn's screen image have been established as quite so appealingly butch, or androgynous if you like, if Cukor and Arzner hadn't been assigned to guide her through most of her early RKO starmaking films, including her screen debut in Cukor's *A Bill of Divorcement* (1932)? In the context of queer film history, it is no coincidence that Hepburn's best post-1930s butch role was in Cukor's *Pat and Mike*, in which she plays a professional athlete.[36]

Arzner's and Cukor's important connection to a star image that has been developed in queer cultures largely without reference to directorial auteurism brings this chapter back to its original question about authorship, queerness, and queer cultures. That is, how compatible are auteurist cult-of-the-director (star, writer, etc.) notions with non-academic and academic queer approaches to mass culture?

Armed with the knowledge of Cukor's and Arzner's queerness (even if we can't always be certain about how they would define it), and knowing of their often highly influential roles in production, we might recognize a queer version of authorship in which queerly positioned readers examine mass culture texts—here Cukor and Arzner films—in order to indicate where and how the queer discourses of both producers and readers might be articulated within, alongside, or against the presumably straight ideological agendas of most texts. These types of queer readings are tricky and interesting because they establish queer authorial discourses by negotiating a range of textual meanings caught somewhere between auteurist considerations of director (or star, writer, etc.) intentionality and cultural/cultural studies considerations of reception practices and uses of texts. Most generally, I hope this chapter has suggested the potential for combining queer cultural history and cultural practices with established critical and theoretical models, such as auteurism and authorship, in order to develop a variety of distinctively queer-inflected approaches to discussing mass culture.

Notes

1 Films cited: *The Women* (1939, MGM, George Cukor), *Craig's Wife* (1936, Columbia, Dorothy Arzner).

2 In his interview with Boze Hadleigh in *Conversations with My Elders* (New York: St. Martin's Press, 1986), Cukor asks what calling a homosexual "gay" means: "Does it mean a homosexual individual is frivolous, light-hearted, or has a good sense of humor?" (p. 138). Except where the material in this chapter refers directly to Cukor's sexual self-definition, however, I will use the term "gay" to refer to Cukor's homosexuality, although I still want to acknowledge the importance of being precise about historical and cultural differences in individual and group definitions of homosexuality, gayness, lesbianism, bisexuality, and queerness.

3 Implicitly in *Now You See It: Studies on Lesbian and Gay Film* (London and New York: Routledge, 1990), and explicitly in "Believing in Fairies: The Author and the Homosexual," in *Inside/Out: Lesbian Theories, Gay Theories*, ed. Diana Fuss (New York: Routledge, 1991), 185–201, Richard Dyer argues for the political and theoretical value of rethinking certain notions of authorship in discussing lesbian and gay filmmaking. While acknowledging the importance of individual and group readers in establishing queer cultural interpretive practices, Dyer's work is centered upon examining production practices and contexts. Of particular interest to Dyer is how and where notions of authorship (as a site of multiple authors "with varying degrees of hierarchy and control") and homosexuality (as "a culturally and historically specific phenomenon") might be applied to formulate a more precise sociocultural understanding of films made by and for lesbians and gays (p. 187).

4 Films cited: *Camille* (1937, MGM, George Cukor), *Little Women* (1933, RKO, George Cukor), *Christopher Strong* (1933, RKO, Dorothy Arzner), *Sylvia Scarlett* (1936, RKO, George Cukor), *Adam's Rib* (1949, MGM, George Cukor), *Dinner at Eight* (1933, MGM, George Cukor), *The Wild Party* (1929, Paramount, Dorothy Arzner), *A Star is Born* (1954, Warners, George Cukor), *A Woman's Face* (1941, MGM, George Cukor), *The Bride Wore Red* (1937, MGM, Dorothy Arzner), *Sarah and Son* (1930, Paramount, Dorothy Arzner).

5 The association of certain Hollywood stars with lesbian culture appears to be international. For example, a scene in the Japanese film *Early Summer* (1951, Shochiku,

Yasujiro Ozu) has Noriko, the central character, being discussed by her boss and her best friend. When the friend mentions that Noriko likes Katharine Hepburn, the boss matter-of-factly asks if Noriko is a lesbian.

6 Margie Adams, "Greta Garbo's 'Mysterious' Private Life," OUT/LOOK 4 (Fall 1990): 25. For another angle on lesbian star cults, see Victoria A. Brownworth's "Just Another Soapbox" column in the PGN: *Philadelphia Gay News* 16, no. 34 (June 19–25, 1992): 43. Brownworth uses the premiere of *Aliens* 3 (1992, Twentieth Century-Fox, David Fincher) as a reason to discuss what she finds problematic about most dyke mass culture icons: "Now I know that this is treason amongst most lesbians who see Sigourney [Weaver] . . . and her 'Alien' character, Ripley, as leading lesbo ladies, but you girls need to get over these straight women and find some nice real-life lesbians to drool over. . . . The problem is this fixation lesbians have with pseudodykes, the great pretenders, the women who tell but don't kiss, the lesbo wanna-be's. . . . First we had this terrible attachment to Katharine Hepburn. Now that she's nearly dead we can adjust to the fact that she hates women other than herself and always has. She may have played a few cross-dressers, but she never was one in real life."

7 Of course, this is not to say some gays haven't made use of the knowledge of Arzner's lesbianism in conducting readings of her films, or that some lesbians haven't done the same with Cukor's "homosexuality" and his films. Here I am discussing more general trends in lesbian and gay cultural reading practices.

8 Two interesting works that examine lesbian cultures, lesbian reading practices, and mass culture (largely film) are Claire (formerly Judy) Whitaker's "Hollywood Transformed: Interviews with Lesbian Viewers," *Jump Cut* 24–25 (1981): 33–35; rpt. in *Jump Cut: Hollywood, Politics, and Counter-Cinema*, ed. Peter Stevens (New York: Praeger, 1981), 106–18; and Jane Cottis and Kaucyila Brooke's video *Dry Kisses Only* (1990). Whitaker's interviewees discuss their changing tastes and readings, and indicate how and where race and class intersect their readings of mass culture. Taken as a whole, these interviews suggest that stars and/or cross-gender identification are central to many lesbian uses of mass culture.

Dry Kisses Only combines mock-academic discussions, "lesbian on the street" interviews, and cleverly edited clips from films such as *The Great Lie* (1941, Warners, Edmund Goulding), *Johnny Guitar* (1954, Republic, Nicholas Ray), *All About Eve* (1950, Twentieth Century-Fox, Joseph L. Mankiewicz), *Mädchen in Uniform* (1931, Deutsche Film-Gemeinschaft, Leontine Sagan), and *The Hunger* (1983, MGM, Tony Scott) to reveal the variety and complexity of lesbian culture's confrontations with mass culture. Throughout the video, Cottis and Brooke suggest readings of films (including Arzner's *Christopher Strong*) that concentrate on lesbian culture and lesbian readers apart from any auteurist influences. Overall, the video implies that most lesbian cultural authorship in mass culture is conducted without reference to directors or even to stars, but rather is achieved by performing "perverse readings" articulating a text's "unconscious logic," "covert narrative," or "homosexual subplots or subtexts" through "searching out the look, the confrontation, the connotative language of the women onscreen," and looking for "disturbances" of the main (hetero-sexual) plot. However, these lesbian reading practices are very much like the interpretive practices of certain auteurist critics (discussed later in this section) who read films "obliquely," looking for "cracks" and "seams" in a text's "apparent formal coherence," which they would then attribute to a particular director's work on the project.

9 Judith Mayne, *The Woman at the Keyhole: Feminism and Women's Cinema* (Bloomington and Indianapolis: Indiana University Press, 1990), 89–123. An earlier version of this chapter

appears as "Lesbian Looks: Dorothy Arzner and Female Authorship" in *How Do I Look? Queer Film and Video*, ed. Bad Object-Choices (Seattle: Bay Press, 1991), 103–35. A companion piece to these works is Mayne's "A Parallax View of Lesbian Authorship," in *Inside/Out: Lesbian Theories, Gay Theories*, ed. Diana Fuss (New York and London: Routledge, 1991), 173–84. This essay (re)considers authorship in relation to lesbian representation through discussions of "films in which the filmmaker herself is written into the text, although not in ways that match the common, easy equation between authorial presence and the fictions of identity" (p. 177).

10 Mayne, *Woman at the Keyhole*, 112–15.

11 Gerald Peary and Karyn Kay, "Interview with Dorothy Arzner," *The Work of Dorothy Arzner: Toward a Feminist Cinema*, ed. Claire Johnston (London: British Film Institute, 1975), 19–29.

12 Ibid., 26.

13 Cukor "outs" Arzner in his interview, telling Hadleigh that "our" Dorothy Arzner had an affair with Alla Nazimova (*Conversations*, 170). Other lengthy interviews with Cukor in books, and book-length studies of the director containing interview material, include Charles Higham and Joel Greenberg, *The Celluloid Muse: Hollywood Directors Speak* (New York: Signet/New American Library, 1969), 60–78; Andrew Sarris, *Interviews with Film Directors* (New York: Avon Books, 1967), 92–126; Gene D. Phillips, *George Cukor* (Boston: Twayne, 1982); Gary Carey, *Cukor & Co.: The Films of George Cukor and His Collaborators* (New York: Museum of Modern Art, 1971); Carlos Clarens, *George Cukor* (London: Secker and Warburg/British Film Institute, 1976); Gavin Lambert, *On Cukor* (New York: G. P. Putnam's Sons, 1972). Clarens also wrote "The Secret Life of George Cukor," containing interview material gathered by John Hofsess, for the gay porn magazine *Stallion* (August 1983). This article was perhaps the first evidence of Cukor's public coming out.

14 Patrick McGilligan, *George Cukor: A Double Life* (New York: St. Martin's Press, 1991).

15 Richard Lippe, "Cukor and Authorship: A Reappraisal," *CineAction!* 21–22 (Summer–Fall 1990): 26, 34.

16 Jean-Luc Comolli and Jean Narboni, "Cinema/Ideology/Criticism," *Film Theory and Criticism*, 4th ed., ed. Gerald Mast, Marshall Cohen, and Leo Braudy (New York and Oxford: Oxford University Press, 1992), 687. This article originally appeared in English in Sylvia Harvey, ed., *May '68 and Film Culture* (London: British Film Institute, 1978).

17 Of course, discussing a director (or star) as a female or feminist auteur and/or as a lesbian, gay, bisexual, or queer auteur is to conduct auteurist analyses from within certain cultural, critical, and theoretical frames. But these practices would not necessarily be any more limited or limiting than other auteurist approaches that implicitly evaluated auteurs in relation to straight, white, male middle- and ruling-class ideological agendas, either to praise or to critique them. Feminist and queer auteurism foregrounds gender and sexuality as the terms of their analyses, and while these analyses can become narrow and restrictive in their politics (for example, certain critics deciding Gus Van Sant is not a good gay auteur because his films aren't "gay" or "gay-positive" enough), female-, feminist-, or queer-inflected auteurism can express as many different positions as there are women and queers.

   One of the challenges for women and queers using auteurism is deciding what they mean by terms such as female, woman, or feminist auteur, or gay, lesbian, bisexual, or queer auteur. Will the directors (stars, writers, etc.) under auteurist consideration be evaluated against certain specific definitions of woman, the female, feminist, gay, lesbian, bisexual, or queer? Or, through a combination of textual analysis, biography, and cultural-historical contextualization, will auteurist critics suggest how they see auteurs defining these gender and sexual identity terms throughout their texts?

18 Films cited: *Dance, Girl, Dance* (1940, RKO, Dorothy Arzner), *Our Betters* (1933, RKO, George Cukor).

19 Perhaps the best straight feminist reading of this film is Lucy Fischer's "*Dance, Girl, Dance*: When a Woman Looks," in *Shot/Countershot: Film Tradition and Women's Cinema* (Princeton: Princeton University Press, 1989), 148–54. Danny Peary also has a section on the film in *Cult Movies* (New York: Dell, 1981), 59–64, where he discusses its reputation as a feminist cult film.

20 Mayne, *Woman at the Keyhole*, 101.

21 On this point, Mayne finds that "Judy's attractions to men are shaped by substitutions for women and female rivalry—Steve Adams is a professional mentor to substitute for Basilova, and Jimmie Harris is an infantile man who is desirable mainly because Bubbles wants him too" (*Woman at the Keyhole*, 103). My reading of these "substitutions" would note that Adams is coded as a feminized man whose trusted associate is the butch Miss Olmstead, and that it is less "female rivalry" than repressed queer desire on Bubbles's part that makes *her* find Jimmie "desirable mainly because" she notices Judy's interest in him. Besides, Judy's wish on a star after a date with Jimmie is for a dancing career, not for him. As for Basilova, it is worth noting in this context that her removal from the plot is accomplished in classic homophobic narrative fashion: she gets hit by an oncoming bus as she takes Judy to her ballet audition. As if to comment on Basilova's (un)expected death, Arzner moves from her body to pan up the phallic building across the street that houses the ballet company.

22 Mayne's reading of this moment is feminist, but not lesbian: "And the catfight that erupts between Judy and Bubbles on stage is less a recuperative move . . . than the claiming by two women of the stage as an extension of their conflicted friendship, rather than as the alienated site of performance" (*Woman at the Keyhole*, 102). Although concerned with examining the "lesbian inflection" in Arzner's treatment of "female bonding" as part of how the director expresses the tensions between female friendships and lesbianism, Mayne discusses Bubbles's and Judy's bond as an example of heterosexual female rivalry.

23 Sarah Halprin, in "Writing in the Margins," *Jump Cut* 29 (1984), notes that there are "two 'minor' characters [in *Dance, Girl, Dance*] who both dress and look remarkably similar to Arzner herself (i.e., tailored, 'mannish,' in the manner of Radclyffe Hall and other famous lesbians of the time), and are placed as mature, single, independent women who are crucial to the career of the young Judy and who are clearly seen as oppressed by social stereotyping, of which they are contemptuous" (p. 32). Basilova is one of these butch women, and Miss Olmstead is the other. It is Olmie who first jumps up to applaud Judy's tirade against the burlesque house audience.

24 Film cited: *Salome* (1922, Nazimova Productions, Charles Bryant).

25 Peary and Kay, "Interview," 25.

26 Hadleigh, *Conversations*, 164.

27 Reviews as quoted in Peary, *Cult Movies*, 331.

28 Ibid., 333.

29 Ibid.

30 Ibid.

31 Ibid.

32 Carey, *Cukor & Co.*, 53.

33 Clarens, *George Cukor*, 143.

34 Lambert, *On Cukor*, 92.

35 Ibid.

36 Films cited: A *Bill of Divorcement* (1932, RKO, George Cukor), *Pat and Mike* (1952, MGM, George Cukor). A related reflection on film history occurs to me here: frequently queer-positioned director Lowell Sherman (*The Greeks Had a Word for Them*, 1932, RKO; Mae West's *She Done Him Wrong*, 1933, Paramount) worked with Hepburn on *Morning Glory*, the film that officially won her the 1932–33 Best Actress Oscar. The finale of *Morning Glory* had Hepburn's character, Eva Lovelace, renouncing the men interested in her so she can devote herself to an acting career. Eva Lovelace is an interesting name, suggestive of woman in her Christian originary state erotically connected to something traditionally feminine. Perhaps Hepburn as Eva is the femme side of Jo March and Cynthia Darrington.

The Oscar voters in 1933 were clearly more comfortable publicly rewarding Hepburn's portrayal of what could be read as a more traditionally feminine character, although just as clearly they were silently casting their ballots for Hepburn's compelling butchness in *Little Women* and *Christopher Strong*, which were released during the same Oscar-qualifying period as *Morning Glory*. Another queer culture Oscar footnote is in order here: the Best Actor winner the same year that butch, man-renouncing Hepburn was named Best Actress was gay actor Charles Laughton, for his near-parodic, tongue-in-cheek portrayal of that notorious, hypermacho, much-married monarch, Henry VIII.

What was happening in the West, and in Western cultural production, in the early 1930s that encouraged such queer goings-on? Are there links to the Depression, with its disruptive challenges to capitalist patriarchal hegemony? Or does it have something to do with the effects of the more liberal pre-1934 Production Code in Hollywood? Or might this situation be the result of a growing sense of community within the film industry on both sides of the Atlantic among prominent queers and queer-positive straights, such as David O. Selznick, producer of certain Arzner and Cukor films? Questions such as these might be researched and explored at greater lengths as part of authoring a queer history of film and other forms of mass culture.

Physique Cinema, 1945–1969

2

Hard to Imagine

THOMAS WAUGH

[. . .]

The "physique cinema" is a unique and somewhat arcane body of work confined historically within a fifteen-year period and merchandised, like physique photography, through a licit mail-order network, though on a somewhat smaller scale. Less accessible than the photos and magazines, the small corpus of physique movies is remembered fondly, if uncritically, by the pre-Baby Boom generations. They provide a sense of the cultural dynamic of gay eroticism in the transitional years leading up to Stonewall, a sense too of the roots of not only gay erotic film and video of the last thirty years but arguably of the legit gay narrative cinema as well.

In comparison to that frozen portrait of corporal perfection that was the still physique photo, physique films provide dreamlike structures of narrative momentum and fulfillment, and thus an even richer document of our sexual imaginary of the period. When beefcake began to move through a projector, the spectator's narrative identification with an unfolding communal impulse transformed his prior fixation on the static presentational image. The gay man became enactor of desire within the narrative instead of external perpetrator of the look of desire. Narrative allowed the storytellers of our burgeoning subcultures to transform the one-way voyeuristic attachment to the representation of the male body into a complex relationship of psychic, dramatic, and political identifications.

Even within the beefcake still, the itch to move and the drive toward narrative were often registered: for consumers bereft of technological apparatus, for example, several of the magazines and studios compensated through photo strips and photo sequences. One enterprising studio even offered "flipcards" that "[made] every muscle seem to move" and a "do-it-yourself feature with 3 male figures to cut out and mount as you see it."[1] Finally, the moment that physique artists and their customers started setting up images in sequences and bodies in relation to each other, the moment they told a story, however oblique, the era of alibis was irrevocably over.

History, capital, and technology

To speak of mail-order physique cinema as a "small corpus" is to speak in relative terms. In comparison with the thousands of still photographs and small magazines inundating the postwar market, the movies were few and far between. Rather than a hundred or so major photo studios on the international scene, the more restricted market for mail-order films allowed at most only a dozen producers in 1960, predominantly American. Furthermore, the film market developed somewhat later than the photo and magazine networks. It is true that prototypes of the films are extant from as early as the 1930s, principally hobby-scale productions for personal use.[2] But the earliest commercial examples the author is aware of date from 1949, an interesting cycle of narratives made by pioneer Richard Fontaine (b. 1923) in New York and New Jersey. Over the next twenty-odd years Fontaine's almost continuous production activity on both the East and West coasts was centered in companies called Apollo Productions, Zenith Productions, and R. A. Enterprises. He was not alone in the field for long. A Cincinnati outfit called Spectrum Films is visible as early as 1953 and became within two years a prominent advertiser of posing and narrative films in the magazines.

The boom in physique cinema didn't come, however, until around 1958, when Bob Mizer of the Athletic Model Guild entered the fray with an assembly-line output which was to continue weekly for more than a decade (and sporadically to his death in 1992). Mizer, by far the most prolific film producer in the whole network, claimed at one point to have produced 1,500 films.[3] But it is possible that the entire corpus by all producers amounts to little more than that number (fewer still if one is referring to extant works). The French "naturist" studio headed by Jean Ferrero in Nice also added film production, principally solo posing films, to its catalogue around the same time as Mizer. By the early sixties, they had been joined by Bruce of Los Angeles, Pacific Films (Albany, Calif.), DSI (Minneapolis), Bob Anthony (New York), and Kris Studio (Chicago) as well as London's Graham Studio, Montreal's "Mark One," and Munich's Hollfelder Studio.

Technically speaking, the physique film corpus has the kind of self-enclosed historical autonomy common to several other short-lived artforms arising from erratic technological proliferation. Although many of the mail-order films were produced originally in 16mm, the vast majority were released in the much cheaper and more accessible medium of Regular 8mm (although they were also available in 16mm at a higher price). The 8mm format was popularized in the early fifties as a mass-market amateur technology just in time for the boom in licit gay eroticism in the physique milieu. Many consumers even did without projectors, occupying both hands during screenings with hand-cranked portable viewers obligingly sold by the studios. At a time when the embryonic gay movement was preaching the privacy of the domestic space, a new leisure technology requiring individuated, private, and domestic consumption seemed just what the doctor ordered.

Posing, wrestling, dreaming

Three main genres within physique cinema have distinct internal iconographies and contexts: the posing film, the wrestling film, and the narrative film. Of the three genres, the posing film was the most naked, frontal enactment of the sexual pleasure of looking at the male body. In the posing films, the static quality of a succession of stiff physique poses, frozen in a moving medium, seemed to exaggerate all the more the pretense and artificiality of the mask, problematizing the spectator's entry into the frame through fantasy or identification. At the same time, undiluted by narrative fantasy or the proto-narrative momentum of combat (mediations cultivated in the other two genres), the posing films often foregrounded the awkward looks of the models at the invisible director, and by extension at the invisible spectator, as if asking for directions or mistrusting the motive. Or else looking is avoided, as if in discomfort at being the object of the look that dares not speak its name, amplifying the usual feeling of selfconsciousness and unease. The presentational, frontal quality of the poses constantly accentuates the spectatorial status of the consumer and the commodity status of the model's exhibition of his strength. What is more, great posers with great bodies were seldom great actors.

Juwa La Vonce, an AMG film from the early sixties and apparently in release as late as 1968, is typical.[4] The systematic elaboration of La Vonce's every muscle proceeds in sequence, including that special undeveloped organ, the face of this not especially cinematic model in close-up, and his fetishized tattoo, that signifier of class and gender affinity (as well as of other cultural and psychological variables).[5] A variation halfway through the film, a jump-cut change of costume from strap to see-through briefs, does not alleviate the embarrassment of a performer uncertain of the quality, nature, terms, and destination of his performance. The display is concluded by an awkward exit stage left, as if both performer and *metteur-en-scène* had forgotten the cinematic format of the performance in their relief at the termination of the look.

Cocktails, a 4½-minute short by Dick Fontaine (1950), one of the earliest films in the corpus, offers an ingenious strategy for accommodating and rechanneling these stresses into humor and narrative. The invisible photographer becomes a persona in the film engaged in flirtatious repartee thanks to coy silent intertitles as full of wit and double entendres as the title itself. The posing session becomes a short seduction narrative, a game of power and complicity between model and voyeur, beginning with classic disrobing and ending with postponed but anticipated gratification. It is unlikely that Cocktails was extensively circulated: certainly the distribution network was not yet in place and, unfortunately, few later examples profited from its graceful and funny inventiveness.

An interesting contrast is Ray Walling (AMG), one of the earlier frontal nude posing films, distributed in 1966 by DSI with an editorial proclaiming the social validity of nudism.[6] This film is considerably less graceful than Cocktails, encumbered both by the weight of formula and by a necessary adjustment to the new demands of the phallus unbound. The addition, for example, of exercises such as handstands to the traditional repertory was part of an aesthetic detour, a perhaps misguided effort to adapt the motion picture medium to the flaccid penis in motion, spawning the short-lived subgenre of the "danglie." With nowhere else to go, the film stumbles clumsily into narrative closure through the model's improvisation of a feigned yawn and make-believe sleep, offering through closed eyelids a less stressful scopophilic activity to the spectator.

More successful on their own terms in the danglie interlude are short solo loops by Bruce of Los Angeles. One featuring model John Manning employs costume and dramatic references to mine the infinite riches of popular culture, camp, and fantasy.[7] Dressed as a Native American warrior complete with feather headdress, tomahawk, and the natural setting of a rocky promontory, the model awkwardly performs several scouting gestures and dangle-inducing war dances. This time, however, the stress is channeled toward a heightening of the same kind of self-reflexive complicity as in Cocktails. Here we have a minority appropriation of the unspoken homoeroticism in majority mythology (cowboys and Indians), hilariously sending up its theatrical artifice, hypocrisy, and prurience at the same time. (The model's aboriginal identity, well known in the physique milieu, of course complicates the circuitry of appropriation, send-up, and self-reflexivity.) The physique alibi is by this time only vestigial (though the fetish of pectoral size already seems to be making its inevitable migration below the waist), perhaps another reason for the loop's agreeable durability.

The posing genre launched the physique movie in the late 1940s, the obvious cinematic extension of the already established still-beefcake format. But it is not surprising that, due to the aesthetic and logistical problems I have emphasized, the posing film soon became eclipsed by the other two genres. By the time of an ambitious GGP inventory of AMG productions in 1965, solo posing films occupied less than 10 percent of the almost 750 titles listed.[8]

The "wrestling film," an obvious spinoff of the posing genre, is one of the more bizarre anomalies in our culture's history of resistance to censorship. This genre was the specialty primarily of AMG, but the regional Ohio studio Spectrum was also known for its rambunctious and authentic wrestling. Merchandised according to the names of the actors, many of whom enjoyed a connoisseur following, the films offered direct continuous representations of (usually) two figures wrestling over the 50 or 100-foot length of the film, usually mounted with a minimal variety of different angles and camera ranges. Mizer offered dozens of these films: of almost 750 titles in the 1965 catalogue, about one-third are straight wrestling films. The listings occasionally tag the films according to surprisingly frank estimations of the "quality" of the wrestling, whether it is particularly violent, posed, etc. (e.g., "Wrestling poor! More violence at a women's department store bargain counter"). The tags often admit baldly to the pretense of the wrestling formula, thus openly inviting customers to play the games of circumventing the censor.

The voyeurism of the spectator reaches a certain apotheosis in the wrestling genre. The strap-clad athletes are forced into every possible positional permutation of vulnerability and accessibility. No doubt the special attraction is the coital simulacrum that is the basis of this sport. Is this in fact the attraction of mainstream wrestling as well? Does it play a part in all mainstream spectator sports of which Mizer's glistening romps are by extrapolation such a telling parody? The climactic narrative momentum of the wrestling loop, unlike with the serial and static posing film, culminates in exhaustion, depletion, and stasis, the sweating and oiled bodies literally collapsed on each other at the moment of quasi-orgasmic fulfillment.

Combat and sport, it goes without saying, are the only allowable formats of same-sex physical contact in Anglo-Saxon society. The enshrinement of wrestling as the privileged licit crypto-erotic formula during the Cold War may be a telling commentary on gay culture during that contradictory period (and since). Yet wrestling may also be a clue to the erotic function of violence, competition, and aggression across patriarchal culture as a whole, with its commercialization of spectatorship and its consecration of war. Many of the wrestling films gleefully deconstruct this mystification, admitting at the same time their game of encoding and compliance through blatant staging and simulation, through blatant zoom-in fragmentation of the erogenous body (especially as the sixties wore on), and through blatantly mock-coital poses in the promotional stills.

A celebration of the minority cultural practice of subtexting, the wrestling film is also a recklessly defiant declaration of the subtext's immunity from censorship and control. Wrestling became Mizer's trademark, the basic formula even of his narrative films, which had their wrestling interludes as predictably as Hollywood musicals would have their musical numbers. Many became indiscriminate frescoes of piled-up bodies and flailing limbs, an allegorical vision of mass riot transfixed by the utopian dream of communal orgy. Does present-day gay male culture seem to privilege noncontact sports *in spite of* or *because of* our traditional extreme awareness of the erotic potential of contact sports?

The narrative film genre, the most developed form of the mail-order cinema, evolved within a decade from minimally anecdotal variations of the posing and wrestling loops to full-length dramatic features aimed at the theatrical market of the post-Stonewall period, arguably the first authentic dramatic film fiction of gay liberation. Most of the early narrative films were thin contrivances for getting the models to disrobe, pose, and fight. Our cultural heritage provided much fodder for such contrivances, however, which soon became as complicated as they were formulaic: innumerable bathing scenes, waking and sleeping scenes, "artist" plots in which the problems of sculptors, photographers, and painters with their nude models invariably provided the hinge of the plot.

Perhaps the most standardized of the formulas were the pretexts provided by homosocial institutional settings (prisons, the armed forces, schools, sports). These usually provided combat stories in which a gay prototype would assert himself through a prolonged wrestling bout against a bullying authority figure, whether warden or officer or stepbrother or castrating father.

A typical item of this category, *Boys in Prison*, a 7-minute film produced by AMG in 1959, presented a cast of about a dozen men in a surprisingly sophisticated outdoor set within the AMG studio courtyard. The official synopsis was as follows:

> The plot is of a young bodybuilder who is thrown into jail with a bunch of roughnecks. When he attempts to work out with his dumbbells and cables they tease and ridicule him. The bully of the group tears his inspirational muscle-man pin-up photo from the wall and destroys it. When the bodybuilder tries to fight the bully, the other prisoners restrain him (for his own good). Then one day in the shower the final humiliation is visited upon the bodybuilder. After being forced to wash the bully's feet, the bodybuilder is given a kick in the rump which sends him sprawling. Fed-up, he tackles the bully, gets some wrestling holds on him which put him out of commission. The other prisoners are quite impressed. Back in the dormitory, the bodybuilder now gets the prized bunk, the other prisoners dutifully read the copies of *Physique Pictorial* which have been provided for them, and the film closes with them all going through their exercises.[9]

Of particular interest, other than the simple celebration of the men's bodies and the boy-next-door eroticization of jockey shorts, are several key mythological functions. The place of the novice and his eventual triumph over the bully would be an obvious allegory of gay self-affirmation even without the blatant labeling mechanism served by the "physique enthusiast" affinity, the pinup idol, and the reading material. This is not, however, the "coming out" formula of post-Stonewall fiction, but a utopian fantasy of an outcast's conversion of a whole social environment. The novice's courage and integrity, his wrestling skill rather than brute strength, transforms a fearful mob into a fraternal community. Group exercise becomes a sacrament of collective identity, consolidated both by looking (that is, reading, by both the spectator with his movie and the characters with their magazines), and by doing (exercise, bathing, and mock-coital combat). Both looking and doing are the stand-ins for erotic exchange and the triggers of arousal.

The sadomasochistic character of this and many of the films is so prevalent that it requires further comment. Though some of the AMG spanking plots are endearingly silly, others are so brutal, even by today's standards, that one can assume that certain producers, probably Mizer, had a special predisposition to S/M fantasy. The titles alone are evocative: *Street Fight*, *Pharaoh's New Slave*, *Aztec Sacrifice*, *The New Recruit*, *Der Nazi und der Judische Junge*, *Cruel Stepbrother*, etc. Yet that is not all. There is such overwhelming evidence of audience approval that one must deduce that the erotic discourses of violence, victimization, and power not only effectively diverted the non-S/M constituency's erotic drives, stymied by censorship, but also tapped on a mythological level the gay constituency's experience of social oppression. Nevertheless, the films do depart significantly in the final analysis from the pure S/M formula of the eroticization of power imbalances. The AMG fantasies normally overturn the terms of power and stage the triumph of the bottom. This dream of vindication is not so much an erotic fantasy proper, but a political fantasy of self-assertion, a revenge fantasy akin to the perennial Charles Atlas myth of the 97-pound weakling giving the beach bully his comeuppance. The internalization of oppression is reversed through the wish-fulfillment of the triumph-over-the-bully formula.

The formulaic quality of this narrative material raises the question of its origins in audience input in a milieu that was, after all, highly interactive. *Physique Pictorial* would continually solicit reader ideas for new movie plots (but not without providing a basic orientation, of course):

WANTED! BASIC IDEAS FOR PHYSIQUE MOVIES, PLOT MOTIVATIONS ETC. One of the easiest basics to work out is a plot centered around a fight. This gives the actors an excellent opportunity to display their physiques under stress and strain.

We have already offered a number of such films such as having a victim fighting a robber, recalcitrant model fighting a photographer, Indians fighting thieving cowboys, new slave fighting court wrestler for his freedom, crooked poker player being pummeled by other players, Triton fighting fisherman who steals his playmate, new "fish" in prison fighting bully, fishermen fighting over treasure they have found. Other fight basics we are working on include a Cop fighting a rebellious hotrodder, hoodlum irritating Marine guard who must stand at stiff attention, sailor needled by his petty officer, marine fights sailor because latter whistles at his girl (girl leaves them both and goes off with another less crude fellow), boys fight when they find they have the same girl's picture, etc., etc.

Now, how about your thinking up some other good reasons that fellows could brawl about. Try to include a trick ending if you can think of one, but even if you can't think of a full plot send the basic idea anyway because often from just a seed an entire story can be built up.[10]

Perhaps the most consistently self-affirming and upfront of the physique films (as well as cinematically most accomplished) came from Chicago's Kris Studio. Strikingly adult in relation to the AMG's puerile stories and generally eschewing the wrestling addiction, Kris's movies were tough-guy narratives on the surface. But beneath their hard edge of humor, latent violence, and the rich fetish possibilities of popular culture, the films dealt with loneliness, romance, and tenderness. *The Hired Hand*, the studio's first movie production (1963), frontally nude ahead of its time, is a delightful case in point. Set in an idyllic farm landscape, the film shows a city slicker lured into joining the homestead by a tricky nude rancher: after the hired hand passes the test of dutifully carrying out the chores, the two men become a romantic couple cartwheeling through a flower-strewn meadow. A subsequent film,

The Fugitive, presents "Cherokee" as an outlaw on the run in a mythical Wild West, who beds down with a hunky homesteader, is recognized and ready to bolt, but passion overcomes the homesteader's civic duty and the two live happily ever after.

One crucial aspect of the narrative films has already been raised in relation to the posing and wrestling films, namely their minority appropriation of majority cultural goods and patriarchal mythology. For in addition to mythologizing political wish-fulfillment and documenting our sexual and sociocultural origins, the narrative films take these operations of appropriation, deconstruction, and subtexting to an exemplary height of expression. What is at stake is of course an early and pristine articulation of the notorious "gay sensibility," quite aside from the films' primary operation of sexual arousal. This is not the place to belabor the many facets of this sensibility that have been proposed by authors such as Babuscio, Dyer, and Bronski.[11] But any of the narratives provide textbook compendia of camp taste, take uninhibited delight in excess, parody, theatricality, and artifice, and, it might be said, offer much naive postmodern textual play before its time.

Fontaine's *Days of Greek Gods* (1954) is a case in point. The film brought together three aspirants to physique stardom, Bob Del Montegue, Artie Zeller, and Jimmy Apollo, in a narrative of three bodybuilders spending a lazy afternoon together comparing themselves to classical statues of Hercules, Narcissus, and Apollo. Filmed on a stage in a New York loft where gay Academy Award parties (organ-accompanied) and underground drag film screenings (*All About Steve!*) were all the rage, *Gods* reveals the liabilities of using primitive 16mm sound technology with performers whose stupendous bodies conceal terrible voices and worse acting. Mercifully, most customers did not have 16mm sound projectors and requested silent 8mm prints. As a result, this father of the gay erotic cinema reached his first audience with silent films whose lustrous images were unspoiled by awkward sound and whose dialogue, delivered through title cards, came off as witty parody of the creaky classical alibi.

It was only to be in Hollywood that Fontaine finally found his stride. There, he enacted his own days of gods with a series of campy but earnest shorts made for his outfit Zenith Films between his arrival in 1956 and the cataclysmic advent of frontal nudity around 1966. Take a particularly rich example of what might be called a costume sub-genre such as Fontaine's *The Captives* (c. 1959). A Roman official interrogates a pair of captive comrades accused of spying and finally frees them in tribute to their devotion to each other under torture: "Because of your bravery you have won your people's freedom. Go in peace!" Even such a minimal synopsis conveys the film's delighted recycling of the Hollywood biblical epic (together with an irreverent jab at the plaster pillars and "classical" iconography of the traditional physique alibi). Tunics are ripped off oiled flesh at swordpoint, heroic gestures of parting are held too long, and set design is the ultimate in pastel vulgarity. Yet this and the other films are not empty pastiche, rather a somehow moving clash of earnest wish-fulfillment with the high artifice and carnal intent of its vehicle. The denouement's affirmation of the couple was certainly Fontaine's personal specialty as well as Kris's. But in fact, affirmations of the couple recur across the board and can even be read into the scores of wrestling films as well, most of which are characterized by as much affection and pleasure as strife.

[. . .]

Notes

1 Ads in *Trim* (August 1959): 40; and *Zing* 1–12 (April 1960): 40.
2 See chapter 4 of Thomas Waugh, *Hard to Imagine: Gay Male Eroticism in Photography and Film from their Beginnings to Stonewall* (New York: Columbia University Press, 1966), especially the section on amateur erotic filmmaker Otis Wade.
3 Paul Siebenand, "The Beginnings of Gay Cinema in Los Angeles: The Industry and the Audience" (Ph.D. diss., University of Southern California, 1975), 43.
4 Collection of the author.
5 See Sam Steward, *Bad Boys and Tough Tattoos: A Social History of the Tattoo with Gangs, Sailors, and Street-Corner Punks, 1950–1965* (Binghampton, NY: Harrington Park Press, 1990) for a semischolarly personal reflection on the meanings and motivations of tattoos by a veteran of homoerotic culture of the pre-Stonewall generation in the United States.
6 Collection of the author.
7 Collection of the author.
8 "Featuring AMG's Physique Film Library, 1965–1975 [sic]," *Grecian Guild Studio Quarterly* (Washington), no. 16 (Winter issue 1965).
9 *Physique Pictorial* vol. 9, no. 1, Spring 1959.
10 *Physique Pictorial* vols 10–12 (August 1960), 8.
11 John Babuscio, "Camp and Gay Sensibility," in Richard Dyer, ed., *Gays and Film*, rev. ed. (New York: Zoetrope, 1984); Dyer, *Heavenly Bodies: Film Stars and Society* (London: Macmillan/British Film Institute, 1987); Michael Bronski, *Culture Clash: The Making of Gay Sensibility* (Boston: South End Press, 1984).

Transgressive Cinema

Lesbian Independent Film

ANDREA WEISS

A young, attractive woman exchanges looks with a nun on the streets of New York's Lower East Side. The nun walks away quickly, but the woman follows her right into a church. And the camera positions our view with that of the bold pursuer, so that we unexpectedly find ourselves guilty of transgressing the taboo, of looking at the nun somehow "differently." But at the same time, the camera's virtually frantic movement, while securing our gaze to that of someone walking quickly down an urban street, also frees our gaze from that which she sees (the nun), thereby disturbing the possibility of an erotic contemplation of the image. What occurs in this one short scene is that we are implicated in the romantic pursuit of a nun, yet the eroticism is not attributable to the object of the look, to the image of Woman to signify sexuality, as it would be in the dominant cinema or in pornography. It is rather the power and intrigue of looking itself which becomes erotically charged. Su Friedrich's *Damned If You Don't* (1987) has imagined lesbian desire outside of the pornographic parameters of the dominant cinema.

This goal—not often achieved—is a primary one for lesbian independent film, and one of its defining characteristics. The growing body of work referred to as lesbian independent cinema has been attempting to control and define lesbian representation in terms other than those offered by the dominant media. These films provide very different perspectives on lesbian desire and, with varying degrees of success, also subvert the ways in which the cinema historically has been constructed for the male gaze. Lesbian independent filmmaking attempts to construct alternative visual codes that more closely derive from the search for lesbian self-definition.

In the United States, lesbian independent film emerged in the early 1970s with the advent of the gay and women's liberation movements. It benefited from a strengthening of the American independent film movement in general in the 1960s, a consequence of that decade's anti-establishment climate, the founding of such granting agencies as the National Endowment for the Arts (giving, however, only piecemeal funding for film production), and the technological development of lighter, more accessible 16mm film equipment. Although the production of lesbian films spans a number of Western countries, the relative lack of government or television subsidy for independent work make for an independent film practice which is particularly American, unrecognized by and marginal to a massive, world-exporting Hollywood film industry. Only in the United States, for example, would the following grassroots fundraising announcement be found in a mid-1970s lesbian journal: "Their budget is $25,000, and they need $5,000 to start the film." This ad in *Lesbian Tide* was for what turned out to be perhaps the most widely screened and recognized lesbian documentary, Iris Films' *In the Best Interest of the Children*.[1] Some of the formal qualities developing out of this independent, marginal position have found their way into the films of non-American Western directors, just as the codes of European art cinema have become discernible in American films. However, lesbian independent films are situated differently in Canada and Europe due to the existence (now unfortunately changing) of complete government or television production subsidy and, in continental Western Europe, a history that fostered a national film culture. In Britain, lesbian films have not had to resort to this kind of panhandling within the lesbian community and have been commissioned for television broadcast virtually without exception, a situation that carries with it certain aesthetic and audience mandates— one thinks of Beeban Kidron's *Oranges Are Not the Only Fruit* (U.K., 1989), Joy Chamberlain's *Nocturne* (U.K., 1990), Pratibha Parmar's *Flesh and Paper* (U.K., 1990). Although there is much that could be said about these works, my focus here is on American films which in form and content declare their complete independence from and opposition to the dominant American film and television industries.

Inspired by the energy and enthusiasm of the 1970s lesbian/feminist movement, the first significant lesbian independent films proclaimed their allegiance to this movement by visually articulating its utopian agenda. Pioneering lesbian filmmakers Barbara Hammer and Jan Oxenberg began in the early 1970s to make short personal films that affirmed their experiences and sexuality, Oxenberg drawing upon narrative and documentary styles and Hammer upon the avant-garde film tradition. *Dyketactics* by Barbara Hammer (1974) and *Home Movie* by Jan Oxenberg (1972) both share the early movement's insistence that lesbianism is not solely a personal, sexual matter, but is a form of social or political liberation. These and other lesbian films from this period had in common their conscious attempts to address a specifically lesbian audience, by relying on the audience's familiarity with the cultural assumptions, symbolism, humor, and radical politics characteristic of the American lesbian-feminist community at that time.

For some filmmakers who subscribed to the lesbian separatist tendencies of the movement and wanted to protect these new images from male appropriation, the film's mode of address was not enough; they insisted on further exclusion of the male viewer by showing their films in women-only spaces, the women's centers and coffeehouses that sprang up across the United States during the early 1970s. Journals such as *Lesbian Tide* and *Amazon Quarterly* carried regular announcements of Barbara Hammer's films, invariably ending with "this program is for wimmin, only."[2] Jan Oxenberg, interviewed in *Amazon Quarterly*, said of one of her films, "Now, this film is not . . . for the general public. It's really entertainment for the lesbian community. As far as I'm concerned, it's not being made for other people to see."[3]

Jan Oxenberg and Barbara Hammer are filmmakers who represented two (frequently overlapping) tendencies within 1970s lesbian-feminism, which could be differentiated by the terms "cultural feminism" and "radical feminism." Both tendencies imbued the definition of lesbianism with significance beyond the sexual: beginning with the Radicalesbians in 1970, "lesbian" began to suggest "woman-identified" in both a personal and political sense.[4] But whereas radical feminists emphasized the political importance of "woman-identified-women" as a threat to patriarchy and as an antidote to male power, cultural feminists moved away from immediate political concerns to explore ancient matriarchies and female forms of power.

Radical feminists argued that, given the narrow patriarchal definitions of woman, being "feminine" and being a whole person are irreconcilable,[5] while cultural feminists embraced the feminine in themselves, and connected lesbianism to the creative, eternal feminine principle. Cultural feminists tried to create a women's culture that came as close to lesbian nirvana and kept as far from patriarchal realities as possible, which radical feminists sometimes criticized as a retreat.[6]

Home Movie takes up the radical feminist position that lesbianism is an antidote to male power. Rather than situate her film completely within a female community (as Barbara Hammer's early films are situated), Oxenberg juxtaposes, and in the course of the short film replaces, images of patriarchal order with images of lesbian pleasure. The film uses home movies of the filmmaker's childhood to call into question the heterosexual socialization process of childhood; familiar images of a little girl dancing for the camera and holding a doll are given new meaning via the soundtrack, in which the filmmaker asks, "I wonder why I was doing this? I look so . . . normal, just like a little girl. And it's really strange, because I didn't feel like a little girl." Over the home movies of herself as a teenager, cheerleading at a high school football game, the filmmaker's voice continues to undermine the convention reading of the image: "The thing I liked best about being a cheerleader was being with the other cheerleaders." As Michelle Citron points out,

> Oxenberg uses home movies to underscore the role of the family and school as institutions that perpetuate patriarchal ideology. In the context of this film, home movies, usually a celebratory recording of family life, ironically become a condemnation of the very institutions filmed.[7]

Not only, as Citron argues, does *Home Movie* directly critique patriarchal ideology, placing it within the radical feminist camp, but it also sees a problematic, even contradictory relationship between the identities "lesbian" and "feminine." Oxenberg's lesbianism, as indicated by her commentary about not feeling like a little girl, is signaled by her difference from a culturally-mandate feminine model, not by identification with a natural, eternal feminine principle. If "feminine" and "whole person" are irreconcilable, the choice is clear. By the end of the film, the woman has abandoned her efforts to fit in to a socially sanctioned role, and this abandonment is depicted in "liberating" imagery. No longer cheering on the sidelines, she is playing a sensuous, non-competitive disorderly game of football with a group of lesbians, an image of strength and a celebration of women's "non-feminine" bodies.

In contrast, Barbara Hammer's work can be seen as embodying the cultural feminist position.[8] Her many lesbian-identified films of this period involve the quest for a lesbian iconography, a visual language not defined by the heterosexual, patriarchal world, but rather based on personal inner truths and the rhythms of her own body. She worked from an intuitive, "female" source of knowledge, claiming that "my body tells me how to shoot or how to edit. I work with a kinesthetic feeling rather than an a-priori plan when it comes to the way I want to express myself with the camera."[9] The lesbian self and lesbian sexuality, long erased from the visual history of patriarchy, became visible in Barbara Hammer's work through matriarchal images and symbols of women's spirituality, a connection with "female" nature (as opposed to "male" culture), and a focus on the lesbian body as a source or power and knowledge, themes which had considerable currency in early and mid-1970s American lesbian communities. In a prolific body of work with such titles as *Moon Goddess*, *Sappho*, *Sisters!*, *Women*

I Love, Menses, Women's Rites, Multiple Orgasm and The Great Goddess, Hammer favored the use of superimposition and a linkage of vaginal and nature imagery, connecting women's bodies to ancient spiritual sites or natural formations, and always, to each other.

Jacqueline Zita describes Hammer's agenda as follows:

> To invert the cultural negations and denials attached to the lesbian body seems the first task at hand. There are two obvious possibilities: the body that has been historically defiled and abhorred can become purified, sanctified, and turned into an object of worship, or the body that has become denigrated as unnatural and sick can be "naturalized" and normalized to fit more intimately into the rhythms of Nature. . . . Both of these tendencies are present in Barbara's films.[10]

[. . .]

Lesbian avant-garde films were often intended as correctives to dominant representations of lesbian sexuality. These films experimented with non-voyeuristic approaches to lesbian sexuality: for example, in Barbara Hammer's Dyketactics and Women I Love, the filmmaker is participant instead of voyeur of lesbian lovemaking, while in Su Friedrich's Gently Down the Stream, words scratched into the film's emulsion take precedence over images occupying only a corner of the frame. Whereas Chantal Akerman's lesbian lovemaking scene in Je Tu Il Elle stars the filmmaker in order to de-aestheticize the lesbian image, Hammer's use of her own body is integral to the lesbian sensibility she was then developing. Akerman's much cooler (anti-) aesthetic in her lovemaking scene is precariously balanced between her strict control as director and her vulnerability as performer, while Hammer's performance in her own films from this period lacks that feeling of vulnerability—and her directing lacks that strict control. There isn't the same tension in Hammer's dual role of filmmaker and performer; they are part of one tactile relationship to the image. As Jacqueline Zita has noted, the filmmaker's participation

> gives the camera itself an altogether different role. Instead of being used to gaze upon the spectacle, it seems to be part of the action, used to capture a loving intimacy by connecting with it and completing its fleeting and primitive pleasure. . . . Barbara's camera is subjective; it participates as does the filmmaker in an orchestrated event between two bodies and a camera.[11]

The filmmaker's participation in the lovemaking scene is not enough alone to counteract the prevalent construction of lesbian lovemaking as cinematic spectacle designed to titillate male desire. But it does begin to break down the barriers between spectators, filmmaker, and image upon which voyeurism relies. Hammer's inclusion of her own body serves a further purpose, to rely on the personal truths of her own body (the only "reliable" source under patriarchy) in order to give universal expression to the lesbian body.

By the early 1980s, feminism had evolved, and so had lesbian independent cinema, which was now starting to embrace more complex theoretical and aesthetic questions. Some feminists had started to question a feminist politic that reinscribed femininity as an essence, as biological and natural rather than historically and culturally constructed, a position which ultimately returns to the place patriarchal culture has assigned to women: outside of culture, in the realm of the emotions, nature, and motherhood. Working-class lesbians and lesbians of color found themselves excluded from both the luxury of utopian, separatist lifestyles and from a "universal" lesbian mythology extrapolated from specific personal (primarily white middle-class) lesbian identity, while more androgynous or "masculine" women were unable to fit within the rigid parameters required by the cult of the feminine. As these voices grew stronger, utopian fantasies eventually gave way to diversity and conflict.

Meanwhile, issues of sexuality and sexual representation were heating up in the early 1980s, dividing the feminist movement into hostile camps on opposite sides of the pornography debate. In the 1970s, feminists viewed pornography rather simply as visual propaganda which advocated violence against women, but then neither pornography nor violence against women received much critical attention outside of feminist circles. By the early 1980s, they, as Dot Tuer so bluntly put it,

> found their struggles co-opted by a moral majority who stepped over battered bodies of women in their rush to manipulate public opinion.[12]

As the New Right moved in on what had been feminist territory, many women were unhappy about feminism's strange new bedfellows, and had serious doubts about whether censorship or 'pro-family' values were any improvement over pornography. The issue was realigning itself as pro- or anti-sex, and many lesbians, rebelling against the political correctness and puritanical aspects of the lesbian-feminist movement, suddenly came out as pro-sex in all its variations of pleasure and perversion. The direct visual representation of these ideas about sexuality is limited primarily to photography and to low-low-budget home video pornography for lesbians (such as those by Blush Productions). The government funding bodies had long overlooked lesbian artists and their proposed film projects; by the late 1980s they were demanding anti-obscenity pledges from all artists receiving government monies. But while this new preoccupation with sex has not become the primary concern for lesbian filmmakers, the visual representations created by the lesbian porn movement and these other changes taking place within the lesbian community still have considerable ramifications for lesbian independent film.

One significant development in recent documentary film is that the idea of a "universal" transhistorical lesbian has been replaced with lesbian specificity and diversity. The lives of lesbians who would have been overlooked or ridiculed by 1970s lesbian-feminists for role-playing, "male-identification" or just not conforming to the feminine ideal, are now documented and celebrated. Storme deLarverie, the subject of Michelle Parkerson's documentary, *Storme: The Lady of the Jewel Box* (1987), is one such woman: she is the talented male impersonator who from 1955 to 1969 fronted the once-famous, multi-racial drag show, the *Jewel Box Revue*.

[. . .]

The representation of black lesbians in independent narrative films is obviously not subjected to the same constraints as in historical documentary. Lizzie Borden's *Born in Flames* (1983) combines 1970s radical feminist politics with a focus on diversity among and differences between women, especially along racial lines, which penetrated feminist thought more consistently in the 1980s. Although the film brings together black, white, Latina, and Asian women characters of different ages, it is especially striking for the power and beauty with which it represents black women, especially through the characters of Adelaide Norris (Jean Satterfield), Zella Wylie (Flo Kennedy), and Honey (Honey), who represent the vanguard of feminism in terms of both political theory and action.

The power of black women in this film is not the power that white American culture has long attributed to relatively powerless black women, the "matriarchal" status that white culture has assigned to black women's lives simply because of their insubordination to black men.[13] The film discredits this cultural mythology in one of its first scenes, where with intended irony we are given the "matriarchal" family background of a black feminist revolutionary as seen by the dominant culture: poverty, female-headed household, eight kids, are all here. Nor is the beauty with which black women are represented that of traditional aestheticized female images, extended since the 1960s to black women but still based on narrow definitions of femininity and race. The power and beauty that black women in Born in Flames emanate, through their insistence on taking power into their own hands, and their physical strength and comfort in their bodies, stands in sharp contradiction to and serves to dismantle these cultural constructions of race and gender.

Born in Flames is a low-budget feature set in what looks like the present, but, we learn, is ten years after a peaceful socialist democratic revolution has taken place in the United States, leaving the basic structures of patriarchy intact. Refusing to be appeased any longer, a "women's army" becomes increasingly militant in its actions against the government, eventually taking over the news media. The narrative is disjunctive, cutting back and forth between several groups of women (representing different feminist tendencies which will eventually unite), between a diverse range of "languages," musical and spoken (punk rock, blues, rap music, informal "black" English, media newspeak, political theory) and between various levels of visual representation which offer different perspectives on the same event.

First we see what seems to be an "insider's" view of the interaction between the women, and then the scene cuts to an image in which this interaction is monitored by the government (police or FBI), to its being debated by other groups of women, and finally to its distortion beyond recognition by the media. In one particularly striking shot, a black and white erotically charged image whose graininess conceals as well as reveals, two naked women's bodies slowly move in concert with each other. But our enjoyment of the image is disrupted as we encounter a freeze-frame and a male voice (which we recognize as that of an FBI agent) is heard; the image becomes a slide projected in FBI headquarters. This shift in representation makes a strong point about how women's personal lives are extremely vulnerable to political surveillance and state regulation, and further suggests our lack of control over the appropriation of lesbian images.

The changes in feminist thinking about sexuality across the decade of the 1980s can be discerned in Lizzie Borden's career. Born in Flames is, among other things, a cautionary tale about the appropriation of women's bodies, while Borden's next film, Working Girls (1986)—about women who work in the sex industry but are "in control" instead of victims—can be found in the porn section of your local video store. What began as a feminist approach to sexual representation was readily appropriated in its marketing campaign as white-collar pornography, in which feminists and "sophisticated" men can find common ground.

[. . .]

In assessing contemporary lesbian independent film, it seems that experimental film forms lend themselves more readily than documentary or narrative to exploring possibilities for and problems in the visual expression of lesbian desire. Although this is not meant to disparage documentary and narrative filmmaking, it does seem that experimental, or avant-garde, film is able to circumvent both the historical problems of documentary film and the repression of lesbianism by classic narrative film conventions, which has insidiously found its way into independent narratives as well.

This is a position which Barbara Hammer alludes to when she asks whether "radical content requires radical form," a question that presupposes that the avant garde is indeed radical, and not also burdened by a heavily masculinist, heterosexist bias, and that documentary and narrative forms are necessarily conventional.[14] This debate cannot be taken up in full here, but Hammer's question is part of her ongoing refinement of a lesbian aesthetic developed within her large body of work. *Sync Touch* (1981) can be seen as Hammer's treatise on lesbian filmmaking, in which she attempts to define in more theoretical terms the aesthetic concerns pervading her work since *Dyketactics* in 1974.

Sync Touch is structured in four sections, each exploring the relationship between touch and sight which the film maintains is the basis for lesbian filmmaking. The first section utilizes handpainted and pixilated photographic images, a rapid montage of finger-painted 16mm frames and contact sheets. The textures of the paint break up and dominate the image, but we see recognizable images fleetingly emerging and disappearing: one is of Hammer hugging her camera, another is of a blindfolded woman and girl sitting at a film projector. Both images convey the primacy of touch over sight, the first for the (female) filmmaking process, the second for the (female) spectator as well.

This idea is developed further in the third section of the film, in which what we conventionally call the "image" is from an old erotic film of Hammer. Here the erotic potential is obscured by the physical, tactile properties of the film medium itself, which prove the stronger: the jumpiness and graininess of the image, the scratches, sprocket holes, emulsion and visible frameline dominate the screen and comprise the "true" image. At one point the film slips in the optical printer gate and becomes completely abstract.

In the film's final sequence, two women are face to face, one (the filmmaker) repeating after the other a French statement about feminism and language. The English subtitles read:

> Feminist language is complete. It reunites mind and body, intellect and reason to physical sensation and emotion. . . . We are in a culture where expression of the heart and the senses are repressed. The heart of the film is the rapport between touch and sight.

This French lesson which concludes the film connects Hammer's articulation of her lesbian aesthetic to French feminism, especially suggesting Luce Irigaray's "When Our Lips Speak Together" (1977), which also insists on the primacy of touch, not sight, in the construction of female sexuality, and which also connotes strong lesbian associations.

Sync Touch was the last film Barbara Hammer made before turning away from explicitly lesbian imagery to explore other visual concerns throughout the 1980s. As Claudia Gorbman has written of her work following *Sync Touch*, "Her recent films . . . have virtually absented human forms; instead they focus on women's vision, a woman's vision, translating/ interpreting/transforming the world."[15] In *Sync Touch* Hammer's long association of visual and tactile senses continues but her previous focus on the lesbian body has changed. In the second section (a lecture on touch, filmed using a macro lens to create an extreme close-up of the speaker) she eroticizes the face; in the third section she obscures the body; in the fourth section she clothes the body and conveys an eroticism through ideas. This last section (the French lesson) visually pairs the two women. They are clothed similarly, both have short brown hair, wear long earrings, and are facing each other; then are facing the camera in a close-up on their eyebrows and eyes, again visually paired. This section continues a lesbian sensibility that was by 1981 rapidly changing—differences between women began to carry a far stronger erotic charge. But other changes occurring in lesbian representation are here: it is clear in the film that the representation of the lesbian body has become far more problematic than its celebration in her films from the 1970s ever implied; perhaps Hammer also felt the need to protect it from the fetishization and voyeurism now also the province of lesbians. In any case, the film takes a strong step toward "displacing" the lesbian body with other kinds of imagery, foreshadowing the change to come, a change which Gorbman describes: "the lesbian body has moved out of the frame to the camera's viewfinder."[16]

Su Friedrich's *Gently Down the Stream*, made the same year as *Sync Touch*, also involves a highly tactile approach to the filmmaking process and also deals with erotic content in a way which obscures rather than reveals women's bodies. The film is black and white and silent, and into black leader Friedrich has scratched words that, one at a time, construct a narrative which recounts the filmmaker's dreams. Although the words serve this narrative function, they work more prominently as a visual image themselves, and one which, as they scratch and disturb the film's emulsion, has strong tactile qualities. As with Hammer's optical printing of an erotic film in *Sync Touch*, the erotic potential of Friedrich's dreams is subjugated to the film's physical properties. The photographic images which intermittently appear have a dream-like association rather than literal relationship to these words.

In one of the dream narratives, we see in the upper-right corner an image of a woman on a rowing machine, while we read that: "A woman sits on a stage hunched over in the corner. She calls up a friend from the audience, asking her: [and at this point the image in the corner disappears, the words occupy full screen, one word at a time] come and make love to me. She does. I can't watch. [The screen goes black for a moment, then in big, full-screen scratched letters] Moans MOANS ROARS roars HOWLS." This sequence effectively raises a double-edged concern: that of the filmic representation of women's sexuality, which it problematizes by banishing the image of the woman from the screen, and that of women's position as film spectator (a position that invariably implicates women in the voyeuristic process), which is problematized by the words "I can't watch," followed by a blackened screen. These concerns are ones Friedrich takes up again and develops more fully in *Damned If You Don't* (1984).

Damned If You Don't successfully avoids the two major traps in which lesbian independent cinema has so often been caught over the past two decades: the "essentialist" trap, on the one hand, that imagines lesbianism to be completely outside of patriarchal definitions and, on the other hand, the trap that situates lesbianism so strictly within patriarchal definitions that it can't imagine any way out from them. In re-imagining lesbian desire, *Damned If You Don't* interrogates the sexual definitions and mandates of the dominant culture and its institutions (specifically the cinema and the Catholic Church) and ultimately dismantles them so that a different story can be told.

Four distinct narratives are interwoven, some spoken and some told visually, three referring to events in the (historical or fictional) past, and one taking place in the film's present. In the film's present, the narrative focuses on the nun (Peggy Healey) and her attractive neighbor (Ela Troyano) whom we met at the beginning of this chapter. This narra-tive, told visually in a black-and-white style that is at once impressionistic and documentary, moves from an exchange of looks, through a romantic pursuit, to the nun's discovery and reluctant acceptance of "hitherto unsuspected emotions," to the seduction and lovemaking scene which ends the film.

The other three narratives consist of a condensed, rephotographed version of the 1946 Powell–Pressburger film, Black Narcissus, watched on a poor quality black-and-white television set by the neighbor/seductress (with an added female voice narrating the plot for us); a woman's offscreen, spoken recollections of nuns in Catholic high school and their importance to the awakening of her sexuality; and the reading aloud from the testimony of Sister Mea Crivelli regarding her "immodest acts" with Sister Benedetta during the Renaissance. The situating of these three narratives in the near or far, historical or fictional past—seventeenth-century, high-school memories, a movie from the Forties with a foregone, unchangeable conclusion—enables us to view the film's present narrative as a sort of contemporary remake of these (hi)stories, with the possibility of a more satisfying resolution, in which desire can be rewarded instead of punished.

The original, color Powell–Pressburger film, Black Narcissus—although itself not exactly "mainstream" in its use of cinema conventions—upholds the mainstream cinema's strict codification of Woman as good/bad, moral/immoral. But the way it is used here, as the film-within-the-film, in its condensed black-and-white silent version on a television with a female voice-over narration, challenges the dominant cinema's construction of sexual difference and its reliance on cultural binarism. Breaking the narrative into fragments on a TV screen and providing a voice-over narration completely alters our relation to the events of the film. First, the poor quality of the image disturbs rather than creates visual pleasure, and directs the viewer more strongly toward the spoken narration—narration which clearly spells out, and thereby deconstructs, the good nun/bad nun polarization, a process which is further assisted by the film's conversion from its original color to the more oppositional black and white. The dark gray horizontal bands which pass over the TV screen, at times forming a kind of black-out bar over the "bad" nun's eyes to signify illicit behavior, serve this same purpose of exposing the ideological apparatus.

Second, by playing the film as a TV movie being watched by the nun's neighbor, Damned If You Don't inscribes the position of the lesbian spectator within the character of this unnamed woman. Her interest wanes during the course of Black Narcissus, perhaps due to the inevitability of the plot (the "bad" nun is punished for her sexual desire, and in a struggle with the "good" nun, falls over a cliff). By the film-within-a-film's end, the "bad" nun is dead and the unnamed woman is asleep, her identification with the "wrong" character, the "bad" nun, firmly established in a shot of her sleeping, surrounded by burning candles, which could possibly also be read as a shot of the "bad" nun laid out for her funeral.

The two verbally revealed narratives in Damned If You Don't challenge the ideological construction and regulation of women's sexuality on another front besides the cinema— here, Damned If You Don't takes on the Catholic Church. In conversation with the filmmaker, a woman recalls her fascination with the eroticism with which Catholicism is imbued; her comments underscore Michel Foucault's position that sexual repression, far from subduing desire, fuels its obsession. In the readings from Immodest Acts: The Life of a Lesbian Nun in Renaissance Italy, the testimony of Sister Mea Crivelli, used to indict and imprison Sister Benedetta for the rest of her life (some 30 years), veils explicitly sexual content in moral language ("she corrupted herself, she corrupted me . . ."), which has the effect of doubling as confessional pornography. The linkage of the testimony against the lesbian nun with confessional pornography exposes the hypocrisy of the moral/immoral binary which could cast Sister Crivelli as the "good" nun and Sister Benedetta as the "bad" nun of this history. The reading of this testimony, interspersed with silence, over images of the nun (of the film's present) riding the subway and visiting Coney Island further breaks down this polarization which is central to the regulation of sexuality. The nun's initial exploration of desire involves looking through symbolic barriers: out of the train window, through sunglasses, through glass aquarium walls, and finally through the vertical convent bars behind which she is imprisoned—she watches the woman who first watched her.

The slow building to the seduction scene, the silence of the women's interaction, and the tension of the taboo being violated all contribute to the eroticism of the final scene in *Damned If You Don't*. The complicated removal of the nun's habit, in itself a liberating metaphor, sustains the eroticism by postponing its enactment. The women start to make love, and shortly after that the film ends, the suggestion all the more powerful for its not being culminated on the screen.

Notes

1 "Iris Films Fundraising for Lesbian Mothers Film," *Lesbian Tide*, 5.4 (March/April 1976), p. 8.
2 One of many such announcements appears in *Lesbian Tide*, 5.4 (March/April 1976), p. 8.
3 Alice Bloch, "An Interview with Jan Oxenberg," *Amazon Quarterly*, 2.2 (December 1973), p. 54.
4 Radicalesbians, "Woman-Identified-Woman" (1970), reprinted in Karla Jay and Allen Young (eds) *Out of the Closets* (New York: Jove/HBJ Books, 1977).
5 Ibid. p. 176.
6 Brooke, "The Retreat to Cultural Feminism," in Redstockings, *Feminist Revolution* (New York: Random House, 1978).
7 Michelle Citron, "Comic Critique: Films of Jan Oxenberg," *Jump Cut*, 24/25 (1981), p. 31.
8 Richard Dyer uses Barbara Hammer's films to define this cultural feminist position. See Dyer, *Now You See It* (London: Routledge, 1990), pp. 194–206.
9 Barbara Hammer, quoted in Jacqueline Zita, "Counter-Currencies of a Lesbian Iconography: Films of Barbara Hammer," *Jump Cut*, 24/25 (1981), p. 29.
10 Ibid. p. 28.
11 Zita, "Counter-Currencies of a Lesbian Iconography," p. 28.
12 Dot Tuer, "Pleasure in the Dark: Sexual Difference and Erotic Deviance in the Articulation of a Female Desire," *CineAction!* (Fall 1987), p. 56.
13 For more on the myth of black matriarchy, see Angela Y. Davis, *Women, Race and Class* (New York: Random House, 1981).
14 Barbara Hammer, "Does Radical Content Require Radical Form?" *Millennium Film Journal*, 22 (Winter/Spring 1989–90).
15 Claudia Gorbman, "Body Displaced, Body Discovered: Recent Work of Barbara Hammer," *Jump Cut*, 32 (April 1986), p. 12.
16 Ibid.

The New Queer Cinema

4

B. RUBY RICH

1992 was a watershed year for independent gay and lesbian film and video. In the spring, on the very same day, Paul Verhoeven's *Basic Instinct* and Derek Jarman's *Edward* II opened in New York City. Within days, the prestigious New Directors/New Films Festival had premiered four new "queer" films: Christopher Münch's *The Hours and Times*, Tom Kalin's *Swoon*, Gregg Araki's *The Living End*, and Laurie Lynd's R.S.V.P. Had so much ink ever been spilled in the mainstream press for such a cause? *Basic Instinct* was picketed by the self-righteous wing of the queer community (until dykes began to discover how much fun it was), while main-stream critics were busily impressed by the "queer new wave" and set to work making stars of the new boys on the block. Not that the moment wasn't contradictory: the summer's San Francisco Gay and Lesbian Film Festival had its most successful year in its 16-year history, doubling attendance from 1991, but the National Endowment for the Arts pulled its funding anyway.

The queer film phenomenon was introduced in 1991 at Toronto's Festival of Festivals, the best spot in North America for tracking cinematic trends. There, suddenly, was a flock of films that were doing something new, renegotiating subjectivities, annexing whole genres, revising histories in their image. All through the winter, spring, summer, and autumn, the message was loud and clear: queer is hot. Check out the international circuit, from Park City to Berlin to London. Awards have been won, parties held. At Sundance, in the heart of Utah's Mormon country, there was even a panel dedicated to the queer subject, hosted by yours truly.

The Barbed Wire Kisses panel put eight panelists on stage, with so many queer filmmakers in the audience that a roll call had to be read. Filmmakers stood, one by one, to applause from the matinee crowd. "Sundance is where you see what the industry can bear," said panelist Todd Haynes, there to talk about *Poison*'s year on the firing line. He stayed to be impressed by earnest 18-year-old Wunderkind Sadie Benning, whose bargain-basement videos, shot with a Fisher-Price Pixelvision and produced for less than $20 apiece, have already received a retrospective at MoMA.

Isaac Julien was suddenly cast in the role of the older generation. Summarizing the dilemmas of marketing queer product to general audiences, he described a Miramax Prestige advertising campaign for his *Young Soul Rebels* that used a bland image of guys and gals hang-ing out, like a Newport ad gone Benetton. Julien got them to change to an image of the black and white boyfriends, Caz and Billibud, kissing on a bed. The box office improved.

Tom Kalin struggled to reconcile his support for the disruptions of Basic Instinct's shoot with his film Swoon's choice of queer murderers as subjects. Australian filmmakers Stephen Cummins and Simon Hunt related the censorship of an episode of The Simpsons, where a scene of Homer kissing a swish fellow at the plant was cut. The panel turned surprisingly participatory. One Disney executive excoriated the industry. Meanwhile, Derek Jarman, the grand old man in his fourth decade of queer activity, beamed. He'd never been on a panel of queers at a mainstream festival.

Try to imagine the scene in Park City. Robert Redford holds a press conference and is asked, on camera, why there are all these gay films at his festival. Redford finesses: it is all part of the spectrum of independent film that Sundance is meant to serve. He even allows that the awards in 1991 to Poison and Jennie Livingston's Paris Is Burning might have made the festival seem more welcoming to gays and lesbians. He could just as easily have said: these are simply the best films being made.

Of course, the new queer films and videos aren't all the same, and don't share a single aesthetic vocabulary or strategy or concern. Yet they are nonetheless united by a common style. Call it "Homo Pomo": there are traces in all of them of appropriation and pastiche, irony, as well as a reworking of history with social constructionism very much in mind. Definitively breaking with older humanist approaches and the films and tapes that accompanied identity politics, these works are irreverent, energetic, alternately minimalist and excessive. Above all, they're full of pleasure.

All the same, success breeds discontent, and 1992 was no different from any other year. When the ghetto goes mainstream, malaise and paranoia set in. It can be ideological, or generational, or genderational. Consider the issues that might disturb the peace. What will happen to the lesbian and gay filmmakers who have been making independent films, often in avant-garde traditions, for decades already? Surprise, all the new movies being snatched up by distributors, shown in mainstream festivals, booked into theaters, are by the boys. Surprise, the amazing new lesbian videos that are redefining the whole dyke relationship to popular culture remain hard to find.

Amsterdam's Gay and Lesbian Film Festival made these discrepancies plain as day. The festival was staged in November 1991, wedged between Toronto and Sundance. It should have been the most exciting place to be, but wasn't, not at all. And yet, that's where the girls were. Where the videos were. Where the films by people of color and ex-Iron Curtain denizens were. But the power brokers were missing.

Christine Vachon, co-producer of Swoon and Poison, is sure that the heat was produced by money: "Suddenly there's a spotlight that says these films can be commercially viable." Still, everyone tries to guess how long this moment of fascination will last. After all, none of this is taking place in a vacuum: celebrated in the festivals, despised in the streets. Review the statistics on gay-bashing. Check out US immigration policy. Add the usual quota of internecine battles: girls against boys, narrative versus experimental work, white boys versus everyone else, elitism against populism, expansion of sights versus patrolling of borders. There's bound to be trouble in paradise, even when the party's just getting going.

Dateline: Toronto

Music was in the air in Toronto in September 1991, where the reputation of queer film and video started to build up. Or maybe I just loved Laurie Lynd's R.S.V.P. because it made my elevator ride with Jessye Norman possible. Lynd's film uses Norman's aria from Berlioz's *Les Nuits d'été* as its madeleine—supposedly Lynd sent Norman the finished film as a belated form of asking permission, and she loved it so much she agreed to attend the world premiere at Toronto (with red carpet in place and a packed house going wild, she sat through the screening holding Lynd's hand). R.S.V.P. suggests that the tragedy and trauma of AIDS have led to a new kind of film and video practice, one which takes up the aesthetic strategies that directors have already learned and applies them to a greater need than art for its own sake. This time, it's art for our sake, and it's powerful: no one can stay dry-eyed through this witty elegy.

Lynd was there as a producer, too, having worked on fellow-Canadian John Greyson's *The Making of 'Monsters'*. In it, Georg Lukács comes out of retirement to produce a television movie and hires Bertolt Brecht to direct it. Along with the comedy and boys in briefs, there's a restaging of the central aesthetic argument of the Frankfurt School as it might apply to the crises of representation engendered by today's anti-gay backlash, violence, and television treatments of the AIDS era.

Both low-budget and high-end filmmaking showed up in Toronto. Not surprisingly, the guys were high end, the gals low. Not that I'd begrudge Gus Van Sant one penny or remove a single frame from *My Own Private Idaho*—a film that securely positions him as heir-apparent to Fassbinder. So what if it didn't get a single Oscar nomination?

At the other end of the spectrum was veteran avant-gardist Su Friedrich, whose latest film, *First Comes Love*, provoked catcalls from its largely queer audience. Was it because its subject was marriage, a topic on which the film is healthily ambivalent, mingling resentment with envy, anger with yearning? Or was it an aesthetic reaction, since Friedrich returns to a quasi-structuralist mode for her indictment of institutionalized heterosexuality and thus possibly alienates audiences accustomed to an easier queer fix? Was it because the director was a woman, since the only other lesbian on hand was Monika Treut, who by now should probably be classified as post-queer? Whatever the reason, Friedrich's elegant short stuck out, a barometer in a pack of audience-pleasers.

The epiphanic moment, if there was one, was the screening of Jarman's *Edward* II, which reinscribed the homosexuality so integral to its sixteenth-century source via a syncretic style that mixed past and present in a manner so arch that the film easily fits its tag, the "QE2." Think pastiche, as OutRage demos and gay-boy calisthenics mix with minimalist period drama. Homophobia is stripped bare as a timeless occupation, tracked across centuries but never lacking in historical specificity. Obsessive love, meanwhile, is enlarged to include queer desire as a legitimate source of tragedy.

For women, *Edward* II is a bit complicated. Since the heroes are men and the main villain is a woman, some critics have condemned it as misogynist. Indeed, Tilda Swinton's brilliance as an actor—and full co-creator of her role—invests her character with more weight, and thus more evil, than anyone else on screen. But the film is also a critique of heterosexuality and of a world ruled by royals and the Tory Party, and Isabella seems more inspired by Thatcher than woman-hating. Annie Lennox is clearly meant to be on the side of girls and angels. Her solo "Every Time We Say Goodbye" accompanies Edward and Gaveston's last dance, bringing grandeur, modernity, even post-modernity, to their tragedy. The song comes from the AIDS-benefit album, *Red Hot and Blue*, in which video Lennox inscribed images of Jarman's childhood in a tribute to his activism and HIV status. Thus does Jarman's time travel insist on carrying the court into today's gay world.

Dateline: Amsterdam

The official car showed up at the airport with the festival's own steamy poster of girls in heat and boys in lust plastered all over it. Amsterdam, city of lights for faggots and dykes, offered the promise of an event purely one's own in the city celebrated for queerness. Expectations were running high, but in fact the festival showed all the precious advantages and irritating problems that life in the ghetto entails. It was a crucible for queer work, all right, but some got burned. How does this event fit into the big picture set by the "big" festivals? Well, it doesn't. The identity that elsewhere becomes a badge of honor here became a straitjacket. But would "elsewhere" exist without the "here"?

Amsterdam was an exercise in dialectics in action, with both pleasures and dangers. Filmmaker Nick Deocampo from the Philippines was planning his country's first gay festival and hoping that the "war of the widows" wouldn't forestall it. Race, status, romance, gender, even the necessity of the festival came up for attack and negotiation, on those few occasions when the public got to talk back. Pratibha Parmar affirmed the importance of a queer circuit—"my lifeline"—sure that it's key to the work. Jarman disagreed: "Perhaps their time is up," maybe life in the ghetto now offers diminished returns. So though Jarman and Ulrike Ottinger got awards here, and though Jarman used the opening night to call for the decriminalization of Oscar Wilde, the meaning of such an event remained contested.

Not that there weren't good films at Amsterdam. But the best work seemed to come from long ago or faraway, like the great shows of German cross-dressing movies or the Mary Wings tribute to "Greta Garbo's lesbian past" or the extraordinary 60s fantasy from Japan, *Funeral of Roses*. There were even two terrific new lesbian films, both deserving of instant cult status. Cleo Uebelmann's *Mano Destra* brought bondage and domination straight to the viewer, serving up knot fetishism and the thrills of specular anticipation with an uncanny understanding of cinema's own powers. From a trio of Viennese filmmakers (Angela Hans Scheirl, Dietmar Schipek, Ursula Puerrer) came *Flaming Ears*, a surreal fable that draws on comics and sci-fi traditions for a near-human love story visualized in an atmosphere of cabaret, rubble, and revenge. Its fresh "cyberdyke" style reflects Austrian sources as diverse as Valie Export and Otto Muehle, but shot through with Super-8 visual rawness and a script that could have been written by J. G. Ballard.

It was a shame that the Dutch press marginalized the festival, because the kind of "scoop" that the *New York Times* and *Newsweek* would later find in Utah could have been theirs right at home. A new kind of lesbian video surfaced here, and with it emerged a contemporary lesbian sensibility. Like the gay male films now in the limelight, this video has everything to do with a new historiography. But where the boys are archaeologists, the girls have to be alchemists. Their style is unlike almost anything that's come before. I would call it lesbian camp, but the species is, after all, better known for camping. And historical revisionism is not a catchy term. So just borrow from Hollywood, and think of it as the Great Dyke Rewrite.

Here's a taste of the new genre. In Cecilia Dougherty's *Grapefruit*, white San Francisco dykes unapologetically impersonate John, Yoko and the Beatles—proving that appropriation and gender-fuck make a great combination. Cecilia Barriga's *The Meeting of Two Queens* re-edits Dietrich and Garbo movies to construct the dyke fan's dream narrative: get the girls together, help them get it on. It's a form of idolatry that takes the feminist lit-crit practice of "reading against the grain" into new image territory, blasting the results on to the screen (or monitor, to be exact). In one episode of Kaucylia Brooke and Jane Cottis' *Dry Kisses Only*, Anne Baxter's back-stage meeting with Bette Davis in *All About Eve* is altered, inserting instead of Baxter a dyke who speaks in direct address to the camera about her life working in a San Francisco lesbian bar, her love lost to Second World War combat. She's cross-cut with Bette's reaction shots, culminating with Davis taking her arm (and taking her home).

Apart from the videos, festival lesbians pinned all voyeuristic hopes on the "Wet" Party, where they would finally get to the baths. Well, sort of. Everyone certainly tried. Outfits ranged from the campiness of childhood-at-the-beach to show-your-leather seriousness. Women bobbed in the pool, playing with rubber rafts and inflated black and white fuck-me dolls. (Parmar would later note that there were more inflatables of color in attendance than actual women of color.) San Francisco sex stars Shelly Mars and Susie Bright both performed, though the grand moment in which Bright seemed to be lecturing us on "Oedipal underwear" turned out to be a cruel acoustical joke: she was actually extoling the virtue of edible underwear. But the back rooms were used for heart-to-hearts, not action. Caught between the states of dress-up and undress, everyone waited for someone else to do something.

Other parties offered other pleasures. At one, Jimmy Somerville, unscheduled, did a Sylvester homage. At another, Marilyn Monroe appeared, frosted on to a giant cake, clutching her skirt, only to be carved up by a gaggle of male chefs. In the end, somehow, Amsterdam was the festival you loved to hate, the place where everyone wanted the world and wouldn't settle for less, where dirty laundry could be washed in public and anyone in authority taken to task, where audiences were resistant to experimental and non-narrative work, and where criticisms were bestowed more bountifully than praise. Still, while the market place might be seductive, it's not yet democratic. Amsterdam was the place where a "Wet" Party could at least be staged, where new works by women and people of color were accorded pride of place, where video was fully integrated into the programing. Amsterdam was a ritual gathering of the tribe and, like a class reunion, filled with ambivalence.

Park City, Utah

Everything came together at the Sundance Film Festival in Park City. Christopher Münch's *The Hours and Times* is a good example. Audiences fell in love with this imaginary chronicle of Brian Epstein and John Lennon's last tango in Barcelona. Münch's camera style and script are a reprise of *cinéma vérité*, as though some dusty reels had been found in a closet in Liverpool and expertly edited, as though Leacock or Pennebaker had turned gay-positive retroactively. Epstein tries to get Lennon into bed, using old-world angst, homo-alienation, Jewish charm. Lennon tries to sort out his life, balancing wife Cynthia against groupie against Epstein, trying to have it all and to figure out whatever will come next. Just a simple view of history with the veil of homophobia pulled back. It's rumored that the dramatic jury at Sundance loved it so much, they wanted to give it the Grand Prize—but since it wasn't feature length they settled on a special jury award.

"Puts the Homo back in Homicide" is the teaser for Tom Kalin's first feature, *Swoon*, but it could easily apply to Gregg Araki's newest, *The Living End*, as well. Where Kalin's film is an interrogation of the past, Araki's is set resolutely in the present. Or is it? Cinematically, it restages the celluloid of the 60s and 70s: early Godard, *Bonnie and Clyde*, *Badlands*, *Butch Cassidy and the Sundance Kid*, every pair-on-the-run movie that ever penetrated Araki's consciousness. Here, though, the guys are HIV positive, one bored and one full of rage, both of them with nothing to lose. They could be characters out of a porn flick, the stud and the john, in a renegotiated terrain. Early Araki films are often too garage-hand, too boychick, too far into visual noise, but this one is different. Camera style and palette update the New Wave. Araki's stylistic end runs have paid off, and this time he's got a queers-on-the-lam portrait that deserves a place in movie history—an existential film for a post-porn age, one that puts queers on the map as legitimate genre subjects. It's quintessentially a film of its time.

And so is *Swoon*, though it might seem otherwise, what with the mock-period settings, the footage purloined from the 20s, and the courtroom-accurate script, based on the 1924 Chicago trial of Leopold and Loeb, the pair of rich Jewish boys who bonded, planned capers, and finally killed a boy. In the wake of the Dahmer case, it would be easy to think of this as a film about horrific acts. *Swoon*, however, deals in different stakes: it's the history of discourses that's under Kalin's microscope, as he demonstrates how easily mainstream society of the 20s could unite discrete communities of outsiders (Jews, queers, blacks, murderers) into a commonality of perversion. The whole look of the film—director of photography Ellen Kuras won the prize for cinematography in dramatic film in Park City—emphasizes this view with the graphic quality of its anti-realism, showing how much Kalin, Kuras, and co-producer Vachon tailored its look.

As part of a new generation of directors, Kalin isn't satisfied to live in the past, even a post-modern past. No, *Swoon* takes on the whole enterprise of "positive images," definitively rejecting any such project and turning the thing on its head. I doubt that anyone who damned *The Silence of the Lambs* for toxic homophobia will swallow *Swoon* easily, but hopefully the film will force a rethinking of positions. Claim the heroes, claim the villains, and don't mistake any of it for realness.

Throughout Sundance, a comment Richard Dyer made in Amsterdam echoed in my memory. There are two ways to dismiss gay film: one is to say, "Oh, it's just a gay film"; the other, to proclaim, "Oh, it's a great film, it just happens to be gay." Neither applied to the films in Park City, since they were great precisely because of the ways in which they were gay. Their queerness was no more arbitrary than their aesthetics, no more than their individual preoccupations with interrogating history. The queer present negotiates with the past, knowing full well that the future is at stake.

Like film, video is a harbinger of that future, even more so. Yet Sundance, like most film festivals, showed none. To make a point about the dearth of lesbian work in feature film and to confront the industry with its own exclusions, the Barbed Wire Kisses panel opened with a projected screening of Sadie Benning's videotape *Jollies*—and brought down the house. With an absolute economy of means, Benning constructed a *Portrait of the Artist as a Young Dyke* such as we've never seen before. "I had a crush. It was 1978, and I was in kindergarten." The lines are spoken facefront to the camera, black-and-white images floating into the frame alongside the words enlisted to spell out her emotions on screen, associative edits calling settled assumptions into question.

The festival ended, of course. Isaac Julien returned to London to finish *Black and White in Colour*, his documentary on the history of blacks in British television. High-school dropout Sadie Benning left to show her tapes at Princeton, and to make another one, *It Wasn't Love*, that proved she's no fluke. Derek Jarman and Jimmy Somerville were arrested for demonstrating outside London's Houses of Parliament. Christopher Münch and Tom Kalin picked up prizes in Berlin. Gregg Araki found himself a distributor. New work kept getting produced: the San Francisco festival found its submissions up by 50 per cent in June. The Queer New Wave has come full circle: the boys and their movies have arrived.

But will lesbians ever get the attention for their work that men get for theirs? Will queers of color ever get equal time? Or video achieve the status reserved for film? Take, for example, Cheryl Dunye, a young videomaker whose *She Don't Fade* and *Vanilla Sex* put a sharp, satiric spin on black romance and cross-race illusions. Or Jean Carlomusto's *L is For the Way You Look*, a definitive portrait of dyke fandom and its importance for, uh, subject position.

For one magical Saturday afternoon in Park City, there was a panel that traced a history: Derek Jarman at one end on the eve of his 50th birthday, and Sadie Benning at the other, just joining the age of consent. The world had changed enough that both of them could be there, with a host of cohorts in between. All engaged in the beginnings of a new queer historiography, capable of transforming this decade, if only the door stays open long enough. For him, for her, for all of us.

PART TWO

FORMS

Introduction

This section contains four case studies examining how cinematic structures—for example, genres or types or styles of filmmaking—figure queerness in specific ways. All of the essays draw on genre theory and structuralist thinking to some degree, and base their observations on the idea that cinematic forms themselves (regardless of specific content) contain their own ideological messages about sexuality. Classical Hollywood narrative form, for example, has had a heterosexist bias since its codification, in that it almost always contains a male protagonist and a female love interest (more rarely one also finds the reverse). As the protagonist defeats the antagonist during the climax of the story, the heterosexual couple is united romantically, signaling a traditional "happy ending." Heterosexual characters—and by extension heterosexuality itself—are privileged by the very form of Hollywood storytelling. Non-straight characters are excluded from the central heroic roles, and queers can thus be frequently found in either marginalized supporting roles (the spinster aunt, the comedic shop clerk) or as antagonists themselves (the lesbian vampire, the effeminate gunsel). Throughout Hollywood history, actors and actresses who exhibited less-than-traditional gender attributes were repeatedly typecast as villains and comic relief, while those who enacted macho men and feminine women were cast as heroes and heroines (Russo 1987; White 1999, 136–193).

Beyond the heterosexist imperatives of Hollywood casting, one might understand the very structure of the antagonist role to be queer, in that he or she (or it) attempts to overturn the *status quo* and disrupt happy heterosexual closure. While classical Hollywood narrative form usually encourages spectators to identify with "normal" characters and not with queer ones, some cinematic forms (such as the musical and the animated film) invite audiences to glory in the chaotic extravagance that occurs when the rigid social conventions of normality are overturned. This is also one of the (albeit equivocal) appeals of the horror film—a genre that seems to revel in attacks upon the so-called "normal" world. In previous decades, such fantastic facades were necessary metaphors for queer lives and forces. Yet, these forms still proliferate in contemporary mainstream entertainment; in fact, it is easier to find metaphoric queers at the movies—hobbits and wookies and vampires and X-Men—than overt homosexuals, bisexuals, or transgendered people. These figures and forces can be decoded as queer by some spectators, and just as easily not by others, a point made by Henry Jenkins in his exploration of queer *Star Trek* fans (in Part Four of this volume).

The first pieces in this section examine how two traditional Hollywood film genres emphasize many of these issues. Harry Benshoff's "The Monster and the Homosexual" and Brett Farmer's "Queer Negotiations of the Hollywood Musical" both arise from the historical fact of lesbian and gay male interest in those genres. They both argue that what makes these two genres so appealing to queer spectators is their use of excess, drawing in audiences by promising moments that will transgress the "normal world" (into the abnormal in the horror film, and into the supernormal in the musical). Working within mainstream business practices, these genres historically were not explicitly homosexual (and both authors point out how they both also promote the superiority of heterosexuality). Yet, the artificiality of the fantasy worlds in these genres, as well as the ineffable quality that seemed to but did not exactly say "homosexual," are precisely what the authors find so queer about the genres.

The last two essays in this section deal with types of cinema that do not easily fit the description of film genres, although some have tried to make them do so. Film noir has been called a genre, a style, and a historical movement. Similarly, the animated cartoon has been approached both as a genre and as an entirely different mode of filmmaking. (Perhaps film noir and the animated cartoon are exemplary queer forms in that they themselves resist easy categorization.) Richard Dyer's "Queer Noir" turns one of the recurrent arguments *against* reading films queerly (that potentially queer figures are rarely denoted as such) into an aspect of what makes noir so thoroughly queer: uncertainty about everything is fundamental to noir, and thus uncertainty about sexual desire is often structured into these films. Sean Griffin's "Pronoun Trouble: The 'Queerness' of Animation" reveals the same potential for queerness that Benshoff and Farmer find in their genres: the Carnivalesque nature of animation makes it hard to claim any specific sexual orientation for certain cartoon characters, as well as creating a general sense of fluidity and anarchy that is often expressed through a play with gender and sexuality.

The Monster and the Homosexual

5

HARRY BENSHOFF

[. . .]

In the 1970s, in a series of essays exploring the horror film, critic Robin Wood suggested that the thematic core of the genre might be reduced to three interrelated variables: normality (as defined chiefly by a heterosexual patriarchal capitalism), the Other (embodied in the figure of the monster), and the relationship between the two.[1] According to Wood's formulation, these monsters can often be understood as racial, ethnic, and/or political/ideological Others, while more frequently they are constructed primarily as sexual Others (women, bisexuals, and homosexuals). Since the demands of the classical Hollywood narrative system usually insist on a heterosexual romance within the stories they construct, the monster is traditionally figured as a force that attempts to block that romance. As such, many monster movies (and the source material they draw upon) might be understood as being "about" the eruption of some form of queer sexuality into the midst of a resolutely heterosexual milieu. By "queer," I mean to use the word both in its everyday connotations ("questionable . . . suspicious . . . strange . . .") and also as how it has been theorized in recent years within academia and social politics. This latter "queer" is not only what differs "in some odd way from what is usual or normal," but ultimately is what opposes the binary definitions and proscriptions of a patriarchal heterosexism. Queer can be a narrative moment, or a performance or stance which negates the oppressive binarisms of the dominant hegemony (what Wood and other critics have identified as the variable of "normality") both within culture at large, and within texts of horror and fantasy. It is somewhat analogous to the moment of hesitation that demarcates Todorov's Fantastic, or Freud's theorization of the Uncanny: queerness disrupts narrative equilibrium and sets in motion a questioning of the *status quo*, and in many cases within fantastic literature, the nature of reality itself.[2]

Sociologically, the term queer has been used to describe an "oxymoronic community of difference,"[3] which includes people who might also self-identify as gay and/or lesbian, bisexual, transsexual, transvestite, drag queen, leather daddy, lipstick lesbian, pansy, fairy, dyke, butch, femme, feminist, asexual, and so on—any people not explicitly defining themselves in "traditional" heterosexual terms. Queer seeks to go beyond these and all such categories based on the concepts of normative heterosexuality and traditional gender roles to encompass a more inclusive, amorphous, and ambiguous contraheterosexuality (thus there are those individuals who self-identify as "straight queers"). Queer is also insistent that issues of race, gender, disability, and class be addressed within its politics, making interracial sex and sex between physically challenged people dimensions of queer sex also, and further linking the queer corpus with the figure of the Other as it has been theorized by Wood in the horror film. Queer activism itself has been seen as unruly, defiant, and angry: like the mad scientists of horror films, queer proponents do want to restructure society by calling attention to and eventually dismantling the oppressive assumptions of heterocentrist discourse. As one theorist has noted,

> the queer, unlike the rather polite categories of gay and lesbian, revels in the discourse of the loathsome, the outcast, the idiomatically proscribed position of same-sex desire. Unlike petitions for civil rights, queer revels constitute a kind of activism that attacks the dominant notion of the natural. The queer is the taboo-breaker, the monstrous, the uncanny. Like the Phantom of the Opera, the queer dwells underground, below the operatic overtones of the dominant; frightening to look at, desiring, as it plays its own organ, producing its own music.[4]

Queer even challenges "the Platonic parameters of Being—the borders of life and death."[5] Queer suggests death over life by focusing on non-procreative sexual behaviors, making it especially suited to a genre which takes sex and death as central thematic concerns.

[. . .]

Earlier critical thinking on the monster movie frequently drew upon metaphysical or psychoanalytic concepts relating to the genre's twin obsessions, sex and death. Some earlier writing on the links between cinematic horror and (homo)sexuality used a Freudian model of repression as a theoretical rubric. In Margaret Tarratt's groundbreaking essay of the early 1970s, "Monsters from the Id," the author examined Hollywood monster movies of the 1950s and persuasively postulated that the monster represented an eruption of repressed sexual desire.[6] Thus, 1951's The Thing (from Another World) develops explicit parallels between the monster in question and the libidinous nature of the film's male lead, Captain Hendry. The monster serves as a metaphoric expression of Hendry's lusts; it is a displaced and concretized figure of phallic desire. Even a cursory glance at the monster movies of this era will repeatedly reveal this trope: The Creature from the Black Lagoon (1954), The Giant Gila Monster (1959), and most of their scaly brethren seem to "pop up" like clockwork whenever the hero and heroine move into a romantic clinch. The ideas put forth by Tarratt became common and useful tools to understanding the functioning of the genre, but what is perhaps less well known was that her essay was initially published in the British journal Films and Filming, which was produced and marketed primarily for and to a gay male readership.[7]

During the 1970s and 1980s, in a series of articles and books, Canadian film scholar Robin Wood further developed Tarratt's ideas, expanding them generally to all horror films, and specifically to the films of 1970s horror auteurs such as Larry Cohen, Wes Craven, and Tobe Hooper. (Robin Wood is himself a gay man who makes certain distinctions between his pre- and post- "coming out" work in film criticism.)[8] Drawing on Herbert Marcuse's and Gad Horowitz's readings of Marx and Freud (in Eros and Civilization and Repression, respectively),[9] Wood invokes concepts of basic and surplus repression to sketch a model of life under patriarchal capitalism. According to this model, society cannot be formed or continue to exist without a certain amount of basic repression. Surplus repression, on the other hand, is used by those in control to keep all "Others" subjugated to the dominant order. The Other reciprocally bolsters the image of "normality": as Simon Watney has observed, "Straight society needs us [homosexuals]. We are its necessary 'Other'. Without gays, straights are not straight."[10] According to Wood's readings of the American horror film, it is easy to see these Others cast in the role of the monster: repressed by society, these sociopolitical and psycho-sexual Others are displaced (as in a nightmare) onto monstrous signifiers, in which form they return to wreak havoc in the cinema. While some have critiqued this model as essentialist, Wood did note the importance of historical parameters in understanding the relationship between normality and monsters, asserting that "[t]he monster is, of course, much more protean, changing from period to period as society's basic fears clothe themselves in fashionable or immediately accessible garments."[11]

For many, the repressive hypothesis explicit in Tarratt's and Wood's readings of the genre was overturned by the work of the French theorist Michel Foucault, who, in *The History of Sexuality* (1978), argued that sexuality is in fact not repressed by society, but rather explicitly constructed and regulated via a series of discourses which include those of the medical, legal, religious, and media establishments. While many of these discourses have the same effect on certain sectors of society as might be argued under the repressive hypothesis (the exclusion from the public sphere, dehumanization, and monsterization of certain forms of sexuality), Foucault argues that "it is a ruse to make prohibition into the basic and con-stitutive element from which one would be able to write the history of what has been said concerning sex starting from the modern epoch."[12] In a by now famous turn of phrase, Foucault noted of "repression" that "[t]here is not one but many silences."[13] (This does not mean that basic psychoanalytic concepts such as sexual repression and egodystonic homosexuality will not be discussed within the following pages. Indeed, homosexual repression—as it might exist within an individual psyche rather than within society at large—is still a potent formulation in how one might understand the homosexual and/or homophobic dynamics of many horror films.)

Like Wood, Foucault was a homosexual cultural critic who drew upon (and eventually expanded) a Marxist understanding of how society regulates human sexuality, developing a more precisely historicized formulation which examines how power and knowledge are embedded in the practice of social discourse. Shifting the debate from the repression of sex to the production of sexuality, Foucault noted that ours is now a culture wherein "the politics of the body does not require the elision of sex or its restriction solely to the repro-ductive function; it relies instead on a multiple channeling into the controlled circuits of the economy—on what has been called [by Marcuse] a hyper-repressive desublimation."[14] As sex and sexuality become more ever present in the public sphere, they are nonetheless regulated into certain cultural constructions through powerful social discourses. Yet, as Foucault further asserts,

> we must conceive discourse as a series of discontinuous segments whose tactical function is neither uniform nor stable. To be more precise, we must not imagine a world of discourse divided between accepted discourse and excluded discourse, or between the dominant discourse and the dominated one; but as a multiplicity of discursive elements that can come into play in various strategies.[15]

As British cultural theorists such as Stuart Hall have pointed out, the multiplicity of these discourses and their multiple sites of reception also allow for the active negotiation of these issues. Thus, when talking about a cultural product or "discursive object" such as a filmic genre system, one would be wise to take into consideration the historical discourses not only of production (where meanings are encoded) but also those of reception (where meanings are decoded according to a multiplicity of different reading positions).[16]

[. . .]

How actual practices of spectatorship interact with the narrative patterns of a genre system must then be considered when discussing the queer pleasures of a horror film text itself. Where does the viewer of monster movies position him/herself in relation to the text? The overtly heterosexualized couple of the classical horror film of the 1930s might be said to represent the most common (or intended?) site of spectatorial identification for these particular films, yet as many theorists have pointed out, it is more likely that specific shot mechanisms within the film's formal construction will link the spectator's gaze to that of the gothic villain or monster.[17] Furthermore, there is more to the processes of spectatorial identification than patterns of subjective shots and cinematic suture.[18] For example, the heterosexualized couple in these films are invariably banal and underdeveloped in relation to the sadomasochistic villain(s), whose outrageous exploits are, after all, the *raison d'être* of the genre. To phrase it in Richard Dyer's terms, in the horror film, it is usually the hetero-sexualized hero and heroine who are stereotyped—painted with broad brush strokes—while the villains and monsters are given more complex, "novelistic" characterizations.[19] As the titular stars of their own filmic stories, perhaps it is the monsters that the audience comes to enjoy, experience, and identify with; in many films, normative heterosexuality is reduced to a trifling narrative convention, one which becomes increasingly unnecessary and outmoded as the genre evolves across the years.

As I shall be arguing throughout this work, the cinematic monster's subjective position is more readily acceded to by a queer viewer—someone who already situates him/herself outside a patriarchal, heterosexist order and the popular culture texts that it produces. [. . .] What does it mean if lesbians identify with the beautiful female vampires of *The Hunger* (1983), or if gay men go to see Tom Cruise bite Brad Pitt in *Interview with the Vampire* (1994)? In what ways does this happen and what is the "price paid" in culture-at-large for yet another depiction of monstrous predatory homosexuals? Identification with the monster can mean many different things to many different people, and is not necessarily always a negative thing for the individual spectators in question, even as some depictions of queer monsters undoubt-edly conflate and reinforce certain sexist or homophobic fears within the public sphere. For spectators of all types, the experience of watching a horror film or monster movie might be understood as similar to that of the Carnival as it has been theorized by Bakhtin, wherein the conventions of normality are ritualistically overturned within a prescribed period of time in order to celebrate the lure of the deviant.[20] Halloween functions similarly, allowing otherwise "normal" people the pleasures of drag, or monstrosity, for a brief but exhilarating experience. However, while straight participants in such experiences usually return to their daylight worlds, both the monster and the homosexual are permanent residents of shadowy spaces: at worst caves, castles, and closets, and at best a marginalized and oppressed position within the cultural hegemony. Queer viewers are thus more likely than straight ones to experience the monster's plight in more personal, individualized terms.

What then exactly makes the experience of a horror film or monster movie gay, lesbian, or queer? There are at least four different ways in which homosexuality might intersect with the horror film. The first and most obvious of these occurs when a horror film includes identifiably gay and/or lesbian characters. These characters might be victims, passers-by, or the monsters themselves, although gay and lesbian people (to this point in time) have never been placed in the role of the normative hero or heroine.[21] Broadly speaking, the appearance of overtly homosexual film characters doesn't occur until the late 1960s and early 1970s, following the demise of the Production Code and its restrictions against the depiction of "sex perversion." Films such as *Blacula* (1972), *Theater of Blood* (1973), or *The Sentinel* (1977) fall into this category. In these films, gay or lesbian characters fall victim to the monster just as straight characters do, although somewhat disturbingly their fates are frequently deemed "deserved" by the films they inhabit, often solely on the basis of their characters' homosexuality. Other films such as *The Fearless Vampire Killers* (1967), *The Vampire Lovers* (1971), or *The Hunger* (1983) characterize their vampires as specifically homosexual or bisexual. These films have perhaps done much to cement into place the current social construction of homosexuals as unnatural, predatory, plague-carrying killers, even as they also might provide a pleasurable power-wish fulfillment fantasy for some queer viewers.

The second type of homo-horror film is one written, produced, and/or directed by a gay man or lesbian, even if it does not contain visibly homosexual characters. Reading these films as gay or lesbian is predicated upon (what some might call a debased) concept of the cinematic auteur, which would argue that gay or lesbian creators of film products infuse some sort of "gay sensibility" into their films either consciously or otherwise. Yet such questions of authorship, which are certainly important and hold bearing on this particular study (for example the films of James Whale or Ed Wood), will herein be of lesser importance, since it is not necessary to be a self-identified homosexual or queer in order to produce a text which has something to say about homosexuality, heterosexuality, and the queerness that those two terms proscribe and enforce.[22] A variation on the homo-horror auteur approach is that in which a gay or lesbian film star (whether "actually" homosexual or culturally perceived as such) brings his/her persona to a horror film. Classical Hollywood cinema is full of such performers, who, regardless of their off-screen lives, bring an unmistakable homo-sexual "air" to the characters they create: Eric Blore, Franklin Pangborn, Robert Walker, George Sanders, Judith Anderson, Eve Arden, Greta Garbo, and Marlene Dietrich, to name just a few. The characters created in 1930s horror films by Charles Laughton or by Vincent Price in the 1960s and early 1970s best typify this type of homo-horror film.

The third and perhaps most important way that homosexuality enters the genre is through subtextual or connotative avenues. For the better part of cinema's history, homosexuality on screen has been more or less allusive: it lurks around the edges of texts and characters rather than announcing itself forthrightly. In films such as *White Zombie* (1932), *The Seventh Victim* (1943), or *How To Make a Monster* (1958), homosexuality becomes a subtle but undoubtedly present signifier which usually serves to characterize the villain or monster. This particular trope is not exclusive to the horror film. It has been pointed out in films *noir*, action films, and in other films wherever homosexuality is used to further delineate the depravity of the villain.[23] Alexander Doty has argued against this model of connotation, suggesting that it keeps gay and lesbian concerns marginalized: "connotation has been the representational and interpretive closet of mass culture queerness for far too long . . . [This] shadowy realm of connotation . . . allows straight culture to use queerness for pleasure and profit in mass culture without admitting to it."[24] Accordingly, in many of these films, queerness is reduced to titillation, frisson, fashion, or fad. The "love that dare not speak its name" remains a shadowy Other which conversely works to bolster the equally constructed idea of a normative heterosexuality.

But it is also precisely this type of connotation (conscious or otherwise) which allows for and fosters the multiplicity of various readings and reading positions, including what has been called active queer (or gay, or lesbian) reading practices. If we adopt Roland Barthes's model of signification wherein the denotative meaning of any signifier is simply the first of many possible meanings along a connotative chain, then we can readily acknowledge that a multitude of spectators, some queer, some not, will each understand the "denotative" events of a visual narrative in different ways. For Doty, then, there is the (fourth) sense that any film viewed by a gay or lesbian spectator might be considered queer. The queer spectator's "gay-dar," already attuned to the possible discovery of homosexuality within culture-at-large, here functions in relation to specific cultural artifacts. As such, "Queer readings aren't 'alternative' readings, wishful or willful misreadings, or 'reading too much into things' readings. They result from the recognition and articulation of the complex range of queerness that has been in popular culture texts and their audiences all along."[25] In the case of horror films and monster movies, this "complex range of queerness" circulates through and around the figure of the monster, and in his/her relation to normality.

These approaches to finding homosexuals in and around the text are hardly mutually exclusive—in fact, these factors usually work in some combination to produce a text which might easily be understood as being "about" homosexuality. James Whale's *The Old Dark House* (1932), directed by and starring homosexual men, would be one such film that combines these approaches: while it might be possible for some spectators to miss the homosexual undercurrents which fuel the plot (since no character is forthrightly identified as overtly homosexual), for other spectators these themes readily leap off the screen. Conversely, other films which have no openly homosexual input or context might still be understood as queer by virtue of the ways in which they situate and represent their monster(s) in relation to heterosexuality. Ultimately, then, this project rests upon the variable and intersubjective responses between media texts and their spectators, in this case spectators whose individualized social subjectivities have already prepared and enabled them to acknowledge "the complex range of queerness" that exists in the English-language monster movie.

A short history of the homosexual and the monster

In many ways, the development of the gothic form and the social understanding of homosexuality have followed concurrent and often commingling paths. Before the codification of the classical Hollywood horror film, and before the late nineteenth-century "invention" of the homosexual as a distinct type of person, it is apparent that Western and non-Western cultures alike had some sort of terminology for and/or knowledge of both the monstrous and same-sex love. In many cultures, such as that of ancient Greece, the two clusters of meaning had little in common; monsters were often terrible beasts encountered on perilous journeys, and (male) homosexual acts were an accepted element of the structuring patriarchy (although overtly sexualized monsters such as the incubus and succubus do date from these eras).[26] Out of necessity and prudence, this work focuses on the distinctly Western, modern/ist, nineteenth- and twentieth-century constructions of the monster and the homosexual, and their considerable overlap. The histories of these concepts are complex, but the origins of Western literary horror are usually traced to the mordant verses of the mid-eighteenth-century Graveyard Poets or the appearance of the "first" gothic novel, *The*

Castle of Otranto, in 1764. In that era, the term "homosexuality" was as yet unknown; if and when same-sex desire was acknowledged as a possible form of human sexuality, it was usually understood as a preference for a specific range of sexual behaviors and not as an entire identity. In many cultural artifacts of the time (including the early gothic novels), contra-straight sexual behavior was often linked to members of the crumbling aristocratic class who had the means to indulge in whatever forms of pleasure they could imagine. Most significantly, when "homosexuality" (which appeared in the scientific lexicon in 1869) reached common English parlance in the 1880s and 1890s, Victorian England was in the middle of a gothic renaissance whose legacy can still be felt in today's horror films.[27]

Still, even before this momentous cultural event, the confluence of contra-straight sexuality with the development of the gothic, both in terms of its production and its thematic concerns, is striking. As Eve Kosofsky Sedgwick has noted, "the Gothic was the first novelistic form in England to have close, relatively visible links to male homosexuality . . ."[28] She points to the fact that many of the writers of the first wave of gothic novels (William Beckford, Matthew "Monk" Lewis, Horace Walpole) might be understood to have been homosexual by today's understanding of the word. A "case can be made about each that he was in some significant sense homosexual—Beckford notoriously, Lewis probably, Walpole iffily."[29] Horace Walpole, author of *The Castle of Otranto*, was certainly eccentric, if not forthrightly homosexual: his personal life exhibited tendencies that we might now view as indicative of a gay camp sensibility. One biographer describes the bachelor dandy as a "gentle, sickly, effeminate boy" who grew into a "whimsical man [who] found it difficult to avoid flights of fancy," such as spending most of his adult life constructing a mock medieval castle, a gothic fantasy world, at his home, Strawberry Hill.[30] Whether or not Walpole was homosexual by today's understanding of the term remains unknowable; however, by virtue of his apparent gender-bending and his focus on the performative aspects of role-playing, he might more readily be called queer, a term more historically distant but perhaps more descriptively accurate.

Many of the gothic works of this first wave (which were more or less satirized in Jane Austen's *Northanger Abbey*, written in 1797–98 but not published until 1818) focused on a young heroine and an older, sexualized male threat. Yet many also contained more obviously queer menaces, albeit in ways displaced through the gothic signifiers of death, decay, and the double. William Beckford, who had been "hounded out of England in 1785 over charges involving a younger man,"[31] published *Vathek* in 1796, and this work can easily be read as an allegory about homosexual proclivity.[32] M. G. Lewis's *The Monk* (also published in 1796) found the form becoming increasingly explicit, and it garishly featured religiously repressed sexual hysteria and a transsexual demon. A few years later at the Villa Diodati, two of history's most enduring monsters entered the literary canon when a rather queer congress decided to write some ghost stories. The sexual eccentricities of John Polidori ("The Vampyre" [1819]), Lord Byron, Percy Bysshe Shelley and Mary Wollstonecraft Shelley (*Frankenstein* [1818]) are well documented, and many read Polidori's sexually predatory Vampyre Lord Ruthven as a thinly disguised portrait of the bisexual libertine Lord Byron. *Frankenstein* itself has become something of a counter-hegemonic classic; feminists and queers alike have plumbed its depths to underscore a scathing critique of male hubris in which the attempt to create life without the aid of procreative sexual union results in disaster for all. Though rarely filmed in any manner approaching the novel's complexity of metaphysical argument, this core idea—that of a mad, male, homosexual science giving birth to a monster—can be found to a greater or lesser degree in almost every filmic adaptation.

After several relatively dormant decades, gothic writing flourished again during the latter half of the nineteenth century. Also at this time, homosexual "underworlds" began to be acknowledged in many European cities, and early sexologists such as Richard von Krafft-Ebing and Karl Heinrich Ulrichs began to argue that same-sex relations should be understood in terms medical rather than criminal. Ulrichs wrote essays on the natural etiology of same-sex feelings, arguing in 1862 that "Urnings" (his word for a passive, effeminate, male homosexual) were a biologically determined "Third Sex." Like the mad scientist of the Hollywood horror film, Ulrichs was interested in the effects of blood transfusion, and wondered in print whether or not exchanges of bodily fluids might make an Urning into a "normal" man, and vice versa.[33] Ulrichs also perhaps unwittingly contributed to the monster–homosexual equation in 1869 when he wrote "Incubus: Urning-love and blood lust" in response to a particularly violent rape and murder of a five-year-old boy.[34] While Ulrichs's aim was to explore and differentiate Urning love from murderous pederasty, the Zastrow case of 1869 (as it became known) and Ulrichs's discussion of it only helped to link same-sex relations with concepts of the monster both ages old (the Greek Incubus) as well as more modern (the sexual psychopath). For years after the trial, the common parlance of the day used the term "Zastrow" (the name of the accused murderer) in place of "Urning."[35] Also less well known is that toward the end of his career Ulrichs wrote an explicitly homosexual vampire story entitled "Manor," which was published in 1885: true to what would become narrative convention, the story ends with its male lovers embracing, but only in death.

Like "Manor," the works of the late nineteenth century's gothic renaissance were even more explicit than their predecessors regarding the conflation of the monstrous with some form of queer sexuality. J. Sheridan Le Fanu wrote his lesbian vampire tale "Carmilla" in 1872, and Robert Louis Stevenson published *The Strange Case of Dr. Jekyll and Mr. Hyde* in 1887. This latter tale has recently received an excellent queer exegesis from Elaine Showalter, who uses unpublished manuscripts to argue that Jekyll's repressed Mr. Hyde was meant to be read as homosexual.[36] Bram Stoker's *Dracula* (1897), which arguably created the most enduring of monsters, features an elegant and seductive count who preys not only upon the bodies of men and women, but also on the very *being* of his victims, transforming them into creatures as sexually monstrous as himself. This might be understood as mirroring the culture's invention of the homosexual: the vampire's victims not only indulge in vampiric sex, but now become a new and distinct type of individual/monster themselves.[37]

Around this same time, the association of homosexual behavior with elitism, death, and decay existed dramatically in an entire movement of poets and painters who became known as "The Decadents." Centering their work on abnormal loves, necrophilia, and the ever-present image of the woman's corpse, the school was simultaneously morbid and queer. As cultural historians have noted, the term "Decadence" itself became "a fin-de-siècle euphemism for homosexuality."[38] The (mostly) male Decadents celebrated themselves as pale, thin, delicate, aestheticized, and emotional creatures, turning upon one popular "scientific" construction of homosexuality at that time: that of gender inversion, "anima muliebris in corpore virili inclusa," a woman's soul trapped in a man's body. The Decadent monster queer is also invariably sad, like the tragic gothic and romantic heroes from whom he descends. This sad young slightly effeminate man can be found throughout the twentieth-century history of homosexuality and is a staple of horror films as well. In the 1950s this character was especially susceptible to the seductions of older, forthrightly "evil" men, and in the 1970s and 1980s he was often figured as an ostracized high-school student and loner.

This image of the pathetic and slightly sinister homosexual dandy was perhaps cemented into place through the life and work of Oscar Wilde. Wilde was linked to the Decadents through social connections as well as through *The Yellow Book*, a literary magazine which was featured heavily in his 1895 trial for sodomy and itself became synonymous with homosexual scandal. But it is Wilde's 1891 book *The Picture of Dorian Gray* that contains the quintessential imagery of the monster queer—that of a sexually active and attractive young man who possesses some terrible secret which must perforce be locked away in a hidden closet. The common gothic trope of the "unspeakable" was now (partially, incompletely) derepressed; it had become, in the words of Wilde's young lover Lord Alfred Douglas, "the love that dare not speak its name."

Monsters, and especially the imagery of the vampire, continued to be linked with homosexuality during the early years of the twentieth century. *Der Eigene*, a German male homosexual magazine published between 1896 and 1931, "contained much vampire imagery in its fiction and at least one complete vampire story."[39] And Lillian Faderman has demonstrated how vampiric imagery crept into a slew of novels at this time in order to pathologize or "monsterize" women's "romantic friendships."[40] In the 1910s, when narrative cinema began to explore the monstrous, the gothic literature of the nineteenth century was pressed into service. Edison filmed *Frankenstein* in 1910, and D. W. Griffith adapted Edgar Allan Poe's "The Tell-Tale Heart" as *The Avenging Conscience* in 1914. However, by far the most filmed horror story of the period was Oscar Wilde's *The Picture of Dorian Gray*. According to horror film historian Gregory William Mank, there were at least seven adaptations of the novel during the 1910s: "a 1910 Danish version; a 1913 US adaptation; a Russian film in 1915, as well as another American version; a British 1916 film, starring Henry Victor, with an appearance by 'the devil'; and, in 1917, versions from both Germany and Hungary (the latter possibly featuring Bela Lugosi)."[41] Whether or not these films (most of them are now lost) focused more on the novel's tropes of pictorial transformation or its thematic queerness, it is nonetheless clear that they did help to construct a very definite image of the monstrous male homosexual. For example, the poster for the 1917 German version of *The Picture of Dorian Gray* shows a figure consistent with that era's understanding of the male homosexual. Dorian Gray stands next to a vase filled with heart-shaped leaves; the figure himself wears a stylish tuxedo, patent leather slippers, bracelets and makeup, has rounded hips, arms akimbo with one on the pedestal and one on a hip, crossed legs, cocked head, flowered lapel, and a slightly bored, bemused expression on his face.[42]

It was the Germans who would ultimately create the distinctive "look" of the horror film by wedding its queer characters and occurrences to a visual style drawn from modernist painting, one that eventually became known as a cinematic style in its own right, German Expressionism.[43] The nightmarish subjectivity explored in the twisted and distorted *mise-en-scène* of these films proved to be a key visual analog to the literature of horror and monsters, as well as to the hidden recesses of the human psyche and sexuality. Many of the German "Schauerfilme" of the era explored gothic themes such as the homosexual creation of life (*The Golem* (filmed in 1914 and 1920)), while others focused on homoerotic doubles and madness (*The Student of Prague* (1913), *The Picture of Dorian Gray* (1917), and perhaps most famously *The Cabinet of Dr. Caligari* (1919)). One of the leading filmic Expressionists of this era, F. W. Murnau, was homosexual; he made film versions of both *The Strange Case of Dr. Jekyll and Mr. Hyde* and *Dracula*, released in Germany as *Der Januskopf* (1920) and *Nosferatu* (1922).[44] German Expressionism and modern art in general was and still is frequently linked with homosexuality, not only through the historical sexuality of many of its practitioners, but also through its subject-matter, and its opposition to "normality" as constructed through realist styles of representation. Nazi Germany made these links most clear in 1937 when it invited its citizens to denounce and mock modernist art at a Berlin exhibit snidely entitled "Degenerate Art." The aim of the exhibit was to demonstrate how Aryan culture had been polluted by primitivism and the modernist style practiced (of course) by Jews, homosexuals, and other social deviants. By that time, however, many of Germany's artists had died or fled the continent. Filmmakers such as Karl Freund and Paul Leni (among many others) brought the German Expressionist style to America and specifically to the horror films of Hollywood's classical period. Once there, it helped to create some of the defining examples of cinematic horror, upon whose foundations almost all of Hollywood's later monster movies have been built.

In citing these historical "facts" I do not mean merely to suggest a rather coarse or knee-jerk auteurism (queer works are produced by queer authors), but rather to point out the confluence of contra-straight sexuality within the development of the gothic/horror genre. [. . .]

Notes

1 Many of these essays have been reworked and published in Robin Wood, *Hollywood: From Vietnam to Reagan* (New York: Columbia University Press, 1986) 79.

2 Tzvetan Todorov, *The Fantastic: A Structural Approach to a Literary Genre*, trans. Richard Howard (Ithaca, NY: Cornell University Press, 1973) especially 25–40; Sigmund Freud, "The Uncanny," in *The Standard Edition of the Complete Psychological Works of Sigmund Freud*, Vol. XVII, trans. James Strachey (London: The Hogarth Press, 1955) 219–252.

This trope of the genre has been theorized by a great many people in a variety of ways. For example, Noel Carroll has focused on rot, ooze, slime, and blood as generic motifs which suggest transition and transgression, concluding that "What horrifies is that which lies outside cultural categories"—in short, the queer. Noel Carroll, *The Philosophy of Horror, or Paradoxes of the Heart* (New York: Routledge, 1990) 35.

3 Louise Sloan, "Beyond Dialogue," *San Francisco Bay Guardian Literary Supplement* (March 1991), quoted in Lisa Duggan, "Making it Perfectly Queer," *Socialist Review* (April 1992) 19.

4 Sue Ellen Case, "Tracking the Vampire," *differences* 3:2 (Summer 1991) 3.

5 Case 3.

6 Margaret Tarratt, "Monsters from the Id," *Films and Filming* 17:3 (December 1970) 38–42 and 17:4 (January 1971) 40–42. Reprinted in Barry Keith Grant, ed., *Film Genre Reader* (Austin: University of Texas Press, 1986) 258–277.

7 For a brief narrative history of *Films and Filming*, see Anthony Slide, ed., *International Film, Radio, and Television Journals* (Westport, CT: Greenwood Press, 1985) 163–164. Slide notes the magazine's "definite homosexual slant" and also the mild controversy it caused in 1971 when some readers began to object. See also "Letters," *Films and Filming* (July 1971) 4.

8 See "Responsibilities of a Gay Film Critic," *Film Comment* 14:1 (January–February 1978), Reprinted in Bill Nichols, ed., *Movies and Methods, Volume Two* (Los Angeles: University of California Press, 1985) 649–660. One might wonder as to the degree his thinking about and writing on the horror film was related to this process.

9 Herbert Marcuse, Eros and Civilization: A Philosophical Inquiry into Freud (Boston, MA: Beacon Press, 1955), Gad Horowitz, Repression: Basic and Surplus Repression in Psychoanalytic Theory: Freud, Reich, and Marcuse (Buffalo: University of Toronto Press, 1977).

10 Simon Watney, Policing Desire: Pornography, AIDS and the Media, 2nd edn. (Minneapolis: University of Minnesota Press, 1987) 26.

11 Wood 79.

12 Michel Foucault, The History of Sexuality, trans. Robert Hurley (New York: Vintage Books, 1978) 12.

13 Foucault 27.

14 Foucault 114. Compare these thoughts with those of Herbert Marcuse in "Chapter Three: The Conquest of the Unhappy Consciousness: Repressive Desublimation," in One-Dimensional Man: Studies in the Ideology of Advanced Industrial Society (Boston, MA: Beacon Press, 1964) 56–83.

15 Foucault 100.

16 For an overview of the theoretical arguments which developed within and from the Birmingham Centre for Contemporary Cultural Studies, see Graeme Turner, British Cultural Studies: An Introduction (Boston, MA: Unwin Hyman, 1990). Many of the most important original essays are collected in Michael Gurevitch, Tony Bennett, James Curran, and Janet Woolacott, eds, Culture, Society and the Media (New York: Methuen, 1982) and Stuart Hall, Dorothy Hobson, Andrew Lowe, and Paul Willis, eds, Culture, Media, Language (London: Hutchinson, 1980).

17 Linda Williams, "When the Woman Looks," in Re-Vision: Essays in Feminist Film Criticism, eds Mary Ann Doane, Patricia Mellencamp, and Linda Williams (Los Angeles: University Publications of America, Inc., 1984) 83–99.

18 For an exploration of some of these issues, see Nick Browne, "The Spectator-in-the-Text: The Rhetoric of Stagecoach," in Movies and Methods, Vol. 2, ed. Bill Nichols (Los Angeles: University of California Press, 1985) 458–75.

19 Richard Dyer, "The Role of Stereotypes," in The Matter of Images: Essays on Representation (New York: Routledge, 1993) 11–18.

20 For a discussion of the Bakhtinian Carnival and how it relates to film (and briefly Halloween), see Robert Stam, "Chapter Three: Film, Literature, and the Carnivalesque," Subversive Pleasures: Bakhtin, Cultural Criticism, and Film (Baltimore: The Johns Hopkins University Press, 1989) 85–121. Although he doesn't specifically talk about horror films, several of the ten criteria he isolates for the cinematic expression of the Carnivalesque are highly relevant to the genre.

21 For an interesting account of how gay and lesbian actors get marginalized both within Hollywood narrative systems and industrial practice, see Patricia White, "Supporting Character: The Queer Career of Agnes Moorehead," in Out in Culture: Gay, Lesbian, and Queer Essays on Popular Culture, eds Corey K. Creekmur and Alexander Doty (Durham, NC and London: Duke University Press, 1995) 91–114.

22 For a fuller discussion of these issues, see Doty in this volume.

23 See Dyer, "Homosexuality and Film Noir," in The Matter of Images: Essays on Representations (New York: Routledge, 1993) 52–72.

24 Alexander Doty, Making Things Perfectly Queer: Interpreting Mass Culture (Minneapolis: University of Minnesota Press, 1993) xi–xii.

25 Doty 16.

26 For a historical overview of these figures, see Nicolas Kiessling, *The Incubus in English Literature: Provenance and Progeny* (Seattle: Washington State University Press, 1977).

27 Elaine Showalter, *Sexual Anarchy: Gender and Culture at the Fin de Siècle* (New York: Penguin Books, 1990) 171.

28 Eve Kosofsky Sedgwick, *Between Men: English Literature and Male Homosocial Desire* (New York: Columbia University Press, 1985) 91.

29 Sedgwick 92.

30 E. F. Bleiler, "Horace Walpole and *The Castle of Otranto*," *Three Gothic Novels: The Castle of Otranto, Vathek, & The Vampyre*, ed. E. F. Bleiler (New York: Dover Publications, Inc., 1966) vii, x.

31 Sedgwick 92.

32 A fuller queer exegesis of *Vathek* was recently offered by Jason Tougaw in his paper "Owning Our Own Devils: Jeffrey Dahmer, *Vathek* and Gay Male Subjectivities," presented at Queer Frontiers: The Fifth Annual National Lesbian, Gay and Bisexual Graduate Student Conference, Los Angeles, 1995.

33 See Hubert Kennedy, *Ulrichs: The Life and Works of Karl Heinrich Ulrichs: Pioneer of the Modern Gay Movement* (Boston, MA: Alyson Publications, Inc., 1988) 77.

34 Kennedy 136–144.

35 Kennedy 138.

36 Showalter 105–126.

37 For a fuller account of the novel's homoerotic aspects, see Christopher Craft, "'Kiss Me with Those Red Lips': Gender and Inversion in Bram Stoker's *Dracula*," *Representations* 8 (Fall 1984) 107–133.

38 Showalter 171.

39 Reported in Richard Dyer, "Children of the Night: Vampirism as Homosexuality, Homosexuality as Vampirism," *Sweet Dreams: Sexuality, Gender and Popular Fiction*, ed. Susanna Ranstone (London: Lawrence and Wishart, 1988) 48.

40 Lillian Faderman, *Surpassing the Love of Men* (New York: Marrow, 1981).

41 Gregory William Mank, *Hollywood Cauldron* (Jefferson, NC: Mcfarland and Co., Inc., 1994) 298.

42 Reproduced in Phil Hardy, ed., *The Overlook Film Encyclopedia: Horror* (Woodstock: The Overlook Press, 1986) 20. For a discussion of "arms akimbo" in relation to queer politics, both historically and today, see Thomas A. King, "Performing 'Akimbo': Queer Pride and Epistemological Prejudice," in *The Politics and Poetics of Camp*, ed. Moe Meyer (New York: Routledge, 1994) 23–50.

43 See Lotte H. Eisner, *The Haunted Screen* (Los Angeles: University of California Press, 1969).

44 See Lotte H. Eisner, *Murnau* (Los Angeles: University of California Press, 1973).

Queer Negotiations of the Hollywood Musical

6

BRETT FARMER

[. . .]

The gay male celebration of the Hollywood musical is one of the most widely noted aspects of gay spectatorial relations. As Al LaValley matter-of-factly puts it: "At the heart of gaycult, the aesthetically stylized genre of the musical reigns supreme."[1] The affinity between gay men and the musical is so intense as to have produced at times marked metaphoric associations. In gay subcultural argot, the term *musical* has long been used as a coded reference to homosexuality; to describe someone as "musical" or "into musicals" is to describe them as homosexual. "It is surely no coincidence," writes Phillip Brett, "that among the many code words and phrases for a homosexual man before Stonewall (and even since), 'musical' . . . ranked with others such as 'friend of Dorothy' [a reference to the 1939 MGM musical, *The Wizard of Oz*] as safe insider euphemisms."[2] In a more personal vein, Wayne Koestenbaum describes how as a child in the sixties and seventies his first incipient gay identifications were made not through a conscious recognition of same-sex erotic attractions but via his fondness for musical comedy: "I worried, listening to records of *Darling Lili*, *Oklahoma!*, *The Music Man*, *Company* and *No, No, Nanette*, that I would end up gay: I didn't know the word 'gay' . . . but I had a clear impression (picked up from where?) that gays liked musical comedy."[3]

Even today, long after the demise of the musical as a central form of popular culture, the symbolic associations between musicals and male homosexuality seem to have lost little of their signifying resonances for gay subcultures. A glance through almost any of the scores of English-language gay magazines will attest to this. For example, a recent copy of *Outrage*, an Australian gay lifestyle "glossy," features two articles on musical-related themes, an essay on "show queens" and an interview with a local musical comedy star, Judi Connelli, as well as laudatory reviews of two new musical recordings. As John Thurfitt writes in one article, "in a culture which sometimes seems dominated by dance floor divas like Kylie and Madonna, it is interesting that musical theater has lost none of its hold over gay men, and musical icons like Merman, Minnelli [and] Streisand . . . are perennial."[4]

It would, of course, be naive to assume that all gay men take the same pleasures in musicals or that these pleasures have somehow remained constant and unchanged over time. The historical marginalization of the musical—especially, perhaps, the Hollywood musical—has meant that it has become an increasingly rarefied taste, even within gay male subcultures. Younger gay or queer men tend not to respond to the musical with the same degree of devotion and personal attachment that often characterizes the receptions of this genre among (some) older gay men. The latter's receptions of the musical have invariably shifted in time, waxing and waning as the musical has moved from mass cultural form to nostalgic object. Even in its heyday during the midcentury, enthusiasms for the musical would not have been universal among gay men, being largely associated with—though, by no means, limited to—those white, middle-class men who composed the most affluent and, therefore, most visible constituency in urban gay subcultures. Nevertheless, the musical has exercised and continues to exercise considerable fascination for gay men with the result that, more than any other cinematic genre, it has developed as a singularly privileged site of and for gay subcultural investments. So much so that, even those gay-identifying men who claim no particular interest in or taste for the musical remain fundamentally subject to its gay associations. As D. A. Miller notes in his recent meditation on the cultural relations between gay men and the Broadway musical, "though not all gay men—nor even most—are in love with Broadway, those who aren't are hardly quit of the stereotype that insists they are, which appropriates their musical taste nonetheless by imposing on it the burden of *having to take a position vis-à-vis* the mythos of male homosexuality for which . . . an extreme devotion to the musical theater is a chief token."[5]

Yet what is it about the musical that has made it such a resonant form for gay male discourses and identifications? One of the most common explanations for the enduring affinity between gay audiences and the musical is the genre's widely recognized status as "escapist entertainment." As Richard Dyer writes, musicals are generally seen to offer "the image of 'something better' to escape into, or something we want deeply that our day-to-day lives don't provide. Alternatives, hopes, wishes—these are the stuff of utopia, the sense that things could be better, that something other than what is can be imagined and maybe realized."[6] For many commentators this is the precise source of gay fascination with the musical. LaValley, for example, asserts categorically that gay men have been drawn to the musical because of its "utopian level of wish fulfillment, charged with bold colors, elegant style, dance, costume, and song." He extends this reading to gay spectatorship in general, arguing that "movies have always held a particular attraction" for gays because "here they found hints of a utopian and alternate world, one more congenial to their sexuality and repressed emotions."[7] More recently, Peter Kemp has argued that the reason the musical has proven "such a compelling source of endless appeal for gay men" is the genre's construction of "a stylised non-naturalism, a formal out-of-this-world-ness that would particularly attract the culturally unconventional, the socially unacceptable." [. . .][8]

These attempts to represent and make sense of gay male fascinations with the Hollywood musical in terms of escapism are widespread, and in many ways the argument they advance is both persuasive and appealing. What I find particularly captivating about these readings is the way they define cinematic spectatorship as a privileged space of fantasmatic expression for gay-identifying subjects. These accounts explicitly suggest that gay men use their spectatorships of the Hollywood musical to articulate and shape their innermost fantasies and desires. As such, they provide a solid entry point for the type of fantasy-based inquiry into gay spectatorships that I am promoting. However, these accounts of gay fascinations with the musical in terms of escapism also present potential difficulties or limitations for a critical analysis.

For a start, these characterizations sound similar to pathologizing descriptions of homosexuality as a flight from reality that circulate with such enduring force in mainstream culture. One cannot help but wonder how much of the widespread popularity and resonance of these characterizations of gay spectatorship as pure escapism stems from how the trope of escapism already figures centrally in dominant constructions of male homosexuality. "The popular view of homosexuality," notes Michael Bronski, "is that it is a flight . . ., variously from women, from masculinity, from the 'responsibilities' of heterosexuality (i.e., wife, children, and a house in the suburbs), from male competition, or from the 'self.'"[9] This discursive tradition provides ample scope for the devaluation of gay spectatorial escapism, whether in relation to Hollywood film, in general, or the musical, in particular. Although most of the writers cited above are careful to avoid this type of reading, other critics have been less cautious and have explicitly interpreted gay subcultural obsessions with so-called escapist forms of entertainment like the musical as an indication of what they see as the vacuousness of much gay culture.[10]

Furthermore, though a reading of gay fascinations with the musical in terms of escapism or utopianism goes some of the way toward explaining the broad-based appeal this genre can hold for marginalized or disempowered groups such as gay men, it does not really tell us very much about the particularity of gay pleasures in the musical. What exactly is it within the musical that has spoken and continues to speak so powerfully to gay spectators? Nor do these accounts allow for a recognition and adequate appreciation of the dynamic, active nature of gay engagements with the Hollywood musical. In fact, these accounts tend to portray gay receptions of the musical as a largely abstract, passive affair. They imply that gay spectators simply and effortlessly escape into a fantasy world that is waiting tailor-made for them in the musical film. This reading ignores the rather obvious fact that, like most forms of mainstream cinema, the Hollywood musical is produced in, by, and for a culture that insists on the definitional primacy of heterosexuality and that, as a result, the utopian idylls it presents are almost universally heterosexual. One need only look at the enshrinement of heterosexuality in the titles of many Hollywood musicals like *Twenty Million Sweethearts* (1934), *For Me and My Gal* (1942), *Royal Wedding* (1951), *The Farmer Takes a Wife* (1953), and *Seven Brides for Seven Brothers* (1954) to gauge the extent to which the musical as genre is predicated on an assumption of heterosexuality as celebratory ideal.

Some scholars have suggested that the musical may in fact be the most heterosexist of all Hollywood film forms. Patricia Mellencamp argues that the musical plays out and celebrates "the ritual of re-creation/procreation of the privileged heterosexual couple"; Steve Neale asserts that, in the musical, "heterosexual desire occupies a central . . . place . . ., its presence is a necessity, not a variable option."[11] The most influential version of this argument is presented by Rick Altman in his detailed 1987 study, *The American Film Musical*, in which he defines heterosexuality as the veritable *sine qua non* of the musical's entire structural organization. Altman argues that, unlike most classical films, which focus largely on the diegetic trajectory of a single character, the Hollywood musical follows a dual-focus structure of gendered parallelism in which a carefully balanced sequence of textual repetition and rhyme plays a masculine paradigm off a feminine one. This is generally represented by a leading male/female character couple—as Altman puts it, "in the musical *the couple is the plot*."[12] This basic sexual duality is overlaid by secondary competing oppositions, with each sex linked to "a particular attitude, value, desire, location, age or other characteristic attribute . . . [that] always begin diametrically opposed and mutually exclusive" but that end up reconciled in the grand utopian finale of hymeneal union. For Altman, the Hollywood musical serves an important ideological function by "fashion[ing] a myth out of the American courtship ritual" and naturalizing heterosexuality as compulsory norm. As he puts it: "The American film musical seems to suggest that the natural state of the adult human being is in the arms of an adult human being of the opposite sex" (24–32).

Such analyses highlight the inadequacy of simply reading off gay spectatorial passions for the musical as a direct effect of the utopian scenarios offered by the musical text, for they demonstrate the extent to which these scenarios assume and promote a heterocentrist economy of meaning/desire. If gay-identifying spectators do in fact use the Hollywood musical as a site to articulate their own utopian or escapist fantasies, then clearly they must engage in active and quite extensive processes of resistance and negotiation. This is not to say that gay spectators are somehow excluded from or incapable of making pleasurable psychocultural investments in a given fantasmatic scenario simply because it is coded as heterosexual. The gay male spectator's homosexuality does not endow him with an intrinsic aversion to or immunity against the appeals of a heterosexual fantasy; relations of desire and identification are never that clear-cut. Furthermore, as critics like Judith Mayne and Rhona Berenstein have argued, part of the appeal and fascination of cinema may actually lie in the very opportunities it provides for assuming sexual identifications different from those ordinarily assumed by the spectator in "real" life.[13] It could be entirely possible, therefore, that a pleasurable invest-ment in and identification with heterosexuality is an integral component of gay receptions of the musical. Nevertheless, given the musical film's dominant tendencies toward supreme heterosexual idealization, there is a point at which one must acknowledge a fundamental misfit or incongruence between the (dominant) desires promoted by the musical text and the desires of the gay-identified spectator; and that, as a result, if the gay spectator is to appropriate the musical film for the construction and exploration of gay-identified fantasies and meanings, then this will require at least some form of textual disruption and refiguration.

For such processes of textual negotiation to work, they would need to open up a space within the musical film for alternative formations of (gay) fantasy and desire. In light of the arguments presented by theorists like Altman about the importance of textual closure in determining the musical film's dominant heteronormative agenda, the most effective strategy for any proposed practice of queer negotiation would be to refuse and under-mine the musical's push toward closure. If the musical is structured to build up to a final, all-embracing moment of heterosexual union as utopian ideal, then a disruption of its linear trajectory toward closure would, perforce, also disrupt its textual path to heterosexual utopianization.

Several critics have suggested that such a resistance to clotural containment may in fact form a standard strategy of gay engagements with mainstream film in general. In her ethnographic-based study of lesbian receptions of *Personal Best*, Elizabeth Ellsworth argues that lesbian spectators consistently rejected that film's attempts at repressing the pos-sibilities of lesbian desire opened up by the narrative within a safe, heterosexual ending.[14] She contends that they did this by focusing on the lesbian character at the close of the film rather than on the heterosexual couple, even though the film clearly defines the lesbian character as marginal and less important. At a more general level, Al LaValley claims that gay spectators habitually reject mainstream cinematic attempts to contain meaning within a heteronormative closure by disordering the dominant linear trajectory of filmic narrative in such a way as to give determinative supremacy not to the final moment of closure as is customary but to other textual features often repressed or marginalized by the recuperative processes of closure.[15]

[. . .]

The issue here is not a reading practice that simply ignores the last ten minutes or so of a film. What the particular practice of gay spectatorial reading suggested here entails, rather, is an active reordering of the text that is both a refusal and a redefinition of the preferred meanings of a film's given clotural scenario. By making certain marginal textual features the organizational pivot of narrative meaning construction, this style of negotiational reading practice produces a radically restructured semiotic economy in which the "earlier" textual features thus privileged come to inflect a text's clotural scenario in such a way as to undermine its dominant significatory agenda and open it up to alternative interpretations. In the case of the musical, this may mean that, by latching on to certain moments or features that are marginal or oblique *vis-à-vis* the demands and concerns of the dominant (straight) narrative and making them central to the organization of their own textual engagements, gay spectators can redefine the clotural scenario of idealized heterosexual union promoted by the musical and refashion it to support the articulation of gay-identified fantasies and desires.

These gay negotiational reading practices are similar to those forms of critical reading "against the grain" proposed by certain film theorists as a way to expose and subvert a film's dominant ideological paradigm. Both forms of reading strategically locate and extend points of disruption in the text, points at which the control of the dominant narrative seems to falter and other potential meanings emerge. Within film theory, these points of textual fracture have largely been theorized in terms of a disruptive "excess"—marks of a signifying surplus that exceed the needs or demands of the dominant filmic narrative.[16] The concept of cinematic excess is based on the proposition that the film-text is the site of a complex semiotic heterogeneity that can never be totally reduced to or exhausted by a film's dominant narra- tive structures, and this heterogeneity is evident whenever the smooth functioning of the dominant representational conventions breaks down and permits a momentary outburst of diegetically unaccommodated signification. These moments of excess appear as a devi- ation from or a going beyond the motivations of dominant narrative demands either at the level of narrative content, such as certain scenes, shots, characters, or actions that have no apparent narrative function and bear little if any relation to dominant diegetic foci, or at the level of textual form, such as unconventional camera work, obtrusive editing styles, extravagant *mise-en-scène*, and the like. The concept of excess, then, allows one to gain greater analytical purchase on some of the specific strategies involved in gay negotiational readings of the musical text. If the moment of textual excess is understood as a symptomatic point of failure, a gap or rip in the fabric of dominant textual homogeneity, then it seems to recommend itself as a fertile point of reference for gay spectatorial resistances to and reconstructions of the heteronormative dynamics of mainstream film.

The musical as excessive text

The Hollywood musical has in fact long been theorized as a privileged genre of excess. Stephen Heath, one of the leading theorists of filmic excess, argues that "the musical is an obvious and extreme example [of excess] with its systematic 'freedom' of space . . . and its shifting balances of narrative and spectacle."[17] As this might suggest, many arguments about cinematic excess and the musical film focus on what is perhaps the genre's defining feature— the deployment of both realist and nonrealist textual modes in its characteristic combination of spoken narrative and musical number—as the primary structure enabling this disruptive excess. With its characteristic "breaks" from linear narrative flow into spectacular song-and-dance sequences, the musical constructs a multileveled system of textual enunciation unique in mainstream film. The admixture of markedly different textual modes employed by the musical is something normally associated with avant-garde and experimental film forms. As a result of this unusual discursive pluralism, the Hollywood musical provides unprecedented scope for the articulation of some of the more heterogeneous dimensions of filmic signification. Jane Feuer, for example, argues that the narrative/number split produces a singular system of "multiple diegesis," a plurality of narrative forms. "The narrative with its third-person mode seems to represent a primary level. . . . But unlike other kinds of movies, a secondary level, presented in direct address and made up of singing and dancing, emerges from the primary level . . . [and] disturbs the equilibrium of the unitary flow of the narrative." Feuer points to the example of backstage musicals directed or, at least, partially directed by Busby Berkeley for Warner Brothers during the 1930s—42nd Street (1933), Gold Diggers of 1933, Footlight Parade (1933)—in which the musical numbers signal a radically different mode from that of the conventional narrative: "a separate universe, a world of cinematic excess and voyeuristic pleasure . . . an absolutely unfettered play of the imagination."[18]

Significantly, these moments of cinematic excess in the musical are frequently understood to signal an anarchic disruption of not only the dominant structures of classical narrative film form but the structures of textual and spectatorial desire as well. In this argument, the subversion of linear narrative form produced by the musical's "break" into song-and-dance occasions a correlative subversion of the text's dominant libidinal forms, a metaphoric slippage into the unconscious that produces a disruptive effusion of ordinarily censored erotic material. Just as the camera in the musical number breaks out of the confines of classical film form into the implausible perspectives and frenetic mobility of crab dollies, crane shots, split-screen montage, and the like, desire—textual and spectatorial—undergoes a similar transformation and is released into a range of libidinal formations. Musical spectacles, argues Patricia Mellencamp, "are momentarily subversive fantasy breaks in the . . . narrative superstructure. These breaks displace the temporal advance of the narrative, providing immediate, regular doses of gratification rather than delaying the pressures until The End. . . . Through this play, the psychical energies of the spectator are granted freer movement and the signifiers are less repressed."[19]

Another way to look at this, one that helps relate this discussion more explicitly to questions of gay specificity, is to think of the libidinal "excessiveness" of the musical number in terms of its representation of non- or even anti-oedipal formations of desire. Indeed, if, as many critics contend, the linear trajectory of narrative represents a structural replaying of heterocentric, oedipal development, then the musical's insistent breaks or deviations, from narrative progression into nonlinear spectacle, seem to all but beg this type of reading.[20] Within such a schema, the move from a teleological structure of narrative into a spatial structure of spectacle signaled by the musical's breaks into song-and-dance numbers becomes readable as a correlative move from a linear, oedipal economy of straight desire into a de-oedipalized framework of perverse desire. This is something suggested by Dana Polan when he writes that the moment of spectacle in the musical number "brings male and female together, but this moment is a moment outside the forward propulsion of time, *outside the impulse of a domestic desire that drives oedipal narrative along.*"[21]

[. . .]

Thus, one could argue that much of the extraordinary force of gay spectatorial receptions and popularizations of the Hollywood musical turns on a structure of engagement invested in what might be called *fantasies of perverse, de-oedipalized desire* or, to put it in another, slightly more user-friendly way, *fantasies of queerness*. By the latter, I mean the full sense of the term queerness as it has been defined in recent critical theory as a shifting space of antinormative difference that resonates profoundly with homosexualities but is not necessarily synonymous with them. Alexander Doty defines queerness as "a wide range of positions within culture that are non-, anti-, or contra-straight . . . a flexible space for the expression of all aspects of non- (anti-, contra-)straight cultural production and reception."[22] Queerness, thus defined, has strong associations with notions of homosexuality as de- or anti-oedipal in that both refer to positional structures of antinormativity. Indeed, in certain respects, queerness may be read as a reproduction of Freudian arguments about perverse desire and unconscious sexuality under a different name.[23] Reading gay receptions of the musical in terms of a broad fantasmatic structure of de-oedipalized desire, or queerness, has the advantage of high-lighting the resonant fascination of the musical for gay spectators/gay readings while stressing the psychic complexities of that fascination. For what the musical number in its excess provides—and what, I would contend, is seized on by gay spectators in their engagements with the musical—is not simply representational formations of homosexual desire (though these do abound in the musical number and they provide important sites of fantasmatic engagement for gay spectators) but formations moreover of queer desire—desire let loose into positions that are aberrant, perverse, or just plain "nonstraight."

The musical number has long been recognized as providing "a covert method of conceiving normally undiscussed aspects of intersexual relationships."[24] Linda Williams correlates the Hollywood musical number to the sexual "number" in the pornographic film wherein, for example, she compares the musical's "solo song or dance of self-love or enjoyment" to masturbation, the trio to a sexual *ménage à trois*, "the choral love songs celebrating the sexual union of a whole community" to orgies, and so on.[25] Taken out of context in this way, such an analogy can seem contrived, but it nevertheless highlights how the excessive dimensions of the musical number can be seen to represent a "queer" libidinal hetero-geneity—something that far exceeds the parameters of the domestic, oedipalized heterosexuality promoted by the narrative.

As suggested, the musical number frequently offers images and sequences that can be read as homosexual or, at the very least, homoerotic. Alexander Doty suggests that part of the appeal of musicals for gay men may be rooted in what he terms their "hidden cultural history of gay erotics."[26] He cites the homoerotic triangles of the "male trio" musicals such as *Take Me Out to the Ball Game* (1949) and *On the Town* (1949), as well as the representation of the male body as erotic spectacle in numbers such as "Is There Anyone Here for Love" in *Gentlemen Prefer Blondes* (1953) and "Y.M.C.A." in *Can't Stop the Music* (1980). To this list could be added the exuberant, sexual duets of male stars such as Gene Kelly and Frank Sinatra in *Anchors Aweigh* (1945); the narcissistic displays of male solo dances such as the "I Like Myself" number by Gene Kelly in *It's Always Fair Weather* (1955); the athletic cowboy dancing routines in *Seven Brides for Seven Brothers* (1954), *Oklahoma!* (1955), and *The Best Little Whorehouse in Texas* (1982); the all-male, balletic gang dances in *West Side Story* (1961); and the orgasmic gyrations of Elvis Presley and his band of male prisoners in the "Jailhouse Rock" sequence from the 1957 film of the same name, or John Travolta and his fellow gang members in the "Greased Lightning" number in *Grease* (1978). These numbers all provide instances of a spectacular eroticization, if not homoeroticization, of the male image that is quite unusual in mainstream cinema. Several critics have claimed that the musical may in fact be "the only genre in which the male body has been unashamedly put on [erotic] display in mainstream cinema in any consistent way."[27] Significantly, these critics contend that this insistent eroticization of the male body in the musical destabilizes traditional gender structures. Both Steve Neale and Steven Cohan, for example, claim that the musical's eroticization of the male image serves to "feminize" that image because it places it in the conventionally "feminine" role of sexual object.[28] [. . .] This "feminization" of the male image in the musical provides strong potentials for empathic identification on the part of gay-identifying spectators, as well as for the projection of gay fantasies of gender disorganization. Male homosexuality has developed strong, even constitutive associations with discourses of femininity in our culture; consequently, many gay spectators would be highly responsive to the musical's aberrant constructions of a spectacular, feminized masculinity and the potentials this extends for gay fantasmatic indulgence.[29] At the very least, the feminization of the male image in the musical film attests to the dynamics of antiheteronormative queerness that I am suggesting run through the excessive space of the musical number.

Further evidence for my claim that the musical number is frequently the site of a liminal breakdown of oedipalized desire and heterosexual normativity resides in the musical's extensive representation of various forms of gender or sexual subversion. The most obvious example here is the widespread use of cross-dressing in the musical number, such as Mickey Rooney's Carmen Miranda routine in *Babes on Broadway* (1941), or Garland and Astaire dressed as tramps for the "Couple of Swells" number in *Easter Parade* (1948), or the "Thanksgiving Follies" routine in *South Pacific* (1958). Other examples are the seemingly ubiquitous musical figure of the androgynous female performer in male tuxedo and tie such as Eleanor Powell in *Broadway Melody of 1936* (1935) and *Lady Be Good* (1941), Garland in *Summer Stock* (1950) and *A Star Is Born* (1954), and Vera-Ellen in *Three Little Words* (1950); the brash butchness of the eponymous female characters in *Annie Get Your Gun* (1950) and *Calamity Jane* (1953), or, conversely, the effeminacy of male characters like the Cowardly Lion in *The Wizard of Oz* (1939) and the long line of sissy boys played by Edward Everett Horton in musicals of the thirties and forties. More recent examples are the explicit celebrations of transvestism in such modern musicals as *Cabaret* (1972), *The Rocky Horror Picture Show* (1975), *Victor/Victoria* (1982), and *The Adventures of Priscilla, Queen of the Desert* (1994). These spectacular moments of gender transgression all point to a profound current of sexual subversion at play in the musical number. With their images of gender and sexual "otherness," they present what Annette Kuhn describes as "a vision of fluidity of gender options," "a utopian prospect of release from the ties of sexual difference that bind us into meaning, discourse, culture."[30] It should not be surprising, therefore, that many of these examples of gender transgression in the Hollywood musical have become privileged images of and for gay subcultural iconographies.

In a rather different vein, the musical number has frequently represented and explored not only sexual differences but racial differences. Altman argues that "from its very beginnings in the *Jazz Singer* (1927), the musical has been associated with black faces."[31] The most obvious example here is the presence of certain iconic African American actors and performers in the Hollywood musical such as Bill Robinson, Ethel Waters, Lena Horne, Louis Armstrong, Pearl Bailey, and Sammy Davis Jr. Significantly, one of the first films featuring an entirely African American cast to find widespread success at the U.S. box office was a musical, *Hallelujah* (1929).

This was followed by several all-black film musicals including such notable successes as *Cabin in the Sky* (1943), *Stormy Weather* (1943), *Carmen Jones* (1954), *Porgy and Bess* (1959), and *The Wiz* (1978). Other examples in this context include the representation of Asians or, at least, "Asianness" in such musical films as *The King and I* (1956) and *Flower Drum Song* (1961), or in numbers such as "Anything Goes" in the 1936 film of the same name and the "Limehouse Blues" routine in both *Ziegfeld Follies* (1946) and *Star!* (1968); the use of Middle Eastern locales and cultures in such films as *The Desert Song* (1953) and *Kismet* (1955); the celebration of Polynesian "exoticism" in the long line of South Seas musicals from *Waikiki Wedding* (1937) to *Pagan Love Song* (1950) to *Blue Hawaii* (1962); or the popularization of Latino motifs, locales, and actors (Carmen Miranda, Don Ameche, Fernando Lamas, Ricardo Montalban) in the range of South American musicals made during the forties such as *Down Argentine Way* (1940), *That Night in Rio* (1941), and *Week-end in Havana* (1941). Although many of these representations are undoubtedly racist—using ethnic difference in a patronizing and objectifying manner, as, quite literally, "added color" and, often, in accordance with the ideological fantasies of Western orientalism—they suggest that the exploration of *queerness* or, to use a slightly more appropriate term in this particular context, *otherness* in the musical number is not limited to sexual differences alone. And just as the formations of sexual queerness in the musical number exceed and disrupt narrative straightness, so, perhaps, this wide-ranging imagery of racial difference may also exceed and disrupt textual discourses of hegemonic "whiteness" in certain ways.

It has in fact been suggested that the musical as a genre turns on a foundational structure of racial mimicry that works in competing ways to both shore up and problematize the stability of hegemonic ideologies and identities. In her critical reading of *Singin' in the Rain*, Carol J. Clover argues that this film—and by extension the entire history of the Hollywood musical that the film knowingly references and represents—depends on an "uncredited" appropriation of African American cultural forms, most notably dance forms, which are subsequently attributed to and possessed by white performers. "The film musical," she writes, "drew heavily and variously on black art and talent. Only in the 'Negro musical' was that talent front and center. The more common pattern was to put it off to the side . . . or behind the scenes . . . or out of 'creditable' range altogether."[32] This act of negated cultural appropriation clearly supports relations of white dominance and black marginality as Clover details, but it potentially problematizes those relations as well. Not only does the most vehement negation of the musical's "black roots" fail to exorcize completely the disavowed "specter" of racial difference that, as the examples cited above suggest, remains to "haunt" and energize the genre in diverse and often spectacular ways, but the very act of racial/cultural appropriation that critics like Clover argue underpins its basic generic structures imbues the musical with an inescapable logic of identificatory masquerade that cuts against the grain of its normalizing operations. Although I in no way want to undercut the full acknowledgment of cross-racial appropriation and mimicry as violent strategies of racist oppression, the dynamics of boundary crossing that inevitably attend the transvestic operations of these practices make them potential agents of what Marjorie Garber terms "category crisis." By this she means "a failure of definitional distinction, a borderline that becomes permeable, that permits of border crossings from one (apparently distinct) category to another: black/white, Jew/Christian, noble/bourgeois, master/servant, . . . male/female."[33] Garber is careful to point out that cross-racial imitation can be mobilized for various political purposes and "signifies differently in different cases and contexts," but she asserts that, as with any instance of categorical transvestism, it contains a powerful potential "to disrupt, expose, and challenge, putting in question the very notion of 'the original' and of stable identity" (303, 16).

It is difficult to define the precise role these dynamics of racial otherness and exchange may play in gay readings of the musical, but Garber's emphasis on the interrelations between otherwise distinct forms of "category crisis"—"category crises can and do mark displacements from the axis of class as well as from race onto the axis of gender [and sexuality]"—suggests a possible homology or isomorphism between the musical's formations of sexual queerness and racial "otherness" that would be broadly appealing and responsive to gay investments (17).[34] The widespread celebration in gay male cultures of African American and Latina musical stars such as Carmen Miranda, Dolores del Rio, Lena Horne, Pearl Bailey, and Rita Moreno, to say nothing of more recent traditions of black disco/pop diva worship, suggests that many gay spectators strongly identify with figures and images of racial/ethnic difference. The resonances of these images of racial otherness would, of course, be further heightened —certainly, more overdetermined—in the case of gay men of color. It is also important not to overidealize the relations of white gay men to these images; such relations can never be entirely free from the discourses of racism and white privilege that frame the production, circulation, and evaluation of racial differences in white contexts. Nevertheless, the dynamics of alterity, marginality, and binaristic disruption that shape the representation and experiences of gayness and blackness alike provide, if not a metaphoric equivalence, then at least a potential affinity between gay spectators and the musical's formations of racial difference.[35]

The fantasmatic lure of the "excessive" musical number for gay audiences appears in other, more abstract ways as well. Recent work in musicology suggests that music itself may, in certain contexts, signify a space of "perverse" or queer desire. Much of this work takes up psychoanalytic arguments about the potential in music to reactivate and/or replicate pre-oedipal modalities and memories. The post-Lacanian analyst Guy Rosolato has argued famously that part of the pre-oedipal bond between mother and child is played out at an aural level. He argues that the mother's voice acts as a "sonorous envelope" surrounding the infant in a soothing and highly pleasurable blanket of sound and that it provides the subject with its "first model of auditory pleasure." Music, he suggests, "finds its roots and its nostalgia in [this] original atmosphere, which might be called a sonorous womb, a murmuring house, or music of the spheres."[36] In a similar vein, Julia Kristeva suggests that the rhythmic flow of music and some poetry has the potential to evoke memories of the maternal voice from the pre-oedipal phase or, what she terms, the "semiotic." She contends that the nonrepresentational properties of these forms replicate the prelinguistic sounds of mother–infant communication and that they, therefore, signal potential points of libidinal disruption, points where the pre-oedipal or semiotic erupts through the dominant discourse of symbolic signification.[37] Theories such as these have prompted some critics to suggest that music may signal a transgressive realm of feminine *jouissance*—in which maternal incantation triumphs over paternal logocentrism. This is why, it is suggested, music is largely coded and marginalized as "feminine" in patriarchal cultures. "Nonverbal even when linked to words, physically arousing in its function as initiator of dance, and resisting attempts to endow it with, or discern in it, precise meanings," writes Phillip Brett, music "represents that part of our culture which is constructed as feminine and therefore dangerous."[38] Although purely theoretical, these arguments provide interesting material for a further analysis of the queer potentials of the excessive musical number.

[. . .]

Notes

1 Al LaValley, "The Great Escape," *American Film* 10.6 (1985): 31.

2 Phillip Brett, "Musicality, Essentialism, and the Closet," in *Queering the Pitch: The New Gay and Lesbian Musicology*, ed. Phillip Brett et al. (New York: Routledge, 1994), 11. See also Wayne R. Dynes, *Homoplexis: A Historical and Cultural Lexicon of Homosexuality* (New York: Gay Academic Union, 1985).

3 Wayne Koestenbaum, *The Queen's Throat: Opera, Homosexuality, and the Mystery of Desire* (New York: Poseidon, 1993), 11.

4 John Thurfitt, "Show Queens," *Outrage* 156 (May 1996): 34.

5 D. A. Miller, *Place for Us: Essay on the Broadway Musical* (Cambridge: Harvard University Press, 1998), 16.

6 Richard Dyer, *Only Entertainment* (London: Routledge, 1992), 18.

7 LaValley, "Great Escape," 29–32.

8 Peter Kemp, "Secret Love (or Gays and Musicals: An Attractive Connection)," in *The Bent Lens: A World Guide to Gay and Lesbian Film*, ed. C. Jackson and P. Tapp (Melbourne: the Australian Catalogue Co., 1997), 18.

9 Michael Bronski, *Culture Clash: The Making of Gay Sensibility* (Boston: South End Press, 1984), 92.

10 Take, for example, a recent article by Larry Galbraith wherein he attacks what he loosely terms *camp culture*, that "eclectic . . . instantly recognisable gay culture which can include off-Broadway shows, Hollywood movies (often the older the better), Broadway block-busters and supper club cabaret." Such a culture is, he suggests, moribund in its "total reliance on nostalgia" and apolitical in its promotion of escapism. He writes: "In a world where gay men can be themselves and live their lives, openly and proudly, there is little need to live their lives through Judy Garland, Hollywood movies or Broadway musicals" ("The Slow Demise of Camp Culture," *Outrage* 146 [1995]: 64).

11 Patricia Mellencamp, "Spectacle and Spectator: Looking through the American Musical Comedy," in *Explorations in Film Theory: Selected Essays from Cine-Tracts*, ed. Ron Burnett (Bloomington: Indiana University Press, 1991), 5; Steve Neale, *Genre* (London: British Film Institute, 1980), 23.

12 Rick Altman, *The American Film Musical* (Bloomington: Indiana University Press, 1989), 35.

13 Judith Mayne, *Cinema and Spectatorship* (London: Routledge, 1993); and Rhona J. Berenstein, *Attack of the Leading Ladies: Gender, Sexuality, and Spectatorship in Classic Horror Cinema* (New York: Columbia University Press, 1996).

14 Elizabeth Ellsworth, "Illicit Pleasures: Feminist Spectators and *Personal Best*," *Wide Angle* 8.2 (1986): 45–56.

15 LaValley, "Great Escape," 29.

16 See Kristin Thompson, "The Concept of Cinematic Excess," in *Narrative, Apparatus, Ideology: A Film Theory Reader*, ed. Phil Rosen (Princeton: Princeton University Press, 1986).

17 Stephen Heath, *Questions of Cinema* (London: Macmillan, 1981), 52.

18 Jane Feuer, *The Hollywood Musical* (1982; rpt., Bloomington: Indiana University Press, 1993), 68–69.

19 Mellencamp, "Spectacle and Spectator," 11.

20 See, for example, Teresa de Lauretis, *Alice Doesn't: Feminism, Semiotics, Cinema* (Bloomington: Indiana University Press, 1984).

21 Dana Polan, *Power and Paranoia: History, Narrative, and the American Cinema, 1940–1950* (New York: Columbia University Press, 1986), 302, emphasis added.

22 Alexander Doty, *Making Things Perfectly Queer: Interpreting Mass Culture* (Minneapolis: University of Minnesota Press, 1993), 3.

23 See, for example, Tim Dean's two essays on queer theory and psychoanalysis: "On the Eve of a Queer Future," *Raritan* 15.1 (1995): 116–34; and "Sex and Syncope," *Raritan* 15.3 (1996): 64–86. See also Christopher Lane, "Psychoanalysis and Sexual Identity," in *Lesbian and Gay Studies: A Critical Introduction*, ed. A. Medhurst and S. R. Munt (London: Cassell, 1997).

24 Altman, *American Film Musical*, 85.

25 Linda Williams, *Hard Core: Power, Pleasure, and the "Frenzy of the Visible"* (Berkeley: University of California Press, 1989), 133.

26 Doty, *Making Things Perfectly Queer*, 10–11.

27 Steve Neale, "Masculinity as Spectacle," *Screen* 24.6 (1983): 14–15.

28 Steven Cohan, "'Feminizing' the Song-and-Dance Man: Fred Astaire and the Spectacle of Masculinity in the Hollywood Musical," in *Screening the Male: Exploring Masculinities in Hollywood Cinema*, ed. Steven Cohan and Ina Rae Hark (New York: Routledge, 1993).

29 As Les Solomon notes when explaining his own fascination with the musical, "there were a lot of gay overtones in the old MGM musicals of the '50s. It was often quite unbelievable to see these supposedly straight men leaping about the place doing some very effeminate things in some cases" (cited in Phillipe Cahill, "Heavenly Knowledge," *Campaign* 227 [1995]: 66).

30 Annette Kuhn, *The Power of the Image: Essays on Representation and Sexuality* (London: Routledge, 1985), 50.

31 Altman, *American Film Musical*, 290.

32 Carol J. Clover, "Dancin' in the Rain," *Critical Inquiry* 21 (summer 1995): 738–39. For a broader reading of the history of white cinematic appropriations of African American cultural forms, and one to which Clover's own analysis is indebted, see Michael Rogin, *Blackface, White Noise: Jewish Immigrants in the Hollywood Melting Pot* (Berkeley: University of California Press, 1996).

33 Marjorie Garber, *Vested Interests: Cross-Dressing and Cultural Anxiety* (Harmondsworth: Penguin, 1992), 16.

34 Adrienne L. McLean provides an interesting reading of possible queer investments in the musical's formations of racial otherness in her recent article on the "orientalist" choreography of Jack Cole. Cole was a gay choreographer who worked on a string of Hollywood musicals in the forties and fifties such as *Moon over Miami* (1941), *Kismet* (1955), and *Gentlemen Prefer Blondes* (1953). Heavily influenced by the "oriental dance" tradition of the twenties and thirties, Cole incorporated Middle Eastern and Asian motifs and movements in his choreography. Although recognizing the problematical "orientalism" undergirding Cole's work, McLean argues that Cole mobilized "his Orientalist dance practice as a Camp discourse" through which he was able to express his queer sexuality and articulate a satirical critique of "the hegemony of the great white fathers by emphasizing the physical power and spiritual authority of Arabs, Asians, and women" (Adrienne L. McLean, "The Thousand Ways There Are to Move: Camp and Oriental Dance in the Hollywood Musicals of Jack Cole," in *Visions of the East: Orientalism in Film*, ed. Matthew Bernstein and Gaylyn Studlar [New Brunswick: Rutgers University Press, 1997], 151).

35 On the complex relations between gay cultures, gay men (both black and white), and representations of blackness see Kobena Mercer and Isaac Julien, "Race, Sexual Politics, and Black Masculinity: A Dossier," in *Male Order: Unwrapping Masculinity*, ed. R. Chapman and J. Rutherford (London: Lawrence and Wishart, 1988); and Kobena Mercer, "Skin Head Sex Thing: Racial Difference and the Homoerotic Imaginary," in *How Do I Look? Queer Film and Video*, ed. Bad Object-Choices (Seattle: Bay Press, 1991).

36 Guy Rosolato, cited in Kaja Silverman, *The Acoustic Mirror: The Female Voice in Psychoanalysis and Cinema* (Bloomington: Indiana University Press, 1988), 84–85.

37 Julia Kristeva, *The Revolution of Poetic Language*, trans. M. Waller (New York: Columbia University Press, 1984).

38 Brett, "Musicality, Essentialism, and the Closet," 12. See also Susan McClary, *Feminine Endings: Music, Gender, and Sexuality* (Minneapolis: University of Minnesota Press, 1991); and Renee Cox, "Recovering Jouissance: An Introduction to Feminist Musical Aesthetics," in *Women and Music: A History*, ed. Karen Pendle (Bloomington: Indiana University Press, 1991).

Queer Noir

7

RICHARD DYER

What are you doing in a neighbourhood like this?

Johnny to Ballin in *Gilda*

They'll be looking for us in every closet.

Fante to Mingo in *The Big Combo*

It is widely known that male homosexuals[1] figure significantly in film noir.[2] By no means all noir films have queers in them, yet many of the most celebrated do or may (*The Big Sleep*, *Gilda*, *Laura*, *The Maltese Falcon*, *Strangers on a Train*) and they stand out in a period (the 1940s and early 1950s) when there was little other such representation. However, when one looks at the films again, it's not always so clear why we think there are queers in them: in noir, some of the most obvious queens are married, some straight guy friendships could just be that while other nominations are hard to swallow. I've had students at each other's throats over whether the relationship of Johnny and Ballin in *Gilda* is really homosexual and I have myself been taken aback by some proposed examples, such as Jack Marlowe in *Phantom Lady* and Walter Neff and Keyes in *Double Indemnity*. One may feel strongly that so-and-so is a queer and he may well be, but it is seldom certain.

In this chapter I want to suggest that such uncertainty is not just the perennial difficulty of reading homosexuality back into past culture, but very much part of the mood, the noirness, of these films. One can explain the uncertainty in part by reference to censorship (one is not going to find explicit physical contact or verbal declaration in the period), but it is also of a piece with noir's general uncertainty about how to decipher the world.

Uncertainty is built into noir's central narrative organization. These are films about finding out. In most cases, what is to be found out is eventually found out, but in the process a world profoundly deceptive and disorienting is revealed: you can't rely on how things look or what people say (not even the innocent); the process of unraveling the mystery is confusing, full of deceptions, detours, blind alleys; the telling involves complicated, sometimes contradictory flashbacks, voice-overs, and dream sequences; the geography of the films can confuse, with rambling residences, mirrors that double the world or turn out to be windows, even literal mazes; and noir's famed chiaroscuro and skewed angles unsettle perception.

As a result, you cannot be sure that the co-ordinates of the film's implicit social world are securely in place. The classic detective story assumes that if you just sort out the crime at hand, that is, this particular disruption of the social order, then the pieces of that order will fall back into place; it assumes that the underlying fabric of society and the means for comprehending it are sound. This is not the case with noir. Here crime and respectability are bedfellows, Anglo-Saxon supremacy is being nudged out by Latin and other (though not yet black) pretenders, women have added money and independence to the power of sexual allure that they always had, and there seem to be all these queers, marginal yet insidiously present.

I begin exploring the latter—all these queers—with the question of reading, of why certain characters might be thought to be queers. I look in detail at two contentious examples (*Kiss of Death* and *The Big Sleep*) before considering other examples even less clear than these. I then look at three aspects of queer noir uncertainty—stereotypes, noir queers' devotion to women, male–male relationships—before situating these representations in relation to noir more generally, considering what it was about noir that facilitated the re-emergence of queers in Hollywood cinema and the role of queers in noir: villainy, uncertainty, unmasculinity.

In *Kiss of Death* (1947), Nick Bianco (Victor Mature), a convict on parole, is persuaded by the police to pick up an acquaintance with psychotic hoodlum Tommy Udo (Richard Widmark) in order to get evidence against him and those he works for. Nick bumps into Tommy accidentally on purpose at a boxing match; they go drinking together at a flash nightclub and Tommy sends his girlfriend away so he can be with Nick alone. There is then a cut from the noisy nightclub to a high-angled shot looking down on a quite spacious, rather old-fashioned, drab and utterly silent entrance hall; a man goes to the door and lets in Tommy and Nick; they walk across the hall into the back, Nick asking, 'What's that smell?' and Tommy replying, 'Perfume'; end of shot.

There is no doubt that this last shot is entirely understandable in terms of heterosexuality: two guys out on the town go to a brothel together. The strangeness of the treatment (the silence, the dowdy *mise-en-scène*, the high-angle shot and single take) can be plausibly accounted for in terms of censorship (you could not make it too clear it was a brothel) or possibly class (it might be an up-market brothel, quiet, unflashy). Yet it is also very easy, inspired by that odd opacity of treatment (what *is* going on here?), to make the case for this as a queer moment.

Tommy, like many noir queers, dresses at once smoothly and showily (very neatly slicked back hair, off-white coat and tie against black shirt and jacket). At the boxing match (with its male flesh display), reaction shots show Tommy slavering as one guy lays into another in the ring. He gets rid of the girl, who could be a fig leaf or beard, a trophy to mask his queerness, and throughout the film he calls Nick 'big man'. Finally, when he says 'Perfume', he evokes something with which, as I shall discuss, queers are often associated in noir film. In short, Tommy takes Nick to a male brothel (even less representable than a female one, which in fact could be somewhat more clearly suggested in the period). This might explain why, in a cut straight from the brothel to the police station, Nick's first line is that it was an evening he 'wouldn't want to go through again': surely, by the conventions of the day, hanging out with a dreary guy who hero-worships you, having a few drinks and going to a (female) brothel is not such a ghastly way of spending an evening for a normal guy—but if the hero-worship is lustful and the brothel queer, not far off a fate worse than death.

None of this is decisive. Bad guys often dress well in noir, straight guys get worked up at boxing matches, getting rid of a clinging female is par for the course for a laddish night on the town, perfume is what women wear (and strong perfume characterizes brothels) and Nick is established as a highly moral character who loathes Tommy and wants family life above all else. But it is precisely the undecidability of the example, the fact that it might be queer, that makes it also so noir.

If *Kiss of Death* is overall relatively straightforward, *The Big Sleep* (1946) is a by-word for uncertainty, some would say incomprehensibility. The basic enigmas are solved: at the start of the film General Sternwood asks private eye Philip Marlowe directly to find out what his younger daughter, Carmen, is up to and, indirectly, what has become of his valet, Sean Regan; by the end we know that Carmen was being blackmailed because she got herself mixed up in pornography and drugs and that Sean Regan has been killed by the very same Carmen, because he didn't return her love. If some of this and a lot of incidental material is elusive, it is partly because much information is delivered fast and only once, people lie or are misinformed and some elements (e.g. pornography) are cryptically signaled. It is also because we are encouraged to put quite a lot of our narrative curiosity into the wrong question about a character who never appears: from the beginning of the film we ought to be asking 'Who killed Sean Regan?' but instead the characters ask on our behalf where he has gotten to; moreover he himself never appears (of course, being dead—but we don't know that till the end). The question 'Where is he?' displaces 'Who killed him?', and there is also a third question that is never quite clearly asked or answered and yet which drives much of the narrative: 'Who was he?'

We know that he worked for General Sternwood and that Marlowe remembers him from his time on the force, but everything else remains enigmatic. Marlowe says to General Sternwood that he'd heard that Sean had been taken on 'as your . . . whatever he was', thus sort of asking the question, but quite what he was remains unclear: employee, friend, son, lover? The first three are explicitly named as possibilities by General Sternwood while other formulations could suggest the fourth, the lover (General Sternwood: 'He left me', 'I was only his employer but I had hoped he'd come to regard me as something more than that'; Mrs Rutledge, General Sternwood's older daughter: 'It broke dad's heart, his going off like that'). It is also obvious to Mrs Rutledge that Sean nor Carmen is the real object of her father's concern in calling on Marlowe's services (she assumes it in her first conversation with Marlowe after he's seen the General and she's even surprised that Carmen has been mentioned at all) and the same thing is obvious to the District Attorney, a Mr Wilde, who feels that Marlowe should carry on looking for Sean to reassure the General that his 'whatever he was' was not mixed up in the pornography and drugs racket that Marlowe has just uncovered.

General Sternwood is himself portrayed as a man who married late (after a no doubt stimulating life among men) but now is not only confined to a wheelchair but has developed a morbid sensitivity. He is thus, in common with other rich queers in noir (and beyond), at once sexless and exquisitely sensitive, metaphorically a hot-house plant but also actually living out his days in a conservatory hot enough to grow orchids. The last detail is interesting. Though orchids are rare and precious, signs of extravagant love during heterosexual court-ship, they are also suspect, over-elaborate blooms with a sickly sweet smell, the product of unnatural cultivation. All of this, especially the scent, is consonant with the representation of queers as decadent.[3] General Sternwood refers to the orchids' scent and how much he loathes it—yet he chooses to live in the midst of it (he could after all have the orchids removed). What conundrum of wallowing in sickliness is at play here?

As with Tommy Udo and the brothel in *Kiss of Death*, none of this is certain, but it's uncertain either way, it's just as plausibly queer as not. The same could be said of Sean, though here we know even less. He is said to have been having an affair with a Mrs Mars and that's why Carmen killed him; but Mrs Mars says there was no affair, they were just friends. In a film peopled with such chronic liars, who knows what is true? Mrs Mars could have good reason to deny the affair, married as she is to the wealthy and menacing Mr Mars; on the other hand, women bonding with queers is also a feature of film noir, as we shall see, in which case Carmen's fury at being rebuffed by Sean might come from his being queer (or, of course, bisexual but, either, as Marlowe notes, a good guy, not wishing to betray General Sternwood with his own daughter, or else, simply not fancying her). We simply don't know.

Tommy Udo, General Sternwood, and Sean Regan are at the very least plausibly read as queers, but other proposed instances might raise eyebrows. Mike Lagana in *The Big Heat* (1953) dresses well, with a carnation in his buttonhole; he has a portrait of his late mother over his fireplace, a good-looking manservant wakes him in the night to answer the phone wearing a dressing gown but no pyjamas, and he does not engage with his henchman in their talk about women.[4] Does all of this make him 'a homosexual type' (Naremore 1998: 222)? One might see Jack Marlowe (Franchot Tone), the killer in *Phantom Lady* (1944), as a queer (ibid.: 99): he's unmarried, a sculptor (artists are often suspect), with a superiority complex (like Waldo Lydeker in *Laura*) and a sense of paranoia (people 'hate me because I'm different'). However, he's a modernist sculptor (his work has none of the feminine fussiness of Waldo's tastes), his sense of superiority is as much Ayn Rand as wounded aesthete and, although paranoia is one of Freud's signs of homosexuality,[5] not every paranoiac—or every unmarried man—has to be read as queer. Besides, Jack's motive for killing the woman he kills, Marcella, is that she'd said she'd go away with him and then laughed at him and said she wouldn't, which doesn't really sound all that queer a motive. However, while it would never have occurred to me to think of him as a queer, it's also true that he could be: perhaps she laughed at him for his presumption (do you really think I'd run off with a queer?), and despite his oh so straight name, Jack Marlowe, there is something epicene about Franchot Tone's performance of him. Other examples seem to me even more tenuous and yet are perhaps touched by noir's endemic uncertainty. What reason has one for thinking that the heavy-featured lugubrious police detective, Ed Cornell, in *Hot Spot/I Wake Up Screaming* (1941) (McGillivray 1997: 173) is queer except the counter-intuitive one that he was obsessed with the murdered woman to the point of making a shrine of her portrait in his dowdy flat? It's true that some noir queers do similar things, but it's not this alone that suggests their queerness.[6]

There is a different kind of reading uncertainty in two films adapted from sources in which the homosexuality is explicit even if it has ostensibly been expunged from the adaptation: *The Lost Weekend* (1945), where homosexuality is not offered as one of the causes of Don Birnam's (Ray Milland) alcoholism, and *Crossfire* (1947), where the motive for murder becomes anti-Semitism not homophobia. Both were based on best-selling novels (*The Lost Weekend* 1944 and *The Brick Foxhole* 1945). As Chon Noriega (1990) points out, audiences could bring a knowledge of the source to the reading of a film, and critics sometimes drew attention to what was missing. Even without such extra-filmic possibilities, the films may still leave room for queer doubt. Vito Russo (1981: 96–97) notes some of the ways *The Lost Weekend* hints that Don Birnam's 'whispered problem might be rooted in greater psychological depths than the typewriter he keeps in his closet would indicate,' such as his becoming 'coyly and cruelly entertaining when drunk' and feyly proposing marriage to a bartender, and the knowing treatment of him by a 'lewdly homosexual' male nurse in the sanatorium for alcoholics. And what, in *Crossfire*, is this man doing befriending soldiers in bars?[7]

To these two examples we may add a third where in the source, too, there is no homosexuality and yet which, like the source, it seems almost impossible not to read as queer: *Christmas Holiday* (1944), based on (part of) Somerset Maugham's 1939 novel. Here a young woman, Abigail Martin (Deanna Durbin), falls in love with a young man, Robert Manette (Gene Kelly); he hints that he has another side he can't talk about but anyway she must meet his mother; the latter welcomes her, hoping that her love may be able to overcome 'certain traits in Robert'; in voice-over Abigail tells us that the formidable Mrs Manette believed her to be 'her last chance to . . . save Robert' (pause as in film), adding 'I've often wondered what would have happened if she'd told me all she knew of Robert that first afternoon'; after they marry, Robert takes to staying out late at night, coming back in the early morning looking pretty rough, refusing to say where's he's been. Certain unmentionable 'traits', a dominating mother, inexplicable nocturnal absences—but it turns out that Robert is a compulsive gambler which leads him into bad company and eventually murder. It is of course easy to forget that gambling was a crime and a sin, and to underestimate the havoc caused by compulsive gambling, yet the whole structure of the film seems to build towards the revelation of something more utterly unspeakable and it is perhaps only the introduction of murder that stops the revelation being bathetic.

All the films discussed above make sense if read in terms of given characters being queer but also if read straight. Uncertainty is the point. These representations appear in chronically uncertain films, but they also emerge at a moment of intensified uncertainty in representing sexuality between men. Homosexuality was at once ever more present in discourse and experience and, for that very reason, ever more unclear and contradictory. On the one hand, despite their extreme marginalization in the output of Hollywood, the idea of queers was becoming more familiar, from at least a half century of science, scandal, literary treatments, louche humour in popular entertainment, and expanding urban queenery. On the other hand World War II had facilitated a widespread encounter with homosexuality, in one's self and in others, temporarily, *faute de mieux* or decisively (Bérubé 1990), developments made concrete by official military policies and then in 1948 by the Kinsey report on male sexuality, which showed that homosexuality was a far more widespread practice than that involving a few obvious fags. All the elements—of science, making visible through scandal, the evidence of experience, political and erotic self-production—promise knowledge of homosexuality but at the same time taken together produce a confusing and contradictory knowledge: queers were that type of man, that 'everyone' knew about but mainstream media didn't mention, and yet queerness was also in all types of men, everywhere, maybe.

In noir, this uncertainty is both assuaged and produced by one of the means by which certain knowledge of homosexuality was supposedly conveyed: stereotyping. This is how the characters in noir most readily recognized as queers are so identified. The males are fastidiously and just a little over-elaborately dressed, coiffed, manicured, and perfumed, their speech is over-refined and their wit bitchy, and they love art, antiques, jewelry, and cuisine: Joel Cairo (*The Maltese Falcon* 1941), Waldo Lydeker (*Laura* 1944), Lindsay Marriott (*Farewell My Lovely* 1945),[8] Hardy Cathcart (*The Dark Corner* 1946), Ballin Mundsen (*Gilda* 1946), Captain

Munsey (*Brute Force* 1947), 'Grandy' Grandison (*The Unsuspected* 1947), Brandon and Philip (*Rope* 1948) and Bruno (*Strangers on a Train* 1951), together with, as already discussed, Tommy Udo, General Sternwood, Mike Lagana, and Jack Marlowe; females[9] are large, big boned, or fat, have cropped or tightly drawn-back hair, wear shapeless or else highly tailored clothes and generally work for a living: Rose (*Cry of the City* 1948) and Martha (*In a Lonely Place* 1950), both masseuses, housekeeper Mrs Danvers (*Rebecca* 1940), cosmetics tycoon Mrs Redi (*The Seventh Victim* 1943), a Chicano leather girl in *Touch of Evil* (1958) and, softer versions of the type, rich girl Amy (*Young Man with a Horn*) and sanatorium director Miss Holloway (*The Uninvited* 1944); later examples include brothel keepers Jo (*A Walk on the Wild Side* 1962) and Frances Amthor (*Farewell My Lovely* 1976).

Both male and female queer stereotypes assume that homosexuals are a particular kind of person. They also draw upon the notions of homosexuality as gender in-betweenism, inversion, and androgyny, notions found not only in homophobic (religious, psychiatric, sociological) discourses but in subcultural practices, sympathetic sexology, and such homosexual rights activism as there was. In this understanding, queer has something to do with not being properly masculine or feminine. That 'properly' is grounded in hetero-sexuality, but it is held together with the assumption that if a person does not have the sexual responses appropriate to his or her sex (to wit, heterosexual ones), then he or she will not have fully the other attributes of his or her sex. This is how signs of effeminacy and mannishness, that have nothing directly to do with sexual preference but with gender, nonetheless come to indicate homosexuality. Moreover, they are a visible indicator of homo-sexuality, something which, short of showing acts, can't otherwise be seen.

The queers in the penultimate paragraph are all constructed through such gender stereotypification and it would not require immense sophistication to spot them. Yet few are as obvious as the earliest, Joel Cairo (signaled by the look given Sam Spade by his secretary Effie when she announces him), and many could be missed. In other words, for all the use of stereotyping, even these representations are not as assuaging of uncertainty as all that; indeed, to some degree, it is actually because of the use of stereotypes, and the peculiarity of homosexual typification, that they end up producing uncertainty.

All stereotyping has the function of fixing our perception of, in the words of the term's coiner, 'the great blooming, buzzing confusion of reality' (Lippman 1956: 96) into recognizable categories in order to gain a measure of control over it. However, queer stereotyping has a particularly odd logic. Stereotypes of, say, blacks or the disabled tell us that people who look like that are like this in character; stereotypes of queers seem to work in the same way (men and women who dress like that are like this), but they are founded on the opposite need, to say people who are like that (queer), even though you can't see that, look like this. Queer stereotypes are posited on the assumption that there is a grounding, an essential being which is queer, but since this is not immediately available to perception, they have to work all the harder to demonstrate that queers can be perceived. In other words, the problem with queers is you can't tell who is and who isn't—except that, maybe, if you know the tell-tale signs, you can. However, given that the whole thing is founded on a far from universally accepted or understood assumption (there are such things as queers), that it is telling us you can tell in the context of fearing you can't and that it does so by referencing gender misfit rather than sexual practice, given all this, it's not surprising that these stereotypes generate uncertainty even as they attempt to produce certainty—which is why one can have such, according to view, enjoyable or fruitless discussions about whether so-

and-so is or isn't a queer. It may also be why they are so relatively widespread in noir, since they suit so well its general sense of uncertainty.

If it was not universally agreed that queers were a type of person, this might be for reasons of morality (homosexuality is a widespread temptation everyone should fight against or, in some bohemian discourse, give a go), experience (notably that made possible through single-sex schooling, prisons, the armed services, and the temporary 'widowhood' caused by overseas military engagement), or even sexological stumbling over such cognitively dissonant categories as lesbian femmes, regular guy homos, effeminate straight men and the many gradations of bisexuality. All of these in turn produce that other construal of the uncertainty of homosexuality, namely that it may be fluid, potential or temporary. This too is glimpsed in film noir, in two forms. One—that some queer males are married or otherwise devoted to women—generally winds up reinforcing the stereotype discussed above. The other, and rarer—that straight-looking guys may be doing it with each other—doesn't.

Hardy Cathcart (*The Dark Corner*) and Ballin Mundsen (*Gilda*) are married, General Sternwood (*The Big Sleep*) is a widower, Waldo Lydeker (*Laura*) adores the eponymous heroine, Jack Marlowe (*Phantom Lady*) wants to run off with Marcella, a friend's wife, Mike Lagana (*The Big Heat*) has a daughter, Ed Cornell (*Hot Spot/I Wake Up Screaming*) has a shrine to the murdered woman in his bedroom. Of the other obvious noir queers, Lindsay Marriott (*Farewell My Lovely*) is very much a woman's best friend, as perhaps was General Sternwood's Sean Regan, while Bruno (*Strangers on a Train*) is at once devoted to and disparaging of his mother. Yet these women-loving men[10] are also, apart from Ed Cornell, all pretty queeny.

Whilst one could read many of these characters as either bisexual or effeminate straight men, they do seem really rather little driven by sexual desire in their nonetheless intense relations with women. Rather they 'adore' women, aestheticizing them and treating them as beautiful creatures. They are refined connoisseurs of women. The two portrayals by the virtually out Clifton Webb,[11] Waldo and Hardy, are definitive.

Waldo is a classically waspish, fussily dressed queen, with rococo and Orientalist tastes in the decorative arts, established in a bravura opening tracking shot through his apart-ment ('it's lavish, but I feel at home'). His by-play with detective McPherson in the opening sequence is suggestive: standing up out of the bath naked before him, or saying 'I've always liked a detective . . . with a silver shinbone' and pausing as indicated to give a slight innuendo to this appreciation of McPherson's prowess (he was shot in the leg in a raid). All very regal. Yet he also mocks McPherson throughout the film, shows only contempt for other men and is obsessed with Laura, even saying (in voice-over) that he is the only man who really knew her, while ducking McPherson's question as to whether he was in love with her. He moulded Laura into the ideal woman, elegant, gracious, cultivated, and, above all, beautiful. Much of his flashback is his account to McPherson of the process by which he effected the transformation of a rather ordinary, if pushy, young woman into the epitome of high-class glamour, a woman worthy to be seen on his arm and to sit among his antiques, so much so that she became, as he says, 'as well known as Waldo Lydecker's walking stick and his white carnation'.

Hardy in *The Dark Corner* is in many ways a re-run of Waldo, an art dealer apparently most relaxed in the company of old women (whom he patronizes) and a blond gigolo, Tony Jardine. The first scene in which he appears establishes his character in a series of bons mots at a party he is throwing: he greets one woman with 'Guten Abend, Frau Keller', then whispers to Jardine in explanation that she is the 'wife of the Austrian critic—she always looks like she's been out in the rain, feeding poultry', a queer cocktail of snobbery, misogyny, and unkindness masquerading as wit; his remark, 'I never confuse business with sentiment—unless it's extremely profitable of course,' is Wildean in its pacing, while, 'As long as I'm amusing you'll forgive me' is surely the queer's credo. Yet Hardy keeps a female portrait by Raphael in his vault, recounting to a group of visitors how he worshiped it until one day he met Mary, its living embodiment, whom he promptly married. He tells the latter that he never wants her to grow old, a sort of transferral on to her of the crypto-queer desire to fix beauty recounted in *The Picture of Dorian Gray*. Mary tells her lover Jardine that, though Hardy gives her 'everything a man can give a woman,' yet 'still it isn't enough'—a fascinatingly ambiguous pronouncement that surely strongly suggests that Hardy does not give her the one thing that it is most commonly assumed men give women within marriage: sex. For Hardy, Mary is a work of art, adored to the point of sickness, providing a grim undertow to his quip to a party guest that 'the enjoyment of art is the only remaining ecstasy that is neither illegal nor immoral'.

Both Waldo and Hardy kill their beautiful women, Laura and Mary, ostensibly because they are showing an interest in other men (hunks that one might speculate would interest Waldo and Hardy), but really because they don't want their works of art to be robbed. This syndrome—queer adoration of women—provides the template explaining the relationship of Ballin (previously so attached to Johnny) to Gilda and even yoking in Jack Marlowe and Ed Cornell.

More broadly, queers share, and sometimes bond with women over, an interest in the artier arts and feminine adornment (though there are no queenly noir hairdressers or couturiers). Lindsay Marriott's queerness, for instance, is established through his dealing in jewelry, the ring on his little finger, the softness of his large overcoat, the almost blowsy quality of his white cravat which he primps up during his conversation with Marlowe, and, especially, his perfume, the very fact of being perfumed. A gag is made out of this: the lift man tells Marlowe he has a visitor and Marlowe assumes it's his hulking client, Moose Malloy; he asks if he's sober and the lift man says yes, adding in a sardonic voice, 'he smells real nice'; when Marlowe reaches his office, he discovers Marriott, reeking of perfume. The whole thing is laid on with a trowel in the re-make, with Marlowe remarking repeatedly to Marriott on the smell, and a character later commenting that all the fatale Mrs Grayle's male friends are "like that." Perfume links Marriott (in the 1944 version) to another queer, Jules Amthor, when Marlowe takes a carnation from Amthor's corpse and sniffs it,[12] and also to Joel Cairo in *The Maltese Falcon*, whom, like Marriott, we are first introduced to via his perfume ('Gardenia,' says Effie archly, handing Sam Cairo's calling card) and, as we've seen, to Tommy Udo and General Sternwood. Perfume is not only feminine, it is insidious: it gets in everywhere, can't be seen or touched or, therefore, controlled, it's a typically female piece of indirection, of a piece with seduction, manipulation, deceit, and the other strategies of fatality.

So, while marriage and adoration generate uncertainty ('But he's a queer!') round the figure of many noir queens, in the end, through notions of sexless adoration and shared, perfumed femininity, noir queens reinforce the in-betweenist stereotype of male queers. If there is uncertainty, it is much more because of noir's general construction of the treacherous and fatale uncertainty of femininity in general than because we can't be sure (though we can't absolutely) whether Waldo, Cairo, or Lindsay really are queers.[13]

Noir also sometimes features a male couple where neither man is stereo-typically suspect, leave alone homosexually obvious. Let me start consideration of this by giving accounts of two such instances.

The narrative of *Dead Reckoning* (1947) is driven by the efforts of Rip to investigate the disappearance of his army buddy, Johnny. The first scene (before Johnny disappears) has them sharing a railway sleeping compartment, with Johnny changing his clothes in front of him; at the end of the film Rip tells Coral, the woman of the film, unequivocally that he 'loved him [Johnny] more' than her. At one point, he describes Johnny, beautifully and hauntingly, as 'tough, laughing and lonesome': why was Johnny lonesome? and what did Rip do to comfort him?

In *The Big Combo* (1955), the two henchmen of the master criminal Mr Brown are called Fante and Mingo. They share a bedroom together (twin beds, but that was common in representing straight couples too); in one scene, Fante is naked to the waist in the bed next to Mingo's; in another they both receive an unexpected visitor wearing dressing gowns.[14] Toward the end of the film, they are holed up in a disused airfield; at one point, Mingo puts his hand on Fante's arm and says, 'When we get out, let's never come back'; Fante looks down at Mingo's hand but does not remove it as he says how worried he is that when they get out 'the cops'll be looking for us in every closet';[15] Mingo drops his hand away, slightly caressing Fante's arm with his thumb first. Mr Brown plants a bomb in their bunker, which kills Fante straight off but leaves Mingo still just alive; when he realizes what has happened, he agrees to tell Leonard, the film's police detective hero, all he knows:

He [Mr Brown] shouldna done it. Fante was my friend. OK, I'll tell you. But not for you.

In both these films the relationship with another man is the main thing in a character's life; both involve declarations of love ('I loved him more than you', 'Fante was my friend') and scenes between the two of semi-nakedness in an intimate, bedroom space. There are however two important differences between them. First, Rip has a girlfriend Coral, as did Johnny before him. Secondly, Rip is the main character played by a star (Humphrey Bogart), whereas Fante and Mingo are minor characters played (rather well) by jobbing actors. *The Big Combo* is a B-picture that can allow itself pretty well unequivocally queer characters in minor roles, but *Dead Reckoning* must supply heterosexuality, not out of any homophobic consciousness, but because main male characters played by stars have to have a woman (it's part of their heterosexual appeal) and because a noir *femme fatale* is never going to be ignored by a hero. *Dead Reckoning* might raise questions about Rip's relationship with Johnny, opening out on to a perception of homosexuality as something that a man might in certain circumstances experience, and experience as intense and profound, without that meaning that he is a queer. And if it does, it leaves it in the past.

One of the exceptional things about the relationship of Fante and Mingo is that, although they do the dirty work for Mr Brown, they show no particular pleasure in cruelty (unlike most of the noir queers and notably Jeff in *The Glass Key* 1942[16] and Captain Munsey in *Brute Force* 1947) and Mingo's conversion to the right side of the law is entirely motivated by his love for Fante (this is what he means when he says he'll tell Leonard all, 'But not for you'). Within its limits, it's a positive image. The other striking thing is the emphasis on their sameness. Perhaps Fante is slightly older, more worldly, less demonstrative than Mingo, but there's not much in it, certainly not as much as Brandon's dominance of Philip in *Rope* or Jeff's pitiful subordination to Johnny in *Johnny Eager* (1941).[17] Fante and Mingo's similarity is underlined by their identical clothes (except for their ties): very light-colored suits where all the other hoodlums wear dark. This emphasis on sameness, and the same masculinity, is much less clear in the most notorious case of queer noir, *Gilda*'s Ballin and Johnny.

In the first scene of *Gilda*, after Ballin has intervened to rescue him from muggers in a dockland district, Johnny asks him, 'What are you doing in a neighbourhood like this?' What indeed? Maybe Ballin has some assignation to do with tungsten (which we later learn he traffics in), but Johnny's question surely raises a much greater likelihood: Ballin's been cruising and has picked Johnny up. This is only one of a number of small remarks and details that suggest the relationship between them is a queer one. Consider this dialogue, prompted by Ballin's description of his cane with a knife in its tip.

> BALLIN: It is a most faithful and obedient friend. It is silent when I wish to be silent, it talks when I wish to talk.
> JOHNNY: That's your idea of a friend?
> BALLIN: That is my idea of a friend.
> JOHNNY: You must lead a gay life.
> BALLIN: I lead the life I like to lead.

The term 'gay' was certainly well established in queer sub-cultural (and therefore certainly Hollywood) circles by the 1930s (Chauncey 1994: 16–20); Vito Russo (1981: 47) notes its use in *Bringing Up Baby* (1938), when Cary Grant, dressed in a fluffy woman's night-gown, explains that he's 'just gone gay all of a sudden'. Its use here in *Gilda* to mean homosexually queer (itself a much better known term in the period) makes sense, allowing Johnny to seem to pick up on the emphasis on sameness and identity in Ballin's evocation of friendship (man and stick/friend are as one) and to allow Ballin to assert implicitly his defiance of morals and convention. The exchange also hints at the sado-masochistic edge to the relationship: a suggestive cane,[18] 'faithful and obedient'. Johnny uses the latter terms later, when asking Ballin to take him on in his casino: 'You've no idea how faithful and obedient I can be . . . for a nice salary'. Glenn Ford as Johnny flashes his eyes and smiles suggestively here, implying some of the ambiguity of the relationship: employment, personal devotion, masochistic obedience, paid consort. Ballin then seems to underline what's at stake:

> BALLIN: This I must be sure of—that there's no woman anywhere.
> JOHNNY: There's no woman anywhere.
> BALLIN: Gambling and women do not mix.
> JOHNNY: Those are the very words I use myself.

As in *Christmas Holiday*, gambling seems to be a metaphor for homosexuality—except that in *Gilda*, gambling and women are mixed. Ballin marries Gilda and it turns out that Johnny has had a relationship with her and by the end of the film does again. In the most obvious sense, the arrival of Gilda seems to confirm that 'gambling' and women don't mix: she breaks up the Ballin–Johnny relationship, signaled by Johnny's returning the key to Ballin's house:

> BALLIN: What's this?
> JOHNNY: Tact.

Yet structurally Gilda also illuminates the Ballin–Johnny relationship. I've already suggested above that Ballin can be thought of alongside Waldo and Hardy as an adorer of beautiful women. He is much less of a queen than them, more commanding in the masculine world, considerably less witty and brilliant (George Macready is no Clifton Webb), yet he is, like them, fastidiously dressed and mockingly perverse. There is never any sign of any marital intimacy between him and Gilda, none of the touching and glances, the closeness in the frame and intense, unspeaking shot/reverse shot patterns, the musical surges and chromaticism, that construct physical 'chemistry' in Hollywood cinema of the period. Like Waldo and Hardy, he parades Gilda for all to see, a sign of his wealth and taste as much as his libido—as Parker Tyler puts it, 'he "owns" rather than "loves"' her (1972: 167).

Simultaneously, Gilda also brings out the femininity of Johnny's position, comparing it to her own. Her mocking looks and teasing remarks to him can be explained as the anger of an ex-lover but might also be because she knows about him and Ballin.

> JOHNNY: I was down and out—he put me on my feet.
> GILDA: What a coincidence.

Johnny himself recognizes the parallel in a bad-tempered exchange with Ballin after his first meeting (in the film) with Gilda. He comments to Ballin on the speed with which he has married her:

> BALLIN: You should know Johnny that when I want something . . .
> JOHNNY: . . . You buy it quick.

Ballin has bought Gilda just as earlier he bought Johnny. There may be a perverse symmetry here: Johnny was definitely paid to be an employee and was probably a lover: Gilda was definitely acquired to be a wife but may not actually be used much as a lover.

The film underscores the similarity between them as covetable items. One hardly needs to go into Rita Hayworth's screen goddess glamor in this, her most famous role, but this is complemented by a glamorization of Glenn Ford as Johnny. Where his previous appearances (mainly in Westerns and action films) used harsh lighting, close-cropped hair, and rough costuming, here he is softly lit (with his weakly sensual mouth in particular highlighted), his hair is crimped and oiled and he is attractively dressed. His desirability is intensified by the fact that he is the object of her reciprocal gaze on their first meeting (in the film). From the moment we first see her, cut in on a movement tossing her hair back and looking straight to where Johnny is standing, each shot of her looking at him is complemented by a shot of him looking at her. Each shot is of equal length; a shot over his shoulder matches a shot over hers, and so on; the sensuous play of light is identical. Her heterosexual gaze licenses a perception of his desirability that could not be given to us so unequivocally through Ballin's eyes. When a bit later she remarks, more than once, on how "pretty" he is, she mocks her own desire and his role as Ballin's kept boy.

Gilda scrambles some of the period's and noir's frameworks for understanding (homo)-sexuality in a way that I, at any rate, find psychologically convincing rather than incoherent. Ballin is a bit of a queen who nonetheless probably has sex with women and men and, in either case, has the masculine power position. Johnny has regular guy good looks, but can swing either way sexually and is in the feminine position in his relationship with Ballin. In short, both Ballin and Johnny are touched by ideas of gender dissonance (Ballin's bit of queenliness, Johnny's pretty boy status) and by notions of regular guys doing it with each other sometimes, for a time.

Noir was one of the first places in Hollywood cinema to produce images of homosexuals on a scale that makes their presence one of its defining characteristics. One may account for this partly by the fact that queers are so ineluctably tied to villainy in the films—if there was going to be a space, it was going to be a negative one. Thus noir queers are accessories to crime (*Farewell My Lovely*, Cairo in *The Maltese Falcon*), bullies (*Brute Force*), henchmen (*The Big Combo*, *The Glass Key*, *Kiss of Death*), murderers (*The Dark Corner*, *Laura*, *Phantom Lady*, *Rope*, *Strangers on a Train*, *The Unsuspected*) or masterminds (*The Big Heat*, Ballin in *Gilda*, Nick Varna in *The Glass Key*, Gutman in *The Maltese Falcon*).

However, noir had no need of queers in order to have villains. We need to look further at what it was about noir that made the complex mid-century construction of homosexuality so serviceable to it.

For the most part, noir was a feature of B-movie production in Hollywood, a stratum of production at once more impoverished and routine than high-budget, high-profile production, but also less surveiled and controlled. Hollywood invested less both economically and culturally in B-movies, which also meant that B-movie production was for the most part left alone. The result was most often dreary banality, with perfunctory scripts and lack-luster *mise-en-scène*, but B-movie production could also be a space for greater exploitation (of sexual and other sensations) and, on occasion, experimentation. Noir displays both these possibilities.

Noir is sleazy, taking pleasure in sex and violence, in perverse sexualities and decadent lifestyles. Intimations of homosexuality suited this perfectly (alongside sado-masochism, kept men and *femmes fatales*). Homosexuality was something most adults knew something about, but it was not represented in popular public media; to do so was intrinsically shocking. Mainstream Hollywood would not cater to the taste for sexual sensation, which left a space for B-movies, including noir. This was not a conscious marketing strategy; rather, in a period of massive film output, an awful lot of things could happen that no-one took much notice of— indeed, most B-movies, and therefore much noir, barely figure in contemporary public discourse at all. Nor probably was the exploitation of homosexuality aimed at a homosexual audience (though one should not assume this did not occur to anyone involved); rather homosexuality, strange and shocking, was part of a wider appeal to sexual sensation aimed at a heterosexual and, if you like, queer audience.

Noir was also experimental,[19] not just in its visual and narrational daring, but in its un-American pessimism. Central to this is the problem of knowledge—the images and stories are confusing because the world is hard to know. I have already indicated the uncertainty of both noir and the representation of homosexuality within it. At the most general level, homosexuality is simply one more trope in the performance of uncertainty. However, homosexuality is also central to the structure of narrative confusion in many of the films; nor is it any old trope of uncertainty.

Homosexuality, and the doubt over it, often contributes to the confusion of the narrative both in terms of being able to follow it and in terms of explaining what has happened. *The Big Sleep* would be much easier to follow if we knew from the start what was at stake in the investigation that General Sternwood employs Marlowe to undertake; all the fuss and anxiety in *Christmas Holiday* would be easier to make sense of if Robert were brought out of the closet. Lindsay Marriott puts Marlowe off the scent (by means of scent) in *Farewell My Lovely*, while Tommy Udo's ambiguities are one of the difficulties facing Nick in coming to terms with life after prison. The peculiarity of Waldo's and Hardy's attachment to women makes them seem sideshows to the central drama of *Laura* and *The Dark Corner* respectively, when they are in fact the heart of it. The endemic confusions of *The Maltese Falcon* stem entirely from the lies and manipulations of the women and queers—we never know where we are because of the shifting webs of truth and untruth spun by women (who have always practiced the wiles of deception) and queers (whose being is constituted in passing, a *ne plus ultra* of deceit).

Many films imply that homosexuality would explain why characters have done what they have done—this is why Johnny is so jealous and cruel in *Gilda*, why Bruno wants to kill his father in *Strangers on a Train*, why Captain Munsey takes such pleasure in inflicting pain in *Brute Force*, why Waldo and Hardy kill women they want to possess but are incapable of having, why Don in *The Lost Weekend* is an alcoholic, why Montgomery (*Crossfire*) kills the man who befriended him, why Johnny Eager is so elusive in his relations with Jeff.

In a much more complex argument, first published in 1947, Parker Tyler (1971: 169–178) suggests that homosexuality may also explain the actions of Neff and Keyes in *Double Indemnity* (1944). Insurance salesman Walter Neff schemes with Phyllis Dietrichson to kill her husband as part of an insurance scam—but why does he turn on her in the end and why does he pour the whole story out to claims adjuster Keyes? Tyler suggests that Neff is a sexual salesman, selling insurance policies by selling his sexual charm; Keyes, unmarried and Neff's mentor, sees through this, through Neff's excessive talk about his success with women; Neff, unable to deliver on the sexual promise to Phyllis after the murder, turns to confess to the one man who has understood him all along. Tyler is careful not to suggest that Neff and Keyes are having an affair, or want to (even unconsciously), though he does make this claim in his later book on homosexuality in the movies (Tyler 1972: 166).[20] Rather the force of his argument is the uncertainty for the characters themselves of their sexual motivations, with murderous consequences.

Making clear the homosexuality of the characters would sort out a lot of mysteries, but there'd be no film then—both in the sense of less mystery but also, more importantly, less evocation of the feeling of not knowing. If homosexuality were definite, then much of the uncertainty—about what is going on, about why people do things—would evaporate. Noir needs homosexuals not as villains but as part of its endemic epistemological uncertainty.

Noir queers constitute a disturbance in knowledge; they unsettle the process of knowing that drives the narrative and contribute to the experience of not knowing that is such a characteristic flavor of noir. They are a gender disturbance: they are like women and often bond with them in a shared femininity, but they also lurk in the foundational institutions of heterosexuality, marriage, and buddiness. In so far as one of the comforts of normal masculinity is to be in possession of knowledge, including and perhaps especially the knowledge of gender, queers are discomforting.

In the opening bedroom scene in *Laura*, detective McPherson plays with a bagatelle game in his hand, whose board depicts a baseball game. He concentrates on this while Waldo prattles on; at one point, there is even a close-up of the game in McPherson's hand, to emphasize that he is looking at it not Waldo, as the latter preens in front of the mirror. Is this because he is too embarrassed, confused, and even disturbed to look Waldo in the face and, indeed, in the body? Maybe, just as the haunted, twitchy quality of Brad (*The Dark Corner*) and the washed out, defeated demeanor of Scott (*Phantom Lady*) might be attributed to their dealing with queers with whom they were professionally but also perhaps erotically involved in their past, and Nick in *Kiss of Death* perhaps protests too much about his awful, never to be repeated night out with Tommy Udo.

Queers may sometimes disturb the central male characters in these oblique ways, just as queerness may disturb our perception of such characters as Johnny in *Gilda* and Neff and Keyes in *Double Indemnity*. More generally, they constitute part of a world whose uncertainty noir heroes fail to master and, because they are often more vivid and more fun, they take attention away from the hero, decentering him. However, it is also the case that often, at any rate, the protagonists don't act like they're disturbed. McPherson does not seem ruffled by the decadent world he has fallen among and any tensions in the encounters of Leonard Diamond with Mingo and Fante (*The Big Combo*) and Dave Bannion with Mike Lagana (*The Big Heat*) seem fully accounted for by the role of the villains in relation to the hero's loved one, that is, respectively, acting as bodyguards to the man whose possession she has become and ordering the murder of his wife. Moreover, the noir protagonist *par excellence*, Humphrey Bogart, seems unfazed in his encounters with queers, including his own attachment to Johnny in *Dead Reckoning* and even to Sean in *The Big Sleep*. Indeed, perhaps the secret of noir as entertainment is that, even as it presents the audience with the discomfort of a queerly uncertain world, it also offers the reassurance of a hero who takes it all in his stride, maybe a little cynical, maybe a little crumpled, but not really, as it were, put out. This is perhaps the most significant reason of all why noir could permit such at times brilliant (Waldo) and touching (Mingo and Fante) epistemological disturbances, namely, that they didn't really seem to dislodge straight masculinity from the center of knowing. Whether they in fact gave a decisive nudge in that direction must remain an imponderable of cultural history.

Notes

1 So does female homosexuality. Though I touch on it at various points here, I focus on male queers. For some more discussion of noir lesbians see Dyer 1993, 1998b.
2 On the definition of film noir see Naremore 1998. In my usage, 'noir' is a characteristic of films, wholly or in part, rather than a category. I stick here to films within the classic period of the 1940s and 50s, though noir can be found in later examples, even in genres less associated with it and notably to represent homosexuality (e.g. *Advise and Consent* 1962, *The Killing of Sister George* 1968).
3 They are used as a metaphor for queerness and its decadence by the Baron de Charlus in Proust's *A la recherche du temps perdu*.
4 I'm grateful to Malcolm Gibb for this last observation. Interestingly, I was watching *The Big Heat* casually with him one afternoon and he wondered at the end whether Lagana was supposed to be gay, whereas this had never occurred to me when I first saw it. See also McArthur 1992: 51.
5 Of course one hardly needs a theory of the unconscious to work out why people liable to be ridiculed, beaten up, and dismissed from employment if known to be queer might feel the world is against them.
6 Other characters tentatively proposed as queer include Jeff (*The Glass Key* 1942) (McGillivray 1997: 173; Naremore 1998: 63), Bart (*Gun Crazy* 1947) (ibid.: 151), Niles (*Cry of the City* 1948) (Walker 1992: 137) and the Paul Henreid character in *Rope of Sand* (1949) (Durgnat 1996: 97).
7 See also Naremore's discussion of how the film 'enables us to "see" . . . many of the things that censorship was trying to repress' (1998: 118).

8 The original US title of this is *Murder My Sweet*; the British title is also the title of the source novel and the 1976 remake.

9 See Note 1. To draw up this list, I've had to stray further from what is usually considered film noir, though all these films have noirish elements. On *Caged*, *Rebecca*, *The Seventh Victim*, *Touch of Evil* and *The Uninvited*, see White (1999) *passim*; note also her discussion (188–189) of *Dark Passage* (1947).

10 The only noir queens who seem at all hostile to women are Joel Cairo (*The Maltese Falcon*) and perhaps Brandon (*Rope*). Cairo's sneering politeness to Brigid O'Shaughnessy could just be because she is a rival for the falcon, but it does seem informed by queer misogyny. There is also, in a cryptic exchange, the implication that they have been rivals for men. Cairo refers to the problem of a boy watching the apartment from the street outside; Brigid: 'I'm sure you could get round him, as you did the one in Istanbul—what was his name?', Cairo: 'You mean the one you couldn't get to come . . .?', at which point she slaps his face.

11 On Webb, see Tyler 1972: 328–330.

12 See Buchsbaum 1992: 96.

13 The consequences of this argument for the representation of women are discussed in Dyer 1998b.

14 Tom Milne considers their visitor, Joe, the boss's henchman, to be perhaps in love with the boss until the humiliation the latter heaps on him turns love into hatred (1980: 80).

15 Although this phrase is too suggestive not to quote, George Chauncey's researches suggest that the term 'closet' in a specifically gay sense was not in circulation before the 1960s (1994: 6, 374–375).

16 I'm not sure if I do see Jeff as queer (*pace* McGillivray 1997: 173 and Naremore 1998: 63), but he is unmarried, enjoys torturing the hero but later becomes drunkenly maudlin with him, and his boss Nick Varna takes him and his other henchman Rusty upstairs with him when he announces to a party of guests that it's time for bed.

17 In this fascinating film, more old-fashioned gangster movie than noir, Van Heflin plays Jeff, long-term room-mate to the glamorous mobster Johnny Eager, clearly in love with him and becoming alcoholic through lack of reciprocity (though perhaps Johnny gives him reason to hope once in a while?). Heflin won a best supporting Oscar for the role.

18 Joel Cairo (*The Maltese Falcon*) also has a suggestive cane, which he caresses to his lips during his first interview with Sam Spade.

19 The intertwining of experimental and sexual sensation also characterized the underground cinema emerging in the US in the same period (cf. Dyer 1990: 111–134).

20 Claire Johnston, writing in 1998 from within a Lacanian perspective, is even less cautious: 'the repressed homosexual desire of Neff for the idealised father [Keyes]', 'the repressed, homosexual desire between the two men' (1998: 91).

References

Bérubé, Allan (1990) *Coming Out Under Fire: The History of Gay Men and Women in World War Two*, New York: Free Press.

Buchsbaum, Jonathan (1992) "Tame Wolves and Phoney Claims: Paranoia and Film Noir," in Cameron 1992: 88–97.

Cameron, Ian (ed.) (1992) *The Movie Book of Film Noir*, London: Studio Vista.

Chauncey, George (1994) *Gay New York: Gender, Urban Culture and the Making of the Gay Male World*, 1890–1940, New York: Basic Books.

Corber, Robert J. (1997) 'Resisting the Lure of the Commodity: *Laura* and the Spectacle of the Gay Male Body', in *Homosexuality in Cold War America: Resistance and the Crisis of Masculinity*, Durham NC: Duke University Press, 55–78.

D'Emilio, John (1983) *Sexual Politics, Sexual Communities: The Making of a Homosexual Minority in the United States* 1940–1970, Chicago: University of Chicago Press.

Durgnat, Raymond (1996) "Paint It Black: The Family Tree of Film Noir," in Palmer, R. Barton (ed.) *Perspectives on Film Noir*, New York: G. K. Hall, 83–98. (First published 1970.)

Dyer, Richard (1990) *Now You See It*, London: Routledge.

Dyer, Richard (1993) "Homosexuality and Film Noir," in *The Matter of Images: Essays on Representations*, London: Routledge, 52–72.

Dyer, Richard (1998a) "Resistance through Charisma: Rita Hayworth and *Gilda*," in Kaplan: 115–122.

Dyer, Richard (1998b) "Postscript: Queers and Women in Film Noir," in Kaplan 1998: 123–129.

Edelman, Lee (1994) "Imagining the Homosexual: *Laura* and the Other Face of Gender," in *Homographesis: Essays in Gay Literary and Cultural Theory*, New York: Routledge, 192–241.

Johnston, Claire (1998) "*Double Indemnity*," in Kaplan, 89–97.

Kaplan, E. Ann (ed.) (1998) *Women in Film Noir* (new edition), London: British Film Institute.

Lippman, Walter (1956) *Public Opinion*, New York: Macmillan. (First published 1922.)

McArthur, Colin (1992) *The Big Heat*, London: British Film Institute.

McGillivray, David (1997) "Homosexuality," in Hardy, Phil (ed.) *The BFI Companion to Crime*, London: Cassell, 173–175.

Milne, Tom (1980) "*The Big Combo*," *Monthly Film Bulletin* 47: 555, 80.

Naremore, James (1998) *More than Night: Film Noir in its Contexts*, Berkeley: University of California Press.

Noriega, Chon (1990) "'Something's Missing Here!': Homosexuality and Film Reviews during the Production Code Era, 1934–1962," *Cinema Journal* 30: 1, 20–41.

Russo, Vito (1981) *The Celluloid Closet: Homosexuality in the Movies*, New York: Harper and Row.

Tyler, Parker (1971) *Magic and Myth of the Movies*, London: Secker and Warburg. (First published 1947.)

Tyler, Parker (1972) *Screening the Sexes: Homosexuality in the Movies*, New York: Holt, Rinehart and Winston.

Walker, Michael (1992) "Robert Siodmak," in Cameron 1992: 110–151.

White, Patricia (1999) *unInvited: Classical Hollywood Cinema and Lesbian Representability*, Bloomington: Indiana University Press.

Pronoun Trouble

8

The Queerness of Animation

SEAN GRIFFIN

In 1993, a small scandal erupted over rumors that Bert and Ernie, the beloved Muppet characters from PBS's long-running series *Sesame Street*, were a homosexual couple.[1] After all, they were two men who had lived together in the same New York apartment since the show began in 1969—and they were never seen dating women. The outcries were numerous, tending to fall into two categories. The first group declared that public television had conspired to actively (if covertly) promote perversion to young children.[2] Conversely, the second group complained that someone was defaming the wholesomeness of Bert and Ernie's friendship by suggesting that they were sexually attracted to each other.[3] Although there were those who found the rumor a positive development, in which a same-sex couple had seamlessly been brought into American homes for over twenty years,[4] the Children's Television Workshop, which produces the series, quickly issued a statement which assured viewers that the duo "do not portray a gay couple."[5]

Concerned parents might have figured that this was only one isolated incident. Yet, current children's fare on TV contains many relationships that seem queer—Ren and Stimpy, Beavis and Butthead, Mr. Burns and Smithers in *The Simpsons*.[6] A full-scale epidemic of heterosexual parents reading everything as queer could have erupted. This possibility was quelled when columnists and late-night talk show hosts began to joke about the development, framing the whole idea as somehow "ludicrous."[7] One letter writer to TV *Guide* about the incident pointed out that, with the relationship between Kermit the Frog and Miss Piggy, it was far easier to claim that "Oh my gosh, *Sesame Street* is promoting bestiality!"[8]

Although the "Bert and Ernie" affair died away relatively quickly, the incident points out how easily it is to read queerness into these texts. Animation, an art form generally conceived as made for children, has always had a history of queerness. Those who made fun of the commotion caused by outing Bert and Ernie used a conventional weapon against queer readings—that too much was being read into the texts, and that any overt moments were isolated and meant only as jokes. Yet, many queer theorists would classify these readings as divergent, subverting the hegemonic preferred subject position that Stuart Hall describes.[9] Furthermore, animation's use of metamorphosis and inanimate objects brought to life creates a constant potential for queerness to be read by audience members. As Alexander Doty claims in his introduction to *Making Things Perfectly Queer*, "I've got news for straight culture: your readings of texts are usually 'alternative' ones for me, and they often seem like desperate attempts to deny the queerness that is so clearly a part of mass culture."[10] What is remarkable about the "Bert and Ernie" affair was that for a moment the queerness was no longer denied by straight culture and threatened to appear everywhere.

This chapter's purpose is to examine closely a few animated texts to explore the queerness of animation. Although I am focusing on American studio animation, I do not feel that this phenomenon is peculiar to this one institutionalized form of animation (especially as a number of American-produced cartoons use cels that are actually painted outside of the United States). The work of Czech animators or independent avant-garde filmmakers, for example, could also be rich in substance when examining how queerness works in these texts.[11] Yet, the queerness of the texts is both culturally and historically specific, and this chapter also will examine how to reconcile historical research with the sometimes ahistorical approach that queer theorists take towards texts.

Queer theory and historical research

A film archivist can find overt references to homosexuality quite easily in American cartoons. For example, in the Max Fleischer cartoon *Any Rags* (1932), one of the rag-seller's male customers buys a nude statue of a male discus thrower, and then sashays off screen. In the Mickey Mouse cartoon *Shanghaied* (1932), a group of pirates sings, "The Captain's got a girl!"— including one sailor with a falsetto voice who bats his eyes. At the end of the Bugs Bunny cartoon *What's Cookin', Doc?* (1944), Bugs waxes enthusiastic when he gets a rabbit-shaped Oscar, saying "I'll even take youse ta bed wit me every night!" The statue comes to life, kisses Bugs on the mouth, and, standing in an effeminate manner, says, "Do you really mean it?" In *Hair-Raising Hare* (1946), Bugs becomes a talkative fey manicurist as he files a monster's nails. Bugs himself has become recognized by many as a constant cross-dresser throughout his long career.[12]

These readings isolate specific moments within cartoons to highlight their representation of homosexuality. Unfortunately, these excessive moments are dissociated from the rest of the texts, and the rest of the animated films under analysis are affirmed as resolutely heterosexual. This type of discussion falls neatly into Eve Sedgwick's "minoritizing" category of sexuality, which views sexuality as an issue of active importance primarily for a small, distinct, relatively fixed homosexual minority, and not needing to be considered by the "normal" heterosexual majority.[13]

A lot of recent scholarly work on animation has begun to discuss how animation creates an "illusion of life" through the illusion of movement. Characters reveal their personality through the rhythm of their walk or the way they manipulate their facial expressions. "Animation thus poses the very questions of life itself, movement itself and their relation ... suggesting that the two ... can only be thought through each other."[14] In this exploration of the importance of motion in the creation of identity, recent animation theory ties directly into current social constructionist arguments about sexual identity, that all genders and sexualities (not just homosexuality) are learned and performed. In contrast to Sedgwick's definition of the "minoritizing" viewpoint, her "universalizing" view sees sexuality "on the other hand as an issue of continuing, determinative importance in the lives of people across the spectrum of sexualities."[15] Sedgwick argues from a "universalizing" standpoint, which forces not only homosexuality to come to terms with its construction but heterosexuality as well. If so, all renditions of heterosexuality in animated films are just as performative as any rendition of homosexuality. As a result, isolating Bugs' turns in drag ignores how Bugs performs masculinity the rest of the time.

The image of Bugs in feminine garb raises another issue unique to animation. Whether in or out of a dress, Bugs Bunny is always in drag as a human being. Although much of early animation featured human characters such as Mutt and Jeff or the Katzenjammer Kids, by the early 1920s, many of the stars of various cartoon series were anthropomorphized animals (even Betty Boop began her career as a humanized dog, complete with long floppy ears). From Felix the Cat to Mickey Mouse and his friends to the menagerie of Warner Bros. characters, these animals only rarely referred to the characteristics of their supposed species. A mouse as large as Mickey or Minnie (standing taller than their dog Pluto) would belong in the *Guinness Book of Records*. Bugs chomps on his carrot as if it were a cigar. Bugs, Mickey, and Minnie also walk upright rather than on all fours. Furthermore, these animals are never drawn with sexual organs.[16] Many never wear clothing, and those that do tend to wear only tops (such as Donald Duck and his nephews). Yet, the sexual organs of the animals are not visible. Walt Disney's studio was even forced to remove a cow's udder by censors in the early 1930s. Without these signifiers, cartoons must rely on voices and attire to assign gender (and it is also possible to deny the existence of sexuality entirely).

Consequently, to see Bugs wearing lipstick and a wig is to see a drawing of a gender-neutral rabbit acting like a human male pretending to be a human female. The levels of impersonation reach the sublime, to the point where boundaries seem impossible to nail down. This breakdown of categories is precisely what Sedgwick and others have attempted to promote through the reinvestment in the term "queer," which Alexander Doty describes as "an attitude . . . that begins in a place not concerned with, or limited by, notions of a binary opposition of male and female or the homo versus hetero paradigm."[17]

Judith Butler's deconstruction of the categories of identity in *Gender Trouble* proposes as an answer to the material oppression of sexuality not some fantasy overthrow of the system, or impossible return to a pre-history that is itself a construction.[18] Rather, Butler sees how the multiple discourses occurring within culture(s) (which attempt to regulate, prohibit, and generate the approved hegemonic discourse) often overlap, complicate, and contradict each other. Hence, possibilities for resistance occur when the complications of these multiple discourses are revealed. The material discourses of power that define identity are subverted by playing them out in such a manner that the various levels reach absurd and parodic extremes, exposing the constructedness of gender, sexuality, and sex itself.

I would argue that a perfect instance of multiple discourses swirling within one text, exposing the constructedness of gender and sexuality through parodic redeployment, is the animated cartoon. For example, the representation of homosexuality in animation as effeminacy in male characters (dressed in drag, swishing, etc.) runs through much of American animation (and in American mainstream film in general). Yet, the ability of supposedly male characters to convincingly move or costume themselves as female characters starts to question the stability of gender. After all, without any sexual organs to mark them different, it only takes a polka-dot skirt, some pumps, and long eyelashes to turn Mickey Mouse into Minnie Mouse (and factoring in the breakdown between animal and human further complicates this stability). Also, the tradition in animation that began as early as French animator Emile Cohl of metamorphosis and transmogrification of objects further emphasizes how shaky the boundaries of identity are.[19] Furthermore, animation has conventionally been used for creating comic narratives, usually using the technique of metamorphosis or putting characters into disguise precisely to parody society's norms. In terms of gender and sexuality, cartoons point up the foibles of all points of view—conventional heterosexual coupling as well as homosexual stereotypes, male as well as female—in a chaotic, ever unstable universe.

This is not to say that Sedgwick's universalizing viewpoint is not without its own problems. Since queer theory deals with breaking down the various definitions or categories, many self-defined homosexuals worry that queer theory might deny them a subject position just at the moment that it begins to become acknowledged in mainstream culture. I would argue that just as constructionist arguments are used in different contexts for divergent purposes (i.e., to show that all sexuality is constructed or, conversely, to claim that homosexuality can be unlearned), the term queer can be used either progressively to deconstruct the stability of straightness, or can be used to minimize specific historical group definitions, depending on the contexts of its use and reception. The purpose here in using the term queer is to challenge and subvert the assumed natural order of heterosexuality "by any means necessary," and not to decenter the lived experience of individuals.

Although queer theory began precisely to create a space for the wide spectrum of lived experience, the use of queer theory in close textual analysis often creates an aura of ahistoricity—that all texts are always already imbued with sexuality. For example, Doty examines mass-media texts, such as *Gentlemen Prefer Blondes* (1953), *Sylvia Scarlett* (1937), and the character Pee-Wee Herman, to examine queerness in the culture. In doing so, there is an implicit assumption that how Doty reads these texts as queer *now* is how they could *always* be read as queer. To be fair, Doty acknowledges that gay or lesbian viewers (amongst others) "enter cultural history at various times and under differing circumstances, which affect how we make sense of the personalities and products within a culture."[20] But he never analyzes how these differing circumstances might alter how queerness is found by these individuals.

A large group of work has been done within the past twenty years reclaiming a history of gay and lesbian lives and cultures, and queer readings need to touch on this vital research to ground their concepts. The groundswell of work that has become known as "cultural studies" is an outgrowth of the ahistoricity of much of poststructuralist theory. The importance this work places on material reception rather than an imagined or ideal reception to texts must be brought to bear on queer readings. "Queerness" attempts to transcend or deconstruct boundaries, but in different eras and cultures what these boundaries are differs. While a gay man in the 1990s may appreciate the queer nature of Bugs Bunny imitating Carmen Miranda on a video screen, that does not necessarily mean that that queer reading is the same that a gay man did in a 1940s movie theater when the cartoon was first released. The wealth of gay and lesbian history now makes such distinctions possible and necessary to analyze.

Animation developed under specific cultural conditions, and the techniques and narrative tropes that animation adopted are imbued with the mutivalenced (and often contradictory) concepts of sexuality that informed the society that the animators lived and worked in. Animation has consistently represented homosexuality as effeminacy in men. Yet, the ways in which these effeminate characteristics could be read by individuals and how that related to, enforced, or threatened hegemonic definitions of heterosexuality differed from time to time, as the conception of sexual orientation was redefined. The following discussions of three different American animated films from different time periods are preliminary exercises, examining how the individual texts attempt to draw boundaries between heterosexuality and its other according to the conceptions of each text's time.

Snow White (1933)

Five years before Walt Disney and his studio would produce a feature-length version of the Grimm Brothers' fairy tale "Snow White," Max Fleischer's studio refashioned the story to create a surreal jazz-influenced cartoon starring their most popular character, Betty Boop. In this tale, the beautiful Betty goes to visit the ugly Queen, who jealously orders her killed. After a number of mishaps, she escapes death, but is encased in a coffin-like block of ice which the seven dwarfs find and carry down into the Mystery Cave. The Queen (disguised as a hag) and Betty's friends Koko and Bimbo follow her to the Cave, where a surreal performance of "Saint James' Infirmary Blues" takes place before Betty is rescued and the Queen defeated.

Eric Smoodin, in his analysis of the multiple discourses that inflect American cartoons, points out how Fleischer and his studio differentiated their product from their main competitor, Disney, by emphasizing adult humor rather than family entertainment.[21] Betty's overt sexuality stands as a perfect example of this. The fetishized distortion of Betty's body, drawn by Grim Natwick, is readily apparent—in addition to a very oversized head, Betty has a small torso, yet ample hips and thighs. In cartoon after cartoon, Betty's sexuality during the early 1930s was on explicit display, as she sang in burlesque houses, did the hula, and was chased around by various predators out to "take her boop-boop-a-doop away."[22]

What also must be acknowledged is the uniquely urban outlook of most of the Fleischer cartoons, specifically New York City—the metropolis that Fleischer's studio was situated in up until the end of the 1930s. Fleischer animator Shamus Culhane has commented, "These were East Side Jewish kids or people like me . . . so they had this very vigorous style . . . kind of earthy, certainly crude, but honest."[23] If the Fleischer cartoons exhibit an overt expression of sexuality, it is defined in terms of how the intersecting cultures of New York City's communities comprehended sexuality during the 1920s and 1930s. The Prohibition era created in New York City a vast underground of speakeasies and gin joints that allowed individuals who had considered themselves law-abiding before Prohibition to mix with minorities and outcasts from society. Consequently, the horizon of sexual possibilities was widely broadened in the city during this period.

Tied to the Prohibition era in New York City was the Harlem Renaissance, which brought urban African American culture in contact with the dominant white American society—in literature, in art, in dance, and especially in music.[24] Fleischer's Snow White is obviously indebted to the "Negro Vogue" of New York entertainment. The trip into the Mystery Cave is underground, much like the entrance to a speakeasy, dark and secret. In the Cave, Cab Calloway and his Orchestra perform "Saint James' Infirmary Blues," the centerpiece of the short, with Calloway singing for Koko the Clown after the Queen turns him into a ghost (or, shall we say, "spook"). The song itself refers to gambling and drinking "booze," with the ghostly figure metamorphosizing into a bottle during this section of the lyric. The ghost shuffles through the Cave using the rotoscoping process invented by Max Fleischer to copy Calloway's movements during the number.[25]

The aura of illicitness that enticed white audiences to go "slumming" in black speakeasies also "encourage[d] middle-class men and women to interact even more casually and to experiment further with the norms governing acceptable public sociability."[26] George Chauncey, in his work on gay life in New York before World War II, finds evidence that speakeasy culture all through New York (not just in Harlem) created a space for lesbians and gay men to exist in public. Nightclub owners noticed that "if whites were intrigued by the 'primitivism' of black culture, heterosexuals were equally intrigued by the 'perversity' of gay culture."[27] Seeing the popularity of drag balls (such as the enormous Hamilton Lodge balls, as well as events held in Madison Square Garden and the Astor Hotel), entrepreneurs began bringing this culture onto their stages. In straight clubs such as the Club Abbey, the Argonaut, the Club Calais, and eventually a place called the Pansy Club, "pansy acts" became the rage of Broadway. According to *Variety*, by the end of 1930, two of Times Square's most successful clubs "depended upon 'pansy personalities' for their main draw."[28]

It should, then, come as no surprise to see the "Pansy Craze" also finding its way into the cartoon—albeit in not so easily read a manner as Calloway's performance. By looking at the Queen as a "queer" figure, one can read the influences of "pansy culture" in the work. The Queen is introduced with a number of signifiers that complicate "her" gender. The film begins with the Queen hidden behind the Magic Mirror, with what looks like cigar puffs emerging from the sides of the Mirror. A side view reveals the visual joke that the puffs are from the Queen powdering the royal nose. Yet, the ugly Queen has no visual signs of makeup—no eyelashes, no lipstick, no rouge—quite unlike the appearance of that paragon of femininity, Betty. When Betty arrives, the Queen literally peers through the Mirror at her, poking "her" head through it. In doing so, the Queen's wig comes off, revealing what appears to be a bald man, who is jealous of Betty's womanly beauty.

It was commonly thought by American society during this period that sexuality was ruled by gender. Homosexual men desired men because they wanted to be women (and, similarly, lesbians wanted to be men). There was no other way to conceive why men would sexually desire other men unless they thought of themselves as women. This definition of homosexuality separated the insertive partner in male–male sex from the label. It was only the man who was in "the woman's position" that was considered homosexual. The drag queens showcased at the Hamilton Lodge balls were reported in New York newspapers with the conception that all the men who watched the show from the balcony were heterosexual, never considering that any of these respectably dressed (i.e., respectably gendered) gentlemen could be defined as homosexual.[29] In 1903, German physician and sexologist Dr. Magnus Hirschfeld termed homosexuals as literally "the third sex." Although his organization in Germany that worked for the rights of homosexuals abandoned this term in 1910, it is obvious in much of the popular representations of homosexuality at the time that straight culture (and many lesbians and gay men themselves) still conceived of homosexuality in this manner.

Consequently, it comes as no surprise that, in thinking of the Queen as a member of "the third sex," the Queen would be jealous of Betty's femininity. Desiring to be a "real" woman, "the fairest of them all," would seem to be of tantamount concern to a homosexual man during this period. Yet, for the Queen to become jealous of Betty's "natural" femininity begs a viewer to question Betty's naturalness, which bears no resemblance to anatomical plausibility. Furthermore, the manic use of metamorphosis in cartoons from the Fleischer studio always heightens the instability of objects and identities. The shape-shifting of the Queen further establishes "her" as a queer figure. When viewing Betty's beauty, the Queen's face turns into a pan with two frying eggs. Later, when entering the Mystery Cave, the Queen passes the Mirror over her body and becomes a hag/goblin. Toward the end of the film, the

Queen is once more transformed, this time into a dragon that chases Betty and her friends until Bimbo, in one final moment of shifting, grabs the dragon by its tongue and pulls the monster inside out.

The moments of transmogrification are not limited to the Queen though, who uses this power to change the rest of the cast as well, exposing their unstable identities. Betty and her friends are turned into statues, and the Queen also turns Koko into the shape-shifting ghost that sings "Saint James' Infirmary Blues." It's almost as if the sheer presence of the Queen in this culture topples the certainty of things. As Chauncey shows, a shift in definition was beginning to occur, complicating the assumed ties between gender and sexuality. As early as the 1910s and 1920s, some men began to "identif[y] . . . themselves as different from other men primarily on the basis of their homosexual interest rather than their womanlike gender status."[30] Gradually, even the persona of the "fairy" came to disturb middle-class men who had previously considered them as a separate gender category. "His womanlike manner challenged the supposed immutability of gender differences by demonstrating that anatomical males did not inevitably become men and were not inevitably different from women."[31] The attempt to "minoritize" the "fairy" had failed, and the "universalizing" view became too apparent and too threatening to the rest of society. After the repeal of Prohibition, the "Pansy Craze" died quickly; seen as part of the widespread degeneracy that contributed to the cause of the Depression, homosexuality was pushed into what now is called "the closet," through arrests, bar closures, and media censorship. It is no wonder that the Queen is pictured as such a threat, and must be vanquished by the trio of protagonists.

Rabbit Fire (1951)

Unlike the culture that Snow White was created in, Chuck Jones' Rabbit Fire (1951) was made for Warner Bros. under completely different circumstances. There was no "Pansy Craze" to speak of—at least, not the type of "Pansy Craze" that Chauncey describes in Gay New York. Rather, after the onset of the Depression and the repeal of Prohibition, homosexual men and women were forced more and more by legal authorities to hide themselves. Furthermore, after World War II, there rose a mass paranoia about homosexuality, its ties to sex crimes (particularly pederasty), and the threat homosexuals could pose to national security.

The beginning of the Cold War in the late 1940s created an air of distrust and fear in the United States, and, as Communism advanced into China and Eastern Europe, many began to fear that a growing internal subversion was out to sabotage the country. The postwar years of McCarthyism made any individual potentially Communist. One wrong opinion expressed or one misplaced association and you could be suspect. An accusation was almost as good as proof. Loyalty oaths and Senate investigations proliferated.

It was in this atmosphere that a renewed and heated attack on homosexuality began. John D'Emilio describes how,

> facing sharp interrogation by members of the State Appropriations Committee, Under Secretary John Peurifoy testified on February 28, 1950, that most of ninety-one employees dismissed for moral turpitude were homosexuals. . . . In the succeeding months, the danger posed by "sexual perverts" became a staple of partisan rhetoric. . . . Finally, in June 1950 the full Senate . . . authorized an investigation into the alleged employment of homosexuals 'and other moral perverts' in government.[32]

Thousands would be banned from serving in the government as a result of these inves-tigations, and many more would be dishonorably discharged from the military or barred from employment by major businesses who followed similar screening procedures during this period. Even the Post Office abetted the persecution of homosexuals, deeming it within their rights to open mail of suspected homosexuals in order to tip off the authorities.[33]

Many film historians have noted how the McCarthy era was represented in American film directly (anti-Communist films like *My Son John* [1952]) and indirectly (such as in *High Noon* [1952] and *On the Waterfront* [1954]). No one has analyzed their effect on the animated cartoons of the period. Jones' remarkable series of cartoons with Bugs Bunny, Daffy Duck, and Elmer Fudd have been analyzed by a number of animation aficionados in terms of their comic structure. What hasn't been analyzed is how they replicate the society in which they were produced. In a series of three cartoons—*Rabbit Fire, Rabbit Seasoning* (1952) and *Duck! Rabbit! Duck!* (1953)—Daffy manically attempts to get Elmer to hunt Bugs instead of himself. The initial ploy is to convince Elmer that it is actually Rabbit Season rather than Duck Season. Bugs, through hilarious trips of language, consistently turns the tables on the duck, and Elmer ends up blasting Daffy's bill off in a number of different ways. Albeit in a consistently humorous fashion, all three cartoons replicate the hyper-paranoid atmosphere of postwar America. Daffy accuses Bugs in order to keep suspicion from falling on himself. Bugs continuously counters by exposing what Daffy has to hide in the first place. And as the impartial punisher, Elmer is willing to shoot at anything. As he announces at one point in *Rabbit Fire*, Elmer is a vegetarian, and hunts only for the sport of it.

While this would fit quite well into a discussion of McCarthyism, the accusations throughout all three cartoons continually revolve around notions of gender and species. Later in the same cartoon, when Elmer has Bugs cornered, Bugs points out that Elmer has an elephant gun, and it can only be used to shoot elephants. Immediately, Elmer turns to find a large, irate, and very fey elephant with his hands on his hips standing behind him, warning "You do and I'll give you such a pinch!" before pounding him into the ground and flouncing off. In *Rabbit Seasoning*, Daffy ends up fighting with Bugs over who Elmer can "take home," forgetting that the one who accompanies Elmer arm-in-arm to his lodge is about to be filled with gunshot. Daffy eventually terms the slippage in the language tricks that Bugs is using against him as "pronoun trouble!" Consequently, these cartoons also speak of the paranoia about sexuality that was part of this era as well.

The paranoia over homosexuality resulted in a new dominant conception of what a "homosexual" was in American society. In 1948, Alfred Kinsey's *Sexual Behavior in the Human Male* was published, revealing a high incidence of homosexual behavior among white American males. Furthermore, his research showed that individuals engaging in homosexual relations consistently did not fit the prevailing stereotype that society had fashioned—the "pansy." Any individual could potentially be homosexual; it was not possible to tell "just by looking." This shift, from conceiving of sexuality as tied to gender roles to conceiving of sexuality as tied to object choice, made the distinctions between homosexuality and heterosexuality both more distinct and more hazy. Now, whether a male was in the dominant insertive role or the receptive role, he was still considered homosexual, making men who were considered masculine in every other conventional way homosexual. The crisis of masculinity that resulted helped fuel the paranoia of the age, reflected in texts such as *Rabbit Fire*.

After Daffy and Bugs accuse and counter-accuse each other of being the truly hunted individual, the two begin a round of cross-dressing. First, Daffy and Bugs disguise themselves as each other in order to evade Elmer's bullets. Daffy finds a bunny suit and chomps on a carrot, while Bugs hides his ears in a rubber swimming cap, puts on flippers, and a homemade bill. Adding yet another level of impersonation to the queerness of animation ("species drag"?), Mel Blanc's vocal performance is stretched to the limits with Bugs trying to imitate Daffy's lisping(!) and Daffy quoting "What's up, Doc?" Then, Bugs rises out of his rabbit hole in drag as a female hunter (complete with Daffy as his/her hunting dog—gender unknown) in order to woo Elmer and escape. Elmer readily falls for Bugs' seduction until a rather erect rabbit ear pops out from under Bugs' blonde wig. The ease with which both Daffy and Bugs assume other identities in the cartoon highlights the performativity of their roles. Butler has pointed out that "drag constitutes the mundane way in which genders are appropriated, theatricalized, worn, done; it implies that all gendering is a kind of impersonation and approximation."[34] The constant removal of Daffy's bill from his face by Elmer's gunshot blasts further emphasizes the importance of costuming and accessorizing in order to create a convincing performance.

Yet, as Daffy and Bugs show, costume and performance can be used by an individual to hide what an individual might not want to reveal. How many men were consciously overperforming masculinity to hide their homosexuality? The queerness of the levels of impersonation ends up implicating the "straight" man, Elmer, as well. After all other strategies have been exhausted and Bugs and Daffy tear off poster after poster claiming it's alternately Rabbit or Duck Season, they reach a poster that proclaims it's actually "Elmer Season." Elmer can easily be read as a gay character, hiding his queerness (his own vocal peculiarities, his vegetarian habits) behind the mask of being a big game hunter. In a fitting climax to such paranoia and confusion, the cartoon ends with Daffy and Bugs, now wearing "Elmer drag" (oversized hunting cap, khaki jacket, and boots), being "vewy, vewy quiet" as they "hunt Elmers." Heterosexuality in American society perceived itself under attack by the shifting definition of homosexuality from gender to object choice, and countered this paranoia with homosexual witchhunts. Just as Elmer's status is compromised by the end of the short, heterosexuality was in danger of being compromised by this new conception of boundaries.

The Lion King (1994)

More than forty years later, day-to-day existence for many lesbians and gay men has changed markedly. Most gay historians describe the Stonewall Riots of 1969 as ushering in a new era in lesbian and gay culture and politics—more outspoken, more explicit, and more confrontational toward the heterosexual community that had oppressed and attempted to ignore lesbians and gay men through much of the century. The 1970s became a decade of liberation as more and more men and women openly acknowledged and celebrated their homosexuality. In the 1980s, as homosexual communities (cultural, political, and otherwise) became aware of the AIDS crisis, the momentum of the 1970s turned to more direct demands for equality and acceptance, looking on this struggle not just over the right to live openly, but increasingly the right to live, period.

With the growth of a visible and vibrant lesbian and gay community has come a conception of this community's buying power. In the 1970s, many lesbians and gay men boycotted Florida orange juice to protest the anti-gay statements of spokesperson Anita Bryant (a strategy that was recently re-employed when Florida orange juice hired conservative funnyman Rush

Limbaugh as their new spokesperson). In 1977, the gay periodical *The Advocate* conducted a survey to create an economic profile of its readers, and repeated the survey in 1980. As Karen Stabiner and Danae Clark have both pointed out, this research interested some businesses in what was now seen as a "gay market." Indicating "that 70% of their readers aged 20–40 earned incomes well above the national median . . . companies such as Paramount, Seagram, Perrier, and Harper & Row [began] to advertise in gay male publications like *Christopher Street* and *The Advocate*."[35] Since Stabiner's article in 1982, this ad trend has only increased, moving out beyond the pages of these specific periodicals. In 1994, for example, the IKEA furniture store began test marketing a TV spot that showed a white gay male couple shopping for a dining-room table. Films have also jumped on the bandwagon. While Stabiner opens her article with an analysis of the ad campaign for the 1981 film *Making Love*,[36] since then, other films with explicit gay subject matter (*Philadelphia* [1993], *The Adventures of Priscilla, Queen of the Desert* [1994]) or appeal (*Madonna: Truth or Dare* [1992]) have placed articles in gay publications and attempted to position lesbians and gay men as a target group, much like "yuppies" or senior citizens.

It is in this culture that the Disney studio has resurrected its animation department. Having coasted through the 1970s and early 1980s on their reputation for and virtual monopoly over animated features, the popularity of non-Disney features—such as *An American Tail* (1986) and *The Land Before Time* (1988)—forced Disney to update its technology, sharpen its storytelling, and include humor that adults would appreciate, even if it was sometimes beyond a child's understanding. Furthermore, the animated features were marketed more toward adults without children. Starting in 1989, with the release of *The Little Mermaid*, Disney's new strategy has consistently resulted in highly-profitable animated features, drawing adults with and without children.

It is impossible not to see how gay audiences figure into this new approach. The songwriting team that helped begin this new era of Disney animation included lyricist Howard Ashman, an openly gay man. When Ashman died of an AIDS-related disease in 1991, the release of *Beauty and the Beast* (1991) was turned into a tribute to his creative genius. Jeffrey Katzenberg, Vice-President in Charge of Production, was quoted as saying, "We have two guardian angels. One is Walt Disney, who continues to touch every frame of our movies. The other is Howard Ashman, who continues to touch every note of our movies."[37] Even after Howard's death, such association of the animation with gay figures has continued. Openly gay animator Andreas Deja has been interviewed by various gay journals, and *The Lion King* featured songs written by Elton John, who officially came out as homosexual while being interviewed by Barbara Walters a few months before the film's premiere. With such attendant publicity, queer readings of these films are not only more possible, but specifically marketed.

Yet, this increased target marketing toward lesbian and gay consumers has its problems. The advertisers have selected mainly one small segment of the homosexual population as their target—"the white, single, well-educated, well-paid man who happens to be homosexual."[38] Clark points out that white well-educated lesbians have also begun to be targeted by advertisers (particularly in the fashion industry). Yet, the term queer attempts to deal with the wide diversity of lived experience, and to acknowledge that the gay community is actually a number of communities that intersect with each other and various straight communities in a number of ways—and advertising to a select group within this diversity tries to deny this complexity.

Disney has begun to discover this diversity and complexity the hard way. Although their animated features have been extraordinarily successful (*Aladdin* [1992] was the first animated feature to make over $200 million domestically, and *The Lion King* has surpassed it to become, at this date, the sixth most successful film of all time), the studio has encountered protests from various individuals for its stereotypical portrayal of women and race/ethnicity. Women were outraged by the mermaid Ariel's dependency on men in *The Little Mermaid* (1989). The studio attempted to respond to these complaints when working on the character Belle in *Beauty and the Beast*, taking care to show her intelligence and independence (although the narrative still focuses on her selecting a suitor). The enormous outcry by Arab Americans over *Aladdin* caused the studio to change a few lyrics before the film's release to video. Just as the protests over *The Little Mermaid* probably had an effect on the studio's hiring a woman (Linda Woolverton) to script *Beauty and the Beast*, the complaints of Arab Americans over *Aladdin* probably influenced the number of Native Americans involved in the production of the studio's 1995 animated feature *Pocahontas*.

The studio might have thought that they would avoid all these problems in *The Lion King* by creating an all-animal cartoon. By hiring many African Americans as voice artists for this story about animals in the African veldt, Disney attempted to be sensitive to racial issues. Yet, the film caused protests from many groups. Even if Ariel was a problematic character for feminists, at least she was the focus of the narrative. In *The Lion King*, lionesses (not to mention females from other species) are barely present. Many African Americans were also disturbed that the film actively refused to show any existence of African civilization— and the use of actor Robert Guillaume to create a mystic baboon with an Uncle Tom accent didn't help matters.

With the songs of Elton John and an ad campaign that included cartoon characters saying that the film was "to die for" or that they would "put on a grass skirt and do the hula," there seemed to be plenty for gay audiences to enjoy. Contrary to the complaints of nonvisibility by women and African Americans, "gay" animals could be found quite easily in the film. The advisor to the lion king is a fussy and pompous bird, who seems to be modeled after actor Clifton Webb. The two friends that the young lion cub protagonist Simba encounters after he is banished from his tribe can be read as a gay male couple, living together, reveling in their marginalization from the rest of jungle society, and looking askance at Simba's budding heterosexual romance with a lioness. The most obvious gay figure is the villainous lion Scar, voiced by Jeremy Irons, an arch portrayal of a physically weak male who makes up for his lack of sheer strength with catty remarks and invidious plotting. Animated by Deja, the character seems to swish (as much as a lion can), disdaining the concept of the heterosexual family in his attempt to usurp the throne for himself.

While Disney's villains have routinely veered toward camp (Captain Hook, Cruella de Ville, Ursula, Jafar), Scar's homosexual signifiers become disturbing when, after initially enjoying his dry wit, he sings a musical solo that becomes an animated version of the Nuremberg rallies, with Scar at the podium as hyena henchmen goosestep in perfect cadence before him. The color scheme turns black-and-white during this section, furthering the similarities to the Nuremberg documentary *The Triumph of the Will* (1936). Also unlike the other villains, Scar actually kills someone (not even the evil Queen in Disney's *Snow White* [1937] did that). His reign over the kingdom seems to directly cause drought, pestilence, and the general destruction of the ecosystem. It is only with the restoration of Simba to the throne that the land comes back to life, in a dissolve that makes the change seem miraculously immediate.

Scar's unforgivable sin seems to be his refusal to support the heterosexual patriarchy that Simba and his father represent. The other gay figures are not seen as monsters, mainly because they help the young straight lion, and see him as the rightful ruler of the land. This would fit directly into how the corporations that target "the gay consumer" would like to define homosexual individuals. John D'Emilio's essay on "Capitalism and Gay Identity" and Clark's on "Commodity Lesbianism" discuss a "constant interplay between exploitation and some measure of autonomy," in which lesbians and gay men are constituted as a market but not as a political social group.[39] A dissatisfied individual is encouraged to create change not through protest and revolt, but through consumption, which only reinforces the established system which made the individual dissatisfied initially. By buying into the society, the gay consumer effectively supports the hegemonic order, much as Simba's gay friends aid his return to power. Queer activism and theory counters this notion of the gay consumer with the recognition that not all homosexuals are white upscale men with the money or the inclination to support Disney's product; indeed, this is rather poignantly pointed out in an article in the West Hollywood gay 'zine *Planet Homo* (in which the author lambastes the film's portrayal of women and its handling of racial issues).[40] In trying to attract the gay consumer, *The Lion King* works against the queerness that animation often displays.

Conclusion

Snow White, *Rabbit Fire*, and *The Lion King* all posit a specific historical formation of gender and sexuality in American culture, attempting to establish specific boundaries that keep heterosexuality separated from its other. Yet, the queerness that has become a dominant characteristic of animation continually begins to break down those boundaries just as they are being erected within the texts. The metamorphoses, transmogrifications, disguises, and levels of impersonation (animal/human, male/female, masculine/feminine, gay/straight) turn the established boundaries into a chaotic playhouse of signification. Even as *The Lion King* tries to establish heterosexual patriarchy as the natural "Circle of Life" (to quote one of the songs from the film), the presence of interspecies couples such as Simba's friends the meerkat and warthog, show that all is not straight in the natural world.

As Alan Cholodenko points out in his introduction to *The Illusion of Life*, conceiving of animation as some subcategory of film is to deny its importance in understanding the workings of all cinema—that cinema was derived from animation, not the other way around, and that live-action film is just another form of animation.[41] In this age when Bob Hoskins interacts with an animated rabbit, Sam Neill and two teenagers run from computerized dinosaurs and Michael Jackson electronically morphs his face into a number of other extras of varying races and ethnicities, the boundaries between animation and film are growing more and more tenuous, creating even more levels of categorical slippage. Consequently, to argue animation from a universalizing queer viewpoint is to argue against "minoritizing" animation and to implicate all cinema. Yet, just as the move toward cultural studies has made it imperative to become aware of the modes of reception that were possible when doing textual analysis, it is important to read texts queerly within these same modes.

Notes

1 "Cheers n' Jeers," TV *Guide*, Vol. 41, No. 52 (Dec. 25, 1993) 6.

2 Ricky L. Hart, from Huntsville, AL, wrote in a letter to TV *Guide*, Vol. 42, No. 3 (Jan. 15, 1994) 45, "We don't want a gay lifestyle portrayed as normal and acceptable to impressionable children."

3 A letter to TV *Guide*, Vol. 42, No. 3 (Jan. 15, 1994) 45, from Pamela Shillingburg, from Roanoke Rapids, NC, said, "It's ludicrous to believe that two fuzzy puppets are gay, but I definitely do not believe the subject of gay couples has any place on a show for preschoolers."

4 The editors of TV *Guide* in the Dec. 25, 1993 article had the opinion that "kids—and parents—need to learn that a person's sexual orientation really shouldn't matter."

5 "Cheers n' Jeers" 6.

6 Also worth mentioning are Grandpa Simpson's flashbacks to his cross-dressing days in World War II.

7 See the letter quoted in Footnote 3.

8 Steven C. Rich, Riverside, CA, TV *Guide* (Jan. 15, 1994).

9 Stuart Hall, "Culture, Media and the 'Ideological Effect,'" *Mass Communication and Society*, eds. James Curran, Michael Gurevitch, and Janet Woolacott (London: Edward Arnold, 1977) 344–346.

10 Alexander Doty, *Making Things Perfectly Queer: Interpreting Mass Culture* (Minneapolis: University of Minnesota Press, 1993) xii.

11 For example, Amy Lawrence's essay, "Masculinity in Eastern European Animation," *Animation Journal*, Vol. 3, No. 1 (Fall 1994) 32–43, although not explicitly addressing "queer" readings, examines the crisis in masculinity in post-Cold War Eastern Europe as it is manifested in their highly-regarded animation.

12 Hank Sartin, "Bugs Bunny: Queer as a Three-Dollar Bill," *Windy City Times*, June 24, 1993, sec. 2, 79.

13 Eve Kosofsky Sedgwick, *Epistemology of the Closet* (Berkeley: University of California Press, 1990) 1.

14 Alan Cholodenko, "Introduction," *The Illusion of Life: Essays on Animation*, Alan Cholodenko, ed. (Sydney: Power Publications, 1991) 15–16.

15 Sedgwick 1.

16 In regards to the "Bert and Ernie" affair, the characters conceivably have no sexual organs since they are never shown below the waist. In this regard, the scandal could easily be read as the introduction of the possibility of sexuality itself.

17 Doty xv. Activist groups such as Queer Nation began to use the term in the late 1980s to be more inclusive of gay men, lesbians, bisexuals, transsexuals—in short, the wide variety of sexualities (and, hopefully, the diverse racial/ethnic and class identities) which are created by the matrices of social discourse. Soon, academia began to use the term to discuss theories of sexuality, specifically the slippage, breakdown, or deconstruction of attempts to categorize individuals according to a gender or sexuality. Lisa Duggan, "Making It Perfectly Queer," *Socialist Review* (April 1992) 11–31, provides a good survey of the development of the term "queer" as it is used by activists and theorists in the late 1980s and 1990s.

18 Judith Butler, *Gender Trouble: Feminism and the Subversion of Identity* (New York: Routledge, 1990).

19 For a history of Cohl's work, see Donald Crafton, *Before Mickey: The Animated Film* (1898–1928) (Chicago: University of Chicago Press, 1993) 59–88.

20 Doty 21.

21 Eric Smoodin, *Animating Culture: Hollywood Cartoons from the Sound Era* (New Brunswick, NJ: Rutgers University Press, 1993). His first chapter, "Studio Strategies: Sexuality, the Law and Corporate Competition," deals directly with Fleischer's and Warner Bros.' attempts to differentiate their product from Disney.

22 The quote is from the short *Boop-Oop-a-Ooop* (1932), when circus performer Betty is sexually menaced by her ringleader boss.

23 Quoted in Leonard Maltin, *Of Mice and Magic: A History of American Animated Cartoons* (New York: McGraw-Hill, 1980) 98.

24 Amongst the sources for a history of the Harlem Renaissance, see Jervis Anderson, *This was Harlem* (New York: Farrar, Straus, Giroux, 1982); Nathan Irvin Huggins, *Harlem Renaissance* (New York: Oxford University Press, 1971); Bruce Kellner, *The Harlem Renaissance: A Historical Dictionary of the Era* (Westport: Greenwood, 1984); and David Levering Lewis, *When Harlem Was in Vogue* (New York: Knopf, 1981).

25 On Max's invention of the rotoscope, see Crafton 169–170.

26 George Chauncey, *Gay New York* (New York: Basic Books, 1994) 307–308.

27 Chauncey 310.

28 "'Pansy' Stuff Slipping," *Variety* (Dec. 31, 1930) 31.

29 For example, "Masquerade Ball Draws 5,000 People: As Usual, Feministic Males Turn Out in Gorgeous Costumes," *Amsterdam News* (Feb. 20, 1929) 2; "Mere Male Blossoms Out In Garb of Milady at Big Hamilton Lodge Ball: Coy Imitators Simper Sweetly at Affair Attended by 7,000," *Amsterdam News* (Feb. 19, 1930) 3; and "Snow and Ice Cover Streets as Pansies Blossom Out at Hamilton Lodge's Dance," *Amsterdam News* (Feb. 28, 1934) 1.

30 Chauncey 101.

31 Chauncey 115.

32 John D'Emilio, *Sexual Politics, Sexual Communities: The Making of a Homosexual Minority in the United States, 1940–1970* (Chicago: University of Chicago Press, 1983) 41–42.

33 D'Emilio 47.

34 Judith Butler, "Imitation and Gender Insubordination," *Inside/Out: Lesbian Theories, Gay Theories*, Diana Fuss, ed. (New York: Routledge, 1991) 21.

35 Danae Clark, "Commodity Lesbianism," *Camera Obscura*, Nos. 25–26 (Jan./May 1991) 182. The data in this quote comes from Karen Stabiner's article, "Tapping the Homosexual Market," *The New York Times Magazine* (May 2, 1980) 34–36, 74–85.

36 Stabiner 34.

37 Quoted in Mimi Avens' article, "Aladdin Sane," *Premiere*, Vol. 6, No. 4 (Dec. 1992) 67.

38 Stabiner 34.

39 John D'Emilio, "Capitalism and Gay Identity," *Powers of Desire: The Politics of Sexuality*, Ann Snitow, Christine Stansell, and Sharon Thompson, eds. (New York: Monthly Review Press, 1983) 102.

40 Todd Hayward, "The Lyin' King," *Planet Homo*, No. 69 (Sept. 21, 1994) 16–17.

41 Cholodenko 9–10.

PART THREE

CAMP

Introduction

Camp is an often confused and confusing term. It has been called a sensibility, a taste, and an aesthetic, and it shares similarities with literary devices such as parody, irony, and satire. Camp can be both a reception strategy as well as a mode of cultural production. As the former, camp is a means through which spectators can queer the "serious" artifacts of dominant culture, ironically critiquing various aspects of mainstream taste, especially those related to issues of gender and sexuality. As a mode of textual production, a camp sensibility can be purposefully encoded into cultural artifacts by their makers. In 1964, in "Notes on Camp," Susan Sontag distinguished between these two types, calling the reception strategy naive or pure camp—"the camp of failed seriousness"—and the mode of cultural production deliberate or intentional camp. A good example of both types are *Valley of the Dolls* (1967) and *Beyond the Valley of the Dolls* (1970). The first was meant to be a straightforward melodrama that audiences found laughably bad (naive camp), while the latter was produced as a self-conscious parody of the former (deliberate camp). More recently, the dreadful "American Idol" musical *From Justin to Kelly* (2003) might be enjoyed as naive camp, while Baz Luhrmann's *Moulin Rouge* (2001) quite clearly partakes of deliberate camp.

Both types of camp have long been associated with queer audiences and filmmakers. Camp style can be traced back to at least the early eighteenth century and the rise of homosexual subcultures within Western European cities. Camp was a way of performing a hitherto unseen identity, and early camp style celebrated a certain degree of gender-bending, wit, and aestheticism. In its self-conscious focus on stylistic construction and performativity, camp was queer long before queer theory claimed it as such. During the first half of the twentieth century, a sort of "cult of camp" coalesced among urban gay men (and some women) in relation to film, theater, and the other expressive arts. This cult laughed at the foibles of heterosexual melodrama, while simultaneously celebrating the indefatigable drive and bigger-than-life personas of actresses on stage and screen, including "bad" actresses such as Maria Montez. Many gay men adopted aspects of the style and bitchiness of these leading actresses, as well as the outlandish stylistic excesses of the musical, the horror film, the melodrama, and the Orientalist fantasy. The Underground Films of Kenneth Anger, Jack Smith, Andy Warhol, the Kuchar Brothers, and John Waters are deliberate camp glosses on Hollywood formula, style, and industrial practice (Suarez 1996; Tinkcom 2002).

As Sontag's essay documents, camp style became somewhat mainstreamed during the 1960s, partly due to the rise of more media-savvy, countercultural audiences and filmmakers. However, many of these texts (including Sontag's) seemed to ignore or dampen camp's queer origins and political ramifications, an error later gay writers and queer theorists have sought to correct. In "Camp and the Gay Sensibility," first published in the 1970s, film critic Jack Babuscio resituated camp within its historically queer framework, exploring how and why camp was dependent on queers' alienation from the mainstream. Such alienation produced irony (between the straight and gay worlds), performative role playing (the need to pass as straight), aestheti-cization (desire to find beauty and truth wherever one could), and bittersweet humor (needed in order to survive in a hostile world). Babuscio was adamant that camp was not a frivolous or apolitical thing—that, in its mocking of the serious, it was also always a critique of heterosexual privilege and presumption.

Although his essay was written before the rise of queer theory *per se*, Babuscio was arguing that camp was a form of queer critique or parody, a position that Moe Meyer expands upon in his essay "Reclaiming the Discourse of Camp." Reviewing previous writings on camp by Sontag (1983) and Ross (1989), and situating camp against the rise of AIDS activism and queer theory, Meyer argues that even the mainstream appropriation of camp (which he helpfully names Pop camp) contains a powerful queer charge. Meyer's argument is especially useful in discussing today's postmodern culture, where camp styles and reception patterns are frequently appro-priated for seemingly un-queer ends. Thus, the overtly queer may be seemingly missing from deliberately campy artifacts such as *Charlie's Angels: Full Throttle* (2003)—or reception practices such as those that celebrate "bad" movies and s/exploitation films—but Meyer argues that such Pop camp texts and reading strategies are nonetheless dependent upon queer praxis. For Meyer, the un-queer spectator is forced to become (in an eloquent turn of phrase) a "drag queen with no other choice but to lipsynch the discourse of the Other." Consistent with other writings on queer media theory, Meyer argues that while it may be constantly elided, appropriated, or denied by heterocentrist texts and reception paradigms, queerness nevertheless endures, abides, and ultimately prevails.

Camp and the Gay Sensibility

9

JACK BABUSCIO

What I aim to do in this chapter is to consider some of the ways in which individual films, stars, and directors reflect a gay sensibility. In the course of this exploration, I hope to accomplish the following aims: to provide a more precise definition of what is, at present, a most confused area of response that goes under the vague label of *camp*; to ascertain the relationship of camp and gayness; to consider some of the social patterns and mechanisms that make for the gay sensibility; to relate these considerations to cinema with the purpose of stimulating discussion of a hitherto neglected aspect of film; to promote solidarity and a greater sense of identification among gays; to remind readers of the fact that what we see in cinema is neither truth nor reality, but fabrications: individual, subjective perceptions of the world and its inhabitants; and, finally, to argue that there is far more fun in art and art in fun than many of us will even now allow.

The gay sensibility

I define the gay sensibility as a creative energy reflecting a consciousness that is different from the mainstream; a heightened awareness of certain human complications of feeling that spring from the fact of social oppression; in short, a perception of the world which is colored, shaped, directed, and defined by the fact of one's gayness. Such a perception of the world varies with time and place according to the nature of the specific set of circumstances in which, historically, we have found ourselves. Present-day society defines people as falling into distinct types. Such a method of labeling ensures that individual types become polarized. A complement of attributes thought to be "natural" and "normal" for members of these categories is assigned. Hence, heterosexuality = normal, natural, healthy behavior; homosexuality = abnormal, unnatural, sick behavior. Out of this process of polarization there develops a twin set of perspectives and general understandings about what the world is like and how to deal with it. For gays, one such response is camp.

Camp

The term *camp* describes those elements in a person, situation, or activity which express, or are created by, a gay sensibility. Camp is never a thing or person *per se*, but, rather, a relationship between activities, individuals, situations, *and* gayness. People who have camp, e.g. screen "personalities" such as Tallulah Bankhead or Edward Everett Horton, or who are in some way responsible for camp—Busby Berkeley or Josef von Sternberg—need not be gay. The link with gayness is established when the camp aspect of an individual or thing is identified as such by a gay sensibility. This is not to say that all gays respond in equal measure to camp, or, even, that an absolute consensus could easily be reached within our community about what to include or emphasize. Yet though camp resides largely in the eye of the beholder, there remains an underlying unity of perspective among gays that gives to someone or something its characteristic camp flavor. Four features are basic to camp: irony, aestheticism, theatricality, and humor.

Camp/irony

Irony is the subject matter of camp, and refers here to any highly incongruous contrast between an individual or thing and its context or association. The most common of incongruous contrasts is that of masculine/feminine. Some of the best examples of this can be found in the screen personalities of stars whose attraction, as camp, owes much to their androgynous qualities, e.g. Greta Garbo in all her films, but particularly *Queen Christina* (1933), where she masquerades as a man; Mick Jagger in *Performance*, where the pop star's persona is achieved through radical neutering via the elision of masculine/feminine "signs"; the Andy Warhol stars Holly Woodlawn, Candy Darling, and Jackie Curtis in films such as *Flesh* and *Women in Revolt* (1972).

Another incongruous contrast is that of youth/(old) age: the Gloria Swanson–William Holden relationship in *Sunset Boulevard* (1950), or that of Bud Cort–Ruth Gordon in *Harold and Maude* (1971); as well as the Bette Davis characters Fanny Trellis and Jane Hudson in *Mr. Skeffington* (1944) and *Whatever Happened to Baby Jane?* (1962): aging, egocentric women obsessed with the romantic illusions of youth and unable to reconcile themselves to the reality of old age.

Other, less frequently employed contrasts are the sacred/profane (*The Picture of Dorian Gray* [1945]), spirit/flesh (*Summer and Smoke* [1961], *The Roman Spring of Mrs. Stone* [1961]), and high/low status, as in dozens of rags-to-riches musicals (*The Countess of Monte Cristo* [1934]) and melodramas (*Ruby Gentry* [1952]).

At the core of this perception of incongruity is the idea of gayness as a moral deviation. Two men or two women in love is generally regarded by society as incongruous—out of keeping with the "normal," "natural," "healthy" order of things. In sum, it is thought to be morally wrong.

Camp/aestheticism

The aesthetic element is also basic to camp. Irony, if it is to be effective, must be shaped. The art of camp therefore relies largely upon arrangement, timing, and tone. Similarly, the ironic events and situations which life itself presents will be more or less effective depending on how well the precision, balance, and economy of a thing is maintained. Camp is aesthetic in three interrelated ways: as a view of art; as a view of life; and as a practical tendency in things or persons:

> It is through Art, and through Art only, that we can shield ourselves from the sordid perils of actual existence.[1]

Wilde's epigram points to a crucial aspect of camp aestheticism: its opposition to puritan morality. Camp is subversive of commonly received standards. As Susan Sontag has said, there is something profoundly "propagandistic" about it:

> homosexuals have pinned their integration into society on promoting the aesthetic sense. Camp is a solvent of morality. It neutralises moral indignation.[2]

Consistently followed as a comprehensive attitude, aestheticism inevitably leads to an ingrown selfishness in life, and to triviality in art.[3] As a means to personal liberation through the exploration of experience, camp is an assertion of one's self-integrity—a temporary means of accommodation with society in which art becomes, at one and the same time, an intense mode of individualism and a form of spirited protest. And while camp advocates the dissolution of hard and inflexible moral rules, it pleads, too, for a morality of sympathy. Its viewpoint suggests detachment from conventional standards. Here again, as R. V. Johnson has pointed out, there is an aspect of aestheticism which diverges from "a puritan ethic of rigid 'thou shalt nots'," preferring, instead, to regard people and ideas with due consideration to circumstances and individual temperament.[4]

A good example of this is found in Jack Hazan's quasi-documentary portrait of artist David Hockney, A *Bigger Splash*. Here the director manages to convey the wry, distancing nature of his subject's visual humor as an integral part of a gay sensibility that is defiantly different from the mainstream. Because Hockney responds to his gay "stigma" by challenging social and aesthetic conventions in life and art, Hazan's concern is to show the various ways in which his subject's private life affects his art—or how art records personal experience and determines our future. Thus, the film relates to the artist's work in much the same way as the paintings do to life. The presence of the unseen beneath the surface is no less important than what one actually sees.

This double aspect in which things can be taken is further emphasized by the semi-documentary nature of Hazan's film. Hockney and his friends appear as themselves, so that the relationships portrayed are much the same as in reality. But the reality is also rehearsed: Hazan occasionally suggests themes for his "characters" to act out, and the line separating being and role-playing becomes blurred. This convention appears to suit Hockney, whose deceptive innocence and disorientating self-created face (platinum blonde hair, owl-rimmed spectacles) exhibit a special feeling for performance and a flair for the theatrical. And though the film remains, in the final analysis, a subjective record of *one* gay life in which the conjunction of fantasy and experience makes common cause, it does effectively isolate the strong strain of protest that resides in the gay sensibility. By wit, a well-organized evasiveness, and a preference for the artificial, Hockney manages a breakthrough into creativity.

This detached attitude does not necessarily indicate an inability to feel or perceive the seriousness of life. In Hockney's case, it is a means of defiance: a refusal to be overwhelmed by unfavorable odds. When the world is a rejecting place, the need grows correspondingly strong to project one's being—to explore the limits to which one's personality might attain— as a way of shielding the inner self from those on the outside who are too insensitive to understand. It is also a method whereby one can multiply personalities, play various parts, assume a variety of roles—both for fun, as well as out of real need.

In film, the aesthetic element in camp further implies a movement away from con- temporary concerns into realms of exotic or subjective fantasies; the depiction of states of mind that are (in terms of commonly accepted taboos and standards) suspect; an emphasis on sensuous surfaces, textures, imagery and the evocation of mood as stylistic devices—not simply because they are appropriate to the plot, but as fascinating in themselves. Such tendencies as these are consonant with the spirit of aestheticism in camp, and also go some way toward explaining the charm which particular film genres have for a certain section of our community.

The horror genre, in particular, is susceptible to a camp interpretation. Not all horror films are camp, of course; only those which make the most of stylish conventions for expressing instant feeling, thrills, sharply defined personality, outrageous and "unacceptable" senti- ments, and so on. In addition, the psychological issues stated or implied, along with the sources of horror, must relate to some significant aspect of our situation and experience; e.g. the inner drives which threaten an individual's well-being and way of life (Tourneur's *The Cat People* [1942], Mamoulian's *Dr. Jekyll and Mr. Hyde* [1931]), coping with pressures to conform and adapt (Siegel's *Invasion of the Body Snatchers* [1956]), the masking of "abnormality" behind a facade of "normality" (Robson's *The Seventh Victim* [1943], Ulmer's *The Black Cat* [1934]), personal rebellion against enforced restrictions (Burrowe's *Incense for the Damned* [1970]).

As a practical tendency in things or persons, camp emphasizes style as a means of self- projection, a conveyor of meaning, and an expression of emotional tone. Style is a form of consciousness; it is never "natural," always acquired. Camp is also urban; it is, in part, a reaction to the anonymity, boredom, and socializing tendencies of technological society. Camp aims to transform the ordinary into something more spectacular. In terms of style, it signifies performance rather than existence. Clothes and décor, for example, can be a means of asserting one's identity, as well as a form of justification in a society which denies one's essential validity.[5] Just as the dandy of the nineteenth century sought in material visibility (as Auden has said of Baudelaire) "a way out of the corrupt nature into which he, like every- one else, is born,"[6] so many in our community find in the decorative arts and the cultivation of exquisite taste a means of making something positive from a discredited social identity. Hence, the *soigné* furniture and furnishings of the flat designed for Franz in Fassbinder's *Fox and his Friends* (1975), or the carefully cluttered modishness of Michael's apartment in William Friedkin's film adaptation of Mart Crowley's *The Boys in the Band*.[7]

By such means as these one aims to become what one wills, to exercise some control over one's environment. But the emphasis on style goes further. Camp is often exaggerated. When the stress on style is "outrageous" or "too much," it results in incongruities: the emphasis shifts from what a thing or a person *is* to what it *looks* like; from *what* is being done to *how* it is being done.

This stress on stylization can also explain why the musical comedy, with its high budgets and big stars, its open indulgence in sentiment, and its emphasis on atmosphere, mood, nostalgia, and the fantastic, is, along with horror, a film genre that is saturated with camp. This can best be seen in the boldly imaginative production numbers of Busby Berkeley, whose work reveals a penchant for total extravagance, voyeurism, and sexual symbolism that is particularly blatant in "The Lady in the Tutti-Frutti Hat" sequence of *The Girls He Left Behind* (1943) (also called *The Gang's All Here*), with its acres of female flesh, outrageously phallic dancing bananas, and Carmen Miranda at her most aggressively self-assertive.

Camp/theatricality

The third element of camp is theatricality. To appreciate camp in things or persons is to perceive the notion of life-as-theater, being versus role-playing, reality and appearance. If "role" is defined as the appropriate behavior associated with a given position in society, then gays do not conform to socially expected ways of behaving as men and women. Camp, by focusing on the outward appearances of role, implies that roles, and, in particular, sex roles, are superficial—a matter of style. Indeed, life itself is role and theater, appearance and impersonation.

Theatricality relates to the gay situation primarily in respect to roles. Gays do not conform to sex-role expectations: we do not show appropriate interest in the opposite sex as a possible source of sexual satisfaction. We are therefore seen as something less than "real" men and women. This is the essence of gay stigma, our so-called "failing." Gayness is seen as a sort of collective denial of the moral and social order of things. Our very lifestyle indicates a rejection of that most cherished cultural assumption which says that masculinity (including sexual dominance over women) is "natural" and appropriate for men, and femininity (including sexual submissiveness toward men) is "natural" and appropriate for women. The stigma of gayness is unique insofar as it is not immediately apparent either to ourselves or to others. Upon discovery of our gayness, however, we are confronted with the possibility of avoiding the negative sanctions attached to our supposed failing by concealing information (i.e. signs which other people take for gay) from the rest of the world. This crucial fact of our existence is called *passing for straight*, a phenomenon generally defined in the metaphor of theater, that is, playing a role: pretending to be something that one is not; or, to shift the motive somewhat, to camouflage our gayness by withholding facts about ourselves which might lead others to the correct conclusion about our sexual orientation.[8]

The art of passing is an acting art: to pass is to be "on stage," to impersonate heterosexual citizenry, to pretend to be a "real" (i.e. straight) man or woman. Such a practice of passing (which can be occasional, continuous, in the past or present) means, in effect, that one must be always on one's guard lest one be seen to "deviate" from those culturally standardized canons of taste, behavior, speech, etc. that are generally associated with the male and female roles as defined by the society in which we live. Because masculinity and femininity are perceived in exclusively heterosexual terms, our social stereotype (and often, self-image) is that of one who rejects his or her masculinity or femininity. Those unwilling to accept their socially defined roles are appropriately stigmatized. Proving one's "manhood" or being a "lady" is thus closely linked to the rejection of gay characteristics. In women, repression is often internalized; in men, it may be externalized in aggressive behavior.

The experience of passing is often productive of a gay sensibility. It can, and often does, lead to a heightened awareness and appreciation for disguise, impersonation, the projection of personality, and the distinctions to be made between instinctive and theatrical behavior. The experience of passing would appear to explain the enthusiasm of so many in our community for certain stars whose performances are highly charged with exaggerated (usually sexual) role-playing. Some of these seem (or are made to seem) fairly "knowing," if not self-parodying, in their roles: Jayne Mansfield holding two full milk bottles to her breasts in *The Girl Can't Help It* (1957); Bette Davis in *Beyond the Forest* (1949); Anita Ekberg in *La dolce vita*; Mae West in all her films; Cesar Romero as the Cisco Kid and in *The Good Fairy* (1935). Others are apparently more "innocent" or "sincere": Jane Russell in *The Outlaw* (1943); Raquel Welch; Mamie van Doren; Jennifer Jones in *Duel in the Sun* (1947); Johnny Weismuller as Tarzan and Jungle Jim; Ramon Novarro, particularly in *Ben Hur* (1927) and *The Student Prince* (*in Old Heidelberg*) (1928).

The time factor is also crucial to one's appreciation of camp theatricality. A good deal of the screen acting which only recently appeared quite "natural" will, in the goodness of time, doubtless become camp for its high degree of stylization (that is, if it is not already camp). Examples: the "method" acting of Rod Steiger and early Brando; so, too, the charming, "dated" styles of George Arliss, Luise Rainer, or Miriam Hopkins. Similarly, a number of personalities from the silent cinema, once revered for their sexual allure, now seem, in the seventies, fairly fantastic: Theda Bara and Pola Negri. Men, as David Thomson has observed, have always had an insecure hold on the camera,[9] so that male sex appeal, e.g. in the case of Rudolph Valentino, vanished much more quickly than did the sway exerted by women. Finding such stars camp is not to mock them, however. It is more a way of poking fun at the whole cosmology of restrictive sex roles and sexual identifications which our society uses to oppress its women and repress its men—including those on screen. This is not to say that those who appreciate the camp in such stars must, *ipso facto*, be politically "aware"; often, they are not. The response is mainly instinctive; there is something of the shock of recognition in it—the idea of seeing on screen the absurdity of those roles that each of us is urged to play with such a deadly seriousness.

Thus, camp as a response to performance springs from the gay sensibility's preference for the *intensities* of character, as opposed to its content: what the character conveys tends to be less important than *how* or *why* it is conveyed. Camp is individualistic; as such, it relishes the uniqueness and the force with which personality is imbued. This theatricalization of experience derives both from the passing experience (wherein, paradoxically, we learn the value of the self while at the same time rejecting it) and from a heightened sensitivity to aspects of a performance which others are likely to regard as routine or uncalculated.[10] It is this awareness of the double aspect of a performance that goes a long way to explain why gays form a disproportionately large and enthusiastic part of the audience of such stars as, most notably, Judy Garland.

In part, at least, Garland's popularity owes much to the fact that she is always, and most intensely, herself. Allied to this is the fact that many of us seem able to equate our own strongly-felt sense of oppression (past or present) with the suffering/loneliness/misfortunes of the star both on and off the screen. Something in the star's personality allows for an empathy that colors one's whole response to the performer and the performance. As Vicki Lester in Cukor's *A Star is Born* (1954), but, especially, as the concert singer in Ronald Neame's *I Could Go on Singing* (1962), Garland took on roles so disconcertingly close to her real-life situation and personality that the autobiographical connections actually appeared to take their toll on her physical appearance from one scene to the next. Such performances as these solidified the impression, already formed in the minds of her more ardent admirers, of an integrity arising directly from out of her great personal misfortunes.

Camp/humor

The fourth characteristic of camp is its humor. This results from an identification of a strong incongruity between an object, person, or situation and its context. The comic element is inherent in the formal properties of irony. There is a basic contradiction or incongruity, coupled with a real or pretended innocence. But in order for an incongruous contrast to be ironic it must, in addition to being comic, affect one as "painful"—though not so painful as to neutralize the humor. It is sufficient that sympathy is aroused for the person, thing, or idea that constitutes the target of an incongruous contrast. To be affected in this way, one's feelings need to clash. It follows, then, that—as A. R. Thompson has argued in his study of irony:

> contrasts which conform exactly to the objective definitions of irony are not ironical at all when they do not arouse . . . conflicting feelings.[11]

Humor constitutes the strategy of camp: a means of dealing with a hostile environment and, in the process, of defining a positive identity. This humor takes several forms. Chief of these is bitter-wit, which expresses an underlying hostility and fear. Society says to gays (and to all stigmatized groups) that we are members of the wider community; we are subject to the same laws as "normals"; we must pay our taxes, etc.; we are, in short, "just like everybody else." On the other hand, we are not received into society on equal terms; indeed, we are told that we are unacceptably "different" in ways that are absolutely fundamental to our sense of self and social identity. In other words, the message conveyed to us by society is highly contradictory: we are just like everyone else, and yet . . . we are not. It is this basic contradiction, this joke, that has traditionally been our destiny.

Not surprisingly, this contradiction has produced, in many, an identity-ambivalence that has found expression in our talk, our behavior, our artistic efforts; in fact, our whole perception of the world and of our place in it. Like other oppressed groups, gays have developed skills out of much the same need to concentrate on strategy when the rules are stacked against us. Those of us who are sufficiently sensitive to criticism of ourselves may develop a commensurate ability to isolate, dissect, and bring into vivid focus the destructiveness and hypocrisy of others. It is thus that in much of our humor lies a strain of irony that is strongly flavored with hostility for society, as well as for ourselves. As Erving Goffman has said:

> Given that the stigmatised individual in our society acquires identity standards which he applies to himself in spite of failing to conform to them, it is inevitable that he will feel some ambivalence about his own self.[12]

This tendency to see ourselves as others do is to some extent changing, and will continue to change as we come to define ourselves in terms that do not assume heterosexuality as the norm. In the past, however, and, to a lesser extent, in the present, our response to this split between heterosexual standards and self-demands has been a bitter-wit that is deeply imbued with self-hate and self-derogation. This can best be illustrated in films such as *Staircase*, *Boys in the Band*, and *The Killing of Sister George*, all of which are perhaps far too maudlin to be called camp, but whose characters do reflect, in exaggerated form, much of that bitter-wit that goes by the name of camp.

For example, in *Staircase*, directed by Stanley Donen, the humor is saturated with the sadness of those perceived as doomed to live their lives with "unsuitable" emotions in a world where such feelings are tacitly recognized but officially condemned. Thus, throughout the film, the dialogue comments on the central couple's awful–funny confrontation with the "normal" world outside; it is riddled with the self-hatred and low self-esteem of those who have successfully internalized straight society's opinion of us. Self-pity and an aching sense of loss are the prevailing themes: "You've been a father," Charlie hisses at Harry, "a privilege denied thousands of us!" Such dialogue, geared for a "superior" laugh, is squarely based on the tacit acceptance of the hegemony of heterosexual institutions. As for Donen's own patronizing view of these proceedings, this finds its most appropriate metaphor in the maudlin tones of Ray Charles pleading in song on the soundtrack over the flickering images of gay *angst* to "Forgive them for they know not what they do." Finally, the very conventions of the commercial cinema provide their own language of lament via the presence of such big-name, belligerently straight-associated types as Rex Harrison (Charlie) and Richard Burton (Harry).

Camp can thus be a means of undercutting rage by its derision of concentrated bitterness. Its vision of the world is comic. Laughter, rather than tears, is its chosen means of dealing with the painfully incongruous situation of gays in society. Yet it is also true that camp is something of a proto-political phenomenon. It assumes gayness to be a category that defines the self, and it steadfastly refuses to repudiate our long heritage of gay ghetto life. Any appreciation of camp, therefore, expresses an empathy with typical gay experiences, even when this takes the form of finding beauty in the seemingly bizarre and outrageous, or discovering the worthiness in a thing or person that is supposedly without value. Finally, camp can be subversive—a means of illustrating those cultural ambiguities and contradictions that oppress us all, gay and straight, and, in particular, women.

Yet because camp combines fun and earnestness, it runs the risk of being considered not serious at all. Usually overlooked by critics of the gay sensibility is camp's strategy of irony. Camp, through its introduction of style, aestheticism, humor, and theatricality, allows us to witness "serious" issues with temporary detachment, so that only later, after the event, are we struck by the emotional and moral implications of what we have almost passively absorbed. The "serious" is, in fact, crucial to camp. Though camp mocks the solemnities of our culture, it never totally discards the seriousness of a thing or individual. As a character in a Christopher Isherwood novel says:

> You can't camp about something you don't take seriously; you're not making fun *of* it; you're making fun *out* of it. You're expressing what's basically serious to you in terms of fun and artifice and elegance.[13]

Camp and the serious: Fassbinder's *Bitter Tears*

As a way of illustrating camp in service of the serious, consider Rainer Werner Fassbinder's *The Bitter Tears of Petra von Kant*. Here, as in almost all of this director's work, the problem of how to make radical social commentary without alienating audiences is resolved by distancing the action—finding a common denominator to anchor the "message." In *Bitter Tears* the mannerist stylization which dominates the *mise en scène*, the grand gestures, comic routines, and the melodramatic tendencies of the plot, constitute the strategy whereby Fassbinder aims to both distance and engage his audience. As Thomas Elsaesser has pointed out in "A Cinema of Vicious Circles," Fassbinder's search for an "unprovocative realism" has led the director to discover for the German cinema "the importance of being artificial" as a strategy for forcing an audience to question its assumptions about society and its inhabitants.[14]

This artificiality is the camp aspect of *Bitter Tears*. A highly theatricalized world devoid of the very passions that constitute its subject is provided by the director's formalized, almost Racinian dialogue; his elaborate, carefully calculated compositions locked into theatrical tableaux; the anachronistic costumes and mask-like makeup that reflect the psychological situation of the characters; the comic pop/classical music references—the incongruous juxtaposition of Verdi, the Platters, and the Walker Brothers; the stylized performances and ritualized division of the film into five acts, each heralded by the heroine's change of dress and wig; the expressive lighting effects that emphasize a world of masters and servants, predators and victims; and, generally, the formalized editing style which makes the most of the film's single set—a studio apartment that is dominated by a huge brass bed, a wall-sized mural-with-male-nude that bears ironic witness to the action below, and a scattered group of bald-pated mannequins whose poses are continuously rearranged as commentary on their human counterparts.

Each scene is so organized as to heighten the irony of Petra von Kant's (Margit Carstensen) inability to reconcile theory (a loving relationship must be free, honest, and non-possessive) and practice. This failure is particularly apparent in Petra's sado-masochistic relationship with the omnipresent Marlene (Irm Hermann), a silent witness to her mistress's jealous possession of the sensual young model Karen (Hanna Schygulla), who ultimately rejects her benefactress in favor of her (Karen's) former husband. When, in the bitterly ironic final scene, an outrageous mixture of comedy and cruelty, the chastened Petra reverses roles and offers "freedom and joy" to Marlene in return for companionship, the chalk-faced "slave" dispassionately packs her bags and makes a hasty exit, pausing only to drop "The Great Pretender" on the gramophone by way of vocal reply.

It is the very artificiality of Fassbinder's *Bitter Tears* which serves to support the characters and their emotions. The camp aspect of the work emerges in the use of calculated melodrama and flamboyant visual surfaces to accentuate the film's complex of interrelated themes: the interdependence of sex and power, love and suffering, pleasure and pain; the lover's demand for exclusive possession, which springs from vanity; the basic instability of love in the absence of a lover's sense of positive self-identity; the value of pose as an escape and protective shield; the inevitability of inequities within relationships so long as love, ego, or insights are distributed in unequal proportions. Such themes as these carry a special resonance for the gay sensibility. As outsiders, we are forced to create our own norms; to impose our *selves* upon a world which refuses to confront the arbitrariness of cultural conventions that insist on sexual loyalty, permanence, and exclusive possession. Fassbinder's film, by paying close attention to the ironic functions of style, aims to detach us, temporarily, from the serious content of the images—but which, later, encourages a more reflective analysis.

Further studies of the gay sensibility in relation to cinema will need to take account of the interaction of camp and genres, auteur theory, images of women, etc. What follows are two brief, tentative case studies concerning camp and the gay sensibility in relation to the work of a single director (Josef von Sternberg) and in various films based on the drama and fiction of Tennessee Williams.

Sternberg as camp

To explain the relation of Sternberg to camp it is necessary to return, briefly, to the phenomenon of passing for straight. This strategy of survival in a hostile world has sensitized us to disguises, impersonations, the significance of surfaces, the need to project personality, the intensities of character, etc. Sternberg's films—in particular, the Dietrich films from *Morocco* (1930) to *The Devil is a Woman* (1935)—are all camp insofar as they relate to those adjustment mechanisms of the gay sensibility. But they are also camp in that they reflect the director's ironic attitude toward his subject-matter—a judgment which says, in effect, that the content is of interest only insofar as it remains susceptible to transformation by means of stylization. What counts in one's view of Sternberg's films as camp, then, is the perception of an underlying emotional autobiography—a disguise of self and obsessions by means of the artificial. One does not need to see these disguises in a strictly literal way. It is enough to sense the irony in the tensions that arise from Sternberg's anguish and cynicism, and his predilection for the most outrageous sexual symbolism as a means of objectifying personal fantasies.

Those who view camp either as a trivialization of taste or a cultural conspiracy will frown on any labeling of Sternberg as camp. Indeed, several of this director's staunchest admirers have already attempted to "rescue" him from ridicule and replace his reputation in a suitably dignified light.[15] For such critics neither the total experience nor the attitudes and emotional philosophy of the sensibility that produces camp are to be taken seriously. The validity of the camp statement, along with its cultural origins and associations, are regarded as of scant significance. Totally ignored is the fact that camp takes a radically different approach to the serious, one which relies heavily on aesthetic rather than moral considerations. Thus, to find camp in Sternberg is not to surrender to the joys of "over-decorated 'aesthetic' nothings."[16] It is, rather, to appreciate the wit by which Sternberg renders his insights artificial; to sense something of an "affaire" between Dietrich and her director; to perceive the deep significance of appearances—a sumptuous surface that serves not as an empty and meaningless background, but as the very subject of the films: a visual context for Sternberg's fantasies.

Sternberg's style is the inevitable result of his need to impose himself upon his material; to control all the elements with which creative work concerns itself. Self-revelation is best accomplished when viewers are left undistracted by the story line. The more hackneyed the material, the better the opportunities for self-projection. There is no place for spontaneity in such a scheme, as one needs always to be in total control of the information conveyed by camera, sets, actors, etc. Thus, the director demanded complete domination over every aspect of his films. His pictures were "acts of arrogance."[17] Not only did the act of creation derive from him, but he, Sternberg, was also the object created: "Marlene is not Marlene," he insisted, "she is me."[18]

Claire Johnston has said of *Morocco* that

> in order for a man to remain at the centre of the universe in a text which focuses on the image, the *auteur* is forced to repress the idea of woman as a social and sexual being (her Otherness) and to deny the opposition man/woman altogether. The woman as sign, then, becomes the pseudo-centre of the filmic discourse.

The incongruous contrast posed by the sign is "male/non-male," which the director established by disguising Dietrich in men's clothing.[19] This is a masquerade which connects with the theme of sexual ambivalence, of central concern to the gay sensibility, and recurrent in Sternberg's work. Dietrich, then, functions principally as a primary motif. It is she, woman, who becomes the focus of Sternberg's symbolism, psychology, and sense of humor. As Amy Joly in *Morocco*; X-27, prostitute and spy, in *Dishonoured* (1931); Shanghai Lily, prostitute, in *Shanghai Express* (1932); Helen Faraday, nightclub entertainer and archetypal mother in *Blonde Venus* (1932); Sophia Frederica, later Catherine II, in *The Scarlet Empress* (1934); and Concha Perez in *The Devil is a Woman* (1935), Dietrich as woman becomes a manifestation of Sternberg's fantasies. The man takes over; the woman recedes into myth and the details of the décor. The image that emerges is man-made. But it is also an integral part of the larger camp structure. Hence, the danger to which camp enthusiasts expose themselves is as inevitable as it is irreducible, i.e. the danger of surrendering to the corroboration of Sternberg's fantasies as each, in turn, is thrown back on us by the male-manufactured image of the star who illuminates the screen.

The gay sensibility in the films of Tennessee Williams

In the films based on the work of Tennessee Williams (I shall refer to these as "Williams's films" since, even when the plays and fiction are adapted for the screen by someone other than the author, they retain the spirit of the original) the image of women is again of central concern in any consideration of camp and the gay sensibility.[20] The point I wish to take up here is one which various critics have used to denigrate both Williams's films and the gay sensibility; namely, that the typical heroine of these films is a "drag queen."[21]

This interpretation is nowhere more relentlessly pursued than in Molly Haskell's *From Reverence to Rape: The Treatment of Women in the Movies*. Haskell perceives Williams's women as products of the writer's own "baroquely transvestised homosexual fantasies." By no stretch of the imagination, she argues, can they conceivably be seen as "real" women. Hence, Vivien Leigh's Blanche DuBois and Karen Stone in *A Streetcar Named Desire* (1951) and *The Roman Spring of Mrs. Stone* (1961); Geraldine Page's Alexandra Del Lago (the Princess Kosmonopolis) and Alma Winemiller in *Sweet Bird of Youth* (1962) and *Summer and Smoke* (1958); Joanne Woodward's Carole Cutrere in *The Fugitive Kind* (1958); Ava Gardner's Maxine Faulk and Deborah Kerr's Hannah Jelkes in *The Night of the Iguana* (1964); Elizabeth Taylor's Flora (Sissy) Goforth in *Boom!* (1968), etc., etc. All these characters, Haskell argues, are "hermaphrodites" who flow from out of "the palpable fear and self-pity, guts and bravura of the aging homosexual." What happens here, the argument further goes, is that the gay author, seething with repressed desires, dons his female mask (Blanche, Karen, etc.) and hungrily heads, in print as on screen, for a host of fantasy males of his own creation: Stanley Kowalski/Marlon Brando, Paolo/Warren Beatty, Chance Wayne/Paul Newman, etc. The "cultured homosexual" (Williams) is thus seen as being compelled, "often masochistically and against his taste," to love brutes and beachboys, natives and gigolos, primitives and peasants—as well as all the other unavailable prototypes of uninhibited sensuality.[22]

There is some truth in all this, of course. Williams has "used" women to his own advantage. His initial passing strategy for coping with the fact of his gayness was productive of deep anxiety which led to a certain conservatism in his work: a desire to protect himself against the prying eyes of others; an unwillingness to parade his feelings as a gay man in public. Thus, in films based on such early work as A *Streetcar Named Desire*, *Summer and Smoke*, and *The Roman Spring of Mrs. Stone*, Williams's crypto-gayness found relief in the form of female guise: Blanche, Alma, Karen. These characters do express their creator's own "unacceptable" emotions as a gay man. They all do declare the nature of Williams's own fantasy life at the time of their creation. In them the artist has found a means of dealing with the tensions that plagued and defined him—tensions that reside in such dualities as flesh/spirit, promiscuity/pride, youth/(old) age.

Yet it is also true that such a strategy of survival in a hostile world constitutes an imaginative act of which any artist is capable. Most male artists, whatever their sexual orientation, assume the habit of it as a necessary qualification in dealing with female emotions. What one needs to be concerned about is not the *fact* of an artist's fantasies; but, rather, the way in which these fantasies are *shaped* so that they speak to and for other people.

Still, there remains the threat from certain critical quarters to reduce the whole of such problems of interpretation to generalities about the limitations of the gay artist. The central assumption of such criticism is that gays, generally, can know little of life as lived by those who take their place in the "real" world of straight, rather than gay, relationships. This point is most succinctly expressed by Adelaide Comerford, who, writing in *Films in Review*, claims that when Williams is not dealing with "sex degenerates or other psychopaths" his "ignorance of life is boringly patent."[23]

This notion that the work of gay artists cannot be taken seriously because it deals with facts of feeling unknown to straights does have a certain awful logic to it.[24] People insufficiently sensitive to those aspects of our situation which give to an artist's work a measure of dignity surely cannot be expected to be open to the understandings that spring from our unique encounters with self and society. Those who malign or reject the existence of a gay sensibility will all too often overlook the fact that the feelings and creative productions of artists, gay or straight, are the sum total of their experiences—education, relationships, repressions, fortunes, and misfortunes—which have entered into their inner lives. To dismiss the creative efforts that spring from such influences on the ground that the artist is gay serves no useful purpose whatsoever. Certainly it is true enough that gays *do* develop a unique perception of the world, just as do all members of minority groups which have been treated, in essential respects, as marginal to society. And since sexuality can be divorced from no aspect of the inner workings of the human personality, it cannot be divorced from creativity. What one wants to know is this: given the nature of our unique situation, what special insights does the gay artist have to offer?

In defining the gay sensibility it is important to remember that gays are members of a minority group, and that minorities have always constituted some sort of threat to the majority. Thus, gays have been regarded with fear, suspicion, and, even, hatred. The know-ledge of these attitudes has developed in us what I have referred to above as a unique set of perspectives and understandings about what the world is like and how best we can deal with it. It is true that gay artists may at times protect themselves from the social pressures imposed upon them by our cultural contradictions and social prejudices. Hence, it may be that fantasies of revenge are sometimes transformed into art as a way of allowing vicarious play to erotic wishes renounced in the interests of social acceptance; resentments are expressed over treatment received; appeals for sympathy are made through the demonstration of damage wrought by continued injustice and oppression; psychic wounds are recorded so that art becomes, as Williams has said of his own work, "an escape from a world of reality in which I felt acutely uncomfortable";[25] female masks are donned; charades enacted; false identities assumed.

But are not such forms of expression—"deceptions"—in fact everywhere the rule? In Freud's formulation of the creative impulse, the artist is originally one who turns away from reality out of a refusal to come to terms with the demand for his or her renunciation of instinctual satisfaction, and who then, in fantasy life, allows full play to erotic and ambitious wishes.[26] Creativity is thus an inevitable outcome of repressed impulses or relationships. As such it constitutes a defiance against "unlived life."[27] True, the insights offered by so many of the female characters in Williams's films are the product of a gay sensibility. But then the gay artist is one who is graced with a double vision—a vision which belongs to all members of oppressed groups. Those on the outside better understand the activities of the insider than vice versa. As Benjamin DeMott has pointed out in his essay, "But He's a Homosexual . . . ," the gay artist often speaks more frankly than the straight on such matters as the tedium of marriage, the horrors of family life, the lover's exploitation of personality, and the slow erosion of character in promiscuity.[28]

If we are not too rigid about drawing the line between thought and fantasy, but, rather, conceive of creative endeavor as encompassing a great range of covert mental processes, then it should be possible to view more sympathetically Williams's female creations as important both to the conservation and change of this artist's own sense of identity, as well as for what they reveal of an aspect of love that is neither gay nor straight, but, simply, human. These are facts of feeling which gays, who have early in life recognized irony in the incompatible demands of gayness and society, cannot easily avoid. Yet these are facts which can scarcely be understood by those oblivious to the peculiarities, past or present, of our situation in the general culture.

To say this is not to suggest that *only* gays can be objective about heterosexual institutions and arrangements. It is, rather, a way of saying that gays, because of the demands constantly made upon us to justify our existence, have never been able to simply accept, passively, the cultural assumptions that non-gays may well take for granted.[29] The insights provided by, for example, the Deborah Kerr and Ava Gardner characters in The Night of the Iguana are not those of "drag queens," as has been suggested. Rather, they spring from a gay sensibility that is not so completely identified with its "masculine" persona roles that it cannot give expression to its "feminine" component. It is also one which refuses to lapse into unthinking acceptance of what others have insisted is appropriate behavior for two people in love. When the Deborah Kerr character (Hannah Jelkes) speaks of her acceptance of the "impermanence" of relationships, Shannon (Richard Burton) chides her, offering up the metaphor of birds who build their nests "on the very highest level." To this Hannah quickly replies: "I'm not a bird,

Mr. Shannon, I'm a human being. And when a member of that fantastic species builds a nest in the heart of another, the question of permanence isn't the first or even the last thing that's considered." Echoing these sentiments precisely, the Ava Gardner character (Maxine Faulk) tells Burton that sooner or later we all reach a point where it is important to "settle for something that works for us in our lives—even if it isn't on the highest kind of level." This is the message advocated time and again by the Williams female, and it is very much an insight of the gay sensibility.

Conclusion

Camp and the gay sensibility have rarely, if ever, been explored in relation to cinema.[30] On the rare occasions when it has (outside of gay periodicals) analyses have tended to draw upon stereotypes of gayness with which we are all, by now, familiar. The term *camp* has been widely misused to signify the trivial, superficial, and "queer." The original meaning and complex associations of the term, some of which I have attempted to outline in this chapter, are ignored. Thus, just as it has always been a sign of worthiness to speak out on behalf of any oppressed minority group *other* than gays, so, it seems, there exists a corresponding reluctance on the part of people who take the cinema seriously (either out of contempt, or of seeming suspect, or whatever) to perceive in camp a means of heightening their appreciation of any particular performance, film, or director.

Camp, as a product of the gay sensibility, has existed, right up to the present moment in time, on the same socio-cultural level as the sub-culture from which it has issued. In other words, camp, its sources and associations, have remained secret in their most fundamental aspects, just as the actual life of gays in our culture has remained secret to the overwhelming majority of non-gays. Many critics have, of course, appropriated the term *camp*, but without any understanding of its significance within the gay community. The sub-cultural attitudes, catalysts, and needs that have gone to produce camp as a creative expression of gay feelings, are never considered. Yet camp is, in its essence, the expression of these feelings.

The real trouble with the usual speculations on what the critics have thought to term *camp* (aside from the fact that most of it is not) is that they never illuminate the gay sensibility, but, rather, go far to reinforce those very standards of judgment and aesthetic excellence which are often antithetical to it. It is thus that critics conclude, by implication, that camp has emerged from out of no intelligent body of socio-cultural analysis.

To say this is not, however, to plead for the application of any narrow sociological analysis. Rather, it is a way of saying that the worth of camp can simply not be understood in critical terms unless some attention is first given to the attitudes that go to produce it—attitudes which spring from our social situation and which are crucial to the development of a gay sensibility.

Notes

1 Oscar Wilde, *The Decay of Lying*, James R. Osgood, McIlvane & Co., London, 1891.
2 Susan Sontag, *Against Interpretation, and Other Essays*, Delta, New York, 1967. This point, and a number of other insights provided by Sontag in her seminal essay, "Notes on Camp," have been most helpful to me in formulating my own ideas on the subject.

3 This point is developed by R. V. Johnson in *Aestheticism*, Methuen, London, 1969.

4 Ibid.

5 Esther Newton has explored the relationship of costume to female impersonators in "The 'Drag Queens': A Study in Urban Anthropology," unpublished PhD thesis, University of Chicago, 1968. I am much indebted to Newton for her insights on the style and humor systems of "Drag Queens."

6 W. H. Auden in his "Introduction" to the *Intimate Journals* of Charles Pierre Baudelaire, translated by Christopher Isherwood, Methuen, London, 1949.

7 A distinction must be drawn here between kitsch and camp. The latter implies fervent involvement—an ability to strongly identify with what is perceived as camp. Not so the former, which refers to the artistically shallow or vulgar, and is marked by sensationalism, sentimentalism, and slickness. With regard to décor, kitsch can be seen in George Schlatter's *Norman . . . Is That You?*, where the furniture, curtains, chandeliers, paintings, ornaments, etc., provided by set decorator Fred R. Price function principally as things to be mocked.

8 I have developed these ideas at greater length in "Passing for Straight: The Politics of the Closet" in *Gay News* No. 62, January 1974.

9 David Thomson, *A Biographical Dictionary of the Cinema*, Secker & Warburg, London, 1975.

10 Erving Goffman discusses the "passing" strategy in relation to stigmatized groups in *Stigma: The Management of Spoiled Identity*, Englewood Cliffs, Prentice-Hall, 1963.

11 A. R. Thompson, *The Dry Mock, A Study of Irony in Drama*, Berkeley, University of California Press, 1948.

12 Erving Goffman, *Stigma . . .* , op. cit.

13 Christopher Isherwood, *The World in the Evening*, Methuen, London, 1954.

14 Thomas Elsaesser, "A Cinema of Vicious Circles" in *Fassbinder*, Tony Rayns (ed.), BFI, London, 1976.

15 See, for example, Robin Wood, *Personal Views: Exploration in Film*, Gordon Fraser, London, 1976; and Andrew Sarris in *The Films of Josef von Sternberg*, The Museum of Modern Art/Doubleday, New York, 1966, and "Summer Camp" in *The Village Voice*, 21.7.75.

16 Wood, *Personal Views*, op. cit.

17 Quoted in Herman Weinberg, *Josef von Sternberg, A Critical Study*, E. P. Dutton, London, 1967.

18 Ibid.

19 Claire Johnston, "Women's Cinema as Counter-Cinema" in *Notes on Women's Cinema*, SEFT, London, 1973.

20 The *Memoirs* of Tennessee Williams, W. H. Allen, London, 1976, have also been useful to me here for the light they throw on the ways in which the author's gayness has affected his creative output.

21 The instances of critics labeling a Williams heroine "drag queen" are too numerous to cite. However, the most extended development of this particular line of interpretation can be found in Molly Haskell, *From Reverence to Rape: The Treatment of Women in the Movies*, Penguin, New York, 1974, and Elaine Rothschild in *Films in Review*, August/September 1964, where the reviewer speaks of Williams's "malformed females" and "anti-female imagination"; see also Marjorie Rosen, *Popcorn Venus: Women, Movies and the American Dream*, Avon, New York, 1974; Foster Hirsch, "Tennessee Williams," in *Cinema* (USA), Vol. 8, No. 1, Issue 33, Spring 1973; the *Guardian*, 27.10.76; *Interview*, April 1973.

22 Haskell, *From Reverence to Rape . . .* , op. cit.

23 *Films in Review*, December 1962.

24 Peter J. Dyer refers to the "difficulty" of taking the film *Summer and Smoke* "at all seriously," other than as "a case-book study in arrested development" (in *Monthly Film Bulletin*, Vol. 29, No. 339); similarly, Molly Haskell in *From Reverence to Rape* writes: "Williams's women can be amusing company if we aren't asked to take them too seriously . . .", p.251.

25 Tennessee Williams in *The New York Times*, 8.3.59.

26 Sigmund Freud, "The Relation of the Poet to Daydreaming," *Collected Papers*, Vol. IV, Basic Books, New York, 1959.

27 See, in this regard, Antonia Wenkart, "Creativity and Freedom," *American Journal of Psychoanalysis*, XXIII.2 (1963).

28 Benjamin DeMott, *Supergrow: Essays and Reports on Imagination in America*, E. P. Dutton, London, 1970.

29 This so-called "communion of touch" in relationships is further developed in the writer's *We Speak for Ourselves*, SPCK, London, 1976.

30 The notable exception is *Gay News*, a fortnightly newspaper published in London.

Reclaiming the Discourse of Camp

10

MOE MEYER

In the last decade, Camp, or queer parody, has become an activist strategy for organizations such as ACT UP and Queer Nation, as well as a focus in utopian movements like the Radical Faeries. As practiced by these contemporary groups, Camp is both political and critical. Defying existing interpretations that continue to define Camp as apolitical, aestheticized, and frivolous, [this author], prompted by its recently foregrounded political usages, attempts a reappraisal of the phenomenon. I suggest that Camp is not simply a "style" or "sensibility" as is conventionally accepted. Rather, what emerges is a suppressed and denied oppositional critique embodied in the signifying practices that processually constitute queer identities. Accordingly, [this author] operates from shared beliefs concerning the construction of Camp. These are: Camp is political; Camp is solely queer (and/or sometimes gay and lesbian) discourse; and Camp embodies a specifically queer cultural critique.[1] Additionally, because Camp is defined as a solely queer discourse, all un-queer activities that have been previously accepted as "camp," such as Pop culture expressions, have been redefined as examples of the appropriation of queer praxis. Because un-queer appropriations interpret Camp within the context of compulsory reproductive heterosexuality, they no longer qualify as Camp as it is defined here. In other words, the un-queer do not have access to the discourse of Camp, only to derivatives constructed through the act of appropriation.[2]

The use of the word "queer" to designate what is usually referred to as "gay and lesbian" marks a subtle, ongoing, and not yet stabilized renomination. It is used by some writers for various reasons. "Queer" does not indicate the biological sex or gender of the subject. More importantly, the term indicates an ontological challenge to dominant labeling philosophies, especially the medicalization of the subject implied by the word "homosexual," as well as a challenge to discrete gender categories embedded in the divided phrase "gay and lesbian." Because Camp, as we are defining it, gains its political validity as an ontological critique, and because its reconceptualization was initiated by observations of queer activist practices, the term "queer" may be the best descriptor of this parodic operation.

The reappropriation of the once derogatory term "queer," and its contemporary use as an affirmative self-nominated identity label, is far from clear in its current applications. Two writers who have attempted to define this term, Teresa de Lauretis (1991: iii–vi) and Simon Watney (1991), both do so by juxtaposing it with and in opposition to the labels of "gay and lesbian." I think that this logic is inadequate to the task of clarifying the meaning of "queer."

Watney, in particular, identifies the emergence of the label as a generational phenomenon, one used by younger gay men and lesbians to differentiate themselves from what appears to be the bourgeois assimilationism rampant among some segments of the gay and lesbian community and to signify that those who have come out in the era of AIDS are somehow different from those who have not. The flaws in this kind of argument should be apparent: first, it indicates that what is at stake is a critique of class, not of sex/gender; second, it conflates middle class with middle age and assumes a unified understanding of the terms gay and lesbian and a singular lifestyle on the part of those who have reached a certain age; and third, it reveals itself as based in the ageism that has been so detrimental within the gay community. If the term queer is indeed based within imagined generational difference, then I would suggest that it signifies nothing more than a potentially destructive, divisive, and ageist maneuver that, in the end, serves to interrupt the continuity of political struggle through an ahistoricizing turn. But once the uncritiqued ageism of current definitions has been revealed and discarded, what remains—the critique of class—is of definite value and can be used to formulate what might be at stake in both the terms "queer" and "Camp."

What I would offer as a definition of queer is one based on an alternative model of the constitution of subjectivity and of social identity. The emergence of the queer label as an oppositional critique of gay and lesbian middle-class assimilationism is, perhaps, its strongest and most valid aspect. In the sense that the queer label emerges as a class critique, then what is opposed are bourgeois models of identity. What "queer" signals is an ontological challenge that displaces bourgeois notions of the Self as unique, abiding, and continuous while substituting instead a concept of the Self as performative, improvisational, dis-continuous, and processually constituted by repetitive and stylized acts. Rather than some new kind of subject constitution that emerges as the result of a generation-specific response to the AIDS crisis, queer identity is more accurately identified as the praxical response to the emergence of social constructionist (sex/gender as ideologically interpellated) models of identity and its, by now overly rehearsed, oppositional stance to essentialist (sexual orientation as innate) models, thus historically situating queer identity in an epistemological rift that predates the advent of AIDS.

Queerness can be seen as an oppositional stance not simply to essentialist formations of gay and lesbian identities, but to a much wider application of the depth model of identity which underwrites the epistemology deployed by the bourgeoisie in their ascendency to and maintenance of dominant power. As such, the queer label contains a critique of a more vast and comprehensive system of class-based practices of which sex/gender identity is only a part. The history of queer practices . . . is a critical maneuver not limited to sexualities, but is one that has valuable applications for marginal social identities in general. Broadening the scope of the queer critique in this manner also constitutes a radical challenge to the entire concept of an identity based upon sexual orientation or sexual desire because the substitution of a performative, discontinuous Self for one based upon the unique individual actually displaces and voids the concept of sexual orientation itself by removing the bourgeois epistemological frames that stabilize such identifications. Queer sexualities become, then, a series of improvised performances whose threat lies in the denial of any social identity derived from participation in those performances. As a refusal of sexually defined identity, this must also include the denial of the difference upon which such identities have been founded. And it is precisely in the space of this refusal, in the deconstruction of the homo/hetero binary, that the threat and challenge to bourgeois ideology is queerly executed.

As the rejection of a social identity based upon the differentiation of sexual practices, queer identity must be more correctly aligned with various gender, rather than sexual, identities because it is no longer based, and does not have to be, upon material sexual practice. Perhaps emerging as a response to certain unaccountable and uncontainable sexualities—such as celibate gay men and lesbians; heterosexuals who engage in same-sex sexual activity without taking on an identity based on that activity; or even closeted gays who maintain multiple, exclusive, and discrete social identities by switching back and forth between performative signifying codes—queer identity is not just another in an inventory of available sexual identities. Because sexual behavior is clearly not the determining factor in finalizing a self-nomination, even for conventional gays and lesbians, queerness contains the knowledge that social identities, including those of sex, but especially those of gender, are always accompanied by some sort of public signification in the form of specific enactments, embodiments, or speech acts which are nonsexual or, in the very least, extrasexual. Accordingly, Judith Butler (1990) has theorized that

> gender is in no way a stable identity or locus of agency from which various acts proceed; rather, it is an identity tenuously constituted in time—an identity instituted through a *stylized repetition of acts*. Further, gender is instituted through the stylization of the body and, hence, must be understood as the mundane way in which bodily gestures, movements, and enactments of various kinds constitute the illusion of an abiding gendered self.
>
> (270)

Butler's definition of gender can provide an explanation of queer identity that not only locates that identity within a performative nexus, but also solves the problems of identity formation involving celibate gay men, etc., listed above.

Because gender identity is instituted by repetitive acts, then queer performance is not expressive of the social identity but is, rather, the reverse—the identity is self-reflexively constituted by the performances themselves. Whether one subscribes to an essentialist or constructionist theory of gay and lesbian identity, it comes down to the fact that, at some time, the actor must *do* something in order to produce the social visibility by which the identity is manifested. Postures, gestures, costume and dress, and speech acts become the elements that constitute both the identity and the identity performance. When we shift the study of gay and lesbian identity into a performance paradigm, then every enactment of that identity depends, ultimately, upon extrasexual performative gestures. Even the act of "coming out," that is, the public proclamation of one's self-nomination as gay or lesbian, is constituted by an institutionalized speech act. I suggest that queer identity emerges as self-consciousness of one's gay and lesbian performativity sets in.

In the sense that queer identity is performative, it is by the deployment of specific signifying codes that social visibility is produced. Because the function of Camp, as I will argue, is the production of queer social visibility, then the relationship between Camp and queer identity can be posited. Thus I define Camp as the total body of performative practices and strategies used to enact a queer identity, with enactment defined as the production of social visibility. This expanded definition of Camp, one based on identity performance and not solely in some kind of unspecified cognitive identification of an ironic moment, may come as a bit of a jolt to many readers. It means that *all* queer identity performative expressions are circulated within the signifying system that is Camp. In other words, queer identity is inseparable and indistinguishable from its processual enactment, or Camp. The historical and material evidence demonstrates that this was clearly the case until Sontag's 1964 essay, "Notes on Camp," complicated the interpretations by detaching the signifying codes from their queer signified.

This definition of Camp can facilitate a rereading of Sontag and the subsequent appearance of Pop camp that emerged from her interpretation. By holding to a definition of Camp as the total body of queer identity performance practices, then, Sontag's essay does not signal the availability of Camp as an un-queer practice, nor does it signal the birth of multiple forms of Camp. Because the process of Camp has for its purpose the production of queer social visibility, the same performative gestures executed independently of queer self-reflexivity are unavoidably transformed and no longer qualify as Camp. Instead, what emerges from Sontag's essay is the birth of the camp trace, or residual camp, a strategy of un-queer appropriation of queer praxis whose purpose, as I will demonstrate, is the enfusement of the un-queer with the queer aura, acting to stabilize the ontological challenge of Camp through a dominant gesture of reincorporation. Thus there are not different kinds of Camp. There is only one. And it is queer. It can be engaged directly by the queer to produce social visibility in the praxis of everyday life, or it can be manifested as the camp trace by the un-queer in order, as I will argue, to provide queer access to the apparatus of representation.

The problem with Joan

There was a new presence in Chicago's last mayoral election. In April 1991, the race for city hall hosted an unexpected surprise in the figure of Joan Jett Blakk, the first official Queer Nation candidate for municipal office in the windy city.[3] Running a drag queen for the office of mayor did not set well with the powers that be. Despite the flurry of activity and grass-roots support, Ms. Blakk's campaign (her slogan was, among others, "putting the Camp into campaign") was ignored by the gay press even though she attracted enough attention to elevate her to international Superqueer status. Assimilationist gays—many in editorial positions—were especially dismayed by Blakk's campaign strategy, one based on the practice of Camp. Taken for granted to be apolitical, Camp was deemed flippant and demeaning as the foundation for a campaign. Many thought that Blakk needed to be silenced, that her Camp strategy was not serious work, and that the Queer Nation candidate would do damage to the gains made by so-called legitimate caucuses. To delineate a basic division in gay politics along the predictable lines of essentialist and constructionist philosophies does not explain the reactions, because the way that Blakk's campaign was evaluated by both of the opposing positions was through an interpretation of Camp. The role of Camp in the formation of these political factions superseded any allegiance to philosophical theories of identity in favor of more immediate issues of praxis, thus identifying this form of parody as a particularly cogent site for an emerging queer critical theory.

The Queer Nation campaign raised some interesting questions. First, if Camp is apolitical why was it appearing in an overtly political and activist situation? Second, if Camp, as generally defined, is merely an aestheticized sensibility characterized by triviality and lack of content, or simply an operation of taste, then why did it so clearly divide gay political opinion, and in such a strongly articulated way? Clearly there was a conflict. And this conflict was between two constructions of Camp. Joan's actions, identified as Camp by all parties, were being interpreted quite differently depending on whether one believed that Camp is political or apolitical.

Are we talking then about the possibility of multiple forms of Camp? The answer is no. In the case of Joan Jett Blakk, each party to the debate identified precisely the same actions as Camp. There was no deviation in formal recognition. Thus the differences of interpretation could be attributed only to variable analyses of content. But this leads to an even more provocative situation. That is, Camp has often been defined as a sensibility devoid of content. The mainstream gay politicos used that definition as the justification for silencing Blakk. In other words, what we heard was the familiar discreditation of Camp using the claim that it has no content. But this was a claim advanced through an analysis *of* the content that isn't supposed to exist.

When Joan decided her primary campaign strategy would be publicized and highly theatrical shopping sprees in the glamor fashion stores of Chicago's wealthy Gold Coast district, everyone recognized the actions as Camp. So the issue was not whether Camp was political, but whether it was appropriate or effective to politicize it. Since the 1980s, when ACT UP consciously and successfully brought Camp to bear on activist politics in its graphics, or now when Queer Nation bases its demonstrations on expressions of Camp executed through street theater, there has been the need to reevaluate gay and queer parody. What I will advance in this chapter is a reconceptualization of Camp prompted by its recent political applications.

Processing the notes

In 1964 Camp was propelled into public consciousness via Susan Sontag's now famous essay, "Notes on Camp." With its homosexual connotations downplayed, sanitized, and made safe for public consumption, Sontag's version of Camp was extolled, emulated, and elaborated upon in a flurry of writing on the subject that lasted until the end of the decade. Though the erasure of homosexuality from the subject of Camp encouraged the public's embrace, it also had a mutational consequence. Earlier versions of Camp were part of an unmistakable homosexual discourse bound together by a shared referent (the "Homosexual"-as-Type). By removing, or at least minimizing, the connotations of homosexuality, Sontag killed off the binding referent of Camp—the Homosexual—and the discourse began to unravel as Camp became confused and conflated with rhetorical and performative strategies such as irony, satire, burlesque, and travesty; and with cultural movements such as Pop.

The adoption, in the 1960s, of the term "Camp" to describe so many diverse strategies produced the impression that there were many different kinds of Camp. This unquestioning attitude toward the existence of multiple forms of Camp has provided writers with access to a successful evasive tactic. By conceptualizing Camp as simply a common nomination shared by unrelated cultural phenomena, writers have been spared the task of studying relationships among the total range of expressions that have been labeled as "Camp," or even of defining the object of study. Jonathan Dollimore, for example, writing on Camp in 1991, claims that "The definition of camp is as elusive as the sensibility itself, one reason being that there are different kinds of camp" (310). Dollimore then proceeds with a partial interpretation of Camp justified by the claim that there is simply a surplus of signification.[4] This has been a familiar tactic, one used to support vastly different, often contradictory, interpretations of Camp. While writers on Pop culture simply deny Camp as a homosexual discourse, finding such a construction contradictory to their arguments, gay writers seeking to reclaim the discourse of Camp through a restoration of its homosexual connotations fail to address issues of non-gay and Pop culture appropriation.[5] These partial interpretations of Camp derive their authority from Sontag's essay. After all, according to Sontag, Camp is a sensibility and "A sensibility (as distinct from an idea) is one of the hardest things to talk about" (106). She adds that sensibility or taste

> has no system and no proofs. . . . A sensibility is almost, but not quite, ineffable. Any sensibility which can be crammed into the mold of a system, or handled with the rough tools of proof, is no longer a sensibility at all. It has hardened into an idea.
>
> (106)

As long as thinkers, whether gay or non-gay, cling to this definition of Camp-as-sensibility, they are invulnerable to critique, forever protected by invoking Sontag's own critical exemption.

In a recent essay, Gregory Bredbeck (1993) has tried to dismantle Sontag's defense system by pointing out the evasive strategy employed by defining Camp as a sensibility: "a 'sensibility,' like that Regency term . . . is something understood perfectly until articulated. Sontag's essay demonstrates this slipperiness through its recourse to the most basic theoretical strategy derived from Aristotle, division and classification" (275). The promulgation of various kinds of Camp, argues Bredbeck, effects Camp's transformation into "the nominalists' *flatus vocus*, an empty universal term. It functions as all parts of speech, all parts of a sentence: verb, noun, adjective, adverb; subject, object, modifier" (276), able to become whatever one needs it to be for purposes of argument while simultaneously claiming exemption from criticism. Bredbeck suggests that "A more productive theorization might start by looking not at what the word means, but how it functions . . . [as a] sign" (275).

In order to produce a new reading of Camp, one that can account for its recent politicization, we need to jettison objectivist methodologies. Objectivism, as I am using it here, refers to an empiricist route to knowledge that "posits a real world which is independent of consciousness and theory, and which is accessible through sense-experience" (Lovell 1983: 10). This real world can be "discovered" by a knowing subject who is the "source of the sense data which validates knowledge" (Lovell 11). An objectivist methodology becomes extremely problematic in theories of social behavior where the human subjects of study are unavoidably transformed into "objects" of knowledge that are used to generate sense-experience for the observer. As a result, human actors are reduced to "thinglike" status as their own knowledge and experience become rendered as a structure of neutral surfaces readable only by the observer. As a mode for interpretation of queer cultural expressions, the one-way dynamic of objectivism most often results in the erasure of gay and lesbian subjects through an antidialogic turn that fails to acknowledge a possibly different ontology embodied in queer signifying practices. Instead, we need to develop a performance-centered methodology that takes into account and can accommodate the particular experience of the individual social actors under study, one which privileges process, the agency of knowledgeable performers, and the constructed nature of human realities. This approach provides a space for individual authority and experience that, regardless of different perceptions of sexual identity, envisions a power—albeit decentered—that is able to resist, oppose, and subvert. Working with a theory of agency and performance, I will attempt the sacrilegious: to produce a definition of Camp.

Such a definition should be stable enough to be of benefit to the reader, yet flexible enough to account for the many actions and objects that have come to be described by the term. Following Bredbeck's cue (that it would be more productive to approach the project through a study of the workings of the Camp sign), I will suggest a definition of Camp based upon the delineation of a praxis formed at the intersection of social agency and postmodern parody.

Broadly defined, Camp refers to strategies and tactics of queer parody. The definition of parody I use is that of Linda Hutcheon (1985). Her postmodern redefinition of parody differs sharply from conventional usages that conflate parody with irony or satire. Rather, as elaborated by Hutcheon, parody is an intertextual manipulation of multiple conventions, "an extended repetition with critical difference" (7) that "has a hermeneutic function with both cultural and even ideological implications" (2). Hutcheon explains that "Parody's overt turning to other art forms" (5), its derivative nature, and its dependence upon an already existing text in order to fulfill itself are the reason for its traditional denigration, a denigration articulated within a dominant discourse that finds value only in an "original." Hutcheon clears a space for a reconsideration of parody through its very contestation of ideas of Romantic singularity because it "forces a reassessment of the process of textual production" (5). At the same time, her redefinition provides the opportunity for a reassessment of Camp, when Camp is conceptualized as parody. Hutcheon's theory of parody is valuable for providing the terms needed to differentiate Camp from satire, irony, and travesty; and to terminate, finally, the conflation of Camp with kitsch and schlock, a confusion that entered the discourse as a result of the heterosexual/Pop colonization of Camp in the 1960s. When subjected to Hutcheon's postmodern redefinition, Camp emerges as specifically queer parody possessing cultural and ideological analytic potential, taking on new meanings with implications for the emergence of a theory that can provide an oppositional queer critique.

While Hutcheon's theory is capable of locating the address of a queer parodic praxis, it still needs to be queerly adjusted in order to plumb its potential for a Camp theory. By employing a performance-oriented methodology that privileges process, we can restore a knowledgeable *queer* social agent to the discourse of Camp parody. While dominant discursive formations of Camp maintain a social agent, that agent is implied, and thus taken for granted to be heterosexual. Camp theorizing has languished since the 1960s when Sontag's appropriation banished the queer from the discourse, substituting instead an un-queer bourgeois subject under the banner of Pop. It is this changeling that transformed Camp into the apolitical badge of the consumer whose *status-quo* "sensibility" is characterized by the depoliticizing Midas touch, and whose control over the apparatus of representation casts the cloak of invisibility over the queer at the moment it appropriates and utters the C-word. Yet, in order to reclaim Camp-as-critique, the critique silenced in the 1960s, which finds its voice solely when spoken by the queer, we cannot reverse the process of banishment by ejecting the un-queer from the discourse. That kind of power does not belong to the queer. All we can do, perhaps, is to produce intermittent queer visibility in our exile at the margins long enough to reveal a terminus at the end of a pathway of dominant power with the goal of foregrounding the radical politic of parodic intertextuality.

When parody is seen as process, not as form, then the relationship between texts becomes simply an indicator of the power relationships between social agents who wield those texts, one who possesses the "original," the other who possesses the parodic alternative. Anthony Giddens (1984) has argued that structures of signification can only be understood in relation to power and domination. In fact, he defines power and domination as the ability to produce codes of signification (31). Accordingly, value production is the prerogative of the dominant order, dominant precisely because it controls signification and which is represented by the privilege of nominating its own codes as the "original." The "original," then, is the signifier of dominant presence and, because dominance can be defined as such only by exercising control over signification, it is only through the "original" that we can know and touch that power. In that case, parody becomes the process whereby the marginalized and disenfranchised advance their own interests by entering alternative signifying codes into discourse by attaching them to existing structures of signification. Without the process of parody, the marginalized agent has no access to representation, the apparatus of which is controlled by the dominant order. Camp, as specifically queer parody, becomes, then, the only process by which the queer is able to enter representation and to produce social visibility.[6]

This piggy-backing upon the dominant order's monopoly on the authority of signification explains why Camp appears, on the one hand, to offer a transgressive vehicle yet, on the other, simultaneously invokes the specter of dominant ideology within its practice, appearing, in many instances, to actually reinforce the dominant order. Gregg Blachford (1981) has reminded us that

> the processes at work in the sub-culture are more complicated than might appear at first glance, for there is some evidence that the gay sub-culture negotiates an oppositional challenge to some aspects of the dominant order. The best way to understand this innovatory style is to examine one phenomenon of the gay subculture—camp—and to show how it transforms conformity into a challenge.
>
> (193–194)

My goal in the remainder of this chapter is to explore that Camp challenge, and to investigate precisely the relationship of Camp praxis to the dominant order.

The queer as historical waste

The queer's invisibility in representation and his/her dependence upon dominant structures of signification are not so much a negative condition to be overcome, but rather, the very strength to exploit. Michel Foucault (1980), in pointing out that power is not monolithic, but multidimensional, argues that

> there are no relations of power without resistances; the latter are all the more real and effective because they are formed right at the point where relations of power are exercised; resistance to power does not have to come from elsewhere to be real, nor is it inexorably frustrated through being the compatriot of power. It exists all the more by being in the same place as power.
>
> (142)

Working from this premise in order to advance a proposal of Camp-as-critique, I want to explore how this can be deployed to reread the literature on Camp and to explain the role of queer visibility production in subversive transformations of dominant culture.

Terry Lovell (1983) has pointed out that

> there are key areas of experience and practical activity which are suppressed, denied, and
> distorted within dominant ideology. While their suppression makes it difficult to give
> them a name, and to understand their significance, they are essential to knowledge
> production and to the critique of ideology.
>
> (50)

The invisible queer subject is an example of such a suppressed and denied area. This
suppression and denial are founded on the distortion and discreditation of the language
of that subject, the language that carries an oppositional critique and the means by which
the subject may be constituted. This discredited language is what I identify as Camp. Often
considered frivolous, aestheticized, and apolitical, the discourse of Camp can be reclaimed
through a rereading of the phenomenon as a signifying practice that not only processually
constitutes the subject, but is actually the vehicle for an already existent—though obscured—
cultural critique.

The first move in uncovering and revealing the queer is the removal of the objectivist bias
from interpretations of Camp. Sontag and her imitators are quick to define Camp as an
attribute of objects. Even when Camp is applied as a description to the actions of persons,
that person is described as *a* camp. This objectivist bias that reduces people to thinglike
status is used to label Camp as extreme aestheticization and therefore apolitical. The
arguments that defuse Camp, that deny it power as a cultural critique, are based, then, on a
denial of agency. Yet Sontag (1964) herself cannot entirely escape from the human activity
that forms the basis of Camp. After giving the reader a list of objects that are considered
"Camp," she reminds us that "the Camp eye has the power to transform experience" (107).
Therefore Camp cannot be said to reside in objects, but is clearly a way of reading, of writing,
and of doing that originates in the "Camp eye," the "eye" being nothing less than the agent
of Camp. By this I do not mean to deny the existence of the object of Camp. Instead, by
applying a performance paradigm to the study, the visible lines of a ghostlike queer agent
manifest themselves in a shift of focus away from the conventional fixation with the object
surface to the process with which the object is handled. When a concept of performance is
used to establish the existence of a knowledgeable social agent who signifies *through* Camp,
then the conventional interpretation of Camp—as a tool used to facilitate the bourgeois
appropriation characteristic of consumer culture—can be overturned.

Andrew Ross's extremely influential essay, "Uses of Camp" (1989), is a noteworthy example
of the dehumanizing results achieved by applying an objectivist methodology to the study of
Camp.[7] Ross brilliantly described the techniques and motives of appropriation that underlie
the formation of Pop camp. But when we cease to define queer Camp and Pop camp as two
different kinds of Camp, seeing instead two halves of a single phenomenon, then Ross's essay
is helpful in explaining the relationship of queer signifying practices to the dominant order.
Because objectivist methodologies overwhelm and obscure the processual signifying
practices through which the queer articulates the discourse of Camp, the queer is erased in
representation at the very moment that Camp is subjected to a dominant interpretation. Pop
camp emerges, then, as the product of a visually biased dominant reading of queer praxis
interpreted through the object residue that remains after the queer agent has been rendered
invisible. Consequently, the bourgeois subject of Pop camp must assume a queer position

in order to account for these dispossessed objects and becomes, in fact, queer himself. As I will explain, Pop camp becomes the unwitting vehicle of a subversive operation that introduces queer signifying codes into dominant discourse.

Ross defines the camp effect as created "when the products . . . of a much earlier mode of production, which has lost its power to dominate cultural meanings, become available in the present, for redefinition according to contemporary codes of taste" (139). Subjecting his definition to a theory of queer agency (entailing a focal shift away from the object) reveals a much different narrative. Remembering that Anthony Giddens has defined dominance as the power to control the construction of cultural meanings, then what Ross calls a "mode of production" is actually a mode of *discursive value* production, not *industrial object* production. Accordingly, what he calls "contemporary codes of taste" is nothing less than the dominant ideology that controls the establishment of signifying codes. When Camp is defined as a specifically queer discourse, it follows that what Ross calls the redefinition of meanings is the appropriation, through the application of unequal power, of queer discourse by the dominant order. This appropriation attempts to defuse the Camp critique by redefining the actions of the queer within the non-threatening context of compulsory reproductive heterosexuality which, because the representational apparatus cannot render a queer subject, constitutes, simply, its erasure. Because the queer has been, as Cynthia Morrill (1994) describes, "hurled out of representation" at the impacting moment of appropriation, all that remains is the object of Camp which now appears, illusorily, as a fossilized remnant. It is never suspected that the act of appropriation itself has killed off the queer. In order to account for the absence, the conclusion is that the previous owner of the object must long since have passed away. Without a voice to claim possession of the object, the social knowledge of the queer can be ignored because s/he has been relocated to the mists of the bygone past. The perceived threat to dominant ideology by the queer's sexual *non*-productivity is then silenced through benign renomination as a *discontinued* productivity. Located in the past, the queer has been assigned to the site of the grave, of death, of non-existence, of non-presence, and no longer needs to be taken into account.

Ross's unreflecting use of interpretive codes, by regarding them as simple acts of perception (the trademark of the visual bias of objectivism), masks and obscures the source of value production (Shapiro 1988: 5–30). Relocating the queer to a past era by defining him/her as a discontinued mode of production is not the neutral act of identification it is made out to be. Rather, it is a dominant performative gesture of incorporation meant to muzzle an opposing voice by substituting the act of appropriation itself as the referent of camp. Because the act of appropriation includes the erasure of the queer, dominant (read Pop) formations of camp translate this activity into a recognition that Camp *was once* a homosexual discourse, but now refers, more correctly, to the redistribution of objects plundered from the "dead" queer's estate. This technique has been called "the spatialization of time" by Johannes Fabian (1983: 25–35). Fabian explained how unequal contemporaneous power relationships between Self and Other become translated into temporal distance by conflating and then substituting the oppositional terms of "now/then" for the directional binary concept of "here/there" (27, 37–69). The "here" and "now" that signifies the praxis of everyday life is replaced by the "there" and "then" signification of the not really real, a substitution of terms that results in a denial of coevalness, or the state of "being-with" the Other (Berger and Luckmann 1966: 22). Situating the queer's signifying practices in the historical past creates the impression that the objects of Camp no longer have owners and are up for grabs. This metaphorical manipulation forms the basis for and justification of heterosexual/Pop colonization of queer discourse and praxis. Thus instead of the harmless reassignment of values to junk store items that Pop theorists have convinced themselves is "camp," the actual maneuver conceals a contemporaneous struggle over meanings and value production by competing discourses.

Importantly, Ross (1989) does identify a knowledgeable social agent in his formation of Camp. This un-queer agent has some remarkable traits. As he describes: "Camp . . . involves a celebration, on the part of cognoscenti, of the alienation, distance, and incongruity reflected in the very process by which unexpected value can be located in some obscure or exorbitant object" (146). Because the queer is rendered invisible at the moment when values are reassigned in the act of appropriation, it looks as if the objects of Camp have suddenly materialized from nowhere (which is precisely where the queer lives), appearing miraculously as an act of discovery. As if receiving manna in the wilderness, the act of appropriation is perceived as mysterious intervention, a sign of manifest destiny that reinforces the moral authority of the dominant order. Having received the divine dispensation, the bourgeois subject of camp *celebrates* the invisibility of the queer, rejoices in the act of appropriation, and, in effect, derives *pleasure* from the erasure of the queer. Ross indicates that the pleasure derived from the act of appropriation stems from the altogether accidental and "unexpected" quality of the exchange, as if to claim a protected space of moral innocence in the silencing of the queer.

However, the celebratory lynching of the queer cannot take place without knowledge. One does not become a "cognoscente" through celebrating random and "unexpected value." On the contrary, the connoisseur is, by definition, an expert in *establishing* value, not *discovering* it. The cognoscente is an authority not to be questioned. His is the voice that nominates "the original," who manifests the presence of the dominant order, controls the apparatus of representation by speaking a signifying code into existence, and plays the role of ideological logos (Price 1989: 7–22). But then you cannot lynch the "dead," and the appropriation is, of course, benign. Nobody is being hurt. Thus the act of queer erasure becomes a valorized salvage effort on the part of the cognoscente appropriator whom Ross then describes as a "camp liberator," who rediscovers "history's waste [read 'the queer']," a kind of nineteenth-century archaeologist who, by "liberating the objects and discourses of the past from disdain and neglect [read 'by appropriating queer signifying practices']," enfuses himself with "glamor [read 'queer aura']" (ibid.: 151). The whole operation becomes a bizarre love affair with the dead queer who, safely contained within the coffin of a distancing metaphorical historicization, can now be loved and cherished as the source of dominant cultural renewal. The act of appropriation is, after all, a source of pleasure, and Ross describes the activity as a "necrophilic economy that underpins the camp sensibility" (ibid.: 152).

But curiously, Ross goes on to say that

> If the pleasure generated by [camp's] bad taste presents a challenge to the mechanisms of control and containment that operate in the name of good taste, it is often to be enjoyed *only* at the expense of others, and this is largely because camp's excess of pleasure has very little, finally, to do with the (un)controlled hedonism of the consumer; it is the result of the (hard) *work* of a producer of taste, and "taste" is only possible through exclusion *and* depreciation.

(ibid.: 153)

This is a confusing statement. On the one hand, he locates the pleasure of Camp in an act of challenge to the dominant order yet, on the other, this challenge is the result of the hard labor on the part of the producer of taste, the cognoscente, who operates through exclusion. But it is the cognoscente who represents, reinforces, and speaks from the site of power. The production of taste is not a challenge to the dominant order, it *is* the dominant order. Ross's glamorous producer of taste has somehow become both challenger *and* challenged. Without queer visibility, Ross's bourgeois "camp liberator" has not only assumed the role of dominance, but has also assumed the queer subject position which, through the act of appropriation, appears now as vacant property that can be restored to circulation within the economy of properly authorized signification. Ross is correct. This is hard work. And it does operate by exclusion. The bourgeois camp cognoscente "liberates" the queer's oppositional signifying practices from their queer identity and substitutes himself as signified. But because the queer constitutes him-/herself processually, the un-queer is now unwittingly performing the queer. The final-effect is the reproduction of the queer's aura by the un-queer camp liberator who has been transformed into a drag queen with no other choice but to lipsynch the discourse of the Other. While Ross's camp cognoscente has successfully appropriated the signifying surface, the lyrics were still written by the queer who has now entered repre-sentation by producing his/her visibility on the back of the un-queer bourgeois subject. It may be the bourgeois subject who sings the aria but, like the terrifying phantom of the opera, it is the queer who taught her how, and who still plays the "organ" accompaniment behind the wall of enforced invisibility in the sewer system of "history's waste."

By providing a detailed description of the actions and motives of the un-queer appro-priator, Ross has located a position to which the queer agent can read him-/herself back into the discourse by establishing a dialogic relationship. This can be achieved by identifying the social knowledge displayed by Camp agency. As Ross describes: "Pop experience already contains the knowledge that it will soon be outdated, spent, obsolescent, or out of fashion" (151). In other words, the power of Camp lies in its ability to be conscious of its future as an appropriated commodity. Possession of social knowledge is not dependent on access to the apparatus of representation. It is the arrogance of the dominant, derived from ownership of the apparatus of representation, that creates a belief in a monologic construction of social knowledge. When we recognize that the queer is not dead, only rendered invisible by a historicizing metaphor, then we can grant the queer agent the same knowledge as the un-queer appropriator. Operating from under the cloak of invisibility, the queer knows his/her signifying practices will be, *must* be appropriated. As a product of queer agency, it is the process of Camp that selects and chooses which aspects of itself will be subsumed into dominant culture. Queer knowledge can then be introduced and incorporated into the dominant ideology because the blind spot of bourgeois culture is predictable: it *always* appropriates. And it appropriates whatever the agent of Camp chooses to place in its path. The invisible queer is at a certain advantage, because whatever is offered to the un-queer will be unquestioningly received as their own invention, taken as a confirmative sign of their right to possess. Like the little cakes that miraculously appeared to Alice in Lewis Carroll's Wonderland epic, it never occurs to the appropriator to ask who was it that wrote the little tag that says, "Eat Me." And like Alice, the appropriator's body uncontrollably changes its shape at the whim of those unseen hands that place irresistible morsels of discovery before it. By inverting the process of appropriation, Camp can be read as a critique of ideology through a parody that is always already appropriated.

[. . .]

Notes

I wish to thank Terry Kapsalis, Northwestern University, for her many comments on and criticisms of this chapter.

1 [Writers] alternatively use the terms "queer," "gay," "lesbian," or "homosexual" depending on historical and cultural context, or to achieve particular effects and focus within an individual essay. Some of the examples of Camp discussed are problematic as regards the selection of appropriate labels. For instance, Liberace who, according to the working definition given in this chapter, might be considered a quintessential queer because of the performative constitution of his identity, has been described both as "homosexual" and more often as "gay" because of the social contexts in which he worked.

2 In order to distinguish between different constructions of Camp, the following usage has been adopted. When Camp is conceptualized as a politicized, solely queer discourse, an upper-case "C" is used. When an un-queer, apolitical, or Pop culture version of Camp is referred to, a lower-case "c" is used. The only exception to this occurs in cited material where it was mandatory to follow the spelling of the original text. For example, Susan Sontag, in "Notes on Camp," used an upper-case "C." But according to the rule of usage employed in this volume, Sontag's version of Camp, because it is an apolitical formation, would be spelt as "camp."

3 My rethinking of Camp was based on observations of Joan Jett Blakk's Chicago mayoral campaign in 1991, before Joan announced her candidacy for the United States presidential election in 1992. My interpretations of the two campaigns are different. Comments about the mayoral campaign do not necessarily reflect my thinking on the presidential campaign.

4 I have cited Jonathan Dollimore in this regard because he is exemplary of the most contemporary writing on Camp.

5 Writers ignore issues of appropriation in different ways. George Melly (1970) recognizes the gay origins of Camp, but fails to question just how Pop culture was able to wrest the discourse from this context (161). Andrew Ross's conspicuous erasure of gay identity in his essay, "Uses of Camp," constitutes an active depoliticization of Camp that leads to an articulated denial of Camp as a gay critique (1989: 137, 142–144, 162–163). Richard Dyer (1981), on the other hand, identifies Camp as a gay discourse, but then proceeds to define the performances of non-gay stars as "Camp." Dyer offers a detailed analysis of Judy Garland as Camp (178ff.), but without addressing the problem of her non-gay sexual identity, and without a political analysis of the relationship between gay discourse and non-gay producers of Camp.

6 It is not my goal, here, to explain the invisibility of the queer in representation. This has been done admirably in two other essays, Sue-Ellen Case's "Tracking the Vampire" (1991) and Cynthia Morrill's "Revamping the Gay Sensibility" (1994).

7 I use Andrew Ross's essay (1989) as the basis for a critique of Pop appropriation of Camp precisely because it has had such a major impact upon Camp theorizing. After Sontag's "Notes," Ross's "Uses of Camp," in my opinion, stands as one of the most significant contemporary documents on the subject. In the current trend to reread Sontag, Ross's essay has been overlooked. Yet, if we are to recover the discourse of Camp from the Sontagian formulation, Ross's essay, grounded as it is on that earlier work, must be included in the ongoing critique of "Notes."

150 MOE MEYER

Bibliography

Berger, Peter L. and Thomas Luckmann. 1966. *The Social Construction of Reality: A Treatise in the Sociology of Knowledge*. New York: Doubleday.

Blachford, Gregg. 1981. "Male Dominance and the Gay World." In Kenneth Plummer (ed.), *The Making of the Modern Homosexual*. London: Hutchinson, 184–210.

Bredbeck, Gregory W. 1993. "B/O—Barthes's Text/O'Hara's Trick: The Phallus, the Anus, and the Text." PMLA. 108/2 (March): 268–282.

Butler, Judith. 1990. "Performative Acts and Gender Constitution: An Essay in Phenomenology and Feminist Theory." In Sue-Ellen Case (ed.), *Performing Feminisms: Feminist Critical Theory and Theatre*. Baltimore: Johns Hopkins University Press, 270–282.

Case, Sue-Ellen. 1991. "Tracking the Vampire." *differences* 3/2 (Summer, 1991): 1–20.

de Lauretis, Teresa. 1991. "Queer Theory: Lesbian and Gay Sexualities/An Introduction." *differences* 3/2 (Summer, 1991): iii–xvii.

Dollimore, Jonathan. 1991. *Sexual Dissidence: Augustine to Wilde, Freud to Foucault*. Oxford: Clarendon Press.

Dyer, Richard. 1981. "Getting Over the Rainbow: Identity and Pleasure in Gay Cultural Politics." In George Bridges and Rosalind Brunt (eds), *Silver Linings: Some Strategies for the Eighties*. London: Lawrence and Wishart, 53–67.

Fabian, Johannes. 1983. *Time and the Other: How Anthropology Makes Its Object*. New York: Columbia University Press.

Foucault, Michel. 1980. "Power and Strategies." *Power/Knowledge: Selected Interviews and Other Writings, 1972–1977*. Ed. Colin Gordon. New York: Pantheon, 134–145.

Giddens, Anthony. 1984. *The Constitution of Society: Outline of the Theory of Structuration*. Berkeley: University of California Press.

Hutcheon, Linda. 1985. *A Theory of Parody: The Teachings of Twentieth-Century Art Forms*. New York: Methuen.

Lovell, Terry. 1983. *Pictures of Reality: Aesthetics, Politics and Pleasure*. London: British Film Institute.

Melly, George. 1970. *Revolt into Style: The Pop Arts in Britain*. London: Allen Lane.

Morrill, Cynthia. 1994. "Revamping the Gay Sensibility: Queer Camp and Dyke Noir." In Moe Meyer (ed.), *The Politics and Poetics of Camp*. New York: Routledge, 110–129.

Price, Sally. 1989. *Primitive Art in Civilized Places*. Chicago: University of Chicago Press.

Ross, Andrew. 1989. "Uses of Camp." *No Respect: Intellectuals and Popular Culture*. London: Routledge, 135–170.

Shapiro, Michael J. 1988. *The Politics of Representation: Writing Practices in Biography, Photography, and Policy Analysis*. Madison: University of Wisconsin Press.

Sontag, Susan. 1964. "Notes on Camp." 1983. *A Susan Sontag Reader*. New York: Vintage Books, 105–119.

Watney, Simon. 1991. "Troubleshooters: Simon Watney on Outing." *Artforum* 30/3: 16–18.

PART FOUR

RECEPTION

Introduction

As Part Three explored, camp is a form of queer reception practice as well as a mode of textual production. Part Four expands upon Part Three, offering some specific case studies in which camp and other queer sensibilities have shaped the reception of media texts, and how and why some media texts have shaped queer sensibilities. It also offers examples of ways in which distribution and exhibition have been and can be queered, how media fan practice has been instrumental in influencing the production and meanings of mainstream texts, and how one might begin to rethink gaze theory itself as being queer. To a certain extent, Part Four encompasses issues explored throughout this volume, finding multiple queer reception practices located at the intersection of queer authorship, queer forms and genres, and camp.

The first three essays collected here are each localized and historicized reception studies that explore the dynamics of queer spectatorship. The first, an excerpt from Richard Dyer's "Judy Garland and Gay Men," uses letters and personal reminiscences to explore how and why Garland was such an important icon to gay men of the 1950s and 1960s. Dyer argues that Garland's drive and sense of "passion-with-irony" are two of the many things that made her resonate with pre-Stonewall gay culture. (It would be interesting to compare Garland's gay appeal with contemporary queers' adulation of Cher or Madonna: just what has changed in three decades and what has remained constant?) Janet Staiger's "Finding Community in the Early 1960s: Underground Cinema and Sexual Politics" explores the queer film work of Jack Smith, Kenneth Anger, Andy Warhol, *et al.*, but also demonstrates how the very act of exhibiting those films was an act of queer community building in an era that had yet to imagine campus groups, professional organizations, or political action committees. Finally, Henry Jenkins's study of science fiction fans demonstrates how and why queer spectators have been historically drawn to the genre, and how they have influenced the production and reception of *Star Trek*.

This section ends with an essay that queers some of the basic tenets of film theory—specifically those of "gaze theory" as they were originally conceived by Laura Mulvey in her groundbreaking essay "Visual Pleasure and Narrative Cinema" (1975, *Screen* 16:3, 6–18). In it, Mulvey argued that classical cinema invariably constructs a "male gaze"—that the gazes of the camera, diegetic characters, and actual spectators all collude to objectify women as erotic spectacles and create a male subject position for those in the audience, regardless of their actual sex. In the following excerpt from Caroline Evans and Lorraine Gamman's "Reviewing Queer Viewing," the authors survey work that complicates Mulvey's basic premises, and offer their own take on what might be called a "queer gaze." What happens when lesbian and gay spectators are asked to view women according to Mulvey's paradigm? What happens when the male body is put on erotic display? While arguing that some representations do invite more queer reception than others, the authors draw upon the concept of "genderfuck"—the deliberate play with incongruous and confusing gender attributes—to argue for a model of the gaze that is itself queer: anti-essentialist, fluid, multiple, and historically constructed.

11

Judy Garland and Gay Men

RICHARD DYER

He once told me about picking up a bloke who said you could always tell a 'queer's' place because they've all got LPs of Judy Garland.

Kenneth Williams, speaking of Joe Orton

The white kids had the counter-culture, rock stars and mysticism. The blacks had a slogan which said they were beautiful, and a party demanding power. Middle America had what it always had: Middle America. The hawks had Vietnam, and the doves the Peace Movement. The students had campus politics, and the New Left had Cuba and the Third World. And women had a voice. I had rejection from all of them. I also had Judy Garland.

Drag Queen in *As Time Goes By*

In the June 1973 issue of the Birmingham Gay Liberation Front newsletter, there was an article about Judy Garland. It was called "Born in a Trunk" and was printed on pink paper. It made no reference to gayness whatsoever. The author did not feel that there was any need to explain why there should be a straightforward fan's account of Garland's life in the publication of a militant gay political group. Nor did the editorial collective, of which I was a member (though I neither wrote nor suggested the article). We had a policy of printing anything anybody in GLF submitted provided that it was not sexist, racist, or fascist. The Garland piece was none of these, and we were as immersed in gay male culture as the author so that printing a piece on Garland seemed like the most natural thing in the world. When we distributed it, however, a number of people, gay and straight, asked us what on earth the piece was doing in the newsletter. A few were objecting on the grounds that Garland belonged to the unliberated days of gay existence before GLF, but the rest were mystified. Why was Garland in a gay magazine? And when they knew the answer—because so many gay men (especially) are into her—the next question was a bemused "why?" This chapter is an attempt to answer that question.

There will not, of course, be one answer, but a variety of ways in which a star's image can be read if it is to attain star-sized currency and appeal. Hence Monroe can be read within different discourses on sexuality and similarly in those other than sexuality. Robeson too had to appeal across white and black audiences, and with far greater differentiation within them than I have described. Similarly, not only did Garland have the requisite massive appeal to non-gay audiences, but various aspects of her image spoke to different elements within male gay subcultures. In this chapter I want to explore how specific aspects of Garland's image could make a particular set of senses for gay men.

What I am describing is specific, both in terms of the subculture referred to and in terms of period. The subculture is particular first of all by being male. Historically lesbian and gay male subcultures have been linked, though often only tangentially; equally, lesbian subcultures have used Hollywood stars as important figures in their discourse (see Meyers 1976; Sheldon 1977; Whitaker 1981; Gramann and Schlüpmann 1981; Weiss 1992; Whatling 1997; White 1999). However, lesbian and gay male cultures are not one, and I have no sense of Judy Garland being an especially significant figure in the lesbian subcultures. Greta Garbo and Marlene Dietrich, on the other hand, have been important for both subcultures, and it would be instructive to draw out the links between their images and the aristocratic dyke culture associated with Radclyffe Hall, Romaine Brooks, Lady Troubridge, Gertrude Stein, and others (see Ruehl 1982 and Dyer 1983). Though this dyke style would be an important reference point for the gay male readings of Garbo and Dietrich, they would still need to be distinguished from lesbian readings.

The relevant male gay culture is further particularized by being urban (indeed usually metropolitan) and white. This does not mean that small-town, provincial, and non-white gay men could not share it, but that it was produced in the developing urban gay male ghettoes (New York, London, San Francisco, Amsterdam, Sydney etc.) and fostered in forms (drag shows, bars) and publications largely controled by whites. Urban white gay men set the pace for this culture, and in the period under consideration largely defined it as gay male culture itself.

The period under consideration occurs after 1950. It was in that year that Judy Garland was sacked by MGM and tried (rather more desultorily than the press allowed) to commit suicide. This event, because it constituted for the public a sudden break with Garland's uncomplicated and ordinary MGM image, made possible a reading of Garland as having a special relationship to suffering, ordinariness, normality, and it is this relationship that structures much of the gay reading of Garland. In part this reading focuses on her subsequent career—the development of her concert appearances beginning at the London Palladium in 1951; her vehicle films, A Star is Born (1954) and I Could Go On Singing (1962), as well as starring in A Child Is Waiting (1962) and having a showy cameo in Judgement at Nuremberg (1961); a series of albums for Capitol records between 1955 and 1965, notably Miss Show Business, Alone, The Letter, Judy in Love and the double album Judy at Carnegie Hall (a recording of her 1961 concert that was the first double album to sell over a million copies); television shows, including two successful specials (The Ford Star Jubilee 1955, The Judy Garland Show 1963) and a less successful series for CBS in 1963; as well as interviews, radio shows, TV chat show appearances and much press coverage, chiefly of the vicissitudes of her life (suicide attempts, divorces, hospitalizations, and the like).

The post-1950 reading was also a reading of her career before 1950, a reading back into the earlier films, recordings, and biography in the light of later years. This was facilitated by the growth of television and, in large cities, of repertory cinemas specializing in nostalgia revivals, both making Garland's films constantly available for reviewing. In addition, much of her post-1950 career deliberately evokes and reworks the early career. Both A Star is Born and I *Could Go On Singing* are clearly based on Garland's life story, and "Born in a Trunk" in the former is like a knowing précis of the image MGM had fostered (cf. Jennings 1979). Equally her concerts were built around her film career, introducing only a limited amount of new material. Medleys of past hits were introduced with verses such as "The story of my life is in my songs." As Christopher Finch (1975: 186) puts it, her concerts were

> a novel kind of Broadway musical, the words and music by various writers and composers, the book by Judy Garland, with the formidable assistance of the entire Hollywood press corps. To the audience, the book was Judy Garland's life story.

Equally important, during this period Garland spoke increasingly about her life before 1950 (notably in an article in *McCall's* in 1952), thus providing still more opportunity of reading those films and images through later knowledge and understandings.

Because of the availability of the earlier work and its importance as a reference point in the later films, concerts, records, and press coverage, the whole of Garland's career is relevant to this chapter, but it is read through the way she was taken up by the gay male subculture after 1950. The fact of the importance of Garland to this subculture was always widely noted. Most of the obituaries mention it, and it was particularly noticeable, for straight observers especially, at the concerts. Al Di Orio Jr (1975: 133–4) quotes from the *Los Angeles Citizen News* review of her 1961 Hollywood Bowl concert:

> They were all there, the guys and dolls and the 'sixth man', sitting in the drizzle which continued throughout the concert . . . After 'Over the Rainbow' the standing, water-soaked audience applauded until Judy came back and sang three more songs. The guys and gals and 'sixth man' wanted more.

"The sixth man" is a reference to Kinsey's findings on the incidence of homosexuality in the American male, a statistic familiar enough to provide the title for a sympathetic exposé of homosexuality by Jess Stearn in 1962. Non-gay observers are often more venomous than the rather neutral *Los Angeles Citizen News* reporter. William Goldman's (1969: 3–4) description of the last night of Garland's 1967 Palace season displays his obvious straightness. A beautiful gay man is a shock to him. He quotes without comment a straight man's reference to Auschwitz, as if the Nazi extermination of gays is of no account, and he includes the same man's gag, presumably for the reader to laugh at; all this laced with the usual vocabulary of homophobia, "boy," "flit," "chatter," "oooh," "flutter," "fags":

> as the lobby filled up entirely, the audience itself began to become insistently noticeable. A stunning blonde walked by, in a lovely green jacket, sexy and confident, undulating with every step, and it comes as a genuine shock to realize the blonde is a boy. Two other boys flit by, chattering. First: 'I got her pink roses and white carnations; you think she'll like it?' Second (angry): 'Now why didn't I bring her flowers? Oooh, it's just too late for me now.' Another flutter of fags, half a dozen this time, and watching it all from a corner, two heterosexual married couples. 'These fags,' the first man says. 'It's like Auschwitz—some of them died along the way but a lot got here anyhow.' He turns to the other husband and shrugs. 'Tonight, no one goes to the bathroom.'

I do not intend to go any further into these straight accounts of gay men and Judy Garland. I mention them here partly to indicate how widely observed the gay–Garland connection was and partly to register the extent to which this was felt as in some way offensive or threatening, an index of the degree to which gay men's use of Garland's image constituted a kind of going public or coming out before the emergence of gay liberationist politics (in which coming out was a key confrontationist tactic). This in fact is how going to a Garland concert in Nottingham in 1960 is remembered by one gay man:

> I shall never forget walking into the Montfort Hall. Our seats were very near the front and we had to walk all the way down the centre gangway of a hall already crowded. I should think every queen in the east Midlands catchment area had made it . . . everyone had put on their Sunday best, had hair cuts and bought new ties. There was an exuberance, a liveliness, a community of feeling which was quite new to me and probably quite rare anyway then. It was as if the fact that we had gathered to see Garland gave us permission to be gay in public for once.
>
> (Letter to author)

I'm going to begin by looking at what gay men have written about Judy Garland and then move on to consider her image in relation to general aspects of the gay male subculture. There will be some overlap—the gay writings stress Garland's emotionality and its relation to the situation of gay men, and I'll relate this to aspects of her image and performance; equally when discussing those aspects of her image that suggest a connection with gay culture—ordinariness, androgyny, camp—I'll refer where possible to other gay writers' observations on these aspects. The difference in the two sections is of degree—the first is concerned with what is characteristically and explicitly referred to in gay writings, the second to what is more evident by putting her image side by side with characteristic features of gay culture in general.

By gay writings I'm referring equally to articles in gay publications and to responses I received to letters I placed in gay newspapers and magazines.[1] In terms of content there is no significant difference between these two kinds of writing. What does need to be pointed out is that all were written after Garland's death and the emergence of the modern gay movement. Many have memories of the earlier period, but are often articulated in terms that may well have been clearer later—for instance, I do not doubt the memory of the writer, quoted above, who speaks of Garland's Nottingham concert giving "us permission to be gay in public for once," but equally to articulate things in terms of the importance of being "gay in public" is very gay liberationist in emphasis. The writings are all informed by an awareness of gay politics, though there is an interesting shift between some of the earlier writings and some of the later. This is signaled by a change in the pronoun used to refer to gay people, from "they" to "us." This goes along with a changed emphasis from Garland representing gay men's neurosis and hysteria to her representing gay men's resilience in the face of oppression. Thus Roger Woodcock (1969: 17), in the first issue of *Jeremy* (a very softly pornographic and, initially, an ostensibly bisexual publication, which appeared just before the development of the gay liberation movement in Britain), wrote:

> Every time she sang, she poured out her troubles. Life had beaten her up and it showed. That is what attracted homosexuals to her. She created hysteria for them.

Barry Conley (1972: 11), writing in an early *Gay News* (which had been started under the impetus of the British gay liberation movement), puts a more positive emphasis ("fighting back") but still refers to "they" and makes a comparison with straight people to the detriment of gay:

> She began to gather a large following of homosexuals at her concerts, who were eager to applaud each and every thing she did . . . Perhaps the majority of those audiences saw in Judy a loser who was fighting back at life, and they could themselves draw a parallel to this . . . One should also remember that she still managed to retain all her 'straight' admirers over the years, though of course these people were less exhibitionistic in their reactions to her concerts.

Nine years later, Dumont Howard (1981: 95) in *Blueboy* (a gay male equivalent of both *Playboy* and *Cosmopolitan*, with that odd mixture of civil rights editorializing and consumer/hedonist copy, plus sexy pictures) took issue with the reading of gay men's enthusiasm for Garland as "hysterical" and "exhibitionistic," at the same time himself owning the positive feelings he was describing by the use of the pronoun "we":

> Garland is often painted as a pathetic figure and her fans—particularly her gay fans—as devotees of disaster . . . Now that we, as gay people, are learning more about ourselves as a group and a culture, we can begin to understand the true attraction of Judy Garland: it is her indomitable spirit, not her self-destructive tendencies, that appeals to gay audiences.

Similarly, in the Gay Sweatshop production *As Time Goes By* (a play concerned with the recovery of the radical moments in gay history of the past century), in the final section (a series of interweaving monologues in a New York gay bar in June 1969),[2] the drag queen, hauntingly played in the original production by Drew Griffiths, says:

> They say we loved her because she mirrored the anguish and loneliness of our own lives. Crap. My parents were straight . . . They were the most anguished and lonely people I ever knew. No. We do not have a monopoly in the anguish and loneliness department. I loved her because no matter how they put her down, she survived. When they said she couldn't sing; when they said she was drunk; when they said she was drugged; when they said she couldn't keep a man . . . When they said she was fat; when they said she was thin; when they said she'd fallen flat on her face. People are falling on their faces every day. She got up.
>
> (Greig and Griffiths 1981: 62)

The interpretation in the early writings of what gays saw in Garland is similar to many of the unpleasantly homophobic observations of critics, particularly in the obituaries. One might say that Woodcock and Conley are victims of a kind of self-oppressive "false consciousness," internalizing straight interpretations of the gay response to Garland. Maybe, but it would be wrong to assume that only the more "positive" readings accurately express the range of ways gay men might take the Garland image. Woodcock and Conley condense several levels of self-oppression which may in fact characterize one way of reading Garland. They are gay fans of Garland who distance themselves from any gay identification ("they," "homosexuals") by putting down gay responses to Garland. At the same time, they can only read Garland in a gay way that is negative ("hysteria," "exhibitionistic")—they are recognizing a quality of emotional intensity that is in fact what the other gay writers also emphasize but they give it a denigratory label. Later readings want to disown all this, quite properly perhaps—but Garland could also be used in this subcultural discourse, more queer than gay, that spoke of the homosexual identity in self-oppressive modes characteristic of oppressed groups—distancing, denying, denigrating. Aspects of Garland's career and performance could be seen as pathetic and God-awful, and gay men could as it were misrecognize themselves in that and hasten, as Woodcock and Conley do, to disown it. I mention this here because they are the only writers to speak of Garland like this, but are also those writing from their most immediate memories of her. In sharing the predominantly positive understandings of what gay men saw in Garland of the other writings, I don't want to discount altogether this negative reading which the gay liberationist context of the later writing may have filtered out.

There is one source of references to Garland written before 1969, but it is difficult to handle. The British film monthly *Films and Filming*, which began in October 1954, quickly established itself as a closet gay magazine. It consistently published pin-ups of half-clothed male stars and starlets, advertised the kind of fashionable/sexy clothes shops patronized by gay men, and ran a lively small ads column that by the sixties had become quite explicit in its correspondence section ("Gay young man wishes to meet another, varied interests including physiques," November, 1964: 31). In *Films and Filming* the gay–Garland connection is clear, if never explicitly referred to. Ads for the Garland fan club appeared every month (and this was not so for any other star) amid ads for physique films and "discreet bachelor apartments." One small ad made the connection as directly as was possible:

> Young man leaving London for Durham in early October seeks similar (age 21–23) living in that area—view to writing initially, meeting soon. Interests: films, music (serious), Judy Garland, photography, driving (own car). Photograph welcomed. Box 856F.
>
> (*Films and Filming*, July 1964)

There was a picture of Garland (on the set of *A Star is Born*) in the first issue and she was on the cover of the third (December 1954), a still of "The Man that Got Away" from *A Star is Born*. Inside there is a long celebratory article by the magazine's editor, Peter Brinson, which, while it does not make any reference to her gay following (which can anyway only have been embryonic then), does write of her positive qualities. I'll refer later to this article; I've brought it in here because it is the one piece of rather fragile evidence from the pre-gay movement period about how gays made sense of Judy Garland, and it is a positive one. Just as I don't want the post-gay liberation readings to drown out the negative self-oppressive readings, so equally I don't want to give the impression that the more positive readings were only possible after the gay movement had started. On the contrary, the only evidence we have suggests the positive reading was always predominant.

The common emphasis in all gay writings on Garland is on her emotional quality. As Dumont Howard (1981: 95) puts it:

> The essence of Judy Garland's art is emotion. She burns right through lyrics, delivering, instead, their pure emotional substance.

Many of the accounts do not refer to the gayness of the emotionality, but rather suggest the immediate, vivid, intense experience of it. This is worth stressing because however much one can see that Garland is appreciated in ways specifically relating to gay culture, she is not necessarily experienced like that. As with any star, the fan's enthusiasm is based on feeling that the star just is wonderful. Thus some of the people who replied to my letter in the gay press said that as gay men they liked Garland because she had, for instance, "star quality" or "great talent and warmth," terms that might be used by an enthusiast for any star. The intensity and excitement of our experience of them outstrips our consciousness of what they stand for.

The kind of emotion Garland expressed is somewhat differently described in the gay writings, but on two points all agree—that it is always strong emotion, and that it is really felt by the star herself and shared with the audience.

> In every song I've heard it gives you something of her as a person, all the tragedy and happiness of her life is echoed in every word she sings.
>
> (Letter to author)

> All the emotions felt inside worn on the outside. The voice a clarion call of power, joy, love, sharing it all with us.
>
> (Letter to author)

Although these are qualities that might be attributed to many stars, it is the particular register of intense, authentic feeling that is important here, a combination of strength and suffering, and precisely the one in the face of the other. Different writers put different stresses on just how the two elements are combined. Some see the strength all but denying the imputed suffering:

> Judy . . . the power, the strength, the defiance of all the washed-up-has-been talk.
>
> (Letter to author)

Peter Brinson's (1954: 4) article in the third issue of *Films and Filming* details MGM's exploitation of her and other personal setbacks, but the keynote is the celebration of her strength:

> One kind of courage I admire is that which keeps going, come what may. Judy Garland is an example.

Others emphasize her openness to suffering, her ability to convey the experience of it:

> gay people could relate to her in the problems she had on and off stage.
>
> (Letter to author)

> it was precisely the quality that was the cause of all the pain that was also appealing to her audience. When she sang she was vulnerable. There was a hurt in her voice that most other singers don't have.
>
> (Bronski 1978: 202)

The least attractive expression of this emphasis, with ugly photos as accompaniment, is Kenneth Anger's (1981: 413–16) reference to Garland in *Hollywood Babylon*, written after her death and even here recognizing the strength while dwelling on the point at which it gave out:

> MGM's Amphetamine Annie really made it at last after so many attempts—pills, wrist slashings years before in her Hollywood bathroom, hack hack with broken glass . . . She was *hundreds* of years old, if you count emotional years, the toll they take, dramas galore for a dozen lifetimes. She was 'She' who had stepped into the Flame once too often.

Wherever the emphasis comes it is always the one in relation to the other, the strength inspirational because of the pressure of suffering behind it, the suffering keen because it has been stood up to so bravely.

Films and Filming's article is headed "The Great Come-Back" and the come-back was the defining motif of the register of feeling I'm trying to characterize, for it is always having come back from something (sufferings and tribulations) and always keeping on coming, no matter what. Repeatedly in the news from 1950 onwards for this or that reason (suicide attempts, failed marriages, drunk and disorderly charges, and so on), Garland repeatedly came back (Oscar nomination for *A Star is Born*, most successful ever double album *Judy at Carnegie Hall*, sell-out at all concerts and cabaret performances). The very act of coming back set off the feeling and it was reprised in countless details.

Both *A Star is Born* and *I Could Go On Singing* end with the Garland character coming back from personal despair (widowhood and rejection by her child, respectively) to a public performance. The latter has her sing at this come-back performance the come-back song that is the title of the film. The opening number of the 1961 concert (and record) is "When You're Smiling," itself a "keep on keeping on" song, with a bridge passage tailor-made for her image. It begins with rueful references to the kinds of problems one should smile in the face of, problems very close to those of Garland herself (marriage, weight, drugs):

> If you suddenly find out you've been deceived
> Don't get peeved
> If your husband bluntly tells you you're too stout
> Don't you pout
> And for heaven's sakes retain a calm demeanour
> When a cop walks up and hands you a subpoena
> If the groom should take a powder while you're marching down the aisle
> Don't weep and moan
> Because he's flown
> Just face the world and smile.

Then as she leads back into the melody, she could be making two references quite specific to herself:

> 'Cos when you're crying don't you know that your make-up starts to run
> And your eyes get red and scrappy?
> Forget your troubles, have yourself a little fun,
> Have a ball

Forget 'em all
Forget your troubles, c'mon, get happy
Keep on smiling
'Cos when you're smiling
The whole world smiles with you.

First, she sings about make-up. In part this is singing about her immediate situation, made up for a performance that was also a come-back. The song itself is a vaudeville standard, associated with Al Jolson, the epitome of the showbiz ethos, with whom Garland, dubbed in the fifties "Miss Show Business," was often compared. It evokes a whole showbiz litany of tears-beneath-the-greasepaint, the show-must-go-on, that gives a resonance of tradition to Garland's coming back. But in addition one of the most frequently repeated stories about Garland was how she used the act of preparing herself for public appearances as an answer to problems. For example, Roger Woodcock (1969: 16) in *Jeremy* writes:

> She knew they said she drank too much and took too many pills and it upset her. 'What do you do when people talk about you like that?' she asks, 'commit suicide? No, that's messy. Get drunk? No, that's no solution.' What Judy did in fact was to put on her lipstick, make sure her stockings were straight, then she marched onto a stage somewhere and sang her heart out.

The make-up reference in "When You're Smiling" suggests the moment of pulling herself together by putting on her make-up.

Second, she interpolates a phrase from another smile-through-your-tears song, "Get Happy"—"Forget your troubles, c'mon, get happy." This was the final number in *Summer Stock* 1950, her last MGM picture. The reference not only reminds the audience of one of the cult numbers from her films, but more generally of her MGM image. It was also widely known, by 1961, that the making of *Summer Stock* had been fraught with difficulties of all kinds, including her perennial weight problems, and that "Get Happy" was in fact shot several weeks after the completion of the rest of the film, as an afterthought. Garland came back for it, much relaxed and rested, noticeably slimmer and rehearsing and shooting in one day a number that is, as Jane Feuer (1982: 20) puts it, "the ultimate in professional entertainment." The facts about coming back to film "Get Happy," the image of a confident slimmer Garland on screen, as well as its lyrics, all encapsulate the come-back motif, and are condensed in the snatch of it included in the come-back song "When You're Smiling" that starts her come-back concert at Carnegie Hall.

This come-back, going on going on, suffering and strength quality could even be read in the performance of the songs, especially toward the end of her career. In the later concerts, the sense of the trials of her life was no longer offstage, in the publicity read beforehand, in what the songs and gags referred to, but could be seen in the frailty of her figure, heard in her shortness of breath and shaky high notes, noted in her lateness or stumbling walk. Yet she was still carrying on with the show. However demanding the melody now seemed for her, she did get to the end of the song and this became a mini enactment of the come-back motif. Al Di Orio (1975: 201) quotes from the *Camden Courier Post* of 21 June 1968 on her delivery of "Over the Rainbow" at the Kennedy Stadium concert in Philadelphia two nights earlier. She speaks/sings:

If happy little bluebirds fly, beyond the rainbow, why—I made it, I made it—why, oh why—thank you, darlings, I made it all the way through, I didn't think I would—oh why, can't I?

Di Orio argues that this is a misquotation:

What she said was, 'I finally made it over the rainbow thanks to you all'. Then she continued with the song, then she yelled, 'We all do it, you know'. Then another phrase of the song, and finally, 'Thank you. God bless you'.

(ibid.)

I do not know whose memory of her exact words is correct, but may it not be that in the concerts getting to the end of the song enacted getting to the end of the rainbow? In her last recording, of a performance at the Talk of the Town in London, her apparent difficulty in getting through "Over the Rainbow" nonetheless ends with her coming through loud and true on the final "I," producing a triumphant last note in the teeth of the ravaged voice that precedes it.

Gay writing returns repeatedly to this emotional quality as in some way representing the situation and experience of being gay in a homophobic society:

[They] saw in Judy a loser who was fighting back at life, and they could themselves draw a parallel to this.

(Conley 1972: 11)

To the gay male, in those days, there was a terrific bond between Miss Garland and her audience, we, the gay people could identify with her . . . could relate to her in the problems she had on and off stage.

(Letter to author)

She appeals to me as a gay person . . . because she tended to sing songs which seem to echo all the doubts and trials of a gay man within an unaccepting social order. 'The Man That Got Away' could almost become the national anthem of gay men . . . Others too express 'our' desires as a minority. The great 'Over the Rainbow' suggests a perfect world in which even we could live without restricting our life-styles and songs like 'Get Happy' tend to express our ability to cope and get along with 'our lot', whatever happens.

(Letter to author)

This gives us then the feel of the gay sense of Judy Garland. Other stars can suggest this quality (Billie Holiday, Edith Piaf, Shirley Bassey), though for none has the come-back been so decisive a motif. Equally, other groups in society carry on in the face of social stigmatization and Garland did appeal in these terms to other people. Why the special felt affinity between *this* "emotional" star and *this* oppressed group?

I want to discuss shortly three aspects of gay culture which are consonant with aspects of Garland's image, but before doing that I want to look at gay writing which links Garland's emotional quality to a general emotional quality of gay life, the idea of a "gay sensibility." The key to this lies in the particularity of gay people's situation, namely that we can "pass for straight":

The experience of passing is often productive of a gay sensibility. It can, and often does, lead to a heightened awareness and appreciation for disguise, impersonation, the projection of personality, and the distinctions to be made between instinctive and theatrical behaviour.

(Babuscio 1977: 45)

This awareness informs responses to Garland in different ways. Jack Babuscio argues that the sense of Garland performing herself, enacting her life on screen or stage, is a recognition of the theatricality of experience that the gay sensibility is attuned to. Vito Russo (1980/81: 15), on the other hand, stresses the nerve and risk involved in living "on the edge" between a stigmatized gay identity and a fragile straight front, evoked in the very act of Garland going on stage in the teeth of disaster:

I'm not sure that people know what it means any longer to watch a performer walk onto a stage stone cold and suddenly be absolutely brilliant. When Garland sang 'If Love Were All' or 'By Myself', her whole life was on that stage, and believe me, that's not nothing . . . That's why I'm so attracted to Garland. She had the guts to take the chance of dropping dead in front of ten thousand people. And won.

Is that a particularly gay response to Garland? Perhaps. Gays take chances all the time in ways straights never do. We have traditionally been forced to put on one face for the world and another in private.

What both Jack Babuscio and Vito Russo bring out is the way that the gay sensibility holds together qualities that are elsewhere felt as antithetical: theatricality and authenticity. Equally I'd want to suggest that the sensibility holds together intensity and irony, a fierce assertion of extreme feeling with a deprecating sense of its absurdity. This is a quality I find in a number of popular songs by gay writers—Cole Porter's "Just One of Those Things," Noel Coward's "If Love Were All," Lorenz Hart's "My Romance," for instance. Garland seemed to have a particular affinity for songs like this. Her version of the Haymes and Brandt song "That's All" (on *Just for Openers*, a collection of songs from her TV series) is a good example. The song uses the extravagant rhetoric of forever-love and is ironically off hand—"I can only give you love that lasts forever, that's all." In the final verse Garland gives a characteristic, all-out, slurred, Jolsoney delivery of the lyrics' demand for absolute love in return, then gives a tiny laugh before the final "that's all":

If you're asking in return what I would want dear
You'll be glad to know that my requests are small
Say it's me that you'll adore
For now and evermore
(hm)
That's all
That's all.

I've spoken personally here, so I'd better make it clear that I'm not claiming that mine is the definitive gay response to Garland—I'm simply using myself in evidence alongside the writings used throughout the chapter. This passion-with-irony is another inflection of the gay sensibility, a doubleness which informs equally Russo's living-on-the-edge, Babuscio's theatricalization-of-experience and indeed the whole suffering-and-strength motif.

[. . .]

One of the letters I received while researching this chapter tells an interesting story.

> When I was 13 or 14 the whole 3rd form at school voted what film they would like to see at the end of term. My friend and I liked Garland and we wanted to see *The Wizard of* Oz. We were labelled as 'poofs' and also laughed at for being childish, unlike many other 3rd formers who thought they were so mature because they wanted to see a sex film. *Dr No* was the film they finally chose.
>
> I have found out since that my friend was gay a couple of years later and I find it interesting . . . that 2 gays, unaware of each other's sexual preferences, remained in solidarity for Garland. Furthermore, while we were not conscious of her as a gay person's film star, it is interesting to note that we were brutally labelled as 'poofs' for our choice of film.
>
> (Letter to author)

This letter suggests that the gay reading of Judy Garland was not just something that gay men would pick up as they entered the gay scene; it suggests rather that a person identifying themselves as gay (or probably "different") would intuitively take to Garland as an identification figure.

There need be no consciousness of the connection. Another letter I received stressed that the writer had had a "teenage love affair with MGM's great star" and at the same time

> I was a gay teenager and well aware of it. In fact I was very active. I did not in any way connect the gay life with the affinity to Judy.
>
> (Letter to author)

Only retrospectively does he see "the reasons for gays being attracted to Judy," which he understands in terms of her appeal to "sensitive males."

What seems to be happening in such cases is a coming together of two homologous structures—a star image with strong elements of difference within ordinariness, androgyny, and camp, and a way of interpreting homosexual identity that is widely available in society in both dominant and subcultural discourses. The gay subculture would develop the most elaborated, the most inward of readings of Garland, would pick up on the nuances and inflections of her image that could be read in a gay way, and it is this that I have been exploring. But the classmates of the letter writer above clearly sensed, without probably having any knowledge of the composition of Garland's audience, that there was something about Garland which chimed with their sense of what "poofs" were, a connection between image and social identity that the writer himself also made intuitively.

There is nothing arbitrary about the gay reading of Garland; it is a product of the way homosexuality is socially constructed, without and within the gay subculture itself. It does not tell us what gay men are inevitably and naturally drawn to from some in-built disposition granted by their sexuality, but it does tell us of the way that a social–sexual identity has been understood and felt in a certain period of time. Looking at, listening to Garland may get us inside how gay men have lived their experience and situation, have *made* sense of them. We feel that sense in the intangible and the ineffable—the warmth of the voice, the wryness of the humor, the edgy vigor of the stance—but they mean a lot because they are made expressive of what it has been to be gay in the past half century.

Notes

1 Namely, *Gay News* and *Him* (Britain), *Body Politic* (Canada), *New York Native* and *The Advocate* (USA). These range from the broadly political/social papers like *Gay News* to more pornographic magazines like *Him*. The letter asked people to write to me about their memories of Judy Garland and why they liked her.
2 The emergence of the contemporary gay movement is commonly dated from an incident at the Stonewall bar in New York in June 1969, also the month and year in which Judy Garland died.

References

Anger, Kenneth (1981) *Hollywood Babylon*, New York: Dell; originally published Paris, J.J. Pauvert, 1959.

Babuscio, Jack (1977) "Camp and the Gay Sensibility," in Richard Dyer (ed.) *Gays and Film*, London: British Film Institute, 40–57.

Bathrick, Serafina (1976) "The Past As Future: Family and the American Home in *Meet Me in St. Louis*," *The Minnesota Review*, New Series 6: 7–25.

Boone, Bruce (1979) "Gay Language as Political Praxis, the Poetry of Frank O'Hara," *Social Text*, 1: 59–92.

Booth, Mark (1983) *Camp*, London: Quartet.

Brinson, Peter (1954) "The Great Come-Back," *Films and Filming*, December: 4.

Britton, Andrew (1977) "*Meet Me in St Louis*: Smith or The Ambiguities," *Australian Journal of Screen Theory*, 3: 7–25.

Britton, Andrew (1978/79) "For Interpretation, Against Camp," *Gay Left*, 7: 11–14.

Bronski, Michael (1978) "Judy Garland and Others, Notes on Idolization and Derision," in Karla Jay and Allen Young (eds) *Lavender Culture*, New York: Harcourt Brace Jovanovich.

Cohen, Derek and Dyer, Richard (1980) "The Politics of Gay Culture," in Gay Left Collective (eds) *Homosexuality, Power and Politics*, London: Allison & Busby, 172–86.

Conley, Barry (1972) "The Garland Legend: The Stars Have Lost Their Glitter," *Gay News*, 13: 10–11.

Di Orio, Al (1975) *Little Girl Lost: The Life and Hard Times of Judy Garland*, New York: Manor Books.

Dyer, Richard (1977) "It's Being So Camp As Keeps Us Going," *Body Politic* 36, September.

Dyer, Richard (1977) "Entertainment and Utopia," *Movie*, 24: 2–13.

Dyer, Richard (1977) "Four Films of Lana Turner," *Movie*, 25: 30–52.

Dyer, Richard (1982) "*A Star is Born* and the Construction of Authenticity," in BFI Education, *Star Signs*, London: British Film Institute: 13–22.

Dyer, Richard (1983) "Seen to be Believed, Some Problems in the Representation of Gay People as Typical," *Studies in Visual Communication*, 9, 2, Spring: 2–19.

Feuer, Jane (1982) *The Hollywood Musical*, London: Macmillan/British Film Institute.

Finch, Christopher (1975) *Rainbow, the Stormy Life of Judy Garland*, London: Michael Joseph.

Goldman, William (1969) *The Season*, New York: Harcourt Brace & World Inc.

Gramann, Karola and Schlüpmann, Heide (1981) "Unnatürliche Akte. Die Inszenierung des Lesbischen un Film," in Karola Gramann *et al.*, *Lust und Elend: das erotische Kino*, Munich & Luzern: Bücher, 70–93.

Greig, Noel and Griffiths, Drew (1981) *As Time Goes By*, London: Gay Men's Press.

Howard, Dumont (1981) "The Garland Legend," *Blueboy*, January 1981.

Jennings, Wade (1979) "Nova: Garland in *A Star is Born*," *Quarterly Review of Film Studies*, Summer: 321–37.

Katz, Jonathon (ed.) (1976) *Gay American History*, New York: Thomas Y. Cromwell.

Marcuse, Herbert (1964) *One Dimensional Man*, Boston: Beacon Press.

Meyers, Janet (1976) "Dyke Goes to the Movies," *Dyke*, Spring.

Ruehl, Sonja (1982) "Inverts and Experts: Radclyffe Hall and the Lesbian Identity," in Rosalind Brunt and Caroline Rowan (eds) *Feminism, Culture and Politics*, London: Lawrence & Wishart.

Russo, Vito (1979) "Camp," in Martin P. Levene (ed.) *Gay Men, the Sociology of Male Homosexuality*, New York: Harper & Row, 205–10; originally published in *The Advocate*, 19 May, 1976.

Russo, Vito (1980/81) "Poor Judy," *Gay News*, 205, (supplement) 14–15.

Sheldon, Caroline (1977) "Lesbians and Film: Some Thoughts," in Dyer, Richard (ed.) *Gays and Film*, London: British Film Institute, 5–26.

Sontag, Susan (1964) "Notes on Camp," *Partisan Review*, XXXI, 4.

Steakley, James (1975) *The Homosexual Emancipation Movement in Germany*, New York: Arno.

Stearn, Jess (1962) *The Sixth Man*, New York: Macfadden Books.

Steiger, Brad (1969) *Judy Garland*, New York: Ace Books.

Watney, Simon (1980) "The Ideology of GLF," in Gay Left Collective (eds) *Homosexuality, Power and Politics*, London: Allison & Busby, 64–76.

Weeks, Jeffrey (1977) *Coming Out: Homosexual Politics from the Nineteenth Century to the Present*, London: Quartet.

Weiss, Andrea (1992) *Vampires and Violets: Lesbians in the Cinema*, London: Jonathan Cape.

Whatling, Clare (1997) "Stars and Their Proclivities" and "Fostering the Illusion" in *Screen Dreams: Fantasising Lesbians in Film*, Manchester: Manchester University Press: 116–59.

Whitaker, Judy (1981) "Hollywood Transformed," *Jump Cut* 24/25, 33–35.

White, Patricia (1999) *Uninvited: Classical Hollywood Cinema and Lesbian Representability*, Bloomington: Indiana University Press.

Wood, Robin (1976) *Personal Views*, London: Gordon Fraser.

Woodcock, Roger (1969) "A Star is Dead," *Jeremy*, 1: 1, 15–17.

Finding Community in the Early 1960s

Underground Cinema and Sexual Politics

JANET STAIGER

In an essay about finding evidence of communities among peoples who believe themselves to be alone,[1] Joan Scott focuses on science fiction writer Samuel Delany's experience of a St. Mark's bathhouse in 1963: "Watching the scene establishes for Delany a 'fact that flew in the face' of the prevailing representation of homosexuals in the 1950s as 'isolated perverts,' as subjects 'gone awry.'" Rather, "he emphasizes not the discovery of an identity, but a participation in a movement."[2]

It is this same potential of finding others like oneself not only for identity but for community building that I believe the space of the underground cinema of the early 1960s provided. Moreover, the Otherness that seemed so threatening in oneself was, as it was for the St. Mark's bathhouses, a sexual Otherness that did not neatly fit the dominant images of these Others as traditionally conveyed in print, television, and mainstream film. The experience of going to the underground cinema contradicted impressions of isolation as it also elevated images of perverts and subjects gone awry. It vaunted sexual Otherness as an avant-garde aesthetic. It posed sexual Otherness as even a popular culture, as play and laughter, set in a complicated difference against a serious bourgeois art culture. The underground cinema of the early 1960s was a space for validation, empowerment, and often ironic resistance that used sexuality, politics, popular cultural iconography, and humor to establish community among subcultures.

What I wish to emphasize in this chapter, then, are three points. One is the clarity with which at least New York intellectuals associated this cinema with the emergence of tacit, if not aggressive, gay sexual liberation activities and with a critique of traditional gendered, heterosexual, same-race/ethnicity sexual norms.[3] Not merely an identity crisis *but a movement* was at stake in the American underground cinema explosion of the early to mid-1960s. The second point is that going to these films after midnight was a declaration of where one stood in these debates. The midnight cinema was—like the St. Mark's bathhouse—an expression of community and a site for community building, which would eventually have its culmination, at least for the mainstream press and for gay men, in the Stonewall events of 1969. Thus I will contribute to refining debates about the history of gay liberation. Third, the ironic appropriations of popular culture were stylistic tactics directed against bourgeois culture but also assertive rhetorical strategies for creating these subcultural community connections. Critical debates about aesthetics and taste were part of this politics of sexual and personal freedom. It was in these years that feminist, civil rights, and gay/lesbian/transgendered/bisexual movements (hereafter *sexual rights movements*) realized that the personal is political. My argument in this chapter, then, is that events do not come from nowhere. While Marxist warnings against teleological historiography need to be respected, simultaneously it is still the case that prior events prepare the conditions for radical transformations. The subtext for this chapter is the emergence, or rather re-emergence, of a visible gay culture in New York City in the mid-1960s that paralleled its existence in the 1910s and 1920s.[4] I need to stress, however, that the gay culture was not homogeneous. Rather, hierarchies existed within it that required toppling for Stonewall to have the meaning it has now.

Several scholars have studied various parts of these events, noting some of these connections. In particular, David E. James writes: "Contemporary accounts of underground film in the popular press tended, more or less sensationally, to stress the coincidence of formal infractions of orthodox film grammar and parallel moral and social transgressions, interpreting the latter either as evidence of the filmmakers' degeneracy or as their social criticism."[5] I will take up James's remarks by looking at some of the dialogue among various members of the New York and mass media as they discussed and evaluated the events around the underground cinema from 1959 to about 1966.[6] I will extend his remarks by emphasizing the functions of popular culture and humor in these discussions, although the opposition James finds is not so definitely resistant when camp and sexual desire enter into the complex.

The scene

What was the contextual scene for the emergence of the underground cinema? New moviegoing behavior, the live theater scene, "beat culture," and politics all influenced the configuration and meaning of the underground cinema.

Mainstream American moviegoing and movie marketing were in a transitional stage. While historical epics, male melodramas, and musicals that harbored homosexual themes as subtexts commanded the venues of first-run theaters,[7] by necessity subsequent-run theaters catered to various subgroups or "niche" markets that opened up taboo areas of content and sometimes violated taste cultures of high art. Art cinemas and 16-mm film societies had been flourishing for the full decade of the 1950s and remained committed to a highbrow approach to contemporary themes. But another clientele was being exploited: the teenager.

Thomas Doherty describes the impact of a rather innocent B movie—*Rock around the Clock* (1956). The physical response in the theaters to hearing "our" music included "screaming, foot-stomping, and the occasional scuffle."[8] The in-house fun could spill into the streets, and even staid children of the Midwest were reported to have "snake-danced downtown and broken store windows" (p. 82). The enthusiasm of teens for the less reputable genres of the teen-pix and science fiction and horror films provoked film companies to exploit those passions.

Besides using color and widescreen technologies to draw audiences out of their living rooms and into theaters and drive-ins, film firms also returned to the old ploys of showmen. Gimmicks that relied on being at a theater made a comeback. When coupled with the fantastic genres of the horror film and science fiction, a play space was created. William Castle's work provides some outstanding examples. In a series of films produced from 1958 through the early 1960s, Castle constructed novel in-house experiences as part of his movies' marketing strategies: a Lloyd's of London insurance policy against death from the shock of watching *Macabre* (1958), reinforced by the stationing of ambulances and nurses near the theaters; a skeleton rigged to fly across an auditorium at the climax of *House on Haunted Hill* (1958); an electric current to buzz the bottoms of patrons during *The Tingler* (1959).[9] Moviegoing for youth in the late 1950s could be serious (reserved seats for major openings of Hollywood films), but often it was fantasy and play in a physically lively environment such as a neighborhood theater that was showing some movie for the teen market or the drive-in that catered to moving around inside and outside the car. Moreover, in these places the space was usually away from adults. It was the teens' grounds for group exchange, just as certain streets were for cruising and drugstore soda fountains were for shakes and fries.

Both the subject matter of these movies and the theater scene became important contexts for the underground cinema. Sexual themes and problems were commonly explicit in the horror films and other favorite teen-pix of the era. The most obvious, and probably most influential, horror-genre example is *Psycho* (1960). Norman Bates is not just a serial killer; his behavior is connected to his mother's sexual choices and his own sexual ambivalences. *Psycho*, of course, does not support Norman's cross-dressing choice, and it places the blame on mother—both sexuality and bad mothers being common 1950s discourse. Two aspects of moviegoing behavior set the stage for the underground cinema, however: the tendency of the teenager movie market to form an isolated community away from adults, and the introduction of sexually explicit themes in fantasy form.[10]

A second salient predecessor for underground movies was the live theater scene, which also introduced sexual topics and a renewed sense of the physical environment. As Parker Tyler notes, underground cinema had as one of its contexts the "happenings" of the late 1950s.[11] The cinema had just as immediately the theatrical context of off-off-Broadway. Historians of American theater date the beginning of off-off-Broadway "somewhat arbitrarily as September 27, 1960."[12] That was when the revival of Alfred Jarry's *King Ubu* opened at Take 3, a Greenwich Village coffeehouse. Following this production came many more café-theater productions.

Off-off-Broadway had multiple connotations for the early 1960s New York scene. It was promoted as nonprofit (as opposed to the increasing commercialization and capital-intensive Broadway and even off-Broadway). It confronted a tacit boundary between the public and the private by intermingling audience and performer and by putting theater into the hands of anyone. Although cafés were the initial sites for the theater troupes of off-off-Broadway, some of the most important groups found homes in friendly local churches, such as the Judson Memorial Baptist-Congregationalist Church on Washington Square and St. Mark's Church-in-the-Bouwerie on the Lower East Side.[13] Off-off-Broadway also produced cutting-edge sexual dramas. Edward Albee's work started within this community, and, as I shall indicate, some of the early underground cinema was exhibited in off-off-Broadway venues.

Albee's work, like that of the underground filmmakers, provoked attacks for its sexual rights representations. In an early 1960 review of *The Zoo Story*, Robert Brustein of the *New Republic* wrote:

> On the other hand, I am deeply depressed by the uses to which [Albee's] talent has been put. In its implicit assumption that the psychotic, the criminal, and the invert [homo-sexual] are closer to God than anyone else, "The Zoo Story" embodies the same kind of

> sexual-religious claptrap we are accustomed to from Allen Ginsberg. . . . I will not bore
> you with a discussion of the masochistic-homosexual perfume which hangs so heavily
> over "The Zoo Story" except to say that Mr. Albee's love-death, like Mr. Ginsberg's poetry,
> yields more readily to clinical than theological analysis.[14]

Indeed, the "beat" culture (led by Allen Ginsberg) and its currents of homosexuality are a third contextual predecessor for the underground cinema, as James and Richard Dyer point out.[15] Dyer writes that many of the beat poets (Ginsberg, Robert Duncan, Jack Spicer) were gay and others (Jack Kerouac and Neal Cassady) thought it "cool." For Dyer, Ginsberg's publication of *Howl* in 1956 associated beatness with "homosexuality with revolt against bourgeois convention" (p. 138). James explains the logical dynamic: "Since sex was the sign of social and aesthetic values suppressed in straight society, it could signify deviance and resistance in general, and so social repression of all kinds could be contested via the codes of sexual representation" (pp. 315–316). As early as 1960, one *Village Voice* writer was arguing that an even more radical break was necessary: although "being spokesman for a kind of literary homosexuality" had been valuable, that action was now only a "romanticism."[16] But the *Voice* also continued to describe the doings of the beat culture. In a front-page article in summer 1962, the pilgrimage of beats to Ibiza was detailed, including the fact that "Domino's steam-bath intimacy is probably an important reason for its success."[17]

The beat's appreciation of alternative sexualities was not, however, as liberated as it might seem. The beat's privileged sexuality was of a particular type. As Catharine R. Stimpson argues, "in the late 1940s and 1950s, the Beats prized candor and honesty, energy and rage," not a homosexuality of "concealment and camp, parody and irony."[18] Their homosexual hero was a "rebel who seizes freedom and proclaims the legitimacy of individual desire" (p. 375), who was " 'fucked in the ass by saintly motorcyclists' and screamed 'with joy' " (quoting *Howl*, p. 388). The underground cinema would not take up such a distinction, blurring the various styles and politics of sexual liberation—beat and camp—into one general manifesto of desire. Indeed, much of this was about politics, a politics of anticonsensus and pro-individual freedoms—my fourth contextual predecessor. Although the fight was fought out in every arena, one important battle site was civil rights for blacks. Another was the critique of restrictions on subject matter and words on the screen and in the theater. Obscenity laws were under attack as perfect examples of the attempt by Republican conservatives to mold everyone into conformists, thinking the same thing and saying nothing. The early 1960s were the years of the arrests of Lenny Bruce in Greenwich Village and Los Angeles cafés. In the specific area of film, parts of even the mainstream film industry worked to loosen up remnants of the Production Code, while more legal forms of restriction were challenged as aftermaths of the Roth case (1957). In 1959, the California State Supreme Court reviewed a case involving Raymond Rohauer's theatrical screening of Kenneth Anger's *Fireworks* (1947) in 1957.[19]

Throughout this scene of context, I have perhaps somewhat reductively, but fairly I believe, characterized a series of oppositions providing at least cultural equivalencies, if not models, for the underground cinema. Alternatives to the dominant modes of the 1950s were showing up all over the cultural map. (1) Modes of human interaction in a cultural space, (2) modes of producing cultural texts, (3) modes of representation, (4) subject matter, and (5) political agendas are lining up in a series of "either/ors." Peter Stallybrass and Allon White offer the important observation that hierarchically constructed binary oppositions that are linked with one another are often similarly evaluated.[20] In one of their examples, the top parts of the human body, like upper parts of geographical maps, are presumed better than the lower halves. Or, if heads are associated with the rational and the good, genitalia are connected to the emotional and the bad.

In the case that I am developing, the following dichotomies are being aligned in a map of oppositions: (1) passive, private involvement with a text versus active, communal participation with a text; (2) capitalist alienated labor versus cooperative group labor; (3) smooth, seamless modes of mass-produced representation (i.e., dramatic Hollywood movies) versus rough, reflexive modes of popularly produced representations; (4) repressed (or monogamous, same-race hetero)sexuality versus sexual exploration and confrontation; and (5) conservative consensus politics that restricts individual rights versus libertarian and liberation politics.

In his excellent analysis of the decade of the 1960s, Fredric Jameson places the start of the era in the late 1950s. In a general methodological statement, he argues that periods are theoretically knowable by their "sharing of a common objective situation, to which a whole range of varied responses and creative innovations is then possible, but always within that situation's structural limits."[21] The underground cinema was one such response to the common situation of the conformist 1950s, but one that would be resisted in certain quarters in part because the quintet of oppositions became "too much" for certain people. As I shall detail in the cases below, whereas some people could invest in all parts of the map, others could not. Specifically, when rough, reflexive popular culture is replaced by sex play and camp humor, some people draw the line. Of course, for others that last taboo is liberating for its creation of community jokes and pleasure.

[. . .]

Flaming Creatures

As a branch of the New American Cinema, underground cinema was in content sexually explicit and in location "underground"—primarily New York City but also Los Angeles and San Francisco. In the early 1960s, the term underground had specific connotations. One Village Voice headline on January 25, 1962, declared, "The Bourgeois Mothers' Underground, On the Rise."[22] The story described a group of seventy-five Village housewives who traveled to Washington, D.C., as a public protest about the dangers of nuclear war. Labeled as part of "the peace movement," the group's members had not known each other until they gathered on the train ride.

The repeated phenomenon of individuals taking resistant political action against the norm and then finding others who were like themselves seems an important recurring event in this period. Similar revelations were operating in civil and sexual rights. In these same years, the Village Voice published several articles indicating a different stance by some gays toward social and civil repression of homosexuals. In March 1959, Seymour Krim published a "Press of Freedom" column titled "Revolt of the Homosexual."[23] Krim did not take the common 1950s view of homosexuality as an aberration or illness, then even the official view of the Mattachine Society. Instead, he asserted the naturalness and acceptability of homosexuality. Turning to Donald Webster Cory's The Homosexual in America to justify his views, Krim claimed:

> We want recognition for our simple human rights, just like Negroes, Jews, and women.
> . . . Courageous gay people are now beginning to realize that they are human beings who

must fight to gain acceptance for what they are—not what others want them to be. . . . In the future you'll see the equally suave acknowledgment of different standards, including the right of the homosexual to fully express himself as a "healthy" individual in terms of his tradition. . . . When this movement becomes powerful enough—and gay people refuse either to hide or flaunt themselves—it will be openly accepted.[24]

Krim was answered the following week in an essay titled "The Gay Underground—A Reply to Mr. Krim."[25] The author discounted Krim's assertion that a movement was possible, but, again, underground refers to the association of minorities not just in resistance against the dominant but also in a common cause unified by a political agenda for change. In fact, several months later, another *Voice* article reported that one gay rights advocate had proposed a third political party for a homosexual voting bloc.[26] Other articles surveying sexual politics for gays continued to appear throughout the period.[27] Thus, for New Yorkers in the early 1960s, the term underground had connotations not of the hidden but of alternative communities and political activism. Additionally, discourse by homosexual men about their rights was beginning to take a different rhetorical tactic than commonly existed in the 1950s.

The movement effect of the underground cinema was partially propelled by the community associations developed through earlier filmgoing connections. As scholars have noted, the post-World War II efforts of Maya Deren, Amos Vogel, and [Jonas] Mekas to create film distribution organizations, venues, and journals for filmmakers helped instill the sense that numerous individuals were involved in nontraditional film work. They also created various alliances and conflicts.[28] Rabinovitz describes several of these; another is mentioned in Calvin Tomkins' 1973 essay on the scene. Tomkins notes that in 1961 Vogel decided not to show Stan Brakhage's *Anticipation of the Night* at his Cinema 16 society. Mekas accepted the piece for his programming, and later with friends began a competitive film distribution system, Film-Makers' Cooperative, in 1962. For various reasons, Cinema 16 went out of business in 1963, and Vogel, with Richard Roud, cofounded the New York Film Festival.

Meanwhile, Mekas was championing much more offbeat work in the late-night shows at various small film theaters. The term "underground" was applied to movies throughout this period in several ways, but eventually it took on a meaning similar to the wider cultural definition—a liberal or radical agenda with overt demonstrations of involvement by groups of individuals. In a summer 1960 *Film Culture* essay, Mekas wrote about the movies he was championing: "The underground is beginning to boil, to open up, to shoot out."[29] (The masculine eroticism of this image is hard to miss!)

The screenings organized by Mekas and others led to festivals and awards, all of which did not go without their own troubles as the underground cinema began bubbling. Andrew Sarris, asked to judge at the September 1962 Film-Makers' Festival at the Charles Theater, reported his general disgust with the whole lot of films:

> I am aware that Parker Tyler has disassociated himself from the deliberations of a jury which merely wanted to get the hell out of the theatre as quickly as possible. I will go Mr. Tyler one better. I wish to disassociate myself from a primitive movement which fancies itself the moral guardian of cinema. I can take the ineptness, but not the cynical exploitation of the ineptness.[30]

From the context, I am not sure what Sarris meant by "cynical exploitation of the ineptness," although he did express gratitude "for little favors like clearly focused images, audible sound tracks, an occasional glimpse of a pretty girl, an infrequent glimmer of intelligence, and most rarely of all, a friendly gesture to the audience" (p. 13).

Indeed, the underground cinema of the early 1960s was different from the first wave of the New American Cinema. What Sarris was likely complaining about are films such as *The Flower Thief* (Ron Rice, 1960), *Little Stabs at Happiness* (Ken Jacobs, 1959–63), *Blonde Cobra* (Jacobs, Jack Smith, and Bob Fleischner, 1959–63), and, to come, *Flaming Creatures* (Smith, 1963), *The Queen of Sheba Meets the Atom Man* (Rice, 1963), *Scorpio Rising* (Kenneth Anger, 1963), and *Christmas on Earth* (a.k.a. *Cocks and Cunts*; Barbara Rubin, 1963). All of these are now regarded as the canonical exemplars of the underground cinema.

What is wrong with these films beyond Sarris' general accusation of technical ineptness? I would argue that, along with all of the other stylistic, production, and political connotations, these films' representations of nonheterosexual sex and interracial sex and their playful, humorous, sometimes campy approach to sex proved hard to take for some people, even devotees of art and experimental cinema. Although Andrew Ross implies that camp became a way for New York intellectuals to deal with popular culture, this was not possible immediately or for all New Yorkers.[31]

Let me begin with a brief counterexample. In the late 1950s, Brakhage had been exploring the "everyday," including sexuality. *Window Water Baby Moving*—the documentary of the birth of his and his wife's child—showed private body parts. As Tyler would note in 1969, "the emergent message of such films is their novelty in terms of according public exhibition to what has been considered strictly domestic and private."[32] Even earlier, Brakhage had recorded his own masturbation in *Flesh of Morning*.

Tyler connects the sources of Brakhage's work to *cinéma vérité* and a longer tradition of highbrow aesthetics, but I wish to stress the effects. Once one creates the binary opposition quintet that I have described above, a series of consequences develops: the verisimilitude of the shooting style of cinema vérité is contrasted with the artificiality of Hollywood fiction filmmaking; the obvious explosion of hidden sexual acts is contrasted with the obvious representational repression of those acts; the privileging of the everyday and the popular is contrasted with high culture; the seriousness of Hollywood and even some experimental and art cinema is parodied. These oppositions then become a rallying point for a rebellion from the underground. Recall the metaphors above—the New American Cinema wanted a cinema "the color of blood"; Mekas noted that the underground was "beginning to boil, to open up, to shoot out." Brakhage's films were the indication of change, the place for some potential transformations, but Brakhage's alliances with high art, normative sexuality,[33] seriousness, and masculinity provided only a launching pad for the revolution.

The rebellion would come from a new set of filmmakers supported by the underground theatrical scene both as movement and play space, described so well by J. Hoberman and Jonathan Rosenbaum in *Midnight Movies*. Mekas' share in this venture, despite allegations that his motives were not pure, needs to be recognized as well. These screenings were much like those for the teen-pix of the era but with a Village beat cast: audiences smoked marijuana and very vocally responded to the films. As one critic of *The Flower Thief* acknowledged, "One of the really delightful aspects of the Charles Theater is that booing, hissing, and applause are all permitted equally, so that one can express one's feelings on the spot." Andy Warhol described these screenings as "a lot like a party."[34]

Beyond the exuberant screening scene, what has not been stressed in the analyses of these films is how linked were nontraditional sexuality, racial civil rights issues, and the fun of popular culture. Each of the canonical films employs variants of these representational materials. The Flower Thief's main character (played by Taylor Mead) wanders through San Francisco accompanied not only by classical music but by progressive jazz and gospel music. Beat poetry provides part of the sound track. Americana in the form of the flag, sparklers, and amusement parks are part of the flower thief's environment. Little Stabs at Happiness associates old popular music with scenes of Jack Smith dressed as a clown with balloons and a mirror. In the opening section, Smith performs oral sex on a doll. Blonde Cobra is a homage to the 1944 Hollywood film Cobra Woman, starring Maria Montez, but Ken Jacobs and Smith's version does not have the reverence and fetishization of Montez that Joseph Cornell brings to Rose Hobart in his Rose Hobart (1939).[35] Instead, Smith camps a performance of Montez. Smith's cross-dressing and erotic storytelling follow the nostalgic opening music, "Let's Call the Whole Thing Off."

The notorious Flaming Creatures also uses older popular music as background to stylized images of masturbation, cross-dressing, seduction, and rape. Here advertising is employed as commentary in a fabulous second movement that describes the benefits of a new lipstick, which is then liberally applied to lips and penises. Performance is doubly stressed throughout: the characters almost perform performers. Fake noses on "females" gesture toward an obvious ironic use of Freudian symbolism, especially in retrospect after the "women" lift their skirts to reveal their own penises. Hollywood genres are travestied to exaggeration: Flaming Creatures references melodrama but also the horror film. As a woman rises out of a coffin, carrying lilies in her hands (a classic image of the femme fatale), the sound track is of the country-and-western "Wasn't It God Who Made Honky Tonk Angels?" Characters appear not only in strange genders but also in odd races. One of the dancers is in blackface. The film closes to an apparent homage to some (to me unknown) classical painting while "Be Bop a Lula, She's My Baby" trails away.[36]

Christmas on Earth explores dynamics of couplings in a more serious but equally provocative way. Dated around 1963, the two reels of film are now supposed to be projected one on top of the other (another sexual congress?). Reel A, to be shown at full size, displays closeups of heterosexuality: penises, anuses, mouths, vaginas. Reel B, to be projected at half of reel A's size and in the middle of the screen over reel A, represents 1960s tabooed sex: interracial and homosexual. These images are partially performances. For instance, a white woman appears not only in blackface but in black body (her breasts and stomach remain white, providing a second "face"). At the end of the film, all of the participants wave toward the camera.[37]

Scorpio Rising is another excellent instance of the combination of homosexuality, popular culture, and camp satire, with Anger's appropriation of images of male buddies from Hollywood movies, television, and comic strips. The Queen of Sheba Meets the Atom Man pairs a black woman with Taylor Mead, invokes several trashy Hollywood genres, and again uses popular music and jazz.

Although many people appreciated this new cinema, others did not. One recurrent theme is how badly shot by Hollywood standards these films are: out-of-focus and overexposed images, lack of establishing shots, and panning too fast, which prevents the viewer's seeing what is likely (or hopefully) there. These were obviously studied effects by underground filmmakers, and easily justified as that.[38] It is also clear that many people missed or resisted the jokes in the films because other things stood in the way.

An obvious problem was the nontraditional sexuality. It was even nontraditional pornography! Stag movies had been a part of a homosocial scene for males since the 1910s, and exploitation cinema began developing during the late 1950s, but both were still quite nonpublic and unavailable to "innocents" unless they were initiated into them at smokers, lodges, or fraternity parties—in scenes with a strong resemblance to underground cinema events as Warhol and others recall them.[39] As Thomas Waugh has discovered, some male same-sex scenes exist in traditional pornography, but they are extremely rare.[40] These male same-sex scenes are used as preludes to heterosexual sex and are treated without much emphasis. Beyond these rare images of male same-sex actions, traditional stag films also have some instances of cross-dressing, but mostly as drag performances with the humorous "surprise" of revealing the performer's penis at the end of the act. This humor, and the general treatment of the rare male same-sex scene, might appeal to an individual gay man, but the general structure of heterosexual stag-film pornography works to disavow a homoerotic address to the male spectator (pp. 14–15).

If this representation of male same-sex sexuality differed from traditional hard-core pornography, it was even nontraditional for the rare examples of early 1960s gay-addressed erotica! Waugh writes that he has found no evidence of any organized gay audience for gay pornography prior to 1960: it was too illegal and taboo (pp. 6–8). However, gay soft-core erotica was being produced by film companies such as Apollo and Zenith in the 1940s and 1950s. This erotica consisted of short narratives justifying nearly complete male nudity (occasionally genitals were displayed). Promises of sexual activities to occur offscreen or after the film's narrative ends may be implicit, but most onscreen same-sex bodily contact was limited to physical sport such as playful wrestling, swimming, or bodybuilding.[41] Thus the rare instances of male same-sex scenes found in heterosexual-addressed stag films were about all the hard-core images of male same-sex sexuality that appear to have existed before 1960.

Thus the underground cinema was multiply confounding in its representation of male same-sex sexuality. It addressed not only heterosexual devotees of avant-garde cinema but gay audiences in a new way. Significantly, it was not using the conventions of a heterosexual stag reel or even standard gay erotica for that audience. Arthur Knight, reviewing *Flaming Creatures* for *Saturday Review* in autumn 1963, objected: "A faggoty stag-reel, it comes as close to hardcore pornography as anything ever presented in a theater. . . . Everything is shown in sickening detail, defiling at once both sex and cinema."[42] Although it would take almost a year from its initial screening for *Flaming Creatures* to be seized by the police for obscenity, when it was and, two weeks later, Jean Genet's *Un Chant d'Amour* was seized as well, *Variety* proclaimed in its March 18, 1964, headline: "Cops Raid Homo Films Again."[43] *Variety* described *Flaming Creatures* as "a 58-minute montage of a transvestite orgy." In a formal statement, Mekas argued that the films were art and thus deserved unrestricted availability for viewing. As Tomkins notes, the March 1964 publicity brought the underground out of Greenwich Village: "The public, which had been largely oblivious of the underground's existence, assumed that 'underground' was synonymous with dirty pictures."[44]

Prior to *Flaming Creatures'* obscenity charges, one way to appreciate the underground cinema had been to associate it with art, which was part of the pre-March 1964 public discourse. In his *New York Times* review of *The Flower Thief* in July 1962, Eugene Archer analyzed the film by finding associations with beat culture, but, more significantly, he uncovered highbrow allusions. Among the intertextual references he discovered were *The Seventh Seal*, the "pose of marines planting the flag on Iwo Jima," and "films by Sergei Eisenstein, Charlie Chaplin, Luis Buñuel and Alain Resnais."[45]

Another pre-obscenity-charge response was to treat the films with amused paternalism. A July 1963 *New Yorker* essay considered Mekas, Ken Jacobs, the Film-Makers' Cooperative, and "underground cinema" as diverting New York-iana: "The results range from 'poetic' color and motion studies to blunt documentary denunciations of Society and the Bomb, but most share a total disdain for the traditional manner of storytelling on film, and also for the 'self-consciously art' experimental films of the twenties and thirties."[46] Pete Hamill in the *Saturday Evening Post* in September 1963 also gave an overall positive representation of all of the New American films, and quoted Jacobs as indicating that what he was producing was "art," although Hamill described *Flaming Creatures* as "a sophomoric exercise in the kind of sex that Henry Miller dealt with 30 years ago" and *Blonde Cobra* as "accompanied by Smith's voice telling fraternity-house stories that presumably are meant to be shocking." Yet the antipathy found in some writers' remarks about these films was not present in Hamill's essay. His conclusion was that by encouraging the filmmakers to be "bad," a new cinema might develop, one that "at least . . . won't be Debbie Reynolds or Doris Day, sailing into a saccharine sunset."[47]

After the charges of obscenity, the descriptions shifted from art or bemusement to a serious debate because now the underground cinema represented a political cause, connected to its representations of sex acts and display of parts of the human anatomy. In an editorial, the *Nation* called for an end to censorship: "even the banning of hard-core commercial pornography invites trouble." Several weeks later the *Nation* published a critical defense of *Flaming Creatures* by Susan Sontag, who ended up calling the film an example of "pop art" in anticipation of within this same year including the film in her essay on camp. Sontag declaimed, "Smith's film has the sloppiness, the arbitrariness, the looseness of pop art. It also has pop art's gaiety, its ingenuousness, its exhilarating freedom from moralism."[48] As Ross suggests, Sontag's move to justify this cinema as pop art and camp was a break with "the style and legitimacy of the old liberal intelligentsia, whose puritanism had always set it apart from the frivolous excesses of the ruling class."[49] Sontag would, however, back off from equating camp with homosexuality in her "Notes on 'Camp.'"

The question of whether the underground cinema's presentations of play and sexual diversity promoted moralism or amoralism was where the film community divided. By mid-1964, two important supporters of experimental and art cinema openly criticized this part of the New American Cinema. In May 1964, Vogel published in the *Village Voice* a statement accusing Mekas and his supporters of inflating the significance of these films and "disregarding even the most advanced and adventurous contemporary artists of the international cinema, such as Antonioni, Resnais, Godard." By promoting only this cinema, Vogel asserted,

> Jonas [Mekas] has become more dogmatic, more extremist, more publicity-conscious. While the flamboyancy and provocative extravagance of the positions taken has [sic] undoubtedly served to make at least one segment of the independent film visible . . . it has also been accompanied by an absence of style and seriousness, a lack of concern for film form, rhythm, and theory which leads many people to view the existing works and pretensions with an indulgent, amused air, smiling at the antics of the movement or somewhat repelled by the "camp" atmosphere of its screenings.[50]

Vogel continued by arguing that Mekas was anticipating and perhaps hurting the possibilities of a true revolution in the American cinema: "however justified an objective, the question of timing and tactics is a crucial one." Moreover, *Flaming Creatures*, "despite flashes of brilliance and moments of perverse, tortured beauty, remains a tragically sad film noir, replete with limp genitalia and limp art" (p. 18). Vogel was clearly supporting repeals of obscenity laws and the promotion of expression. What Vogel objected to was the use of what he considered to be a less than high art, less than serious film, an unmasculine cinema as the test case for obscenity, for fear the masses would not support the cause.

Predictably, letters to the *Village Voice* divided over Vogel's remarks. Two letters supported Vogel, even calling for the *Voice* to drop Mekas' column; a third argued that Vogel was blind to an important evaluative prejudice: "The reason why Genet's film 'Un Chant d'Amour' has been praised by those who cannot stomach 'Flaming Creatures' is not that it is a smoother construction but that it evokes pity: a nice, warm, serious, recognizable emotion. Homosexual love on the screen, yes; a comic conception of human sex, no."[51] "Brooks Brothers" gayness, yes; drag queens, no.

Dwight Macdonald was another critic of the purported tone of this cinema. In July 1964, he called *Flaming Creatures* and *Un Chant d'Amour* "two sexually explicit, and perverse, movies."[52] However, his view of the problem was opposite that of Vogel: "Like the Beat littérateurs, the movie-makers of the New American Cinema are moralists rather than artists" (p. 361). Macdonald's widely known attacks against mass culture and in defense of high art and his concern for the social threats of mass culture as standardization informed his opinion. Here Macdonald was responding to many aspects of the underground cinema, but the pop art features were likely highly influential in his evaluation, as much as the representation of the "perverse."[53]

These debates continued through the summer of 1964, as Macdonald and other leftist colleagues, including Lewis Jacobs, Edouard de Laurot, and Peter Goldfarb, issued a statement:

> The New American Cinema is a movement much vaster in quantity and quality than its restricted and distorted image insistently publicized throughout the world by the New York Village Group of filmmakers (Joanas [sic] Mekas, Adam [sic] Sitney, et al.).
>
> This misrepresentation is all the more regrettable since the films of the New York Group are on the whole characterized by (a) in their content a solipsistic alienation from reality and society (b) in their form by a lack of originality and professional level (c) in their documentation . . . by a specious or superficial realism—justifying these inadequacies with a mystique of spontaneity which in fact hides creative impotence, more often than not.[54]

This split continued through the 1966 New York Film Festival, run by Vogel, Sarris, and others. Sarris justified not showing some of the New American films that were connected to this trend by claiming many people and critics were opposed to it: Warhol was "pointedly excluded from the proceedings so as not to offend the regular reviewers."[55]

Vogel, Macdonald, Lewis Jacobs, and many others were supporters of cinema and radical politics. Yet how cinema might produce radical change was constantly debated among these people. Indications in the rhetoric and discourse of these writers are that part of their difficulties with the underground cinema had to do with its representations—as not serious enough; as pop art and camp; as perverse.[56] Thus to the set of oppositions, in opposition to high art play and laughter need to be added in a new category of "attitude," an attitude that was too gay—in the double sense of that term. Some of the antagonisms were probably also personal, against Mekas. The debates over *Flaming Creatures* did not end underground cinema; however, the movement took an interesting permutation when the movies of Warhol, excluded from the 1966 New York Film Festival, began to receive national acclaim.

The Chelsea Girls

Andy Warhol's films provide the break from the underground as political movement to aboveground—even general—cinema. It may be a bit too much to claim that his films permitted the acceptance by a counterculture generation of soft-core and hard-core pornography. Yet the play with sexual desire explicit in *Blow Job*, *My Hustler*, *The Chelsea Girls*, *Lonesome Cowboys*, and so many others of his films took away some of the threat that nontraditional sexuality presented to the middle class. When even *Newsweek* and *Life* could report on this cinema in a somewhat enthusiastic way, a sexual liberation seemed tolerable, maybe even fashionable.

Warhol's early involvement with the Mekas underground screenings has been detailed by Hoberman and Rosenbaum, among others.[57] Warhol liked to play with his affection for this cinema as he played with his love of dominant Hollywood and consumer culture. In an interview published in spring 1966 in *Film Culture*, David Ehrenstein asked Warhol:

> DE: Who in the New American Cinema do you admire?
> AW: Jaaaacck Smiiiittttth.
> DE: You really like Jack Smith?
> AW: When I was little, I always . . . thought he was my best director . . . I mean, just the only person I would ever try to copy, and just . . . so terrific and now since I'm grown up, I just think that he makes the best movies.[58] [Ellipses are Warhol's pauses, not deletions of the text.]

By the time Sontag defended *Flaming Creatures*, pop art had become the next New York art fashion, so her stance was a smart tactic for justifying the film. *Film Culture* was also promoting pop art as an iconography worth considering within the New American film scene. In fact, it could even find pop art in the old enemy Hollywood. In *Film Culture*'s summer 1963 issue, Charles Boultenhouse published what I take to be a partially ironic essay, "The Camera as God," in which he declared that "Hollywood is the Original Pop Art and is GREAT because IT IS WHAT IT IS. Gorgeous flesh and mostly terrible acting! Divine! Campy dialogue and preposterous plots! Divine! Sexy fantasy and unorgasmic tedium! Divine!"[59] Three issues later, Michael McClure did a tribute to Jayne Mansfield in something of the same tone and much like Smith's earlier homage to Maria Montez.[60] Warhol's first films for the underground were *Kiss*, shown weekly as the "serial" at the Gramercy Arts Theater. *Kiss* was three-minute kisses with variant pairings, some heterosexual, others homosexual.[61] The Kuchar brothers rapidly learned the discourse of Hollywood advertising, and their promotions of their forthcoming films are among the most amusing documents of the cinema.[62]

The pop art and camp inflections of the underground and trends in the New York art scene were—although different—connected,[63] and suspiciously incorporated old Hollywood as part of their subject matter rather than the subject matter many New York intellectuals privileged: the foreign art film and the auteur cinema promoted by Sarris. This makes sense. If foreign art films, auteurs who transcend the mundane of Hollywood, and segments of the New American Cinema were praised for realism and seriousness, then in this binary inversion, grade-B Hollywood could become a "good" object again, albeit inflected by camp humor or exaggerated as commodity by pop art. Aligned with the foreign art film was also high modernism—the American abstract expressionism that Warhol discusses as a "macho" world from which he was excluded as "too swish."[64]

Pop art and camp were contextually associated by opposition to the dominant, and so too were pop art and sexual diversity. In fact, in their cases, a dangerous subversion was occurring. In April 1966, Vivian Gornick published in the *Village Voice* an article, "It's a Queer Hand Stoking the Campfire," arguing a homosexual control over pop art: "Popular culture is now in the hands of the homosexuals. It is homosexual taste that determines largely style, story, statement in painting, literature, dance, amusements, and acquisitions for a goodly proportion of the intellectual middle class. It is the homosexual temperament which is guiding the progress of Pop Art."[65] Gornick outlined this influence in a bitter essay, deriving her authority from earlier *Voice* discussions of gay rights and gay sensibilities. Moreover, she declared that camp was not, as Sontag described it, "tender" but rather a "raging put-on of the middle classes," "a malicious fairy's joke" (p. 1). Thus, whether praised or condemned, the connections of pop art, play, and a camp gay aesthetic were explicitly being made.

Although the exhibition of Warhol's *The Chelsea Girls* in a midtown theater in December 1966 is a good marker of public acceptance of underground cinema, the way was paved earlier. Two years before, in December 1964, *Newsweek* did a long story on Warhol as pop painter and described his unconventional work in film.[66] Then in January 1965, Shana Alexander described for mass circulation *Life* readers what it was like to watch *Flaming Creatures*, *Scorpio Rising*, and other such films underground. She began:

> The other night I infiltrated a crowd of 350 cultivated New York sophisticates who were squeezed into a dark cellar staring at a wrinkled bedsheet. The occasion was the world premiere of *Harlot* [Warhol], yet another in the rash of "underground movies" which have become the current passion of New York's avant garde. . . . if a bunch of intelligent people will spend two solid hours and $2.50 apiece to see a single, grainy, wobbly shot projected onto a bedsheet of a man dressed up as Jean Harlow eating a banana (that's what we saw in the cellar), then the movie business must be in worse shape than anyone has any idea.[67]

Alexander noted the value of Warhol's paintings, retrospectives occurring at the Metropolitan and Carnegie Museums, and Ford Foundation grants to underground filmmakers, although she concluded with some expressions of concern, not about possible effects of pornography, but about "fake artists, phony art, and pompous, pretentious critics" (p. 23). Mekas and his "cinematheque" made the *New York Times Sunday Magazine* later in 1965.[68]

By this time "expanded cinema" was beginning to replace "underground cinema" as the mid-1960s transition to hippie and acid drug countercultures developed. In late 1965, Mekas did a two-week, mixed media show; in February 1966, Warhol staged "Andy Warhol, Up-Tight," with the Velvet Underground and with multiple images projected on walls and ceilings. Simultaneously on the West Coast, Ken Kesey, the Merry Pranksters, and the Grateful Dead conducted a series of "acid tests," and Bill Graham staged a large public one at the Fillmore.

In April 1966, the famous "Erupting-Exploding-Plastic Inevitable" production with a revolving mirrored ballroom globe and multimedia marked a high point in pop history.

The expanded cinema maintained the tradition of mixed responses. Howard Junker in the *Nation* complained, "How many ill-conceived, half-baked, technically incompetent, faggoty, poetic films can anyone see before announcing: 'I've made that scene. And never mind about the art form of the age.'" Stanley Kauffmann, reviewer for the *New Republic*, opined, "many of [the underground filmmakers] equate radicalism with personal gesture and style–revolt consummated by bizarre hair and dress, unconventional sexual behavior, flirtations with drugs."[69]

It was in September 1966 that *The Chelsea Girls* debuted at Mekas' cinematheque.[70] In a real sense, the praise by *Newsweek* reviewer Jack Kroll marked a mass-media acceptance of these films as potentially art, despite all the other connotations: "it is a fascinating and significant movie event."[71] Warhol's characters were compared with Gelber's, Albee's, and John Updike's—all icons of 1960s contemporary aesthetics, and Kroll encouraged the distribution of the film to film societies and universities.[72]

Several months later, *Newsweek* published another long essay by Kroll, "Up from Underground," that also brought these films positive recognition as an "'official' avant-garde movement" as in other arts. Kroll declared, "the underground has at last surfaced and is moving into public consciousness with a vengeance."[73] Likewise, *Time* in the same month produced an extended examination of the scene. After describing images from an underground film, the writer indicated that the filmmaker "calls it a work of art. The startling thing is that a great many Americans now agree with him." Pop art, camp art was, finally, Art.[74]

In the history of underground cinema, the commercial success of *The Chelsea Girls* indicates at least a growing toleration of these types of images and attitudes. The success also provided sufficient hopes for packaging underground films and distributing them on a routine basis, first attempted by Mike Getz in late 1966 and then in mid-1967 in London by Raymond Durgnat.[75] The most obvious legacy of this distribution of cinema was the late-1960s explosion of feature-length soft-core and hard-core pornography, eventually crossing many prior lines of sexual prohibition, and more generally the commercialization of the sexual revolution in mainstream cinema. Some stylistic tactics of the underground cinema also found their way into mainstream film, particularly the head movies of the late sixties and other "independent" films such as *Easy Rider*.[76]

The critical and commercial success of underground cinema also marked the conclusion of the most lively time for underground cinema as a community film exhibition movement. In 1969, Brakhage filmed *Love Making*; Tyler calmly wrote:

> the second part of the new film, showing two hippie-type males making standardized love (one active, one passive) and featuring unmistakable fellatio, does supply some human interest. . . . For the strictly built-in audience at this premiere, the routine homosexual acts passed with no more than a few semisilent gloats, some scattered, suppressed gasps. So far as stirring up articulate moral or emotional reflexes could be observed, they passed like the eight hours Warhol devoted to looking at the Empire State building.[77]

Admittedly, Tyler's fellow viewers were a "built-in" audience, but something significant had happened in the decade between *The Flower Thief* and *Love Making* to allow Tyler to compare an explicit representation of homosexuality with *Empire*.[78]

The emergence of underground cinema was decisively tied to, and I believe participatory in, sexual liberation politics. That is not to suggest that underground cinema was totally liberated itself. As scholars have pointed out, the representation of women fared badly at times. James notes that Carolee Schneemann was moved to create her own representation of lovemaking after being dissatisfied with Brakhage's images, and Mellencamp argues rightly that this avant-garde provides little or no place for the female spectator.[79] Moreover, the degree to which camp reverence for and homages to Hollywood, stars, and popular culture in general was truly resistant and oppositional is worth reflection, as is the commercialization to which this pop/camp culture was put. This is why I initially labeled this a complex situation.

Yet that the underground cinema was able to so penetrate American culture still deserves notice. Obviously the social conditions of a counterculture and the appropriation of pop culture and comedy made many of the films palatable to people who might otherwise have turned away from them. In fact, the joy and play overrunning the seriousness underpinning the representations likely helped to bind the community and spread it to a larger scene. Although some people may have thought the middle class was unaware of the joke being played on them, I'm not so sure that at least the youth of the middle class were not ready to participate in that joke. All those laughing together at the underground scene created a gay community across sexual orientations.

Waugh argues that the gay address of these films was obvious by 1967. Roger McNiven notes that underground movie "camp" was a "pretext for pornography."[80] I believe this study of New York's reception of its underground cinema indicates that the gay address—at least among Villagers—was apparent right away. Moreover, and however, this gay address set up the events at Stonewall in two significant ways. For one thing, these films were not embarrassed by their sexual deviance. They flaunted it and played with it. For another, the sexual deviance was, within its contemporary gay hierarchies, the most underprivileged—it was directed toward fairies and drag queens, not respectable middle-class gay men.

Studies of Stonewall seek to explain that 1969 event. In one of the major historical contributions, John D'Emilio suggests that two conditions created the "fairy revolt": a new discourse on gay life, replacing the 1950s pathological rhetoric, and a new militancy.[81] The militancy, led by individuals such as Franklin Kameny, derived from increasing general resentment of government interference in personal lives. In 1961, Kameny formed a branch of the Mattachine Society and argued for a civil rights approach (marches, sit-ins) to securing rights for gays and preventing persecution (such as being fired for supposed security reasons). In New York City in 1962, Randy Wicker founded the Homosexual League of New York, with some good publicity in Newsweek, the New York Times, and the Village Voice. The spring 1965 much publicized abuse of homosexuals in Cuba also set up a valuable contrast for U.S. citizens.

These actions and related court petitions, as valuable as they were, were conducted by a small number of people in fairly respectable ways. As Elizabeth Lapovsky Kennedy and Madeline D. Davis argue, this homophile movement was still "accommodationist."[82] Kennedy and Davis suggest that the movement needed to incorporate the wide variety of gays and lesbians—men from leather bars, drag queens, butches and femmes—and to refuse "to deny their difference" in order, finally, to achieve the gay pride symbolized by the events at Stonewall. Most historians of Stonewall stress that it was the transvestites and drag queens who finally fought back, creating the transformation known as the gay liberation movement.

I believe that part of this flaunting of difference derives from the self-identities created in the space of underground cinema in the early 1960s. Several times, screenings flowed into the streets, and confrontations with police or censors at screenings were part of the possible evening events. But most significantly, this underground cinema took up the repressed—even by some homosexuals—images and played with them, had fun, and threw them into the public arena for common consumption. Recognition of this cinema and its makers—from Jack Smith and Andy Warhol to Kenneth Anger—set the stage for validating camp as high style, and gays by association. The underground cinema was not the only early-1960s space for gay play, but it was one that endorsed and even rewarded resistance. It was a scene that "'flew in the face' of the prevailing representation of homosexuals in the 1950s as 'isolated perverts,' as subjects 'gone awry'"—or at least the subjects gone awry were having fun going there! Watching underground movies in New York City in the early 1960s was the beginning of a "participation in a movement"; it was building a community that would later erupt into a revolution.

Notes

This chapter is dedicated to Roger McNiven, who introduced me in the mid-1980s to some of these ideas and who died too early of AIDS. I would also like to thank the audience at the 1996 Conference of the Society for Cinema Studies, Allan Campbell, and Anne Morey for helpful comments, and David Gerstner for his continuing support and friendship.

1 Cindy Patton discusses the problems with using *community* to describe groups of gays, but chooses to use the term in lieu of a better one. I do as well. See her "Safe Sex and the Pornographic Vernacular," in *How Do I Look? Queer Film and Video*, ed. Bad Object-Choices (Seattle: Bay Press, 1991), 32n.

2 Samuel Delany in *Motion of Light in Water*, described in Joan Scott, "The Evidence of Experience," *Critical Inquiry* 17, no. 4 (Summer 1991): 773–74.

3 The claims I make in this chapter apply only to the reception of this cinema in New York City. I do not assume that people outside of New York were as cognizant as those around the Greenwich Village scene of these connotations. It is the case, however, as Thomas Poe pointed out at the 1996 Society for Cinema Studies conference, that some gay men outside of New York City were aware of these events and took them as signposts for themselves and their future.

4 See the groundbreaking work of George Chauncey, *Gay New York: Gender, Urban Culture, and the Making of the Gay Male World, 1890–1940* (New York: Basic Books, 1994).

5 David E. James, *Allegories of Cinema: American Film in the Sixties* (Princeton: Princeton University Press, 1989), 95 n.7. Also published recently with a similar argument is Juan A. Suarez, *Bike Boys, Drag Queens, and Superstars: Avant-Garde, Mass Culture, and Gay Identities in the 1960s Underground Cinema* (Bloomington: Indiana University Press, 1996).

6 As I indicate below, I use the term "New American Cinema" to describe the widest range of non-Hollywood film practices being produced at this time. I reserve the term underground cinema for a specific subset of films that explicitly displayed nondominant sexualities in nonnarrative form and style. To count as underground cinema for the purposes of this chapter, a film needs to contain some sexually explicit material and not look like a narrative Hollywood film.

7   The obvious reference is Vito Russo, *The Celluloid Closet: Homosexuality in the Movies* (New York: Harper & Row, 1981), especially 76–77, 108.

8   Thomas Doherty, *Teenagers and Teenpics: The Juvenilization of American Movies in the 1950s* (Boston: Unwin Hyman, 1988), 82.

9   William Castle, *Step Right Up! . . . I'm Gonna Scare the Pants off America* (New York: G. P. Putnam's Sons, 1976), 136–59. I am indebted to Alison Macor's research for this information. Castle's activities need to be used to contextualize Alfred Hitchcock's *Psycho* (1960) gimmick of preventing people from entering the theater after the movie started.

10   I shall discuss stag movies and gay erotica of the period below.

11   Parker Tyler, *Underground Film: A Critical History* (New York: Grove Press, 1969), 11.

12   Nick Orzel and Michael Smith, Introduction, in *Eight Plays from Off-Off Broadway*, ed. Orzel and Smith (New York: Bobbs-Merrill, 1966), 6.

13   The fact that the troupes' mode of production was often cooperative and communal is important. These were groups of people organizing to produce many plays together, which also marks an alternative politics from that of commercial theater.

14   Robert Brustein, quoted in Nat Hentoff, "No Paul Whiteman?" *Village Voice* 5, no. 21 (March 9, 1960), 6.

15   James, *Allegories of Cinema*, 120, 315–16; Richard Dyer, *Now You See It: Studies on Lesbian and Gay Film* (London: Routledge, 1990), 138.

16   John Fles, "The End of the Affair, or Beyond the Beat Generation," *Village Voice* 6, no. 8 (December 15, 1960), 4.

17   Louise Levitas, "Beats Meet at Ibiza," *Village Voice* 7, no. 34 (June 14, 1962), 1.

18   Catharine R. Stimpson, "The Beat Generation and the Trials of Homosexual Liberation," *Salmagundi*, nos. 58–59 (Fall 1982–Winter 1983): 375.

19   Russo, *Celluloid Closet*, 118.

20   Peter Stallybrass and Allon White, *The Politics and Poetics of Transgression* (London: Methuen, 1986), 2–3.

21   Fredric Jameson, "Periodizing the 60s," in *The 60s without Apology*, ed. Sohnya Sayres, Anders Stephanson, Stanley Aronowitz, and Fredric Jameson (Minneapolis: University of Minnesota Press, 1984), 178.

22   "The Bourgeois Mothers' Underground, On the Rise," *Village Voice* 7, no. 14 (January 25, 1962), 3.

23   Seymour Krim, "Revolt of the Homosexual," *Village Voice* 4, no. 21 (March 18, 1959), 12, 16. Also see Dyer, *Now You See It*, 134–38.

24   Krim, "Revolt of the Homosexual," 12, 16, also remarks, "The old categories of a man being Mars and a woman Venus are artificial: only insensitive people or poseurs pretend to a cartoon image of masculinity vs. femininity" (16).

25   "The Gay Underground—A Reply to Mr. Krim," *Village Voice* 4, no. 22 (March 25, 1959), 4–5.

26   Stephanie Garvis, "Politics: A Third Party for the Third Sex?" *Village Voice* 7, no. 49 (September 27, 1962), 3. For more context for this proposition, see my conclusion.

27   See, most immediately, Stephanie Garvis, "The Homosexual's Labyrinth of Law and Social Custom," *Village Voice* 7, no. 51 (October 11, 1962), 7, 20; Soren Agenoux, "City of Night," *Village Voice* 8, no. 41 (August 1, 1963), 5, 15.

28   Lauren Rabinovitz, *Points of Resistance: Women, Power and Politics in the New York Avant-Garde Cinema, 1943–1971* (Urbana: University of Illinois Press, 1991), 80–84; J.R. Goddard, "'I Step on Toes from Time to Time,'" *Village Voice* 7, no. 8 (December 14, 1961), 1, 18 [on Amos

Vogel and Cinema 16]; J. Hoberman and Jonathan Rosenbaum, *Midnight Movies* (New York: Harper & Row, 1983), 39; Calvin Tomkins, "All Pockets Open," *New Yorker* 48, no. 46 (January 6, 1973), 36–37.

29 Tomkins, "All Pockets Open," 37; Nat Hentoff, "Last Call for Cinema16," *Village Voice* 8, no. 18 (21 February 1963), 4; "Cinema of the New Generation," *Film Culture*, no. 21 (Summer 1960): 9. Stan VanDerBeek used "underground" a year later likewise to describe a filmmaking trend; his discussion concerned many experimental filmmakers who eventually were not categorized in quite this way. Stan VanDerBeek, "The Cinema Delimina: Films from the Underground," *Film Quarterly* 14, no. 4 (Summer 1961): 5–15. Also see Hoberman and Rosenbaum, *Midnight Movies*, 40n.; James, *Allegories of Cinema*, 94–95; Patricia Mellencamp, *Indiscretions: Avant-Garde Film, Video, and Feminism* (Bloomington: Indiana University Press, 1990), 3–4. James captures the revolutionary connotation of the term better than VanDerBeek.

30 Andrew Sarris, "Movie Journal: Hello and Goodbye to the New American Cinema," *Village Voice* 7, no. 48 (September 20, 1962), 13. Sarris continued to voice his displeasure over this cinema, including an oration at the 1966 New York Film Festival; see below.

31 Andrew Ross, *No Respect: Intellectuals and Popular Culture* (New York: Routledge, 1989), 135–36.

32 Tyler, *Underground Film*, 37. Tyler notes that Deren objected to the films as an invasion: "woman's privacy had been deliberately, tactlessly invaded."

33 Although masturbation may not have been publicly approved, it was on the way to being considered normal. It was certainly masculine. Brakhage's heterosexuality was also not in doubt.

34 Tomkins, "All Pockets Open," 31–35; Hoberman and Rosenbaum, *Midnight Movies*, 40–43; David McReynolds, "'The Flower Thief'—Invalid or Incompetent," [Letters to the Editor], *Village Voice*, 7, no. 40 (July 26, 1962), 13; Andy Warhol and Pat Hackett, POPism: *The Warhol '60s* (New York: Harper & Row, 1980), 49. Tomkins notes, as others have, that Mekas started out his career with a different aesthetic. In 1955, Mekas attacked experimental cinema as permeated by "the conspiracy of homosexuality that is becoming one of the most persistent and shocking characteristics of American Film poetry today"; Jonas Mekas, "The Experimental Film in America," *Film Culture*, no. 3 (May–June 1955), rpt. in *Film Culture Reader*, ed. P. Adams Sitney, 23. Also see Rabinovitz, *Points of Resistance*, 84; Dyer, *Now You See It*, 102.

35 By 1960, the Cornell film was a recognized masterpiece in the American avant-garde. Thus *Blonde Cobra* seems a camp version of *Rose Hobart*. This is reinforced by Smith's homage to Maria Montez in *Film Culture*, which might be read as a parody of auteur/high art criticism; for example, "Don't slander her [Montez's] beautiful womanliness that took joy in her own beauty and all beauty—or whatever in her that turned plaster cornball sets to beauty" (28). Jack Smith, "The Perfect Filmic Appositeness of Maria Montez," *Film Culture*, no. 27 (Winter 1962/63): 28–32+.

36 Smith apparently created *Flaming Creatures* to be a comedy, an effect that works for me. However, as J. Hoberman reports, "Smith himself felt burned, bitterly complaining that his film, 'designed as a comedy,' was transformed into 'a sex issue of the Cocktail World'"; J. Hoberman, "The Big Heat," *Village Voice*, November 12, 1991, 61. Also see Michael Moon, "Flaming Closets," *October*, no. 51 (1989): 19–54.

37 For background on the director, Barbara Rubin, see J. Hoberman, *Vulgar Modernism: Writing on Movies and Other Media* (Philadelphia: Temple University Press, 1991), 141–42.

38 For criticisms of competence, see George Dowden, "'The Flower Thief'—Invalid or Incompetent," [Letters to the Editor], *Village Voice*, 7, no. 40 (July 26, 1962), 11; Pete Hamill, "Explosion in the Movie Underground," *Saturday Evening Post* 236, no. 33 (September 28, 1963), 82, 84. For arguments that this is an intentional choice, see Ron Rice, "Foundation for the Invention and Creation of Absurd Movies," *Film Culture*, no. 24 (Spring 1962): 19; P. Adams Sitney, "'The Sin of Jesus' and 'The Flower Thief,'" *Film Culture*, no. 25 (Summer 1962): 32–33.

39 Linda Williams, *Hard Core: Power, Pleasure, and the "Frenzy of the Visible"* (Berkeley: University of California Press, 1989), 58–152.

40 Thomas Waugh, "Homoerotic Representation in the Stag Film, 1920–40," *Wide Angle* 14, no. 2 (1992): 14–15. Female same-sex scenes are quite common and, like male same-sex scenes, are usually preludes to heterosexual couplings. See Williams, *Hard Core*.

41 My special thanks to David Gerstner for alerting me to this cinema. I have viewed a compilation of these films under the general title *Gay Erotica from the 1940s and 1950s: One to Many* (Apollo), *The Beach Bar Nightmare* (Apollo), *Auntie's African Paradise* (Zenith), *Cellmates* (Zenith), *The Cyclist* (Apollo), *Cocktails* (unknown), *Ben-Hurry* (Zenith), *The Captive* (Zenith), and *Fanny's Hill* (Pat Rocco for Bizarre).

42 Arthur Knight, quoted in Hoberman, "Big Heat," 61.

43 "Avant-Garde Movie Seized as Obscene," *New York Times*, March 4, 1964; Stephanie Gervis Harrington, "City Sleuths Douse 'Flaming Creatures,'" *Village Voice* 9, no. 21 (March 12, 1964), 3, 13; "Mekas Gaoled Again, Genet Film Does It," *Village Voice* 9, no. 22 (March 19, 1964), 13; "Cops Raid Homo Films Again," *Variety* 234, no. 4 (March 18, 1964), 5. *Variety*'s labeling of these films as "homo" was not without cause: Mekas had previously publicly represented the underground cinema as connected to homosexuality. See his *Village Voice* columns reprinted in *Movie Journal*: "*Flaming Creatures* and the Ecstatic Beauty of the New Cinema" (April 18, 1963), 82–83; "On the Baudelairean Cinema" (May 2, 1963), 85–86; "On *Blonde Cobra* and *Flaming Creatures*" (October 24, 1963), 101–3. *Flaming Creatures* premiered on April 29, 1963. Its seizure occurred on March 3, 1964 as part of a New York City cleanup for the 1964 World's Fair; see Hoberman, "Big Heat," 61, and Hoberman and Rosenbaum, *Midnight Movies*, 59–60, for excellent accounts of the film's legal history. Also see Dyer, *Now You See It*, 145–49; Tomkins, "All Pockets Open," 38–39; and, of course, Jonas Mekas, *Movie Journal: The Rise of a New American Cinema, 1959–1971* (New York: Collier Books, 1972). Tomkins notes that when Mekas brought *Flaming Creatures* to the December 1963 Knokke-le-Zoute International Experimental Film Competition, he showed it privately to Jean-Luc Godard, Roman Polanski, and others. Mekas' version is in "*Flaming Creatures* at Knokke-le Zoute," *Village Voice*, January 16, 1964, rpt. in *Movie Journal*, 111–115.

44 Tomkins, "All Pockets Open," 40. These films were also being seen and seized in Los Angeles. Arthur Knight had viewed the film there, and Mike Getz was found guilty on March 13, 1964 of screening "the obscene film" *Scorpio Rising* on March 7 at the Cinema Theater in Hollywood; Hoberman and Rosenbaum, *Midnight Movies*, 59–60. Mekas' versions are in "On Obscenity," *Village Voice*, March 12, 1964; "Underground Manifesto on Censorship," *Village Voice*, March 12, 1964; "Report from Jail," *Village Voice*, March 19, 1964, rpt. in *Movie Journal*, 126–30; "On the Misery of Community Standards," *Village Voice*, June 18, 1964, rpt. in *Movie Journal*, 141–44.

45 Eugene Archer, "*The Flower Thief*," *New York Times*, July 14, 1962, 11.

46 "Cinema Underground," *New Yorker* 39 (July 13, 1963), 17.

47 Pete Hamill, "Explosion in the Movie Underground," *Saturday Evening Post* 236, no. 33 (September 28, 1963), 82, 84.

48 "Flaming Censorship," *Nation* 198, no. 14 (March 30, 1964), 311; Susan Sontag, "A Feast for Open Eyes," *Nation* 198, no. 16 (April 13, 1964), 374–76; Susan Sontag, "Notes on 'Camp,'" [*Partisan Review*, 1964], rpt. in *Against Interpretation* (New York: Delta, 1978). Hoberman and Rosenbaum state that the editor who assigned Sontag the *Nation* piece was fired for doing so; *Midnight Movies*, 61. It is not clear to me why this would occur, but the decision may have had to do with the subsequent debates over morality. Do note that the *Nation* published filmmaker Ken Kelman's positive views on New American Cinema within the month: Ken Kelman, "Anticipations of the Light," *Nation* 198, no. 20 (May 11, 1964), 490–94. An excellent later analysis of *Flaming Creatures* is in Grandin Conover, "'Flaming Creatures': Rhapsodic Asexuality," *Village Voice* 9, no. 40 (July 28, 1964), 9 and 15.

49 Ross, *No Respect*, 147–65. Sontag was not the first to make the connection between this cinema and pop art; see Mekas, *Movie Journal*: "On Andy Warhol" (December 5, 1963), 109–10; "On Andy Warhol's *Sleep*" (January 30, 1964), 116.

50 Amos Vogel, "*Flaming Creatures* Cannot Carry Freedom's Torch," *Village Voice* 9, no. 29 (May 7, 1964), 9. See Mekas' response, "Movie Journal," *Village Voice* 9, no. 30 (May 14, 1964), 15.

51 Elizabeth Sutherland, "Flaming Cause," *Village Voice* 9, no. 30 (May 14, 1964), 4.

52 Dwight Macdonald, *On Movies* (New York: Berkeley Medallion Books, 1969), 341.

53 Also see Dwight Macdonald, "A Theory of Mass Culture," *Diogenes*, no. 3 (Summer 1953): 1–17; Dwight Macdonald, "Objections to the New American Cinema" in *The New American Cinema*, ed. Gregory Battcock (New York: Dutton, 1967), 197–204. On Macdonald and taste, see Ross, *No Respect*, 42–64.

54 "In Camera," *Films and Filming* 11, no. 2 (November 1964): 37.

55 Andrew Sarris, "The Independent Cinema" [1966], rpt. in *The New American Cinema*, ed. Battcock, 51. Also see Fred Wellington, "Liberalism, Subversion, and Evangelism: Toward the Definition of a Problem" in *The New American Cinema*, ed. Battcock, 38–47. Annette Michelson did not take the festival's prevailing position, siding with Sontag; see her festival address, "Film and the Radical Persuasion" [1966], rpt. in *The New American Cinema*, ed. Battcock, 83–102.

56 It is perhaps difficult to return to this time for film scholars who are now so familiar with representations of sexuality. Consider that the defense for the 1964 Los Angeles obscenity trial concerning Getz's screening of *Scorpio Rising* was pleased with an all-woman jury: "he feared that a male juror with anxieties about his masculinity might respond hysterically to the homoerotic undertones of Anger's film." Fred Haines, "Art in Court: 1. *City of Angels vs. Scorpio Rising*," *Nation* 199, no. 6 (September 14, 1964), 123. The women found Getz guilty.

57 On Warhol's involvement, see Stephen Koch, *Stargazer: Andy Warhol's World and His Films* (New York: Praeger, 1973); Dyer, *Now You See It*, 149–62; Calvin Tomkins, *The Scene: Reports on Post-Modern Art* (New York: Viking Press, 1976), 35–53; Hoberman and Rosenbaum, *Midnight Movies*, 58–75; Matthew Tinkcom, "Camp and the Question of Value," Ph.D. diss., University of Pittsburgh, 1995. Warhol's version is in Warhol and Hackett, *POPism*, 25–35 and throughout.

58 David Ehrenstein, "Interview with Andy Warhol," *Film Culture*, no. 40 (Spring 1966): 41.

59 Charles Boultenhouse, "The Camera as a God," *Film Culture*, no. 29 (Summer 1963), rpt. in *Film Culture Reader*, ed. P. Adams Sitney (New York: Praeger, 1970) 137.

60 Michael McClure, "Defense of Jayne Mansfield," *Film Culture*, no. 32 (Spring 1964), rpt. in *Film Culture Reader*, ed. P. Adams Sitney (New York: Praeger, 1970), 160–67.

61 Hoberman, *Vulgar Modernism*, 181. And an echo of the famous 1896 film *The Kiss*.

62 "An Interview with Kuchar Brothers" (March 5, 1964) in Mekas, *Movie Journal*, 122–26.

63 Ken Jacobs was later to indicate that he and Smith "hated" pop art. Distinguishing between pop art and camp, or, as Jacobs put it, his and Smith's "'Human Wreckage' aesthetic," is important for a finer discussion of these features. See Jacobs' 1971 interview quoted in Carel Rowe, *The Baudelairean Cinema: A Trend within the American Avant-Garde* (Ann Arbor, MI: UMI Research Press, 1982), 39. Also see Sasha Torres, "The Caped Crusader of Camp: Pop, Camp, and the *Batman* Television Series," in *Pop Out: Queer Warhol*, ed. Jennifer Doyle, Jonathan Flatley, and José Esteban Muñoz (Durham: Duke University Press, 1996), 238–55. Torres writes that although pop, camp, and gay sensibilities were by 1966 linked, they were not equivalents. She argues that camp was going through a "de-gaying" in the mid-1960s by Sontag and others, a de-gaying that permitted the potentially suspect *Batman* series to be considered "camp" but not gay.

64 Warhol and Hackett, POP*ism*, 12–15. Ironically, American abstract expressionism, while perhaps macho, was not immune to attacks by conservatives. In the early 1950s, some right-wingers accused creators of these paintings of hiding information in them to pass on to U.S. enemies. William Hauptman, "The Suppression of Art in the McCarthy Decade," *Artforum* 12, no. 2 (October 1973): 48–52.

65 Vivian Gornick, "It's a Queer Hand Stoking the Campfire," *Village Voice* 9, no. 25 (April 7, 1966), 1, 20.

66 "Saint Andrew," *Newsweek*, December 7, 1964, 102–4.

67 Shana Alexander, "Report from Underground," *Life* 58 (January 28, 1965), 23. See Mekas' reaction, "On the Establishment and the Boobs of the Shana Alexanders," *Village Voice*, February 11, 1965, rpt. in *Movie Journal*, 176–78.

68 Alan Levy, "Voice of the 'Underground Cinema,'" *New York Times Sunday Magazine*, September 19, 1965. Also see Eugene Boe, "Lights! Camera! But Where's the Action?" *Status*, March 1966, 71–74; Elenore Lester, "So He Stopped Painting Brillo Boxes and Bought a Movie Camera," *New York Times*, December 11, 1966.

69 Howard Junker, "The Underground Renaissance," *Nation* 201, no. 22 (December 27, 1965), 539; Stanley Kauffmann, *A World on Film* (New York: Dell, 1966), 424. Also see Robert Hatch, "Media-Mix," *Nation* 202, no. 5 (January 31, 1966), 139.

70 Hoberman and Rosenbaum, *Midnight Movies*, 68–69; Koch, *Stargazer*, 70–71.

71 Jack Kroll, "Underground in Hell," *Newsweek*, November 14, 1966, n.p. This preparation goes through an interest in pornography by mass media in 1965. See "On Perverts and Art," *Village Voice*, April 22, 1965, rpt. in Mekas, *Movie Journal*, 183–84.

72 But see the review by Dan Sullivan, "*The Chelsea Girls*," *New York Times*, December 2, 1966, 46.

73 Jack Kroll, "Up from Underground," *Newsweek*, February 13, 1967, 117–19.

74 "The New Underground Films," *Time*, February 17, 1967, 94–99. Bosley Crowther continued to disagree; see his review of *My Hustler*, *New York Times*, July 11, 1967, 29, in which he pointed out that the Cinematheque had moved to a new theater that used to show burlesque and nudie films. This was fitting for another "homosexual strip-tease." Also see Rosalyn Regelson, "Where Are 'The Chelsea Girls' Taking Us?" *New York Times*, September 24, 1967. These reviewers were a bit late in noticing this trend. In 1962, Rudy M. Franchi,

discussing X-rated movies, predicted the underground cinema would be "art" and "exhibited widely in art houses, playing with quality foreign and American films." "The Coming of Age in the X-Film," *Cavalier* (July 1962), 85.

75 Hoberman and Rosenbaum, *Midnight Movies*, 73; "In Camera," *Films and Filming* 13, no. 10 (July 1967), 38.

76 The late 1960s also was the beginning of the development of erotic films for gay audiences, in part because of changing obscenity laws. See Paul Alcuin Siebenand, *The Beginnings of Gay Cinema in Los Angeles: The Industry and the Audience* (Ann Arbor: UMI Press, 1980). On connections between these events and the development of hard-core pornographic exhibition, both hetero and homo, see Hoberman and Rosenbaum, *Midnight Movies*, 76; Tomkins, "All Pockets Open," 45.

77 Tyler, *Underground Film*, 224.

78 Critics of Warhol suggest that *Empire* was a camp joke: eight hours of a hard-on.

79 James, *Allegories of Cinema*, 317; Mellencamp, *Indiscretions*, 21 and throughout.

80 Thomas Waugh, "Cockteaser," in *Pop Out*, ed. Doyle *et al.*, 59–73; Roger McNiven, Ph.D. comprehensive exam, New York University, April 1987.

81 John D'Emilio, *Sexual Politics, Sexual Communities: The Making of a Homosexual Minority in the United States*, 1940–1970 (Chicago: University of Chicago Press, 1983), 129–75. Also see Neil Miller, *Out of the Past: Gay and Lesbian History from 1869 to the Present* (New York: Vintage Books, 1995), 340–54.

82 Elizabeth Lapovsky Kennedy and Madeline D. Davis, *Boots of Leather, Slippers of Gold: The History of a Lesbian Community* (New York: Routledge, 1993), 372–73.

"Out of the Closet and into the Universe"

Queers and *Star Trek*

HENRY JENKINS

> *Star Trek* celebrates its 25th anniversary in 1991. In that quarter century, one of the most important aspects of the series . . . has been the vision that humanity will one day put aside its differences to work and live in peace together. *Star Trek*, in its various television and motion picture forms, has presented us with Africans, Asians, Americans and Andorians, Russians and Romulans, French and Ferengi, Hispanics and Hortas, human and non-human men and women. In 25 years, it has also never shown an openly gay character.
>
> (Franklin Hummel, *Gaylactic Gazette*)[1]

> Perhaps someday our ability to love won't be so limited.
>
> (Dr Beverley Crusher, 'The Host', *Star Trek: The Next Generation*)

"2, 4, 6, 8, how do you know Kirk is straight?" the Gaylaxians chanted as they marched down the streets of Boston on Gay Pride day. "3, 5, 7, 9, he and Spock have a real fine time!" The chant encapsulates central issues of concern to the group: How do texts determine the sexual orientation of their characters and how might queer spectators gain a foothold for self-representation within dominant media narratives? How has *Star Trek* written gays and lesbians out of its future, and why do the characters and their fans so steadfastly refuse to stay in the closet? The chant captures the play between visibility and invisibility which is the central theme of this chapter and has, indeed, been a central theme in the struggle against homophobia in contemporary society.

The Boston Area Gaylaxians is a local chapter of the international Gaylactic Network Inc., an organization for gay, lesbian, and bisexual science fiction fans and their friends.[2] Founded in 1987, the group has chapters in many cities in the United States and Canada. Adopting the slogan, "Out of the closet and into the universe," the group has sought to increase gay visibility within the science fiction fan community and "to help gay fans contact and develop friendships with each other."[3] The group hosts a national convention, Gaylaxicon, which brings together fans and writers interested in sexuality and science fiction. Although only recently given official recognition from the Network, group members have organized a national letter-writing campaign to urge Paramount to acknowledge a queer presence in the twenty-fourth-century future represented on *Star Trek: The Next Generation*. Their efforts have so far attracted national attention from both the gay and mainstream press and have provoked responses from production spokespeople and several cast members. Gene Roddenberry publicly committed himself to incorporate gay characters into the series in the final months before his death, but the producers never delivered on that promise. The series *has* featured two episodes which can loosely be read as presenting images of alternative sexuality, "The Host," and "The Outcast." Although the producers have promoted these stories as responsive to the gay and lesbian community's concerns, both treat queer lifestyles as alien rather than familiar aspects of the Federation culture and have sparked further controversy and dissatisfaction among the Gaylaxians.

The fans' requests are relatively straightforward—perhaps showing two male crew members holding hands in the ship's bar, perhaps a passing reference to a lesbian lover, some evidence that gays, bisexuals, and lesbians exist in the twenty-fourth century represented on the program. Others want more—an explicitly gay or lesbian character, a regular presence on the series, even if in a relatively minor capacity. As far as the producers are concerned, homosexuality and homophobia are so tightly interwoven that there is no way to represent the first without simultaneously reintroducing the second, while for the fans, what is desired is precisely a future which offers homosexuality without homophobia.

What is at stake for these viewers is the credibility of Gene Roddenberry's oft-repeated claims about the utopian social vision of *Star Trek*. Roddenberry's reluctance to include queer characters in *Star Trek*, they argue, points to the failure of liberal pluralism to respond to the identity politics of sexual preference. As one fan wrote, "What kind of a future are we offered when there is no evidence that we exist?"[4]

[. . .]

Children of Uranus[5]

> During the course of our production, there have been many special interest groups who have lobbied for their particular cause. It is Gene Roddenberry's policy to present *Star Trek* as he sees it and not to be governed by outside influences.
>
> (Susan Sackett, executive assistant to Gene Roddenberry)[6]

> We had been the target of a concerted, organized movement by gay activists to put a gay character on the show.
>
> (Michael Piller, *Star Trek* writing staff supervisor)[7]

> In the late 1960's, a 'special interest group' lobbied a national television network to renew a series for a third season. If those networks had not listened to those with a special interest, *Star Trek* would not have returned and today *Star Trek* might very likely not be all of what it has become. You, Mr. Roddenberry, and *Star Trek* owe much to a special interest group: *Star Trek* fans. Perhaps you should consider listening to some of those same fans who are speaking to you now.
>
> (Franklin Hummel)[8]

The people who organized the national letter-writing campaign to get a queer character included on *Star Trek: The Next Generation* were not "outside influences," "special interest groups," or "gay activists." They saw themselves as vitally involved with the life of the series and firmly committed to its survival. As Hummel asserts, "we are *part* of *Star Trek*." They saw their goals not as antagonistic to Roddenberry's artistic vision but rather as logically consistent with the utopian politics he had articulated in *The Making of Star Trek* and elsewhere. Fans had long drawn upon Roddenberry's own comments about the program and its ideology as criteria by which to evaluate the series texts' ideological consistency. If fan writers often sought to deflect anxieties about ideological inconsistencies from producer (Roddenberry) to character (Kirk), the Gaylaxians had no such option. What was at stake was Roddenberry's refusal to act *as a producer* to reinforce the values he had asserted through extra-textual discourse. The fans reminded Roddenberry that he had said:

> To be different is not necessarily to be ugly; to have a different idea is not necessarily wrong. The worst possible thing that can happen to humanity is for all of us to begin to look and act and think alike.[9]

When, they asked, was *Star Trek* going to acknowledge and accept sexual "difference" as part of the pluralistic vision it had so consistently evoked? They cited his successful fight to get a black woman on the *Enterprise* bridge and his unsuccessful one to have a female second-in-command, and wondered aloud 'why can't *Star Trek* be as controversial in educating people about our movement as they were for the black civil rights movement?" (James).[10]

The people who organized the letter-writing campaign were *Star Trek* fans and, as such, they claimed a special relationship to the series, at once protective and possessive, celebratory and critical. Frank Hummel, one of the key organizers of the campaign, described his decision to take on Roddenberry:

> We expected more of *Star Trek*. A lot of the letters came from a simple, basic confusion. We didn't understand why *Star Trek* hadn't dealt with it. Here was *The Next Generation*. Here was a new series. Here was the late 1980s–1990s. Why didn't *Star Trek* deal with this? Why didn't they approach it the same way they approached casting an inter-racial crew? It was a puzzle.

Frank, like many of the others I interviewed, had started watching *Star Trek* as a child, had grown up with its characters and its concepts. *Star Trek* provided him with a way of linking his contemporary struggle for gay rights with successful campaigns in the 1960s on behalf of women's rights and black civil rights. The producers' refusal to represent gay and lesbian characters cut deeply:

> They betrayed everything *Star Trek* was—the vision of humanity I have held for over 25 years. They betrayed Gene Roddenberry and his vision and all the fans. They didn't have the guts to live up to what *Star Trek* was for.

Even here, we see evidence of a desire to deflect criticism from Roddenberry onto those (the unidentified "they") who "betrayed" his "vision."

Others might point to a series of compromises Roddenberry had made in the program ideology as evidence of a certain duplicity, or, more globally, as a failure of liberal pluralism to adequately confront issues of sexual identity:

Todd: 'I think Gene Roddenberry was this prototypical liberal—and I am not saying that in the most flattering terms. Just like the characters on *Star Trek*, he wanted to convince himself he was open minded and thoughtful and growing so he would do things to present that image and make superficial changes but when it came to something that really counted, really mattered, that wasn't going to go at all.'

In both versions, Roddenberry as *Star Trek*'s "author" embodies certain myths about 1960s' activism and its relationship to contemporary social struggle.

To understand the intensity of the Gaylaxians' responses, we need to consider more closely what science fiction as a genre has offered these gay, lesbian, and bisexual fans. David, a member of the Boston group, described his early experiences with the genre:

I wasn't very happy with my world as it was and found that by reading science fiction or fantasy, it took me to places where things were possible, things that couldn't happen in my normal, everyday life. It would make it possible to go out and change things that I hated about my life, the world in general, into something that was more comfortable for me, something that would allow me to become what I really wanted to be. . . . Being able to work out prejudices in different ways. Dealing with man's inhumanity to man. To have a vision for a future or to escape and revel in glory and deeds that have no real mundane purpose. To be what you are and greater than the world around you lets you be.

Lynne, another Gaylaxian, tells a similar story:

I wasn't very happy with my life as a kid and I liked the idea that there might be someplace else where things were different. I didn't look for it on this planet. I figured it was elsewhere. I used to sit there in the Bronx, looking up at the stars, hoping that a UFO would come and get me. Of course, it would never land in the Bronx but I still had my hopes.

What these fans describe is something more than an abstract notion of escapism—the persistent queer fantasy of a space beyond the closet doorway. Such utopian fantasies can provide an important first step toward political awareness, since utopianism allows us to envision an alternative social order which we must work to realize ("something positive to look forward to") and to recognize the limitations of our current situation (the dystopian present against which the utopian alternative can be read). Richard Dyer has stressed the significant role which utopian entertainment plays within queer culture, be it the eroticism and romanticism of disco, the passion of Judy Garland, the sensuousness of ballet and opera, or the plenitude of gay pornography.[11] Utopianism, Dyer writes, offers "passion and intensity" that "negates the dreariness of the mundane . . . and gives us a glimpse of what it means to live at the height of our emotional and experiential capacities."[12] The Gaylaxians describe their pleasure in science fiction both in terms of what utopia feels like (an abstract conception of community, acceptance, difference, fun) and what utopia looks like (a realist representation of alternative possibilities for sexual expression within futuristic or alien societies).

Science fiction represents a potential resource for groups which have had very limited stakes in the *status quo*, for whom the possibility of profound social change would be a desirable fantasy. Many of the Gaylaxians argue that science fiction is a particularly important genre for gay and lesbian readers:

> James: 'To me the purpose of fantasy and science fiction is to go where no one has gone before, to open our minds and to expand our intellect. The future is wider, bigger, larger and therefore that is a fertile ground for opening up possibilities that are now closed. I think it's the perfect genre to find a place where you can have your freedom because anything can happen here and anything is visible here.'

Science fiction offered these readers not one but many versions of utopia, sometimes contradictory or exclusive of each other, but that was part of the pleasure. Confronted with a world which seemed all too narrow in its acceptance of a range of sexualities, they retreated into a genre which offered many different worlds, many different realities, many different futures.

> Dana: 'Science fiction allows us the flexibility to be ourselves.'

The historic relations between science fiction and gay culture are complex and varied. Eric Garber and Lyn Paleo's *Uranian Worlds* lists more than 935 science-fiction stories or novels which deal with gay and lesbian themes and characters, starting with Lucian's *True History* (AD 200) and ending in the late 1980s.[13] Some of the stories they cite adopt homophobic stereotypes, yet they also see science fiction as a genre which was historically open to gay, bisexual, and lesbian writers who could express their sexuality in a disguised but potent form. As Garber and Paleo note, science-fiction fandom in the 1950s was closely linked to the emergence of homophile organizations, with fanzines, such as Lisa Ben's *Vice Versa* and Jim Kepner's *Toward Tomorrow*, amongst the first gay community publications in the United States. Writers like Marion Zimmer Bradley, Joanna Russ, and Samuel R. Delany were writing science-fiction novels in the 1960s which dealt in complex ways with issues of sexual orientation and envisioned futures which held almost unlimited possibilities for gays and lesbians.[14] These writers' efforts opened possibilities for a new generation of queer authors, working in all subgenres, to introduce gay, bisexual, and lesbian characters within otherwise mainstream science-fiction stories. A key shift has been the movement from early science-fiction stories that treated homosexuality as a profoundly alien sexuality toward stories that deal with queer characters as a normal part of the narrative universe and that treat sexuality as simply one aspect of their characterization.[15]

Many of these new writers, such as J. F. Rifkin, Melissa Scott, Susanna L. Sturgis, and Ellen Kushner, have been actively involved with the Gaylaxians and have been featured guests at their national convention. The Boston group holds regular meetings where professional science-fiction writers do readings or where struggling amateurs share their writings and receive feedback. Reviews of new books by queer writers appear regularly in the group's newsletters, helping to alert members to new developments in the field.

For many of the Gaylaxians, fandom represented an immediate taste of what science-fiction's utopian future might feel like. Fandom was a place of acceptance and tolerance. Asked to describe what science fiction offered queers, their answers focused as much on fandom as on any features of science fiction as a literary genre. The gay men contrasted belonging to fandom to the alienation of the gay bar scene and particularly to their inability to express their intellectual and cultural interests there. The female members contrasted fandom with the "political correctness" of the lesbian community, which they felt regarded their cultural interests as trivial since science fiction was not directly linked to social and political change. Belonging to the Gaylaxians, thus, allowed them a means of expressing their cultural identity (as fans), their sexual identity (as queers) and, for some at least, their political identity (as activists).

The conception of science fiction which emerges in such a context is highly fluid as a result of the group's efforts to provide community acceptance for all those who shared a common interest in science fiction, fantasy, or horror. If the MIT students offered a fairly precise and exclusive conception of the genre, one which preserved their professional status and expertise, the Gaylaxians struggle to find inclusive definitions:

> Betty: 'Science fiction is almost impossible to define. . . . Everyone you ask has a different definition.'
> Lynne: 'It can be anything from hard science to fantasy.'
> Dana: 'The author can do all kinds of things as long as the work is stable within its own universe. It can be close to present Earth reality or it can be as far-fetched as an intergalactic war from Doc Smith.'
> David: 'It's all out there! No matter what your vision of the future is it's out there in science fiction and fantasy. It's all available to us.'

Push harder and one finds that science fiction, for these fans, is defined less through its relationship to traditional science than through its openness to alternative perspectives and its ability to offer a fresh vantage point from which to understand contemporary social experience:

> John: 'Science fiction doesn't limit its possibilities. You can constantly throw in something new, something exciting. . . . Science fiction can be as outlandish as someone's imagination.'
> James: 'My definition of science fiction would be something alien, either the future, the past, different cultures, different worlds, different realities. It would have to be different from our perspective.'

Many of these fans had been drawn to science fiction through *Star Trek* and saw its universe as fully embodying these principles. Nobody had expected the original *Star Trek* series, released in a pre-Stonewall society, to address directly the concerns of gay, lesbian, and bisexual fans. They had taken it on faith that its vision of a United Federation of Planets, of intergalactic cooperation and acceptance, included them as vital partners. Yet, when *Star Trek: The Next Generation* appeared, at a time when queer characters had appeared on many American series, they hoped for something more, to be there on the screen, an explicit presence in its twenty-fourth century. "Everybody had a place in his [Roddenberry's] future," explained one fan. "It didn't matter if you were a man or a woman, white, black, yellow or green. If they can't take it one step further and include sexual orientation! God, if they don't have it under control in the twenty-fourth century, then it will never happen!" (James). Underlying this discussion lies a more basic concern: if *Star Trek* isn't willing to represent gay and lesbian characters in the 1990s, when would it be able to do so? As they watched a series of dramatic shifts in American attitudes towards gay and lesbian politics in the late 1980s and early 1990s, discussion of Star Trek provided them with one focal point for the group's discussion and comprehension of those changes, for talking about issues such as scientific research into the biological basis of sexual desire or efforts to abolish the ban on gays and lesbians serving in the United States military or the successes and setbacks of the Religious Right's campaign against Gay Rights legislation. Discussing Star Trek could provide a common ground for thinking through their conflicting feelings about this process of social transformation.

Where no [gay] man has gone before

> Mr. Roddenberry has always stated that he would be happy to include a character of *any* special interest group if such a character is relevant to the story.
>
> (Susan Sackett)[16]

> Were Uhura and LeForge included because the fact they were black was relevant to a story? Was Sulu included because the fact he was Asian was important to the plot? Were Crusher and Troi and Yar included because the fact they were female was relevant to an episode? I do not think so. These characters were included because they were important to the *spirit* of Star Trek.
>
> (Franklin Hummel)[17]

"We expected Star Trek to do it because we expected more of Star Trek than other series," one fan explained. They looked around them and saw other series—LA Law, Heartbeat, Thirtysomething, Quantum Leap, Northern Exposure, Days of Our Lives, Roseanne—opening up new possibilities for queer characters on network television, while their program could only hint around the possibility that there might be some form of sexuality out there, somewhere beyond the known universe, which did not look like heterosexuality. Star Trek was no longer setting the standards for other programs.

"Sooner or later, we'll have to address the issue," Roddenberry had told a group of Boston fans in November 1986, while Star Trek: The Next Generation was still on the drawing boards: "We should probably have a gay character on Star Trek."[18] "For your information, the possibility that several members of the Enterprise crew might be gay has been discussed in a very positive light. It is very much an area that a show like Star Trek **should** address," acknowledged David Gerrold, the man assigned to prepare the program Bible for Star Trek: The Next Generation.[19]

What were the Gaylaxians to make of the absence of gays and lesbians in the program universe, of Roddenberry's silence on the subject, as season after season came and went? Steve K., writing in The Lavender Dragon, a fan newsletter, saw only two possibilities consistent with the fan community's realist reading of the series:

> As a U.S. Navy veteran, I have had firsthand experience with the military's discrimination against gays and lesbians. It could be that the United Federation of Planets also bans homosexuals from serving in Starfleet. . . . That would explain the large number of never-married officers on board the Enterprise. Except for Dr. Crusher, none of the regular officers have been married (chiefs, e.g. Chief O'Brian, are non-commissioned

officers like sergeants). Does Starfleet have a huge closet? Still, this does leave the problem of civilian homosexuals. Since many of the episodes involve interaction with non-Starfleet characters, you would think that occasionally a gay or lesbian character would be somewhere in the 24th century. Has the Federation found a 'cure' for homosexuality?[20]

Invisibility meant either that gays were closeted or that they had ceased to exist. Neither was an attractive alternative to a group, whose motto, after all, is "Out of the closet and into the universe."

If they had listened more carefully, the fans might have recognized the slippage in Roddenberry's original comments, from including gay people as *characters* to dealing with homosexuality as an *issue*. What the Gaylaxians wanted was to be visible without being an "issue" or a "problem" which the script writers needed to confront and resolve. What they wanted was to see gays and lesbians treated as any other character would be treated within the program narrative, defined in terms larger than their sexuality while acknowledging a broader range of possible identities than would be acceptable within the contemporary social climate. As Theresa M. wrote:

> I want to see men holding hands and kissing in Ten-Forward. I want to see a smile of joy on Picard's face as he, as captain, joins two women together in a holy union, or pain across his face when he tells a man that his same-sex mate has been killed in battle. I want to hear Troi assure a crew member, questioning their mixed emotions, that bisexuality is a way to enjoy the best of what both sexes have to offer. I want to see crew members going about their business and acting appropriately no matter what their sexual orientation in every situation.[21]

Such moments of public affection, community ritual, or psychological therapy were common aspects of the program text; the only difference would be that in this case, the characters involved would be recognizably queer. The fans wanted to be visible participants within a future which had long since resolved the problem of homophobia. They felt this utopian acceptance to be more consistent with the program's ideology than a more dystopian representation of the social problems they confronted as gays, lesbians, and bisexuals living in a still largely homophobic society.

The program's producers would seem to agree, since their public responses to the letter-writing campaign often presuppose that queers would have gained tolerance and acceptance within *Star Trek*'s future, yet they evaded attempts to make this commitment visible on the screen. Curiously, the producers never acknowledged the economic risks in representing homosexuality on contemporary television, risks that might, arguably, involve alienating potential segments of their viewing public, but rather, like the fans, sought to justify their actions on the basis of appeals to the program's liberal ideology. Perhaps a public recognition of the political and economic context of the program's production would too directly undercut the authorial myth of Roddenberry as a crusading producer, which, for their own reasons, they saw as essential to *Star Trek*'s public image. The issue of gay identity on *Star Trek* was thus constructed by producers as a problem of representation rather than one of media access.[22] One can identify a series of basic assumptions about the representation of gay identities which underlie the producers' responses to the letter-writing campaign:

(1) The explicit representation of homosexuality within the program text would require some form of labeling while a general climate of tolerance had made the entire issue disappear. As Roddenberry explained in a statement released to the gay newspaper, *The Advocate*, "I've never found it necessary to do a special homosexual-theme story because people in the time line of *The Next Generation*, the 24th century, will not be labeled."[23]

(2) The representation of homosexuality on *Star Trek* would necessarily become the site of some form of dramatic conflict. As Richard Arnold, the man appointed to serve as *Star Trek*'s liaison with the fan community, explained:

> In Gene Roddenberry's 24th century *Star Trek* universe, homosexuality will not be an issue as it is today. How do you, then, address a non-issue? No one aboard the starship could care less what anyone else's sexual preference would be. . . . Do not ask us to show conflict aboard the Enterprise when it comes to people's choices over their sex, politics or religion. By that time, all choices will be respected equally.[24]

The producers, in a curious bit of circular logic, were insisting that the absence of gays and lesbians in the *Star Trek* universe was evidence of their acceptance within the Federation, while their visibility could only be read as signs of conflict, a renewed eruption of homophobia.

(3) Representation of homosexuality on *Star Trek* would make their sexuality "obvious" and therefore risk offence. As Arnold explained,

> Although we have no problem with any of our characters being gay, it would not be appropriate to portray them as such. A person's (or being's) sexual preference should not be obvious, just as we can't tell anyone's religious or political affiliations by looking at them.[25]

The signs of homosexuality, if they are there to be seen at all, automatically become too "obvious" in a homophobic society while the marks of heterosexuality are naturalized, rendered invisible, because they are too pervasive to even be noticed.

(4) Representation could only occur through reliance on easily recognizable stereotypes of contemporary gay identities. With a twist, the group which the producers didn't dare to offend turns out to be not the religious right (which has often put pressure on producers to exclude gay or lesbian characters) but the gay fans who are demanding representation within the program: "Do you expect us to show stereotypical behavior that would be more insulting to the gay community than supportive?"[26] Arnold asked a room of 1,200 *Star Trek* fans at Boston's Sheraton Hotel: "What would you have us do, put pink triangles on them? Have them sashay down the corridors?"[27]

(5) Representation of gay characters would require the explicit representation of their sexual practice. Arnold asked, "Would you have us show two men in bed together?"[28] Since a heterosexist society has reduced homosexuals to their sexuality, then the only way to represent them would be to show them engaged in sexual activity.

(6) Representation of gay characters and their relationships would be a violation of genre expectations. Adopting a suggestively feminine metaphor, Arnold asked, "Would you have us turn this [*Star Trek*] into a soap opera?" To deal with homosexuality as part of the character's lifestyle would be to transform (and perhaps, emasculate) *Star Trek* while to deal with heterosexuality as part of the character's lifestyle would be to leave its status as a

male-targeted action-adventure program unchanged. Any sort of concerted effort to respond to this logic requires an attempt to make heterosexuality rather than homosexuality visible, to show how its marks can be seen on the characters, the plots, and the entire environment:

> Frank: 'How do we know any of the characters are heterosexual? How do you know? Because you see them interact with other people, especially in their intimate relations. *Star Trek* has done that over and over and over again. You know Picard is heterosexual. You know Riker is heterosexual. Why? Because they've had constant relationships with people of the opposite sex. This has been done systematically as character development. Why not this same development of a gay character?'

(7) As a last resort, having failed to convince the Gaylaxians with their other arguments, the producers sought to deny their own agency in the production of the program and their own control over its ideological vision. "Should a *good* script come along that allows us to address the problems that the gay and lesbian community face on the planet today, then it will very likely be produced."[29] But, in fact, there had been a script, called "Blood and Fire," written by David Gerrold, in the very first season of *Star Trek: The Next Generation* at a time when producers were desperately looking for material to keep the fledgling series on the air. Gerrold's script used Regalian Blood Worms as a metaphor to deal with the issue of AIDS and included a gay couple as secondary characters. David Gerrold explained:

> All I had was a medical technician working with the doctor and a security guy. At no point do they do anything overt. But someone turns to them and says, 'How long have you two been together?' The other guy says, 'Since the academy.' That lets you know that they're gay, but if you don't know about gay people, like if you're under the age of 13, they're just good friends.[30]

Gerrold's script went through multiple revisions before being scuttled. The producers have consistently insisted that their decision not to produce "Blood and Fire" was based on its merits, not its inclusion of gay themes and characters. Gerrold, who parted company with Roddenberry shortly after this incident, has repeatedly challenged this account, charging that the episode was never filmed because the producers were uncomfortable with his attempts to introduce the issue of homosexuality into the *Star Trek* universe: "People complained the script had blatantly homosexual characters. Rick Berman said we can't do this in an afternoon market in some places. We'll have parents writing letters."[31]

Gerrold told his story at science-fiction conventions, on the computer nets, and to lots and lots of reporters. Copies of the script have circulated informally among Gaylaxians and other fans. "Blood and Fire" became part of the fan community's understanding of the program history and was a key factor in motivating the Gaylaxians to adopt more aggressive strategies in lobbying for their cause. "Good scripts are accepted, and this script was deemed not to be a good script," said Ernest Over, an assistant to the executive producer.[32]

The producers had said, repeatedly, in so many different ways, that the only way that queers could become visible within *Star Trek* was by becoming a problem, and so, gay, lesbian, and bisexual *Star Trek* fans became a problem for the producers. They organized a national letter-writing campaign; they posted notices on the computer nets; they went to the queer press and made their dissatisfaction with the producers' responses a public issue. Ernest

Over, himself a gay community activist, told *The Advocate* that the *Star Trek* office had received "more letters on this than we'd had on anything else."[33]

In the midst of the publicity, just a few months before his death, Gene Roddenberry issued a statement: "In the fifth season of *Star Trek: The Next Generation*, viewers will see more of shipboard life in some episodes, which will, among other things, include gay crew members in day-to-day circumstances."[34] An editorialist in the *Los Angeles Times* reported,

> This season, gays and lesbians will appear unobtrusively aboard the Enterprise. . . . They weren't 'outed' and they won't be outcasts; apparently they'll be neither objects of pity nor melodramatic attention. Their sexual orientation will be a matter of indifference to the rest of the crew.[35]

Leonard Nimoy, the actor who played Spock on the original *Star Trek*, responded that Roddenberry's decision was "entirely fitting" with the spirit and tradition of the series.[36]

When the Gaylaxians sought confirmation of Roddenberry's statements, they received no response. When reporters from the *Washington Blade* called, they received only a tape-recorded message from executive producer Rick Berman: "The writers and producers of *Star Trek: The Next Generation* are actively exploring a number of possible approaches that would address the issue of sexual orientation."[37] Once again, "the issue of sexual orientation" had substituted for the promise of queer characters.

[. . .]

Q for queer?

> What about non-human species homosexuality? A Klingon male in drag would surely be a highlight of the TV season. Or maybe a lesbian Vulcan, who logically decided that sex with men was unnecessary. Or even a Betazoid chicken hawk after the virginal Wesley Crusher. The ST:NG Enterprise has been the home of some homosexual stereotypes. Tasha Yar was at times the ultimate in butch female, not afraid of any man. Data is more anally retentive than even the *Odd Couple*'s Felix Unger. And Worf sometimes wears more leather than an entire issue of *Drummer*.
>
> (Steve K., *The Lavender Dragon*)[38]

> I'm sure we're just as strange to them.
>
> (Deanna Troi, "The Outcast")

[. . .] As D. A. Miller writes, queer connotation has the

> inconvenience of tending to raise this ghost all over the place. For once received in all its uncertainty, the connotation instigates a project of confirmation. . . . Connotation thus tends to light everywhere, to put all signifiers to a test of their hospitality.[39]

The constant promise and deferral of a gay character colored the Gaylaxians' relationship to the series and invited them to constantly read a gay subtext into the episodes. *Star Trek* seemed always on the verge of confessing its characters' sexual preferences, only to back away yet again.

If the producers have trouble thinking of ways to make homosexuality visible within *Star Trek*, if they couldn't seem to find a "good script" to tell that particular story, the Gaylaxians have no trouble locating possibilities. Watch any episode with them and they will show you the spot, the right moment, for a confession of previously repressed desire to come out from hiding:

> Lynne: 'Geordi realizes that the reason he can't seem to work things out with women is that he's gay. . . . Picard goes on shore leave and meets this great woman. Why can't he go on shore leave and meet this great man? It doesn't mean he always prefers men. He can mix it up a little. . . . And it [bisexuality] would probably flourish on board the *Enterprise*. They're real open minded there.'

Soon the entire group is participating within this carnival of outlaw signifiers, partaking of what Miller calls "the dream (impossible to realize, but impossible not to entertain) that connotation would quit its dusky existence for fluorescent literality, *would become denotation.*"[40]

For these fans, the text's silences about characters' sexuality or motives can be filled with homosexual desire, since, after all, in our society, such desire must often go unspoken. Straight fans, on the other hand, are apt to demand conclusive evidence that a character is homosexual and otherwise, read all unmarked characters as straight by default. What's at stake is the burden of proof and the nature of evidence within a culture where homosexuality most often appears within connotation rather than denotation. Such speculations cannot sustain direct challenge and often are not taken literally by those who advance them, but open up a fleeting possibility of imagining a different text existing in the margins of that which Paramount delivers.

Sometimes, the possibilities seem to cohere around a particular character, who appears to embody the richest potential for queer visibility, who builds upon the iconography and stereotypes of queer identity. Here, bids for character sexuality can be more strongly maintained since the text offers precisely the type of evidence that is most commonly presented within popular culture to indicate a character's potential homosexuality. Rumors surrounded the arrival of Tasha Yar as a character in *The Next Generation*'s first season. Maybe this is the queer character Roddenberry had promised: "Tasha Yar—an obvious bisexual character. . . . Considering what she went through as a child, she should be a lesbian" (Betty). Tasha Yar—tough, independent, security chief with short-cropped hair, from a planet where she was repeatedly gang-raped by men, able to fight against any and all adversaries, was the classic Amazon: "She could easily be conceived as being a lesbian" (David). But, as the fans are quick to note, she goes to bed with Data in the program's second episode, "The Naked Now": "When they decided to straighten her, they used an android. So we ended up hetero-sexualizing two perfectly wonderful characters. . . . Even if they had left the character alone and not heterosexualized Tasha Yar, we would have been farther ahead than we are now" (David).

The marks of heterosexuality, normally invisible, are made "obvious" by this interpretation, an act of violence committed against otherwise potentially queer characters, a reaction of homosexual panic which seeks to stabilize (or even to deny) their sexuality. Characters' sexualities do not remain unmarked for long within the world of *Star Trek* or, for that matter, the world of popular culture, which insists that characters be undeniably heterosexual even if their sexual preference is totally irrelevant to their narrative actions.[41] "Data has been assigned a sexual orientation, basically" (James). Data has been "heterosexualized." Yar has been "straightened."

Yet, again, how stable is that orientation? "Data is someone where bisexuality can be explored" (James). And, soon, the speculations are all open again:

James: 'Data is a scientist.'
David: 'Not only is he a scientist, he is an android and literally he could not have any qualms in the persona they have cast him. If he is fully functional, he's fully functional and would be able to function with another male.'
John: 'One of the primary roles of the Data character is to explore humanity, to learn about humanity. It would not only be plausible. It would be probable that he would want to explore all aspects of humanity including—'
All: 'A homosexual relationship.'
John: 'Having had a heterosexual relationship, he must be curious. He has this underlying curiosity about all aspects of humanity. He wanted to witness the marriage between O'Brian and his bride. He wanted to understand that institution. He must surely be interested in a homosexual relationship. Even interested in why prejudices—if they don't exist in the future—once existed against this type of relationship.'

Here, in a subversion of the producers' logic, a character can prove his interest in homosexuality by the insistence with which he investigates heterosexuality.

But there are more possibilities still:

John: 'I don't think they've ever approached Geordi's sexuality.'
Lars: 'Yes, they have.'
James: 'They've approached everyone's sexuality. . . .'
Lars: 'If they had an episode where Wesley seriously questioned and explored his sexuality—'
James: '—With Data.'
John: '—With Worf. What about the Klingons? Can't they conceivably be a homosexual race?'
James: 'I can't picture a gay Klingon.'
John: 'Historically, there have been many times when you've had extremely masculine warrior groups and there was a lot of homosexuality among them. The Greeks. The Romans. Ancient Japan. Ancient China.'

John moves beyond the terms of the text's own construction of character to evoke the discourse of gay history, itself just gaining a foothold within popular debates about sexuality but a powerful tool for challenging a straight society's ability to naturalize its own sexual categories.

And what about Q? That campy adventurer appears in Picard's bed in one episode and speaks enviously of that woman Picard is chasing: "If I had known this was a way I could get at you, I would have taken that form a long time ago." Could Q, who minces and swishes his way through every episode, be a Queen? Was Q, the outrageous shape shifter, Queer?

Dana: 'He's a flaming fag. He is and I love him. I think he's wonderful.'
Lynne: 'I think he's got a thing for Picard. I really do.'

The one point on which almost all of the Gaylaxians seemed to agree was that Q was possibly, though you can't be certain, queer, with the evidence residing as much in his evocation of subcultural codes of camp performance as in anything specifically said about his character within the series.

And that was precisely the problem which *Star Trek*'s producers hadn't foreseen. In refusing to demarcate a certain denotative space for homosexuality within the text, they left *Star Trek* open to wholesale reclamation. "They could have introduced a character a long time ago and it just comes out, two, three years later, that he's gay" (John). Soon, all of the characters are potentially queer—at least on the level of connotation:

David: 'A large percentage of the people who settled the west—the cowboys, the frontiersmen—pushed a path away from civilization because they were gay.'
James: 'Using that same analogy, it is not theoretically impossible that once we will start migrating into outer space, gay people will form their own outer space societies and colonies. I don't think that's far-fetched at all.'

Yes, it is "not theoretically impossible" that any or all of these characters could be bisexual. But, the double negative here is suggestive of the fans' insecurity about their own interpretive moves. The speculations can crumple almost as fast as they appear. At most, you can claim, we don't know for sure whether he or she is straight:

James: 'Q can be campy, campy to the campiest, but he would not be *the* homosexual character.'
Lars: 'No, No, No, No.'
David: 'I don't get any feelings of homosexuality from Q. Not at all. I don't get any feelings of heterosexuality from Q either. The best I could do would be to describe the character as asexual.'
John: 'It's more just plain fun, just the writers having fun.'

For a split second, the screen seemed open to all kinds of possibilities and there appeared to be gays and lesbians everywhere in *Star Trek*. Look again and all you see is "the writers having fun."

And so, for many, the experience has been one of tremendous frustration and disillusionment. Some hardcore members continue to write letters, hoping to make their case once again at a time when the production staff on *Star Trek* is undergoing another transition in the wake of Roddenberry's death or hoping that their concerns may surface and be better met within *Star Trek Deep Space 9*. For many others, the myth of *Star Trek* as a progressive alternative to commercial television seems to have dissolved into a new recognition of the ideological constraints on the representation of gay identities within mainstream entertainment.

[. . .]

Reconsidering resistant reading

Resistance is futile. You will be assimilated.

(*Science Friction*)[42]

Cultural studies' embrace of the model of resistant reading is a logical response to theoretical traditions which spoke of readers only in terms of textually constructed subject positions. Resistant reading, as a model, addresses many important questions about the ideological power of the mass media and the relationship between "the viewer and the viewed." Resistant reading, however, only describes one axis of a more complex relationship between readers and texts. The reading practices characteristic of fandom are never purely and rarely openly resistant to the meanings and categories advanced by program producers. Often, as we have seen, the fans' resistant reading occurs within rather than outside the ideological framework provided by the program and is fought in the name of fidelity to the program concepts. The consummate negotiating readers, fan critics work to repair gaps or contradictions in the program ideology, to make it cohere into a satisfying whole which satisfies their needs for continuity and emotional realism. Fandom is characterized by a contradictory and often highly fluid series of attitudes towards the primary text, marked by fascination as well as frustration, proximity as well as distance, acceptance of program ideology as well as rejection. The fans feel a strong identification with the programs, the characters, the producers, and their ideological conceptions, even when they feel strong frustration with the failure of the producers to create stories they would like to see told.

As I have discussed the Gaylaxians with non-fan friends, they often demand to know why these fans don't simply walk away from *Star Trek*, shift their attention to some other text which more perfectly responds to their political agendas or gratifies their desires. Leaving aside the problems which all gay, lesbian, and bisexual viewers face in finding any commercially available text which explicitly acknowledges their sexual identities, this question fails to grasp the particular character of their relationship to the program. *Star Trek* has been a consistent presence in their lives for more than twenty-five years, a text which has offered them endless amounts of pleasure and fascination, even if it has not always delivered all they wanted from it. *Star Trek* continues to be important as a utopian space for their fantasies, still offering them a taste of "what utopia feels like" even if it refuses to show them what (*their*) utopia might look like.

A model of resistant reading cannot, therefore, accurately describe the group's relationship to such a series, nor can their engagement with *Star Trek* be reduced to the politics of the letter-writing campaign itself. Indeed, many group members were reluctant to engage in the letter-writing campaign for fear that it might tarnish their long-term relationship to the series and might politicize their relationship to fandom, a space they had sought out specifically to escape the more doctrinaire corners of the gay and lesbian community. Bob, for example, objected that the letter-writing campaign had "forced the issue" and, as a result, the episodes which had been produced were equally "forced." Resistant reading describes only one side of the ebb and flow of desire which links these viewers to the texts of television science fiction.

Moreover, we need to identify ways in which resistant reading is not necessarily a sufficient response to dissatisfaction with the images currently in circulation. As many writers have noted, resistant reading risks becoming a catch-all solution for all the problems within popular culture, a way of escaping the need for ideological criticism or research into the political economy of media institutions. A model of resistant reading quickly becomes profoundly patronizing if it amounts to telling already socially marginalized audiences that they should be satisfied with their ability to produce their own interpretations and should not worry too much about their lack of representation within the media itself. Resistant reading can sustain the Gaylaxians' own activism, can become a source of collective identity and mutual support, but precisely because it is a subcultural activity which is denied public visibility, resistant reading cannot change the political agenda, cannot challenge other constructions of gay identity and cannot have an impact on the ways people outside of the group think about the issues which matter to the Gaylaxians. Slash, or K/S fiction, represents a long-standing tradition in the women's fan-writing community which poses ways of constructing homoerotic fantasies employing the series characters. Slash, as many writers have now noted, represents a powerful form of resistant reading, an active appropriation and transformation of dominant media content into forms of cultural production and circulation that speak to the female fan community's needs and interests. Slash has proven empowering to its female fan readers and writers, helping them to articulate and explore their sexual fantasies, bringing them together into a community across various barriers which isolate them. Slash, by translating politics into the personal, gave them a way to speak about their experiences and commitments. Some members of the Gaylaxians have embraced slash as a form which can also express their fantasies about the series and their desires for its future development. *Science Friction*, a *Star Trek: The Next Generation* slash zine distributed at the 1992 Gaylaxicon, specifically presented itself as a response to the failure of the letter-writing campaign: "Our motto is: If Paramount can't give us that queer episode, just make it so!"[43]

For many group members, however, slash does not represent the appropriate response to this issue. The fantasy of slash is not their fantasy, does not speak to their desire for visibility and recognition. The circulation of slash within their subcultural community cannot adequately substitute for their lack of access to the media, since the aired episodes, even within fandom, enjoy an authority which cannot be matched by any subcultural production and since, as they often stress, their push for a gay character on the aired episodes is intended as much for the consumption of closeted gay teenagers or straight parents, friends, and co-workers as for the group itself.

Cultural studies' embrace of the model of resistant reading, then, only makes sense in a context which recognizes the centrality of issues of media access and media ownership. Resistant reading is an important survival skill in a hostile atmosphere where most of us can do little to alter social conditions and where many of the important stories that matter to us can't be told on network television. It is, however, no substitute for other forms of media criticism and activism. The Gaylaxians' reception of *Star Trek* points to the importance of linking ethnographic research on resistant readers or subcultural appropriations with a political economy of media ownership and control and with the ideological analysis of program content. If earlier forms of ideological analysis worked from the assumption that texts constructed reading subjects, this new mixture would assume that readers play an active role in defining the texts which they consume but: (a) they do so within a social, historical, and cultural context that shapes their relative access to different discourses and generic models for making sense of the program materials; (b) they do so in relation to institutional power that may satisfy or defer audience desires; and (c) they do so in regard to texts whose properties may facilitate or resist the readers' interpretive activities. The relationship between readers, institutions, and texts is not fixed but fluid. That relationship changes over time, constantly shifting in relation to the ever-changing balance of power between these competing forces.

Notes

1 Franklin Hummel, "Where None Have Gone Before," *Gaylactic Gazette*, May 1991, p. 2. I am indebted to John Campbell for his extensive assistance in recruiting members of the Gaylaxians to participate in the interviews for this chapter. Interviews were conducted both in informal settings (members' homes) as well as more formal ones (my office), depending on the size and the needs of the groups. As it evolved, the groups were segregated by gender.

2 For more information on the Gaylaxian Network, see Franklin Hummel, "SF Comes to Boston: Gaylaxians at the World Science Fiction Convention," *New York Native*, October 23, 1989, p. 26.

3 Gaylaxians International, recruitment flier.

4 Theresa M., "*Star Trek: The Next Generation* Throws Us a Bone . . .," *The Lavender Dragon*, April 1992, 2: 2, p. 1.

5 The nineteenth-century word, Uranian, was coined by early German homosexual emancipationist Karl Ulrichs and used popularly through the First World War to refer to homosexuals. As Eric Garber and Lyn Paleo note, "It refers to Aphrodite Urania, whom Plato had identified as the patron Goddess of homosexuality in his *Symposium*."

6 Susan Sackett, executive assistant to Gene Roddenberry, letter to Franklin Hummel, March 12, 1991.

7 Mark A. Altman, "Tackling Gay Rights," *Cinefantastique*, October 1992, p. 74.

8 Franklin Hummel, Director, Gaylactic Network, letter to Gene Roddenberry, May 1, 1991.

9 Ibid.

10 The analogy John and other Gaylaxians draw between the black civil rights movement of the 1960s and the queer civil rights movement of the 1990s is a controversial one. But it is hardly unique to these fans. This analogy has been part of the discursive context surrounding Bill Clinton's efforts to end the American military's ban on gay and lesbian enlistment.

11 Many of Dyer's most important essays on this topic can be found in Richard Dyer, *Only Entertainment* (New York: Routledge, Chapman and Hall, 1992). On Judy Garland and gay audiences, see Richard Dyer, *Heavenly Bodies: Film Stars and Society* (New York: St. Martin's Press, 1986). For another central text in arguments about the politics of utopian entertainment, see Fredric Jameson, "Reification and Utopia in Mass Culture," *Social Text*, Winter 1979, pp. 130–48.

12 Richard Dyer, "In Defence of Disco," *Only Entertainment* (London: Routledge, 1992), p. 156. What Dyer describes here as "banality" is what fans refer to as "the mundane," while making a similar argument about the pleasures of fandom as a repudiation or movement away from "the mundane."

13 Eric Garber and Lyn Paleo, *Uranian Worlds: A Guide to Alternative Sexuality in Science Fiction, Fantasy and Horror* (Boston: G. K. Hall, 1990).

14 Several of the writers associated with the original *Star Trek* series made important contributions to the development of gay and lesbian science fiction: Theodore Sturgeon,

who wrote "Amok Time" and "Shore Leave," two of the best-loved episodes, had been dealing with issues of alien sexuality and homosexuality in his fiction as early as 1957; David Gerrold, who wrote "Trouble with Tribbles" and was closely involved in the development of *Star Trek: The Next Generation*, was the author of a 1973 science-fiction novel, *The Man Who Folded Himself*, which dealt with the auto-erotic and homoerotic possibilities of time travel; Norman Spinrad, the author of "The Doomsday Machine," wrote stories which dealt, not always sympathetically, with alternative sexualities and had included gay characters in his fiction prior to his involvement in *Star Trek*.

15 Clearly, these newer representations of gay characters, rather than the older representations of the problem or issue of gay sexuality, set expectations about how *Star Trek* might best address the concerns of its gay, lesbian, and bisexual viewers.

16 Sackett, op. cit. Roddenberry has, at various times, acknowledged that he saw his inclusion of Uhura on the original series as a contribution to the civil rights movement, that he had added Chekhov in response to a *Pravda* editorial calling for an acknowledgment of Soviet accomplishments in space, and that he introduced the blind character, Geordi, on *Star Trek: The Next Generation* as a response to the many disabled fans he had encountered through the years. Given such a pattern, it was not unreasonable for the Gaylaxians to anticipate a similar gesture towards gay, lesbian, and bisexual viewers.

17 Hummel, *Gaylactic Gayzette*, op. cit.

18 Edward Gross, *The Making of The Next Generation* (Las Vegas: Pioneer Books) as reprinted in *Gaylactic Gayzette*, May 1991.

19 David Gerrold, letter to Frank Hummel, November 23, 1986.

20 Steve K., "Gays and Lesbians in the 24th Century: *Star Trek—The Next Generation*," *The Lavender Dragon*, August 1991, 1: 3, p. 1.

21 Theresa M., ibid.

22 The commercial success of programs like *Northern Exposure*, *LA Law*, *In Living Color* or *Roseanne*, all of which had previously included gay, lesbian, or bisexual recurring characters, might have substantially decreased the risk of including similar characters on *Star Trek*, though the industry's understanding of audience acceptance of queer visibility was shifting at the time this debate occurred.

23 "*Star Trek*: The Next Genderation," *The Advocate*, August 27, 1991, p. 74.

24 Richard Arnold, letter to J. DeSort Jr, March 10, 1991.

25 Richard Arnold, letter to J. DeSort Jr, September 10, 1989.

26 Ibid.

27 Mark A. Perigard, "Invisible, Again," *Bay Windows*, February 7, 1991, p. 8.

28 Richard Arnold, letter to J. DeSort Jr, March 10, 1991.

29 Ibid.

30 Clark, p. 74; see also Gross, op. cit.; Altman, (1992) pp. 72–3.

31 Altman (1992), p. 72. Note that Berman or the other producers have never made similar arguments in their public statements about the controversy, always suggesting other reasons for their failure to introduce gay, lesbian, or bisexual characters into the series.

32 Clark, p. 74.

33 Ibid.

34 Ibid.

35 Ruth Rosen, "*Star Trek* Is On Another Bold Journey," *Los Angeles Times*, October 30, 1991.

36 Leonard Nimoy, "Letters to the Times: Vision of *Star Trek*," *Los Angeles Times*, November 6, 1991.

37 John Perry, "To Boldly Go . . . These Are the Not-So-Gay Voyages of the Starship Enterprise," *The Washington Blade*, September 20, 1991, p. 36.

38 Steve K., *The Lavender Dragon*, August 1991, 1: 3, p. 2.

39 D. A. Miller, "Anal *Rope*", in Diana Fuss (ed.), *Inside/Out: Lesbian Theories, Gay Theories* (New York: Routledge, Chapman and Hall, 1991), p. 125.

40 Miller (1991), p. 129.

41 The Gaylaxians note, for example, a similar pattern in the introduction and development of Ensign Ro in *Star Trek: The Next Generation*'s fifth season: Ro, like Yar, drew on iconography associated with butch lesbians, and appearing in the midst of the letter-writing campaign was read as the long-promised queer character. Within a few episodes of her introduction, however, the program involved her in a plot where the *Enterprise* crew loses its memory and Riker and Ro become lovers. As one Gaylaxian explained during a panel discussion of the series at Gaylaxicon, "Oops! I forgot I was a lesbian!"

42 *Science Friction* (Toronto, 1992).

43 "Editorial: Welcome to Science Friction," *Science Friction* (Toronto, 1992).

Reviewing Queer Viewing 14

CAROLINE EVANS AND LORRAINE GAMMAN

[. . .]

In this chapter we want to shift the course of the debate about the gaze by engaging with what Constantine Giannaris has described as "genderfuck".[1] By importing some queer notions into the world of critical theory, it may be possible to begin to acknowledge many perverse but enjoyable relations of looking. Our reasoning is not only that today's complex visual iconography requires the sort of theory that can comprehend it, but that previous models of the gaze have produced some very one-dimensional accounts of viewing relations.

[. . .]

The male body as erotic spectacle—women and sexual looking

[Laura] Mulvey bases many of her arguments on the assumption that "the male figure cannot bear the burden of sexual objectification."[2] It is true that when she wrote this in the 1970s there were fewer eroticized images of men in circulation, although Steve Neale has pointed out instances of covert male objectification in mainstream cinema, specifically in Hollywood epics involving gladiators and cowboys.[3]

In "Don't Look Now: The Male Pin-Up" Richard Dyer looks at the circumstances in which the eroticization of the male body is sanctioned, and the conditions under which women are permitted to look. He argues for the instability of the male pin-up, first, because the pin-up denies he is the object of the female gaze by the direction of his look. Second, the pin-up denies his passivity as an object for the gaze by being active. Third, the pin-up wants to be the phallus but can't; his flaccid penis can never match the mystique and power of the phallus. "Hence the excessive, even hysterical, quality of so much male imagery. The clenched fists, the bulging muscles, the hardened jaws . . ."[4]

Whereas Richard Dyer's article considers the heterosexual eroticization of the male body, Steve Neale's article looks at the homoerotic component of the male gaze and, while agreeing with many of Mulvey's premises, he argues that mainstream cinema has to deny the possibility of an erotic relationship between the male spectator and the protagonist. This argument about the disavowal of the explicitly homoerotic in representation has also been made by

Michael Hatt and D. A. Miller.[5] Yet Miller, unlike Neale, argues that the gay male cult of developed musculature is an "explicit aim . . . to make the male body visible to desire."[6] Miller differentiates

> the macho straight male body and the so-called gym-body of gay male culture. The first deploys its heft as a *tool* (for work, for its potential and actual intimidation of other, weaker men or of women) – as both an armoured body and a body wholly given over to utility. . . . The second displays its muscle primarily in terms of an *image* openly appealing to, and deliberately courting the possibility of being shivered by, someone else's desire.[7]

Many writers, among them Andy Medhurst and Yvonne Tasker, have argued that the degree of objectification of men in cinema has become more overt than ever before.[8] Male stars such as Rudolf Valentino and Cary Grant had always achieved the status of sex objects but over the last twenty years, from Richard Gere to Mel Gibson, the naked male body has been increasingly displayed and sexualized.

This objectification of the male body is not only confined to cinema. Throughout the 1980s and 1990s men's bodies were increasingly featured in advertising and fashion imagery. Examples include: the first Calvin Klein advertising campaign; Nick Kamen in the Levi's ad; fashion spreads in magazines such as *i-D* and *The Face*; the work of photographer Bruce Weber and stylist Ray Petri, and fashion designers such as Jean-Paul Gaultier. Frank Mort describes how, in the 1980s, young men were sold advertising images in which they were "stimulated to look at themselves—and other men—as objects of consumer desires . . . getting pleasures previously branded taboo or feminine."[9]

By the 1990s "porn" magazines for women, such as *For Women* and *Women Only*, founded in 1992 and 1993 respectively, were utilizing codes about male objectification previously only found in gay magazines aimed at homosexual men. These women's magazines created eroticized images of men specifically for women to consume, perhaps for masturbatory purposes. Their founding editor, Isabel Koprowski, says that even though they

> can't show an erection . . . we found that many women do want to see the Chippendale type, very muscular, oiled bodies. They also want to see men who look as though they've got personality: men who perhaps aren't as well developed: and they want, you know, dark men, fair men, red-headed men – all kinds of men. The thing that really impressed me was that for a men's magazine you could fill it with busty blondes and with very little editorial and men would buy it. You cannot do that with women . . .[10]

Despite the appearance of male sex objects in the early 1980s, some feminist critics continued to argue that men cannot bear the burden of sexual objectification and that the male gaze cannot be simply inverted to produce a straightforward female gaze. Mary Ann Doane, for example, in her first essay on female spectatorship, suggested that when a woman looks at male striptease her first reaction is to associate this body with a female role and to imagine a woman stripping. This is because, she argues,

> the male striptease, the gigolo – both inevitably signify the mechanism of reversal itself, constituting themselves as aberrations whose acknowledgement simply reinforces the dominant system of aligning sexual difference with a subject/object dichotomy.[11]

Suzanne Moore, in "Here's Looking at You, Kid,"[12] was among the first critics to differ from Mary Ann Doane and to draw attention to the voyeuristic heterosexual female gaze as well as to shifts, in the last ten years, in representations of men and masculinity. Moore points out that gay porn had always eroticized the male body. She argues that the codes and conventions associated with gay porn, taken up by photographers like Bruce Weber (whose work was regularly featured in magazines in the 1980s), created a different space for women (as well as men) as active voyeurs of erotic male spectacle.

The British style magazines of the 1980s (The Face, i-D, Blitz) were the first magazines that were marketed to both sexes and recognized that pictures of pop stars and fashion models were "polysemic." They could speak, for example, both to a gay man and a straight woman at the same time. (Linda Williams has discussed pornography which is targeted equally at gay men and straight women in the USA.)[13] More and more images in contemporary culture make many forms of address to more than one audience, and allow the possibility of multiple identifications by the spectator. Of course, images have always been capable of speaking differently to different spectators, but the new style magazines of the 1980s were more knowing. They gave readers "permission" to be promiscuous with images, and they permitted images to function ambiguously, and thereby to speak to a range of different subject positions. Indeed in the 1980s advertisers used images of "new men" to promote products to men—who were now discovered to be shopping—as well as to women, whom they recognized would also enjoy them, because traditionally women were found to make 85 per cent of consumer purchases.[14] While Moore did not overtly make the case for a ubiquitous female gaze, she argued that "homoerotic representations, far from excluding the (voyeuristic) female gaze, may actually invite it."[15]

Lesbian/gay spectators and lesbian representations

Many lesbian and gay critics have argued that gay and lesbian representations and gay and lesbian desire pose a challenge to the Mulveyian framework.[16] All have utilized psychoanalytic models to some extent, either using Freud, Lacan, or debates informed by psychoanalysis from film theory. Two main themes emerge throughout this work. The first concerns the dynamics of sexual desire of the audience in relation to images. The second concerns the way in which individuals narcissistically identify with images of people in all sorts of ways, including people not of the same sex. (For instance, Richard Dyer has discussed the way some gay men identify with Judy Garland.)[17] These questions often get conflated and below we discuss Jackie Stacey's paper on the lesbian spectator to illustrate how such conflation is problematic.

Jackie Stacey's analysis of two mainstream Hollywood films from different periods, All About Eve (1950) and Desperately Seeking Susan (1985),[18] reviews the psychoanalytic framework of film. This project, for virtually the first time, includes the lesbian spectator in the debate and looks at sexual desire in relationship to sexual "similarity" as opposed to sexual difference. Her approach is different from that of Richard Dyer, who writes about identification. Although Stacey does ask how lesbian women identify with male protagonists she suggests this approach can be too narrow:

> one of the limits of this approach may be that a more detailed analysis of the lesbian audience would reveal a diversity of readings and pleasures or displeasures in relation

to mainstream cinema. . . . There is likely to be a whole set of desires and identifications with different configurations at stake which cannot necessarily be fixed according to the conscious sexual identities of the cinematic spectator.[19]

Stacey goes on to argue that "the rigid distinction between *either* desire *or* identification, so characteristic of psychoanalytic film theory, fails to address the construction of desires which involve a specific interplay of both processes."[20] So Stacey's approach frames lesbian desires partly in relationship to similarities between women on the screen and the possibilities for identification this creates for women in the audience. She stresses that lesbian spectatorship, like all spectatorship, is often a "contradictory" experience. Teresa de Lauretis is one of several writers who criticize Stacey's account. She argues that Stacey has "desexualized" the lesbian spectator, and instead made the case for female narcissism, rather than erotic contemplation of women by women.[21]

Nevertheless, Stacey's article highlights the psychoanalytic point that all forms of looking are sexually charged because of the scopic drive. As Jacqueline Rose argues:

> there can be no work on the image, no challenge to its power of illusion and address which does not simultaneously challenge the fact of sexual difference. . . . Hence one of the chief drives of an art which addresses the presence of the sexual in representation – to expose the fixed nature of sexual identity as a phantasy and, in the same gesture, to trouble, break up, or rupture the visual field before our eyes.[22]

Furthermore, Stacey relies on the specifically Lacanian point that looking itself is split between sexual objectification and narcissistic identification. Obviously in sexual relationships there may be elements of narcissism coexisting with voyeuristic objectification. Stacey, like Metz and Mulvey, suggests a connection between the mirror and the cinema screen and the capacity individuals have to identify with objects (the mirror image or the cinematic image). Her model of spectatorship returns to Lacan's point that the mirror image of the mirror stage is both an adversary (a specular opposite) and an identical image.[23] Lacan argues that identification is partly made through aggression and rivalry—hence objectification and identification may be closely meshed and not opposites.

Additionally some feminist critics have found Stacey's paper on lesbian spectatorship limited. The equation of complexity and fluidity specifically with the lesbian spectator is thought to be a problem, not least because all spectators may be both complex and fluid in their identificatory processes. Judith Mayne has argued that no adequate model of lesbian spectatorship has yet been found. Lesbian desire may disrupt the psychoanalytic model but, she says:

> Quite honestly, I have some ambivalance about a theory of lesbian spectatorship. The models of female spectatorship that have been elaborated in feminist film theory disturb me on two counts. First, female spectatorship becomes the process of displacement itself: contradiction, oscillation, mobility. Though I'm as interested in contradiction as the next person, there is too great a tendency to valorise contradiction for its own sake. So, second, the female spectator becomes the site at which contradiction itself is embodied and it begins to appear that the female spectator functions very much like the Woman in classical cinema – as the figure upon whom are projected all the messy,

troublesome, complicated things that don't fit elsewhere. I would rather start from the assumption that all spectatorship is potentially contradictory, so contradiction doesn't have to carry this utopian burden as proof of some kind of resistant force.[24]

We would take Mayne's arguments about lesbian spectatorship further and suggest that no adequate model of spectatorship has been posited for any individual or social group. But certainly it seems far too simplistic to argue that who you sleep with may determine how you identify with cinematic images.

However, while there may be no such thing as an essentially "lesbian" gaze, there is certainly lesbian imagery in circulation.[25] Suzie Bright has observed,[26] lesbian porn videos featuring butch/femme relationships (women without bouffant hair and long fingernails, enthusiastically performing sex) are experiencing a consumer boom in the USA. Evidently, many lesbians enjoy these videos which eroticize women for women. Some would argue that this is because there is a different gaze at work within them. We would argue, however, that there is no essential "lesbian gaze" at work here, but that lesbian filmmakers and lesbian audiences bring different cultural competences[27] to bear on the production and consumption of lesbian imagery. This is why, as Bright points out,[28] mainstream porn producers don't seem to be able to get it right; they don't know lesbian subcultural codes and fail adequately to address the lesbian market.

We would also argue that the "cultural competence" of the lesbian spectator (and lack of such competence in other viewers) may influence the way representations are viewed and understood by some women. Using Foucault's model of discourse we would argue against any essentialist model of the lesbian gaze and instead suggest that lesbian viewers may bring certain subcultural experiences and knowledge to the reading of specific texts. This may give these women a different perspective on the erotic images in question.

The point we are making is that there are many visual clues and "cultural competences" which generate interpellation, identification, and voyeurism in the cinema. And these visual signs need more analysis and investigation, rather than relying on ideas about "authentic" sexual aims.

On looking at the photographs of British-based photographer Della Grace in her book *Lovebites* Reina Lewis has commented:

> There is an element of being looked at in this collection that does not simply relate to the stereotypical gaze of the (male) voyeur . . . [it] forces us to theorise a lesbian gaze . . .[29]

But when we looked at this overtly "lesbian" collection we, like Reina Lewis, found it impossible to pin the photographs down to any fixed reading. Although Grace may deliberately be celebrating lesbian imagery, Lewis makes the point that it is not only lesbians, or straight women, who may find the images erotic. Indeed, there is no controling, single, ubiquitous, female gaze that excludes heterosexuals but a range of possibilities for spectatorship offered by the photographs. Similarly, lesbian films from *Lianna* (1982) to *Desert Hearts* (1984) appear to invite a multiplicity of spectator positions, including lesbian spectatorship, and certainly do not simply equate with popular notions about the male gaze or any simple "inversion" of it.

With regard to Della Grace's photographs it is possible that the spectator may not necessarily "understand" the relationship of particular "signs," specific haircuts, footwear, and clothing, that have subcultural meaning in some lesbian communities. What we are arguing, then, is that some codes associated with visual images of women (which are often overt in lesbian representation but perhaps require subcultural knowledge in order to recognize or even eroticize them) may be central to constructing lesbian subjectivity.

The s/m scenarios and subcultural fashion codes of Della Grace's work may interpellate "lesbian spectators" as well as other knowing viewers (be they heterosexual, bisexual, lesbian, or homosexual in their "real" lives) and so address and form the spectator because of the spectator's relationship to knowledge about specific objects and products. These items, as a consequence of activities and histories associated with contemporary sexual subcultures, carry heavy symbolic meanings and connotations, not least because they have been used by gay men and lesbian women to carve out more fluid gender identities for themselves.[30]

[. . .]

Identity politics and gaze theory

Laura Mulvey's influential writing on the gaze was about the spectatorship of "classic narrative cinema." Subsequent writers developed and critiqued her theme of how cinematic representations constructed spectatorial positions for gendered subjects. Their emphasis on "essential" identities, particularly of groups that gaze theory has *missed out*, has proved productive but also problematic. Such a model serves to fix identity rather than to understand how promiscuous and contradictory the processes of identity formation may be. Somewhere along the way a theory of cinematic representation bumped into identity politics. Questions about gendered spectatorship and the cultural construction of identity converged.

Given that questions of identity—i.e. gay, straight, male, female identities, etc.—have been raised in relation to film theory about gendered spectatorship, for better or worse, it is necessary to consider the relationship between the gaze and "identity politics." Quite simply a collision has occurred and assumptions have been made in various approaches to film and we can't go backwards. Even the best of those texts, such as writing by Richard Dyer,[31] have sought to define identities—sexual or otherwise—as social constructs which are articulated, even formed, through cinema. Here, identities have been posited straightforwardly as gay, female, black, say, as if there were no intersection between them, and also as if there were no significant differences between people in specific groups.[32]

It is here that queer politics may help us; for as Alan McKee argues, "queer politics is, explicitly, no longer the identity politics of [the] 1970s . . . where a transcendental and essential 'gay identity' stabilised homosexual subjects."[33] Certainly throughout the 1970s and 1980s some people who were gay, female, black, or whatever, needed to articulate a group identity (even if an illusory one) in order to organize. Without the illusion of cohesive group identity group resistance would be impossible. McKee cites Gayatri Spivak's idea of "operational essentialism," which she describes as "a false ontology of women as a universal in order to advance a feminist political programme"; likewise he cites Stuart Marshall's "necessary fiction," as a way of understanding how individuals are often involved in "accepting what is known to be untrue in order to facilitate action."[34] And of course imaginary fictions also frame the way we understand unified categories of gender and sexual orientation.

A homosexual identity or a homosexual identification, as Foucault pointed out, is very different from a homosexual act.[35] Nowadays, one might identify politically, and with pride, as gay, lesbian, female, or black, but in reality the sense of unity and sameness on which such identification is predicated might be illusory. Alan McKee states: "Queer politics has come with the realisation that, to quote Derek Jarman, 'There never was a [homosexual] community, in fact.'"[36] Perhaps the differences between us are as great as the similarities.

In homophobic society, the necessary fiction of a cohesive identity must be spoken in order for political communities to maintain any sort of presence. But there are obviously problems with the articulation of any sort of fixed identity. Judith Butler has argued that even within the field of gay and lesbian studies there are problems with essentialism. This is because a kind of discourse of sexual identities emerges and "identity categories tend to be instruments of regulatory regimes, whether as the normalising categories of oppressive structures or as the rallying points for a libratory contestation of that very oppression." But she adds: "This is not to say that I will not appear at political occasions under the sign of lesbian, but that I would like to have it permanently unclear what precisely that sign signifies."[37] Indeed, this deconstructive mode, which may produce ambiguity, can itself be a political strategy:

> it is no longer clear that feminist theory ought to try to settle the questions of primary identity in order to get on with the task of politics. Instead, we ought to ask, what political possibilities are the consequence of a radical critique of the categories of identity?[38]

If one formulates identity as a more fluid category, one might then be able simultaneously to talk of queer identifications and to acknowledge the complexity and variety of different subjectivities. The impact of these ideas on gaze theory is that, because identity itself is not fixed, it is inappropriate to posit any single identification with images.

If we deconstruct the subject we must by implication also deconstruct the subject's reading/viewing position and, therefore, the text also:

> because subject-positions are mutiple, shifting and changeable, readers can occupy several 'I-slots' *at the same time* . . . there is no 'natural' way to read a text; ways of reading are historically specific and culturally variable, and reading positions are always constructed. . . . Readers, like texts, are constructed. . . . If we read from multiple subject-positions the very act of reading becomes a force for dislocating our belief in stable subjects and essential meanings.[39]

[. . .]

Our reasoning in aligning ourselves with a sort of Judith Butler mode of analysis is that anti-essentialist discussion of identificatory processes actually challenges the fixity of notions about gay, lesbian, or straight identities. It also challenges essentialist ideas that relations of looking are determined by the biological sex of the individual/s you choose to fornicate with, more than any other social relations (such as those associated with ethnic or class subjectivities). We would argue that the heterosexual subject position is equally as unnatural, and more importantly, as *fluid*, in terms of gender identifications, as homosexual or lesbian subjectivities. This collection is politically important because it looks at gaze theory from a gay and lesbian perspective.

[. . .]

Our political stance here is that all sexuality is a construct and sexual categories and definitions impinge on us all. Rethinking gaze theory to include lesbian and gay perspectives means rethinking heterosexual perspectives too, not least because the responsibility for radical sexual politics should be a heterosexual as well as a homosexual imperative. As the "closet" heterosexuals of this collection, we feel gaze theory as it stands cannot explain all our experiences of viewing. We are probably as perverse in our looking habits as many "essentially" gay or lesbian spectators, and only by introducing some queer notions can we begin to explain our experiences beyond the dogma of ideas associated with the meaning of specific sexual orientations.

Further, we recognize that most women dress up as "women" every day and yet, like us, frequently feel they are in drag. As Judith Williamson has written:

> often I have wished I could . . . appear simultaneously in every possible outfit, just to say, how dare you think any one of these is *me*. But also, see I can be all of them.[40]

If we have such a strong sense of our identity as being constructed through appearances, even though we are biologically as well as culturally defined as women, how therefore can we identify in any straightforward or "authentic" way with images of women? Queer theory, perhaps, gives us the space to start to rethink difficulties with cohesion of identity or iden-tification through viewing, and to look for greater fluidity in terms of explanation. It also raises critical questions about cross-gender identifications. Kobena Mercer has talked about inhabiting "two contradictory identifications at one and the same time" and this idea of multiple and simultaneous identification, we would argue, has always been part of the female experience of viewing.[41] This idea of ourselves as split subjects can also be extended into the metaphor of genderfuck where the free floating signifier, biological sex, is detached or cut loose from its signified, cultural gender.

Genderfuck

Della Grace's images of "lesbian boys" cause gender trouble, not least because often her images of lesbian women look so much like gay men that they have attracted a large, gay, male following. Evidently, in one gay bar when the lesbian "object of desire" was revealed not to be a biological man the picture was removed from the wall: genderfuck was not to be allowed in this bar.[42] Conversely, in the 1990s some gay men have adopted the opposite strategy, and have celebrated finding images of lesbian women whom they mistake for "boys" as perversely attractive. Here, then, "genderfuck" or "gender trouble" is created not only by the image but by the subjectivity of the viewer, who likes playing games with political hierarchies as well as those of gender.

June L. Reich has suggested that genderfuck is

> the effect of unstable signifying practices in a libidinal economy of multiple sexualities. . . . This process is the destabilisation of gender as an analytical category, though it is not, necessarily, the signal of the end of gender. . . . The play of masculine and feminine on the body . . . subverts the possibility of possessing a unified subject position.[43]

She aligns the notion of genderfuck with the end of identity politics and makes the case for a politics of performance (exemplified for her in butch/femme role-playing). She goes on to argue:

We are defined not by who we are but by what we do. This is effectively a politics of performance. It neither fixes nor denies specific sexual and gendered identifications but accomplishes something else. . . . Genderfuck . . . 'deconstructs' the psychoanalytic concept of difference without subscribing to any heterosexist or anatomical truths about the relations of sex to gender. . . . Instead, genderfuck structures meaning in a symbol-performance matrix that crosses through sex and gender and destabilises the boundaries of our recognition, of sex, gender, and sexual practice.[44]

Queer viewing . . . queer texts?

These ideas about "fluidity" of gender identifications may be accommodated by two things. First, that we are at a specific moment in history in which television images have copulated wildly with film and other visual texts. Today ideas about the interrelationship or inter-textuality of visual images are generally accepted. Second, new generations of gays and lesbians have articulated their experiences differently from before, and what is being called "queer cinema" and the "queer gaze" has come into being as a consequence of that experience.[45] Although we would argue against the idea of an essentially gay or lesbian gaze, we do not want to make the case for the "queer gaze" either. Rather, we want to make the case for identifications which are multiple, contradictory, shifting, oscillating, inconsistent, and fluid. But does the queer gaze always reconstitute the visual text as queer? Or do some images encourage polymorphous identifications more than others? As we argued in the first section of this chapter, context is important, but the text also is a structuring discourse. Cultural meanings are actively generated through representation,[46] and as Michèle Barrett has argued, "Cultural politics are crucially important because they involve struggles over *meaning*."[47]

The visual text alone cannot exclusively construct spectator positions or identities and in the first section we criticized the fixity of Mulvey's analysis as opposed to the notions we raise here about spectatorial fluidity. There we shifted the focus from filmic text to spectatorial context, minimizing the determining power of the texts and therefore by implication questioning the political usefulness of a Mulveyesque analysis, one committed to a structural analysis of the ideological character of the filmic or other text.

In this section we criticize the essentialism of the subject implied in gaze theory, in order to suggest a "queerer" or more fluid model of identifications, and consequently of the text. If we accept that visual texts do produce meanings to some extent, regardless of arguments about viewing competences and contexts, we need to decide whether these texts encode dominant meanings (which then allow for the possibility of reading against the grain) or whether all texts can be read anyhow, that is, "queerly."[48] Media effects research, as well as some of the theoretical writings associated with Stuart Hall, has discussed the way that some texts present material in order to construct a "preferred reading."[49] Despite examination of how the cultural codes that frame representation achieve this, most cultural studies critics are rarely able to identify causal mechanisms. This is perhaps because structuralist method-ology never sought to explain why things existed but instead focused on the way codes were arranged.

So Roland Barthes on codes is helpful in thinking through whether a textual code is a system of signs governed by rules agreed explicitly or implicitly, or whether these codes are unstable and open to different interpretations. Barthes's early work focuses on cultural codes, which he describes as dominant or conventional ways of reading the signs in the text, whereas his later work moved toward the idea of reading as a "writerly" process "because it can involve the production of plural texts, with different meanings."[50] Despite the apparent rigidities of semiotic analysis, with its suggestion of a universal language of codes, Barthes's model gives us a way of thinking through the ambiguities as well as the clarity of visual texts. For while there might be consensus on the denoted meaning, there is always ambiguity in the realm of connotation.[51] For example, in texts with a homosexual subtext D. A. Miller has argued that the love that dares not speak its name, except ambiguously, is relegated by virtue of its very ambiguity to a system of connotation. He argues that even in Barthes's writing homosexuality is nowhere proclaimed but everywhere inflected as "a gay voice."[52] Elsewhere he argues that the trouble with connotation is that homosexuality simply disappears, becomes invisible.[53] In Hitchcock's *Rope* (1948), for example, homosexuality is "consigned to connotation . . . to a kind of secondary meaning. . . . Connotation will always manifest a certain semiotic insufficiency. . . . It suffers from an abiding deniability" because you can refuse a connoted meaning, just by saying, " 'but isn't it just . . .?' before retorting the denotation."[54] In *Rope* homosexual meaning is elided at the same time as it is being elaborated. Miller goes on to say that connotation is the signifying process of homophobia, denying homosexuality even as it reiterates it, although we would not necessarily agree that this process amounts to homophobia *per se*.

But this suggests ambiguity which is "coded" in the text, which is different from reconceptualizing the reader as "queer" in his/her identifications. We have said above that some images encourage polymorphous identifications and perhaps it could be implied that any text can become an object of a queer gaze. However, this suggests (by semantic implication) that some texts do *not* encourage such identifications. Again we are back to asking questions about the definition of particular texts, how they are structured and what kinds of spectatorial positions they authorize or elicit. What exactly does it mean for a text to encourage "polymorphous identifications" and how do we recognize the characteristics of such a text? Do some texts discourage queer viewing?

In short, because we are arguing that identification is fluid in terms of gender identification, we recognize that we are virtually saying that all texts can be viewed queerly. Some texts do seem to "encourage" queer viewing (e.g. Madonna's "Justify Your Love" pop promo) because the sexualized images are so ambiguous. But even texts which have overt heterosexual narratives can come over time to be seen as queer. This is because such re-readings are not ahistorical but the product of a queer cultural moment in which images have been subject to so much renegotiation (including subcultural renegotiation) that the preferred heterosexual reading has been destabilized.

So our point is that some representations, what we call "queer" representations, seem to share in common the capacity to disturb stable definitions. As Judith Butler points out, many such representations cause "gender trouble." What she means is that such images mobilize "subversive confusion and proliferation of precisely those constitutive categories that seek to keep gender in its place."[55]

These new images from queer cinema shatter and fragment images of "normative" gender, and "essential" gender. For example, in the film *Paris is Burning* (1990)[56] the act of "passing" as a particular gender or profession is not an index of authenticity. The term "realness" is used simply to mean "convincing" image rather than "real" image. The implications of this categorization system are that gender is constantly changed and remade in and through the process of performance and representation.[57] This is because representation is an arena in which meanings about gender can be and are contested and constantly renegotiated. Queer representations are important not least because they offer wider opportunities for viewing/identification than those associated with the more stereotypical cinematic representations, even though we note some lesbian film critics like Pratibha Parmar have argued that queer film usually means homosexual (rather than lesbian) film in terms of the funding of such productions.[58]

But what do we mean by a queer representation? In cinema, the term has come to mean a representation that is not necessarily right on. Queer representations may not always be positive; they are frequently ambiguous, slippery, and in total don't add up to a coherent whole. They often leave the spectator/viewer questioning.

This type of imagery crops up in advertising and fashion photography too. What do we make of advertisements which use a heterosexual couple who look like lesbians (to one of us) and gay men (to another), to sell jeans? What viewing position is the male or female spectator supposed to take when Thierry Mugler uses drag queens to model women's clothes on the Paris catwalk and when Naomi Campbell says she would kill for RuPaul's legs? Or when Bette Midler on stage pretends to be a type of woman based on her viewing of gay men in drag? Or in the film *The Crying Game* (1992) when the "female" lead turns out to be a biological man acting as a transsexual complete with male genitalia? Perhaps the answer is that we enter some sort of "drag" when viewing, but what sort of drag is it?

Carole-Anne Tyler argues that the transvestite look of Mulvey's theory may be an option for men too. She argues that the concept of the phallic woman, embodied by a drag queen with an erection, is a queer concept, citing the scene in *Pink Flamingos* (1972) where a "beautiful woman" lifts up her skirt to reveal a penis.[59] The question raised here is one of authenticity. If anti-essentialist notions of the self construct identities as fictions,[60] then what's the difference between a lesbian boy and a gay man in terms of the transvestism of the spectator? Is there a difference between a woman with a dildo and a man with an erection, or a drag queen and Mae West? Or between mimicry and masquerade? None of the examples is authentic. As Tyler says, "Style is the wo/man: there is no authentic, 'real' self beyond or before the process of social construction."[61] If all identities are alienated and fictional how can we differentiate parody, mimicry, camp, imitation, and masquerade? Yet words like "masquerade" or "parody" both imply there is an opposite, i.e. a "real," and posit a binary opposition between Mae West and a drag queen. As Diana Fuss has usefully pointed out, anti-essentialism is in a dependent relationship to essentialism, so the two positions are not opposites but mutually dependent:

> what is *essential* to social constructionism is precisely this notion of 'where I stand', of what has come to be called appropriately enough, 'subject positions'.[62]

But genderfuck is about play and performance which destabilize subject positions. In playing with binary opposition it moves toward a model of gender as a simulacrum (without an original). These questions about essential identities cannot be answered within the confines of this chapter. Nevertheless, by raising them we recognize that we are invariably challenging the essential categories that frame models of gendered spectatorship. Ultimately, such questions bring us back to two familiar debates. First, the idea that the underlying model of human sexuality is "polymorphously perverse." Second, that debates about identification in the cinema necessarily raise questions about gender, masquerade, and identity—questions unanswered by film theorists to date.

Notes

1 Constantine Giannaris, "The New Queer Cinema," *Sight and Sound*, September 1992, p. 35.
2 Laura Mulvey, "Visual Pleasure and Narrative Cinema" (first published in *Screen*, vol. 16, no. 3, Autumn 1975), reprinted in Laura Mulvey, *Visual and Other Pleasures*, Macmillan, Basingstoke, 1989, p. 20.
3 Steve Neale, "Masculinity as Spectacle: Reflections on Men and Mainstream Cinema," in Screen Editorial Collective (ed.), *The Sexual Subject: A Screen Reader in Sexuality*, Routledge, London and New York, 1992, pp. 277–87 (first published 1983).
4 Richard Dyer, "Don't Look Now: The Male Pin-Up," in Screen Editorial Collective (ed.), op. cit., p. 270 (first published in 1982).
5 Michael Hatt, "The Body in Another Frame," *Journal of Philosophy and the Visual Arts* ("The Body" issue, ed. Andrew Benjamin, Academy, 1993); D. A. Miller, "Anal *Rope*," in Diana Fuss (ed.), *Inside/Out: Lesbian Theories, Gay Theories*, Routledge, New York and London, 1991; D. A. Miller, *Bringing Out Roland Barthes*, University of California Press, Berkeley, Los Angeles, London, 1992.
6 Miller, op. cit., 1992, p. 30.
7 Ibid., p. 31.
8 Andy Medhurst, "Can Chaps Be Pin-Ups?," *Ten 8*, vol. 8, no. 17, 1985; Yvonne Tasker, *Spectacular Bodies: Gender, Genre and the Action Cinema*, Routledge, London and New York, 1993.
9 Frank Mort, "Boys Own? Masculinity, Style and Popular Culture," in Rowena Chapman and Jonathan Rutherford (eds.), *Male Order: Unwrapping Masculinity*, Lawrence & Wishart, London, 1988.
10 Isabel Koprowski, unpublished interview with Lorraine Gamman, 1992, available in Central St. Martin's College of Art & Design Library.
11 Mary Ann Doane, "Film and the Masquerade: Theorising the Female Spectator," *Screen*, vol. 23, nos. 3/4, September/October 1982, p. 77.
12 See Lorraine Gamman and Margaret Marshment (eds.), *The Female Gaze: Women as Viewers of Popular Culture*, The Women's Press, London, 1988, p. 55.
13 At "On/scenities: Looking at Pornography: A Conference at the NFT," Summer 1993.
14 Rosemary Scott, *The Female Consumer*, Associated Business, London, 1986.
15 Gamman and Marshment (eds.), op. cit., p. 55.
16 Teresa de Lauretis, *Alice Doesn't: Feminism, Semiotics, Cinema*, Macmillan, Basingstoke, 1984; Dyer, op. cit.; Doane, "Masquerade Reconsidered: Further Thoughts on the Female Spectator," *Discourse*, 11, Fall/Winter 1988/89, pp. 42–54. See also Mark Finch, "Sex and Address in *Dynasty*," *Screen*, vol. 28, no. 1, Winter 1987; Jackie Stacey, in Gamman and Marshment (eds.), op. cit.; Teresa de Lauretis, "Sexual Indifference and Lesbian Representations," *Theater Journal*, vol. 40, no. 2, May 1988.
17 See Richard Dyer, "Judy Garland and Gay Men," in *Heavenly Bodies*, St. Martin's Press, New York, 1987.

18 Jackie Stacey, "Desperately Seeking Difference," in Gamman and Marshment (eds.), op. cit. (first published 1987).

19 Ibid.

20 Ibid.

21 Teresa de Lauretis, "Film and the Visible," in Bad Object-Choices (ed.), How Do I Look? Queer Film and Video, Bay Press, Seattle, 1991, pp. 223–64.

22 Jacqueline Rose, Sexuality in the Field of Vision, Verso, London, 1986, pp. 226–7.

23 Jane Gallop, Reading Lacan, Cornell University Press, New York and London, 1985, pp. 59–61.

24 Judith Mayne, "Lesbian Looks: Dorothy Arzner and Female Authorship" and subsequent "Discussion," in Bad Object-Choices (ed.), op. cit., p. 136.

25 In Tessa Boffin and Jean Frazer (eds.), Stolen Glances: Lesbians Take Photographs, Pandora, London, 1991, lesbian critics and photographers offer a variety of approaches to explaining the meaning of overtly lesbian representations. But none offer an adequate model of lesbian spectatorship or significantly move beyond the contribution Jackie Stacey has made.

26 In Every Conceivable Position, Clare Bevan (Director), Mandy Merck (Producer), roughcut never broadcast by the BBC, London, 1991.

27 Elizabeth Ellsworth, in "Illicit Pleasures: Feminist Spectators and Personal Best," Wide Angle, vol. 8, no. 2, 1986, pp. 45–56, discusses "interpretive communities" in terms of the cultural competences brought to a viewing situation. See also Alan McKee, "Review," Screen, vol. 34, no. 1, Spring 1993, p. 91.

28 In Claire Bevan (Director), Mandy Merck (Producer), op. cit.

29 Reina Lewis, "Dis-Graceful Images: Della Grace and Lesbian Sado-Masochism," Feminist Review, no. 46, Spring 1994, pp. 76–91; Della Grace, Lovebites, Aubrey Walters, London, 1991.

30 For historical accounts of butch/femme codes see Joan Nestle, A Restricted Country, Sheba Feminist, London, 1988 and Lillian Faderman, Odd Girls and Twilight Lovers: A History of Lesbian Life in Twentieth-Century America, Penguin, Harmondsworth, 1992. For a discussion of the way gay men and lesbian women use clothing to carve out identities see "Chic Thrills," in Elizabeth Wilson, Hallucinations: Life in the Postmodern City, Hutchinson Radius, London, 1988.

31 Richard Dyer, Gays and Film, Zoetrope, New York, 1984.

32 This issue is discussed by Kobena Mercer, "Skin Head Sex Thing: Racial Difference and the Homoerotic Imaginary," in Bad Object-Choices (ed.), op. cit., pp. 169–222. See in particular p. 193 where Mercer criticizes "the mantra of 'race, class, gender' (and all the other intervening variables)" which does not deal with "the complexity of what actually happens 'between' the contingent spaces where each variable intersects with the others." See also pp. 215–17.

33 McKee, op. cit., p. 89.

34 Ibid., p. 90.

35 Michel Foucault, The History of Sexuality. Volume I: An Introduction, trans. Robert Hurley, Penguin, Harmondsworth, 1981, p. 43 (first published 1976).

At a Marxism Today conference, in June 1992, Suzanne Moore described a gay New York journalist who had an affair with a military cadet. The military cadet said he wasn't "gay," he just enjoyed homosexual sex (which is not surprising given the penalties for being gay in the army). The point of her argument was that the sussed-out New York journalist said that in relation to the military cadet he felt "straight" too . . .

36 McKee, op. cit., p. 89.

37 Judith Butler, "Imitation and Gender Insubordination," in Henry Abelove, Michele Aina Barala, David M. Halperin (eds.), *The Lesbian and Gay Studies Reader*, Routledge, New York and London, 1993, p. 308, reprinted from Fuss (ed.), op. cit., 1991.

38 Judith Butler, *Gender Trouble: Feminism and the Subversion of Identity*, Routledge, New York and London, 1990, p. ix.

39 Fuss, op. cit., 1989, p. 35.

40 Judith Williamson, "A Piece of the Action: Images of 'woman' in the photography of Cindy Sherman," *Consuming Passions*, Marion Boyars, London and New York, 1986, p. 91.

41 Mercer, op. cit., p. 180.

42 Reina Lewis, op. cit., p. 89.

43 June L. Reich, "Genderfuck: The Law of the Dildo," in Cheryl Kader and Thomas Piontek (eds.), *Discourse*, vol. 15. no. 1, Fall 1992, p. 125.

44 Ibid., p. 113.

45 See Cherry Smyth, *Queer Notions*, Scarlet Press, London, 1992.

46 This point was made in response to this paper by Gavin Butt who lectures in fine art and teaches a course on "Homovisibilities" at Central St. Martin's College of Art and Design. He also argued "that what is lost in the shift from determining text, to determining context, is an analysis of the way images structurally encode power relationships, which of course was the strength of Mulvey." The reason why he took such an analysis to be important is because it enables us to comprehend how, for instance, homophobic representations consistently encode and disavow "queer pleasure." He went on to argue that in homophobic culture the queer look is still largely an illegitimate one, relying on D. A. Miller's notion that in many representations homosexuality is disavowed in so far as it is "pushed" into the shadowy realm of connotation. (See D. A. Miller, op. cit., 1991 and 1992.) In this context Gavin Butt also cited the arguments of Michael Hatt, op. cit. Hatt argues that the homosocial and the homosexual must be kept apart in cultural representations in order for the erotic to be disavowed in the homosocial so that it can be contained by the homosexual.

47 Michèle Barrett, "Feminism and the Definition of Cultural Politics," in Rosalind Brunt and Caroline Rowan (eds.), *Feminism, Culture and Politics*, Lawrence & Wishart, London, 1982, p. 37.

48 See Alexander Doty, *Making Things Perfectly Queer: Interpreting Mass Culture*, University of Minnesota Press, Minneapolis, 1993.

49 There has been so much media effects research that discusses ideas about "preferred readings." This debate has been summarized by Tim O'Sullivan *et al.* (eds.), *Key Concepts in Communication*, op. cit., as follows:

> **preferred reading** . . . **a text** is open to a number of potential readings, but normally 'prefers' one (or, occasionally more). Analysing the internal structure of the text can identify this preference.
> Texts according to Eco (*The Role of the Reader*, Hutchinson, London, 1981), can be open or closed. A *closed text* has one reading strongly preferred over others; an *open text* requires a number of readings to be made simultaneously for its full 'richness'

or 'texture' to be appreciated (to use literary critical terms). Open texts tend to be highbrow, high culture, whereas closed texts tend to the more popular, mass culture. Most mass media texts are closed in so far as they prefer a particular reading.

Alternative readings to the preferred one usually derive from differences between the social positions and/or the cultural experience of the **author** and the **reader**, or between **reader** and **reader**. Eco uses the theory of **aberrant decoding** to account for this but Hall and Morley produce subtler and more sophisticated accounts based on Parkin's theory of **meaning systems**. Hall *et al.* (S. Hall, D. Hobson, D. A. Lowe, P. Willis (eds.), *Culture, Media, Language*, Hutchinson, London, 1980) propose three main types of decodings or readings of tv texts which correspond to the reader's response to his/her social condition, not to the structure of the text. These are:

(1) *The dominant-hegemonic* which accepts the text 'full and straight' according to the assumptions of the encoder. This is the preferred reading, and corresponds to F. Parkin's (*Class Inequality and Political Order*, Paladin, St Albans, 1972) dominant meaning system.

(2) *The negotiated reading* which acknowledges the legitimacy of the dominant codes, but adapts the reading to the specific social condition of the reader. This corresponds to Parkin's subordinate meaning system.

(3) *The oppositional reading* which produces a radical decoding that is radically opposed to the preferred reading, because it derives from an alternative, oppositional meaning system. (Radical meaning system in Parkin's terminology.)

50 Diana Saco, "Masculinity as Signs: Poststructuralist Feminist Approaches to the Study of Gender," in Steve Craig (ed.), *Men, Masculinity and the Media*, Sage Publications, California, London, New Delhi, 1992, p. 31.

51 Miller, op. cit., 1991 and 1992.

52 Miller, op. cit., 1992, pp. 24–5.

53 Miller, op. cit., 1991, p. 123.

54 Miller, 1991, ibid., pp. 123–4.

55 Butler, op. cit., 1990, pp. 33–4.

56 *Paris Is Burning*, Jenny Livingstone, 1990.

57 Teresa de Lauretis, *Technologies of Gender*, University of Indiana Press, Bloomington and Indianapolis, 1987, p. 3, argues that:

gender is (a) representation – which is not to say that it does not have concrete or real implications, both social and subjective, for the material life of individuals. On the contrary . . . the representation of gender *is* its construction – and in the simplest sense it can be said that all of Western Art and high culture is the engraving of the history of that construction.

Janet Wolff, *Feminine Sentences*, Polity Press, Oxford, 1990, p. 1:

culture is central to gender formation. Art, literature, and film do not simply represent given gender identities, or reproduce already existing ideologies of femininity. Rather they participate in the very construction *of* those identities.

Second (and consequently), culture is a crucial arena for the contestation of the social arrangements of gender.

58 This is not to say that there haven't always been transvestite effects in theater and cinema. For a wide-ranging survey see Marjorie Garber, *Vested Interests: Cross-Dressing and Cultural Anxiety*, Routledge, New York and London, 1992.

59 Carole-Anne Tyler, "Boys will be Girls: The Politics of Gay Drag," in Fuss, op. cit., 1991, pp. 32–70.

60 See Butler, op. cit., 1990 and *Bodies that Matter: On the Discursive Limits of 'Sex'*, Routledge, New York and London, 1993, and Fuss, op. cit., 1989.

61 Tyler, op. cit., p. 53.

62 Fuss, op. cit., 1989, p. 29.

Select Bibliography

Aaron, Michele, ed. (2004) *New Queer Cinema: A Critical Reader*, Edinburgh: Edinburgh University Press.

Abelove, Henry, Michele Aina Barale, David M. Halperin, eds. (1993) *The Lesbian and Gay Studies Reader*, New York: Routledge.

Bad Object-Choices, eds. (1991) *How Do I Look? Queer Film and Video*, Seattle: Bay Press.

Barrios, Richard (2003) *Screened Out: Playing Gay in Hollywood from Edison to Stonewall*, New York and London: Routledge.

Bell-Metereau, Rebecca (1993 [1985]) *Hollywood Androgyny*, Second edition, New York: Columbia University Press.

Benshoff, Harry M. (1997) *Monsters in the Closet: Homosexuality and the Horror Film*, Manchester and New York: Manchester University Press.

Berenstein, Rhona J. (1996) *Attack of the Leading Ladies: Gender, Sexuality, and Spectatorship in Classic Horror Cinema*, New York: Columbia University Press.

Bergman, David, ed. (1993) *Camp Grounds: Style and Homosexuality*, Amherst: University of Massachusetts Press.

Bérubé, Allan (1991) *Coming Out Under Fire: The History of Gay Men and Women in World War Two*, New York: Plume.

Booth, Mark (1983) *Camp*, New York: Quartet Books.

Bourne, Stephen (1996) *Brief Encounters: Lesbians and Gays in British Cinema 1930–1971*, London: Cassell.

Brasell, R. Bruce (1997) "A Seed for Change: The Engenderment of A *Florida Enchantment*," *Cinema Journal* 36.4: 3–21.

Bronski, Michael (1984) *Culture Clash: The Making of Gay Sensibility*, Boston: South End Press.

Bryant, Wayne (1997) *Bisexual Characters in Film: From Anais Nin to Zee*, Binghamton, New York: Haworth.

Burston, Paul and Colin Richardson (1995) *A Queer Romance: Lesbians, Gay Men and Popular Culture*, London and New York: Routledge.

Butler, Judith (1990) *Gender Trouble: Feminism and the Subversion of Identity*, New York: Routledge.

Butler, Judith (1993) *Bodies That Matter: On the Discursive Limits of "Sex,"* New York: Routledge.

Capsuto, Steven (2000) *Alternate Channels: The Uncensored Story of Gay and Lesbian Images on Radio and Television*, New York: Ballantine Books.

Case, Sue-Ellen (1988–89) "Towards a Butch-Femme Aesthetic," *Discourse* 11.1: 55–73.

Champagne, John (1995) *The Ethics of Marginality: A New Approach to Gay Studies*, Minneapolis: University of Minnesota Press.

Chauncey, George (1994) *Gay New York: Gender, Urban Culture and the Making of the Gay Male World 1890–1940*, New York: Basic Books.

Corber, Robert (1993) *In the Name of National Security: Hitchcock, Homophobia, and the Political Construction of Gender in Postwar America*, Durham, NC: Duke University Press.

Corber, Robert (1997) *Homosexuality in Cold War America: Resistance and the Crisis of Masculinity*, Durham, NC: Duke University Press.

Creekmur, Corey K. and Alexander Doty, eds. (1995) *Out in Culture: Gay, Lesbian, and Queer Essays on Popular Culture*, Durham, NC: Duke University Press.

DeAngelis, Michael (2001) *Gay Fandom and Crossover Stardom: James Dean, Mel Gibson, and Keanu Reeves*, Durham, NC: Duke University Press.

de Lauretis, Teresa, ed. (1991) "Queer Theory: Lesbian and Gay Sexualities," special volume of *differences* 3:2.

de Lauretis, Teresa (1994) *The Practice of Love: Lesbian Sexuality and Perverse Desire*, Bloomington: Indiana University Press.

D'Emilio, John and Estelle B. Freedman (1988) *Intimate Matters: A History of Sexuality in America*, New York: Harper & Row.

Dixon, Wheeler Winston (2003) *Straight: Constructions of Heterosexuality in Cinema*, Albany: State University of New York Press.

Doty, Alexander (1993) *Making Things Perfectly Queer: Interpreting Mass Culture*, Minneapolis: University of Minnesota Press.

Doty, Alexander (2000) *Flaming Classics: Queering the Film Canon*, New York and London: Routledge.

Doyle, Jennifer, Jonathan Flatley, and José Esteban Muñoz, eds. (1996) *Pop Out: Queer Warhol*, Durham, NC: Duke University Press.

Duberman, Martin, Martha Vicinus, and George Chauncey, Jr., eds. (1989) *Hidden from History: Reclaiming the Gay and Lesbian Past*, New York: Penguin Books.

Duggan, Lisa (1992) "Making It Perfectly Queer," *Socialist Review* (April): 11–31.

Duggan, Lisa and Nan Hunter (1995) *Sex Wars: Sexual Dissent and Political Culture*, New York: Routledge.

Dyer, Richard, ed. (1977) *Gays and Film*, London: BFI.

Dyer, Richard (2002 [1993]) *The Matter of Images: Essays on Representation*, Second edition, London and New York: Routledge.

Dyer, Richard (2002) *The Culture of Queers*, London and New York: Routledge.

Dyer, Richard (2003 [1990]) *Now You See It: Studies on Lesbian and Gay Film*, Second edition, London and New York: Routledge.

Ehrenstein, David (1998) *Open Secret: Gay Hollywood 1928–1998*, New York: William Morrow and Company, Inc.

Faderman, Lillian (1992) *Odd Girls and Twilight Lovers: A History of Lesbian Life in Twentieth-Century America*, New York: Penguin Books.

Farmer, Brett (2000) *Spectacular Passions: Cinema, Fantasy, Gay Male Spectatorships*, Durham, NC: Duke University Press.

Foucault, Michel (1990 [1977]) *The History of Sexuality*, Vol. 1, An Introduction, Robert Hurley, trans., New York: Vintage Books.

Freedman, Eric (1998) "Producing (Queer) Communities: Public Access Cable TV in the USA," in *The Television Studies Book*, Christine Geraghty and David Lusted, eds., London: Arnold.

Fuss, Diana, ed. (1991) *inside/out: Lesbian Theories, Gay Theories*, London and New York: Routledge.

Gamson, Joshua (1998) *Freaks Talk Back: Tabloid Talk Shows and Sexual Nonconformity*, Chicago: University of Chicago Press.

Garber, Marjorie (1992) *Vested Interests: Cross Dressing and Cultural Anxiety*, New York: Harper Perennial.

Garber, Marjorie (1995) *Vice Versa: Bisexuality and the Eroticism of Everyday Life*, New York: Simon & Schuster.

Gever, Martha, John Greyson, and Pratibha Parmar, eds. (1993) *Queer Looks: Perspectives on Lesbian and Gay Film and Video*, London and New York: Routledge.

Gittings, Christopher (2001) "Zero Patience, Genre, Difference, and Ideology: Singing and Dancing Queer Nation," *Cinema Journal* 41.1: 28–39.

Griffin, Sean (2000) *Tinker Belles and Evil Queens: The Walt Disney Company from the Inside Out*, New York: New York University Press.

Hadleigh, Boze (1986) *Conversations with My Elders*, New York: St. Martin's Press.

Hadleigh, Boze (1993) *The Lavender Screen: The Gay and Lesbian Films: Their Stars, Makers, Characters, and Critics*, New York: A Citadel Press Book (Carol Publishing Group).

Hadleigh, Boze (1994) *Hollywood Lesbians*, New York: Barricade Books.

Hadleigh, Boze (1996) *Hollywood Gays*, New York: Barricade Books.

Hankin, Kelly (2001) "Lesbian Locations: The Production of Lesbian Bar Space in *The Killing of Sister George*," *Cinema Journal* 41.1: 3–27.

Hanson, Ellis, ed. (1999) *Out Takes: Essays on Queer Theory and Film*, Durham, NC: Duke University Press.

Hocquenghem, Guy (1993 [1978]) *Homosexual Desire*, trans. Daniella Dangoor, Durham, NC: Duke University Press.

Hollinger, Karen (1998) "Theorizing Mainstream Female Spectatorship: The Case of the Popular Lesbian Film," *Cinema Journal* 37.2: 3–17.

Holmlund, Chris (1991) "When is a Lesbian not a Lesbian? The Lesbian Continuum and the Mainstream Femme Film," *Camera Obscura* 25–26: 145–178.

Holmlund, Chris (2002) *Impossible Bodies: Femininity and Masculinity at the Movies*, New York and London: Routledge.

Holmlund, Chris and Cynthia Fuchs, eds. (1997) *Between the Sheets, in the Streets: Queer, Lesbian, and Gay Documentary*, Minneapolis: University of Minnesota Press.

Jackson, Claire and Peter Tapp (1997) *The Bent Lens: A World Guide to Gay & Lesbian Film*, Australia: Australian Catalogue Company.

Jackson, Earl (1995) *Strategies of Deviance: Studies in Gay Male Representation*, Bloomington, IN: Indiana University Press.

Jump Cut 16 (1977), special section on "Gay Men and Film."

Jump Cut 24/25 (1981), special section on "Lesbians and Film."

Katz, Jonathan Ned (1992 [1976]) *Gay American History: Lesbians and Gay Men in the U.S.A.*, Revised edition, New York: Meridian.

Katz, Jonathan Ned (1995) *The Invention of Heterosexuality*, New York: Dutton.

Lang, Robert (2002) *Masculine Interests: Homoerotics in Hollywood Film*, New York: Columbia University Press.

Lugowski, David M. (1999) "Queering the (New) Deal: Lesbian and Gay Representation and the Depression-Era Cultural Politics of Hollywood's Production Code," *Cinema Journal* 38.2: 3–35.

Madsen, Axel (1995) *The Sewing Circle: Hollywood's Greatest Secret: Female Stars Who Loved Other Women*, New York: A Birch Lane Press Book (Carol Publishing Group).

Mann, William J. (1998) *Wisecracker: The Life and Times of William Haines, Hollywood's First Openly Gay Star*, New York: Viking.

Mann, William J. (2001) *Behind the Screen: How Gays and Lesbians Shaped Hollywood, 1910–1969*, New York: Penguin Books.

Mayne, Judith (1994) *Directed by Dorothy Arzner*, Bloomington, IN: Indiana University Press.

Medhurst, Andy and Sally Munt, eds. (1997) *Lesbian and Gay Studies: A Critical Introduction*, London: Cassell.

Meyer, Moe, ed. (1994) *The Politics and Poetics of Camp*, London and New York: Routledge.

Miller, D. A. (1998) *Place for Us: Essay on the Broadway Musical*, Cambridge, MA: Harvard University Press.

Noriega, Chon (1990) "Something's Missing Here! Homosexuality and Film Reviews during the Production Code Era, 1934–1962," *Cinema Journal* 30.1: 20–41.

Parish, James Robert (1993) *Gays and Lesbians in Mainstream Cinema: Plots, Critiques, Casts and Credits for 272 Theatrical and Made-for-Television Hollywood Releases*, Jefferson, NC: McFarland & Co.

Radel, Nicholas F. (2001) "The Transnational Ga(y)ze: Constructing the East European Object of Desire in Gay Film and Pornography after the Fall of the Wall," *Cinema Journal* 41.1: 40–62.

Ringer, R. Jeffrey, ed. (1994) *Queer Worlds, Queer Images: Communication and the Construction of Homosexuality*, New York: New York University Press.

Robertson, Pamela (1996) *Guilty Pleasures: Feminist Camp from Mae West to Madonna*, Durham, NC: Duke University Press.

Rose, Jacqueline (1986) *Sexuality in the Field of Vision*, London: Verso.

Ross, Andrew (1989) "Uses of Camp," *No Respect: Intellectuals and Popular Culture*, New York: Routledge: 135–170.

Russo, Vito (1987 [1981]) *The Celluloid Closet: Homosexuality in the Movies*, Revised edition, New York: Harper & Row Publishers.

Saunders, Michael William (1998) *Imps of the Perverse: Gay Monsters in Film*, Westport, Connecticut: Praeger.

Screen Editorial Collective, ed. (1992) *The Sexual Subject: A Screen Reader in Sexuality*, London and New York: Routledge.

Searle, Samantha (1997) *Queer-ing the Screen*, Sydney: Moving Image.

Sedgwick, Eve Kosofsky (1985) *Between Men: English Literature and Male Homosocial Desire*, New York: Columbia University Press.

Sedgwick, Eve Kosofsky (1990) *The Epistemology of the Closet*, Berkeley, CA: University of California Press.

Sedgwick, Eve Kosofsky (1993) *Tendencies*, Durham, NC: Duke University Press.

Signorile, Michelangelo (1993) *Queer in America: Sex, the Media, and the Closets of Power*, New York: Doubleday.

Smith, Patricia Juliana, ed. (1999) *The Queer Sixties*, New York and London: Routledge.

Smyth, Cherry (1992) *Queer Notions*, London: Scarlet Press.

Somerville, Siobhan B. (2000) *Queering the Color Line: Race and the Invention of Homosexuality in American Culture*, Durham, NC: Duke University Press.

Sontag, Susan (1983) "Notes on Camp," *A Susan Sontag Reader*, New York: Vintage Books: 105–120 (originally published 1964).

Straayer, Chris (1996) *Deviant Eyes, Deviant Bodies: Sexual Re-Orientations in Film and Video*, New York: Columbia University Press.

Suarez, Juan A. (1996) *Bike Boys, Drag Queens, and Superstars: Avant-Garde, Mass Culture, and Gay Identities in the 1960s Underground Cinema*, Bloomington and Indianapolis: Indiana University Press.

Tinkcom, Matthew (2002) *Working Like a Homosexual: Camp, Capital, Cinema*, Durham, NC: Duke University Press.

Tropiano, Stephen (2002) *The Prime Time Closet: A History of Gays and Lesbians on TV*, New York: Applause.

Tyler, Parker (1992 [1972]) *Screening the Sexes: Homosexuality in the Movies*, New York: Da Capo Press.

Walters, Suzanna Danuta (2001) *All the Rage: The Story of Gay Visibility in America*, Chicago, IL: University of Chicago Press.

Warner, Michael, ed. (1993) *Fear of a Queer Planet*, Minneapolis, MI: University of Minneapolis Press.

Watney, Simon (1987) *Policing Desire: Pornography, AIDS and the Media*, London: Methuen/Comedia.

Waugh, Thomas (1996) *Hard to Imagine: Gay Male Eroticism in Photography and Film from their Beginnings to Stonewall*, New York: Columbia University Press.

Waugh, Thomas (2000) *The Fruit Machine: Twenty Years of Writings on Queer Cinema*, Durham, NC: Duke University Press.

Weeks, Jeffrey (1989) *Sexuality and Its Discontents*, London: Routledge.

Weiss, Andrea (1992) *Vampires and Violets: Lesbians in Film*, New York: Penguin.

Whatling, Clare (1997) *Screen Dreams: Fantasizing Lesbians in Film*, Manchester: Manchester University Press.

White, Patricia (1999) *unInvited: Classical Hollywood Cinema and Lesbian Representability*, Bloomington and Indianapolis: Indiana University Press.

Wilton, Tamsin, ed. (1995) *Immortal/Invisible: Lesbians and the Moving Image*, London: Routledge.

Wittig, Monique (1992) *The Straight Mind*, Boston, MA: Beacon.

Index